The
Ten Commandments

The
Ten Commandments

Manual for the Christian Life

J. Douma

TRANSLATED BY
NELSON D. KLOOSTERMAN

P&R PUBLISHING

P.O. BOX 817 • PHILLIPSBURG • NEW JERSEY 08865-0817

Originally published in Dutch, in three volumes, as *De Tien Geboden: Handreiking voor het Christelijk leven,* by Uitgeverij Van den Berg, Kampen, 1992

English translation © 1996 by Nelson D. Kloosterman

Published by P&R Publishing Company, P.O. Box 817, Phillipsburg, New Jersey 08865-0817

Co-published in Canada by Inheritance Publications, Box 154, Neerlandia, AB Canada T0G 1R0

Printed in the United States of America

Composition by Colophon Typesetting

Library of Congress Cataloging-in-Publication Data

Douma, Jochem, 1931–
    [Tien geboden. English]
    The Ten commandments : manual for the Christian life / J. Douma ; translated by Nelson D. Kloosterman.
        p.   cm.
    Includes bibliographical references and indexes.
    ISBN 0-87552-237-8
    1. Ten commandments—Criticism, interpretation, etc. 2. Christian ethics—Reformed (Reformed Church) authors. 3. Reformed Church—Doctrines. I. Title
    BV4655.D6513   1996
251.5'2—dc20   96-34326

Contents

Preface to the Dutch Edition

I am delighted to see my discussion of the Ten Commandments, originally published in three separate volumes, now appearing in one volume. Evidently interest continues to be expressed in this commentary on the Ten Commandments, even after the individual volumes were reprinted several times.

I am aware that I stand at the back of a long line of other writers who have produced studies of these ground rules and their comprehensive significance for Israel and the Christian church. Many have found in these precepts the basis for their Christian ethics, convinced as they were that Jesus Christ has not set aside these commandments but rather has taught them to us in their fullest depth. The Sermon on the Mount and the Ten Commandments do not stand in tension with one another. For that reason, a commentary on the Ten Commandments can contribute to our reflection concerning how we must live today.

The three separate volumes have come to be termed a "miniature ethics." Although it is true that not all ethical problems can be treated solely in reference to the Ten Commandments, we could nevertheless affirm that within these commandments lie the fundamental pointers we need for our concourse with God and our neighbors. I view them as a manual for the Christian life, as the subtitle indicates.

My thanks to Professor J. P. Lettinga, whose "Notes on the Hebrew Text of the Ten Commandments" could be included in this edition as well. They are designed for readers who have some knowledge of Hebrew. But it appears to me that even without such knowledge people may still profit from them.

I would also thank Mr. Barend Meijer for the care with which he read through the various manuscripts before they went to the publisher.

Mr. Joost Smit compiled the indices which considerably enhance the book's usefulness as a reference work.

Except for a number of minor corrections, the text of this single volume edition is the same as that of the latest three-volume edition.

J. Douma
Kampen, June 1992

Translator's Preface

Professor Dr. J. Douma (pronounced *Dow-ma*) is a minister among the Reformed Churches in the Netherlands (liberated), and since 1970 has been Professor of Ethics at their Theological University in Kampen, the Netherlands. Dr. Douma has written a fifteen-volume series entitled *Moral Reflection* (*Ethische bezinning*), where he discusses various fundamental and up-to-date subjects in the area of ethics. These subjects include abortion, marriage and sexuality, the Christian lifestyle, homosexuality, environment and technology, political responsibility, and nuclear armament. Three of these fifteen volumes constituted a commentary on the Ten Commandments, volumes that were later combined and published as a single volume.

Dr. Douma is respected internationally for his thoughtful interpretation and careful application of Scripture, of the church's creeds, and of church history, in relation to contemporary moral problems. In this volume he provides a modern commentary on the Ten Commandments, which still serve today as a manual for the Christian life.

The reader should be aware of several differences between this English translation and the Dutch original.

In the original edition, Dr. Douma begins each chapter with a translation of the Hebrew text of the prologue or commandment, provided by his colleague, Professor J. P. Lettinga, emeritus professor of Semitic Languages at the Theological University in Kampen. (Professor Lettinga has authored a Hebrew grammar that is widely used today throughout Europe.) Dr. Douma had included, as an appendix to each of the initial three volumes and in the single volume edition, Professor Lettinga's "Notes on the Hebrew Text of the Ten Commandments," which provide the reader with a valuable scholarly treatment of the Hebrew text and its translation. We have chosen to provide an English translation of Professor Lettinga's rendering of the prologue and each commandment, but to omit his rather technical explanations of them. (An English translation of Lettinga's notes on the Hebrew text may be obtained for a nominal fee by writing to The John Calvin Foundation, 5734 191A Street, Surrey, BC, Canada V3S 7M8.)

We should also alert the reader to the function of footnotes and endnotes in the English translation. Although the original contains only footnotes, we have placed in the endnotes references that are generally bibliographical. By contrast, the footnotes contain interpretive expansions of material found in the text itself, and related bibliographical information.

Finally, this English translation includes an Appendix, entitled "The Use of Scripture in Ethics," which does not appear in the Dutch original. This helpful companion essay could profitably be studied before reading the commentary exposition of the Ten Commandments, since here Dr. Douma explains his hermeneutical principles and method, distinguishing four valid ways in which the Bible can be used in moral reflection.

This authorized and independent translation of the Dutch original has made grateful use, at several points, of the preliminary translation work of R. Koat. Barbara Lerch and Thom Notaro of P&R Publishing Company deserve our appreciation as well for their enthusiastic persistence in shepherding this manuscript along the road to publication.

Nelson D. Kloosterman
Mid-America Reformed Seminary
Dyer, Indiana
U.S.A.

The Prologue

I am Yahweh your God, who has freed you from
Egypt, the house of slavery.(Ex. 20:2)

Covenant Charter

Any treatment of the Ten Commandments must deal with the prologue
or preamble, since it clearly belongs to the words that God spoke when He
proclaimed the Ten Commandments on Mount Horeb. Orthodox Jews
ascribe so much value to these words that they make them the first commandment. But that can hardly be right, since nothing is commanded in
the prologue. Rather, God begins commanding in the subsequent words:
"You shall have no other gods before Me" (Ex. 20:3). Moreover, in order
to come up with ten commandments, the Jews must combine several later
commandments. Along with Roman Catholics and Lutherans, they combine what we take to be the first and second commandments into one, and
then identify the third through tenth commandments in the same way as
Reformed believers. We hope to show in our treatment of the second
commandment that this combination is improper. At this point, we
would simply say: Do not make the prologue a distinct commandment, but
do pay special attention to it.

Why? Because this prologue helps to shed light on the fact that in the
Decalogue we possess a charter of the covenant that God made with Israel
at Sinai. As we read in Deuteronomy 4:13, the Lord made known His covenant: "So He declared to you His covenant which He commanded you
to perform, that is, the Ten Commandments; and He wrote them on two
tablets of stone." From extrabiblical sources, we know that during this period, other nations also used tablets for establishing a covenant. Moreover, there are also points of striking similarity between what we find in
the Ten Commandments as a covenant document and what we come

1

across elsewhere. For example, a Hittite king might begin his covenant treaty, made with his subject vassals, this way: "Thus speaks the Sun king Mursilis, the great king, the king of the land of Hatti. . . ." That calls to mind the magnificent introduction of the covenant with Israel: "I am Yahweh your God. . . ." A mighty prince is introducing himself to his subjects. A Hittite covenant treaty might continue by narrating the favors shown by the great king to his vassal princes. In a similar way we read that Yahweh has delivered Israel from Egypt, the house of slavery. The Hittite suzerain would go on to stipulate the obligations that his vassals were to fulfill. In a similar sense, we find in the Decalogue—with its repeated "You shall not"—the regulations that Israel had to observe in order to be faithful to her covenant with Yahweh.[1]

God—Liberation—Holy Living

Let us look a little more closely at the three elements just mentioned.

In the first place, God announces Himself in His majesty. His revelation at Sinai was accompanied by claps of thunder and flashes of lightning "so that all the people who were in the camp trembled" (Ex. 19:16). The Israelites were called to assemble at the mountain that was blazing with a fire that reached to heaven itself, to hear God's words "that they may learn to fear Me all the days they live on the earth, and that they may teach their children" (Deut. 4:10). They were to give *honor* to this God (Pss. 24:7, 9; 29:1–2; 96:6–10). A son honors his father, and a servant his master. Therefore God could say, "If then I am the Father, where is My honor? And if I am a Master, where is My reverence?" (Mal. 1:6). This message is no less valid for the New Testament church. This church, according to the writer of Hebrews, has not come near a physical mountain blazing with fire, covered with darkness and surrounded by stormy winds; but the church is called to serve God with just as much honor and respect, "for our God is a consuming fire" (Heb. 12:18–21, 29).

Second, we notice that God announces Himself as the great Liberator. In the prologue of the Decalogue, He is unlike a despotic Hittite king who compels respect from his vassals. The summons, that Israel fear and honor God, obtains a special flavor. In the prologue, God introduces Himself as the Lord, as Yahweh, who has led Israel out of Egypt, the house of slavery.

For that reason, He is called Yahweh. This name means "I am who I am"; that is to say, "I am the saving and liberating One, who fulfills the promises that I gave to your fathers Abraham, Isaac, and Jacob." God had bound Himself by oath to Abraham, promising to make his descendants numerous and to make them a blessing for all the nations of the earth (Gen. 22:15–18). When He introduced Himself to Moses, God was thinking back to that covenant. The God of Abraham, Isaac, and Jacob did not look down dispassionately when their descendants were being oppressed in Egypt. He demonstrated who He was: the active, acting God who showed Pharaoh and Israel that He kept His promises. God listened to the complaint of Israel in Egypt and remembered His covenant with Abraham, Isaac, and Jacob. He saw how the Israelites were being oppressed and what was being done to them (Ex. 2:23–25).

This covenant, established long ago with the fathers, was being renewed here at Sinai. The nation had been liberated from Egypt and knew what kind of God had delivered them: "I am Yahweh, whom you have come to know as the God who keeps His covenant."

This liberation appears in still sharper relief when we recall that Yahweh delivered the Israelites *in spite of* their own conduct. They were stubborn when their deliverance from Egypt did not proceed quickly enough to suit them (Ex. 5:21–23; 6:9). They turned against Moses as they stood on the shore of the Red Sea:

> Then they said to Moses, "Because there were no graves in Egypt, have you taken us away to die in the wilderness? Why have you so dealt with us, to bring us up out of Egypt? Is this not the word that we told you in Egypt, saying, 'Let us alone that we may serve the Egyptians?' For it would have been better for us to serve the Egyptians than that we should die in the wilderness." (Ex. 14:11–12)

This mentality would surface repeatedly in the wilderness. "You have been rebellious against the LORD from the day that I knew you" (Deut. 9:24). The desire to return to the fleshpots of Egypt was often stronger than the desire to enter the Promised Land. At Sinai, Moses' intervention was required to prevent God from destroying His people. But there we see immediately and clearly why Yahweh spared His people. This is how Moses pleaded with the Lord for the people: "Remember Your servants, Abraham, Isaac, and Jacob; do not look on the stubbornness of this people, or on their wickedness or their sin. . . . Yet they are Your people and Your inheritance, whom You brought out by Your mighty power and by Your outstretched arm" (Deut. 9:26–29). The covenant, of which the Ten Commandments are the charter, is a covenant of grace, and the liberation from Egypt is an undeserved deliverance!

In the third place, God announces Himself as the Lawgiver. The prologue is followed by ten commandments that the Israelite must keep.* But in the light of what happened earlier, these commandments obtain a very special character. The commandments follow the gospel of undeserved deliverance. These are not the commandments of a despot who lays down his law in the sense of "obey and be quiet," for these are commands of Yahweh the Liberator, who wants His people to *stay* free. First occurs the exodus to freedom, then the giving of the law. Here freedom and limits coalesce. For its growth, a fish is limited to water, its proper element. Similarly, people are free—like a fish in water and a bird in the air—only when they listen to God's law. In his epistle, James characterizes the law as a law of liberty (James 1:25).

In this context, we should mention Deuteronomy 6:20–25 as a very relevant passage. In subsequent generations, when a son asked his father, "What is the meaning of the testimonies, the statutes, and the judgments which the LORD our God has commanded you?" the father was *first* to tell the story of Israel's deliverance from Egypt, before coming to the commandments themselves. The purpose for keeping these commandments is clear enough: "And the LORD commanded us to observe all these statutes, to fear the LORD our God, for our good always, that He might preserve us alive, as it is this day" (Deut. 6:20–25). For the one who keeps the law, things will go well. That is a recurring theme (Deut. 4:40; 10:13; 12:28, to mention a few references). As someone has said, the law is the melody whose notes consist of joyful living before God.[2] Poems were composed in praise of the law (Pss. 19; 119). Speaking metaphorically, it is not thunder, but dew, that best characterizes the law given at Horeb.[3] In the foreground of the law is not its strictness, but its concern to keep the one who has been liberated from falling back into slavery.

To this we must add the observation that life in accord with the law is a *holy* life. Especially the book of Leviticus tells us clearly that this holy life is closely tied to liberation from Egypt. In this book of the Bible, we hear the prologue of the Ten Commandments resounding regularly, often connected with the exhortation, "Be holy, for I am holy" (Lev. 11:45; cf. 19:2; 22:31–33). What does this mean concretely? It indicates that Israel cannot behave

---

* In our opinion, whether one speaks of Ten Words or of Ten Commandments makes no difference at all. We read of "words" (Ex. 20:1; Deut. 5:22) or of "ten words" (see the Hebrew of Ex. 34:28; Deut. 4:13; 10:4); but one can also speak of the two stone tablets as containing the *law* and the *commandment* (Ex. 24:12). See also Matt. 19:17–19 and Rom. 13:9. It really comes down to how the concept of "commandment" is interpreted.

like the people of Egypt, and even less like those in Canaan, where Israel was headed (Lev. 18:3). Yahweh had *separated* Israel from the nations so that this people would belong to Him (Lev. 20:26). Yahweh Himself is holy, which means that He is completely different from all other gods; but then His people likewise could no longer live in the style of Egypt, the land from which they had been led. Israel would have to practice another style in every dimension of her life, a style different from those she encountered either in Egypt or among the pagan population in Canaan. Enjoying freedom means living the antithesis.[4] To a separate God belongs a separate people: "a kingdom of priests and a holy nation" (Ex. 19:6).

From Old to New Testament

The three striking elements in the prologue that we have mentioned above stand out in still sharper relief when we move from the Old to the New Testament. Moses, the mediator of the old covenant at Sinai, makes room for Jesus, the Mediator of the new—and better—covenant (Heb. 8:6; 9:15; 12:24). Fundamentally, the better covenant is not *another* covenant, not even with regard to the Ten Commandments. We have written elsewhere about the abiding validity of the Ten Commandments.[*]

Along with Calvin, we insist that the covenant with Israel does not differ in "essence and substance" from the New Testament covenant, but that these two differ only in administration. The new covenant is no longer established with one nation (Israel), but extends to believers and their descendants from all nations of the world (Acts 2:39; Rom. 9:24–26; Eph. 2:11–22). Moreover, worship practices associated with priests, animal sacrifices, and feast days ended when these "shadows" were replaced as the reality of all these things appeared in Christ (Col. 2:16–17; Heb. 5–10).[†] Due to these and other changes, it is no longer possible to speak about the Ten Commandments without relating them to the work of Jesus Christ. Now they receive a broader and deeper interpretation than was possible at the foot of Mount Sinai.

---

* *Christian Morals and Ethics* (Winnipeg, 1981), chap. 5. We will not be discussing again in this volume what we treated there, namely, the abiding validity of the Decalogue, the law as norm for living rather than as way of salvation, and the three uses of the law.

† The relationship between Old and New Testaments is crucial for Christian ethics; among the best discussions is John Calvin, *Institutes of the Christian Religion*, ed. John T. McNeill, trans. Ford Lewis Battles, The Library of Christian Classics, vol. 20 (Philadelphia, 1960), 2.11.1–14, "The Difference Between the Two Testaments."

That must impress us when we read the prologue. We pointed out earlier that in the first place, God announces Himself in the prologue in all His majesty. Subject to this majesty is not only Israel, but the whole world. That was true also when Yahweh established His covenant with Israel at Sinai, for even then He declared that the whole earth belonged to Him (Ex. 19:5). But with the light of the New Testament we see better how *all* things are of Him and through Him and to Him (Rom. 11:36), and how He is worthy to receive glory, honor, and power from *all* nations (Rev. 4:11; 21:26). We see as well how all authority in heaven and on earth has been given to Christ (Matt. 28:18), and that before Him every knee must bow and every tongue confess that "Jesus Christ is Lord, to the glory of God the Father" (Phil. 2:10–11).

Furthermore, what the prologue says about God as the great Liberator receives much deeper content in the New Testament. Already the Old Testament moved beyond the impressive deliverance from Egypt. Jeremiah announced that the day would come when people would no longer say, "The LORD lives who brought up the children of Israel from the land of Egypt," but rather, "The LORD lives who brought up the children of Israel from the land of the north and from all the lands where He had driven them" (Jer. 16:14–15). But the great deliverance accomplished through Jesus Christ would surpass every other deliverance. The old Passover is replaced by the new one, for which Christ Himself has become the sacrificed Passover Lamb (1 Cor. 5:7). The deliverance from Egypt became our deliverance from the power of darkness, from the slavery of sin, so that we might receive a place in the kingdom of Christ (Col. 1:13; 1 Peter 2:9).

Here too, the gracious character of this deliverance must impress us: "For by grace you have been saved through faith, and that not of yourselves; it is the gift of God, not of works, lest anyone should boast" (Eph. 2:8–9). Just as Israel did not escape the slavery of Egypt by her own efforts, so too the great deliverance accomplished by Christ must be described as undeserved. Once again the promises given long ago to Abraham came to fulfillment. God demonstrated His mercy in Christ to Abraham and his descendants forever and ever (Luke 1:55), and remembered the oath He had sworn to Abraham (Luke 1:73). What God once declared to Abraham—"In you all the families of the earth shall be blessed" (Gen. 12:3)—now reaches fulfillment among those who believe in Christ. In this respect, the distinctions no longer matter between Jew and Greek, slave and free, or male and female. They are one in Christ, and whoever is of Christ is a child of Abraham and an heir according to the promise (Gal. 3:7–14, 28–29).

In the third place, we must see clearly that the God who announces Himself as the Lawgiver does so as our Deliverer in Christ more explicitly than under the old covenant. Appealing to the mercies of God, Paul summons us to present our lives to God as a holy sacrifice (Rom. 12:1). We have been chosen *in order that* we might live holy and blameless before God (Eph. 1:4). God has created us in Christ *for* doing good works, which He has prepared beforehand for us to walk in them (Eph. 2:10). First comes the gospel, then the law. People must stand firm in their freedom and not allow themselves to be enslaved again (Gal. 5:1). We must say good-bye to the old, sinful life and not permit ourselves to be seduced by desires from an earlier time when we did not know better. For as the One who called us is holy, so too we must be holy in all our walk, as Peter says, appealing to the Old Testament verse, "Be holy, for I am holy" (1 Peter 1:15–16).

That holy walk of life is also in contrast to the worldly walk from which we have been delivered. We must be blameless and unspotted, children living without fault in the middle of a crooked and perverse generation, and we must be shining stars in the (dark) world (Phil. 2:15). Deliverance from Egypt, or from any house of bondage to whatever sin, requires a visible antithesis in lifestyle between then and now.

No Liberation Theology

Writing about the Ten Commandments involves writing about the Lord's *commands* and about His *law*, which have not lost their relevance in the new covenant. But we cannot properly discuss this law without also speaking continually about liberty and liberation. The prologue prevents us from turning the Decalogue into a set of prescriptions used to order slaves around. They are instead rules of life for liberated people, people who must not be foolish enough to fall back into slavery.

Nevertheless, one could write about this deliverance from Egypt, and about the Ten Commandments given in connection with that deliverance, in a way that leads us down the wrong path. We have in mind modern liberation theology. Central to that theology is deliverance from various social injustices. Just as Israel left Egypt, so too oppressed humanity must overthrow various oppressors. Oppressed groups are to flee from the bondage of apartheid, of capitalism, of patriarchal society, of heterosexual mores, and the like. Blacks in South Africa, the poor in South America, women, and homosexuals all want to be free. Theologians come to their aid with the message that God is the great Liberator, who frees people from all sorts of slavery. Just listen to the exodus motif in the Bible!

Without doubt, *liberty* is an important word in connection with interpreting the prologue and the Ten Commandments themselves. So we too will be using that word often in what follows. The laws of Moses have social implications for foreigners, slaves, orphans, and widows (e.g., in Deut. 15 and 24). Anyone who has been liberated from Egypt must realize how a foreigner and a slave should be treated. But for that reason, it can be quite one-sided (and in its application quite unacceptable as well) to make the Decalogue the Magna Charta of liberation.[5] Why?

Because this incorrectly elevates human liberation to the main theme of the Decalogue. The prologue does not say "*You* are the liberated ones whom I have delivered from Egypt, the house of slavery," but "*I* am the LORD who delivered you from Egypt, the house of slavery." That—or rather, He—is the main theme of the Decalogue. This is confirmed when, immediately after the text of the Ten Commandments (as we find it in Deut. 5), we read about the heart of the matter: the fear of Yahweh. "You shall love the LORD your God with all your heart, with all your soul, and with all your might" (Deut. 6:2, 5). When He quotes this text, Jesus calls this the first and great commandment (Matt. 22:38). But placing human freedom at the center yields an interpretation of the Decalogue that is anthropocentric rather than theocentric.

Respect for God is a unique matter, with its own expressions of faith, gratitude, and praise. The first four commandments were not put first by accident. Liberation theology is not real *theo*-logy, because it overemphasizes human liberation and underemphasizes the indispensable condition for all true liberation: complete surrender to God. In the Bible we learn precisely the opposite. Peter was familiar with the heavy yoke borne by subjects and slaves. But without assuming that they had to throw off this yoke, Peter proceeded from the premise that his readers already *possessed* freedom. They were called to live as free men and to serve God with their freedom (1 Peter 2:13–20).

Moreover, we must not interpret the deliverance from Egypt as a social-political contest between the haves and the have-nots, or between those who ruled and those who were ruled. If it had been a social-political matter, why then were not thousands of other slaves living in Egypt at that time also liberated?[6] Furthermore, we have already seen that if it had been left up to them, the Israelites would never have left Egypt. The pots of meat, the bread and fish, and all the melons (see Ex. 16:3 and Num. 11:5–6) were more attractive than the risks connected with trusting in Yahweh!

Any search for the main point of the Exodus will have to yield more than simple resistance to a despotic Pharaoh and his yoke of slavery. At a time when Israel still had it good in Egypt, Joseph—who was no slave, but a prince—longed for the land of Canaan, extracting an oath that his bones would be brought there when God would one day be moved by the plight of Joseph's people (Gen. 50:24–25). And Moses, who enjoyed just as prominent a position in Pharaoh's court, would rather have suffered evil along with God's people than enjoy the passing pleasures of sin. He considered the reproach of Christ worth more than the treasures of Egypt (Heb. 11:24–26).

The exodus from Egypt cannot serve as a model for various liberation movements, but serves rather as the model of genuine freedom that rests in God's promises, of slavery to *sin* and of the exodus out of that bondage through *Christ*. Anyone who ignores these aspects will offer merely a superficial analysis of Israel's exodus from Egypt. He will gladly cry out with the Israelites about bondage (Ex. 2:23), but then easily complain with them in the wilderness when freedom and bread are tied inextricably to faith and obedience toward God.

Finally, liberation theology cannot be our guide when it comes to holy living, to which the Decalogue summons us. Freedom is a calling, but it must not be used as an opportunity for the flesh (Gal. 5:13). Whether one is slave or free, what matters is keeping God's commandments (1 Cor. 7:17–19). Both rich and poor, freedmen and slaves, can stand on the side of the beast of the antichrist and therefore come under condemnation (Rev. 13:8; 14:16–20; 19:18). Yes, we must defend the poor, but anyone who argues—even if those arguments are wrapped in the holy garments of theology—that the poor are permitted to rise up against the rich as they pursue their rights in a revolutionary way, is not talking any longer about the freedom that Peter was discussing (referred to above). Anyone who defends free sexual expression, who denies that marriage is a divine ordinance, and who defends the right of a homosexual lifestyle, may well be talking about freedom, but then not the kind of Christian freedom that the Bible ties to a holy and modest lifestyle. Even though these are all called liberation theologies, what do they really have to do with theology if they no longer speak biblically about *God* and His *holy* people?

The Personal and the Negative

To all of this we might add as well that the Decalogue is directed to the Israelite in the second person singular. To put it more colloquially, the prologue says, "I am Yahweh, *your* [singular] God who freed *you* [singular] from Egypt, the house of slavery." We could render the commandments the same way: "*You* [singular] shall have no other gods before me, not make any graven images, and not misuse Yahweh's name. *You* [singular], along with your family, must personally rest on the Sabbath, and honor *your* [singular] father and mother. *You* [singular] must not kill, not steal, not commit adultery, and not set your desires on your neighbor's house or possessions."

Yahweh established a covenant with His people, but if this free people wished to remain free, then each one personally had to understand his or her responsibility. Every social ethic is doomed to failure if it is blind to personal responsibility. You can draw all sorts of blueprints for social change in the world and even expect that people will be liberated by following them, but that is pure illusion. Evil resides in structures (also), but it is invented in the human heart. Every person has a special relationship to God. Just as each individual is going to be judged personally in the final judgment (2 Cor. 5:10), so too each one is addressed personally in the law. Nobody can transfer personal responsibility to somebody else.[7] If "everybody" wants to go against what Yahweh says, then He reminds us, "You [singular] shall not follow a crowd to do evil" (Ex. 23:2). This kind of reminder sheds clear light on the real meaning of freedom. People are free when they obey God, even if that leads to social isolation.

In connection with this matter of "freedom," we would like to mention something about the negative character of the commandments. Eight times we hear "You shall not," and the two other commandments (the fourth and fifth commandments) clearly indicate from their positive instruction that certain things are forbidden. In view of so many negative formulations, is it still possible to speak of the law of *liberty*? Do we not lose the freedom to which the prologue bears testimony, as soon as we come to the commandments?

We may certainly deduce from the negative formulations that man is a sinner inclined to transgress the law. In the law we have a mirror in which we look to see ourselves as we really are: you shall not kill, because you are a murderer; you shall not commit adultery, because you really are an adulterer![8]

It is absolutely necessary that we come to know the law in this unmasking function (*usus elenchticus*). For then it delivers us from all conceit and self-righteousness. We might also put it this way: the law of God *liberates* us from conceit and self-righteousness. It tells us rather clearly that we had better not look for our salvation in being decent or moral or law-abiding, but that we can be declared righteous only through a living bond with Christ—who has fulfilled the whole law. Apart from Christ, the law condemns us; but in the hands of Christ, the law remains the charter of our liberty. It functions this way as the fountain for knowing our misery (it drives us to Christ) and as the rule for gratitude (it teaches us the form of Christian living).

To this we would add one more observation: A rule that prohibits one particular thing still permits many others. In the Garden of Eden, eating from one particular tree was forbidden, but Adam and Eve were permitted to eat from all the other trees.[9] The gates of freedom provide a permanent opening in a wall that you may not climb over. Traffic signs do not so much restrict travel, as provide for its safe and orderly movement.

Ten Commandments—Two Tables

Before leaving the prologue to consider the Ten Commandments, we would like to conclude with a few general observations.

The first concerns the precise division of the Ten Commandments. There is quite a divergence of opinion about this. Which commandments belong to the first table and which to the second? Or is it the case that all ten belonged originally to one table, of which the other was simply a duplicate? That last notion was put forth when scholars drew a rather extensive comparison between the Sinai covenant and the Hittite suzerain-vassal treaties. The suzerain and the vassal each received a copy of the covenant stipulations. These were naturally identical copies. In this case, as in other covenants between two parties, Yahweh supposedly wrote one copy of the Ten Commandments for Himself and another identical one for His people.

This view strikes us as too speculative, especially since we read that both tables were later placed in the ark (Deut. 10:1–5). Exactly what was written on one tablet or the other is nowhere mentioned. What we do know is that *ten* commandments were given (although even here there is not complete agreement).* We might also mention that the Ten Commandments are summarized in two commands: love toward God and love toward neighbor, as Christ has taught us (Matt. 22:37–40). But this is not yet to say that each of these two commandments summarizes one of the tables.

---

* For example, B. Reicke, *Die zehn Worte* (Tübingen, 1973), 5, argues that these commandments originally were not numbered and divided as we have them today, but rather a round number (ten) was used "according to ancient Hebrew custom."

The fact that the division of the Ten Commandments varies for Jews, Roman Catholics, Reformed, and Lutherans will become evident when we discuss the individual commandments. We have already learned that the Jews view the prologue as a separate commandment. Our treatment of the Ten Commandments follows the division commonly used by other Reformed theologians.

Rules for Interpretation

A proper treatment of the Ten Commandments is possible only within the context of the whole Scripture. We no longer stand at the foot of Sinai, but we live after Christ. For that reason, we cannot read the Ten Commandments without taking into account the Sermon on the Mount. When we consider "You shall not kill," we must discuss anger and verbal abuse as well. When we seek to understand the meaning of "You shall not commit adultery," we must talk about looking at a woman lustfully (Matt. 5:21–26, 27–32). We cannot confine ourselves simply to the letter of the Ten Commandments. They must be apprehended in all their depth and breadth, as we have already indicated.

Often commentators provide specific rules for interpreting the Ten Commandments. Here are the most important ones:

1. The Decalogue must be interpreted spiritually. That fits what we just wrote: the law is understood in its depth only when we see it fulfilled in Christ and when we interpret it in a "Christian" manner. Spiritual interpretation recognizes as well that we cannot suffice with an external obedience, but that the law demands of us our *heart* (Matt. 22:37–40; 1 Tim. 1:5).
2. The negative commandments ("You shall not . . .") include positive commands, and vice versa.
3. Each commandment must be interpreted *per synecdoche*, which means that where one sin is mentioned, the commandment intends to cover the entire range of related sins.
4. Those commandments concerned specifically with love toward God weigh more heavily than those commandments concerned specifically with love toward neighbor. For example, love for God outweighs love for parents.
5. The starting point and goal of all the commandments is love.[10]

Several of these rules will require further comment in our discussion of specific commandments.

Endnotes

1. J. L. Koole, *De Tien Geboden*, 2d ed. (Kampen, 1983), 10–11; also G. van Rongen, *Zijn vast verbond* (Goes, 1966), 51ff.

2. J. W. Tunderman, *'t Beginsel der eeuwige vreugde* (Goes, 1949), 2:110.

3. H. Veldkamp, *Zondagskinderen*, 3d ed. (Franeker, 1957), 2:138.

4. J. L. Koole, *De Tien Geboden*, 25–26.

5. This term is used by J. M. Lochman, *Wegweisung der Freiheit* (Gütersloh, 1979), 17. Lochman's book is a clear example of interpreting the Decalogue within the context of a (moderated) theology of liberation. Our appreciation and criticisms of this work appear in "L'actualité de l'éthique du Décalogue," *La revue réformée* 33 (1982): 72ff.

6. F. H. von Meyenfeldt, *Tien tegen een* (Hilversum, 1978), 1:58ff.

7. J. Vermeer, *De Leere der Waarheid* (Nijkerk, 1857), 1:155.

8. Helmut Thielicke, *Theological Ethics*, ed. William H. Lazareth, vol. 1: *Foundations* (Philadelphia, 1966), 290–91.

9. A. Maillot, *Le Décalogue* (Paris, 1976), 14.

10. See Calvin, *Institutes of the Christian Religion*, 2.8.10. In his *Institutes of Elenctic Theology* (trans. George Musgrave Giger, ed. James T. Dennison, Jr. [Phillipsburg, N.J., 1994]), Francis Turretin gives seven rules (2:34–36). The Westminster Larger Catechism mentions eight rules (Answer 99). Interestingly, Gisbert Voetius (1589–1676), in his *Catechisatie over den Heidelbergschen Catechismus* (2:756–57), distinguishes between absolute commandments to which God can never grant exceptions (such as the first and third commandments), and commandments to which God can grant exceptions.

The First Commandment

You shall have no other gods beside Me. (Ex. 20:3)

Are There Other Gods?

When you read the Bible, you will meet numerous gods. Upon entering Canaan, Israel encountered residents serving Baal. During the time of the judges, Israel forgot Yahweh, forsaking Him to serve the Baals and the Asherahs (Judg. 2:11; 3:7; 8:33). The plural number indicates that these male and female deities were worshiped in various ways according to geographical regions. Baal Berith lived next to Baal Hermon (Judg. 8:33; 3:3). Later, Elijah would wage a bitter struggle against the Baal worship propagated by Ahab and Jezebel (1 Kings 18:20–40). Other gods were enshrined in the land of Israel. Think of Solomon's idolatry, which led him—under the influence of his many foreign wives—to permit shrines to be built in honor of the Ammonite god Milcom and the Moabite god Chemosh (1 Kings 11:4–8).

Regarding these and numerous other deities, the Lord says in the first commandment that Israel may not have these gods beside Him. From this formulation you might conclude that although these "other gods" were not to be *worshiped* alongside Yahweh, they nevertheless *existed* alongside Him. Just as Yahweh exists, so too do Baal, Milcom, and Chemosh. In a world parceled out by the gods, each nation and region had its own deity! If this were so, the first commandment would come down simply to denying *Israel* the right to kneel before other gods—deities exercising over their nations the very same demand for exclusive worship that Yahweh is here pressing upon His people.*

---

*If this were true, then we should really be speaking not of *monotheism* (there is but one God and other gods do not exist), but of *henotheism* (for *Israel* there is but one God, whereas the other nations have their own—real—gods).

15

In the preceding chapter, dealing with the prologue, we pointed out that at Sinai, Yahweh declared that the whole world belonged to Him (Ex. 19:5). This means that other gods wielded the scepter of power that belongs to Yahweh alone. But we must add another ingredient: actually, these gods had no reality as gods. People called them gods, but they were just like their images: the work of human hands, wood and stone that could not see or hear, eat or smell (Deut. 4:28). Elijah and Isaiah mocked them (1 Kings 18:27; Isa. 40:18–20; 45:20). They are called "nothings," nonentities (Isa. 2:8, 18, 20).

If we continue reasoning along this line, it might even seem that the first commandment is a waste of ammunition: its warning aims at other gods that do not exist. Yet we all know how seriously the entire Scripture warns against idols. John says that faith in Jesus Christ overcomes the world (1 John 5:5), but he concludes his epistle with these words: "Little children, keep yourselves from idols" (1 John 5:21). Apparently, someone who acknowledges Jesus Christ as Lord of the universe must still be on guard against associating with idols!

How can we fit these two things together: on the one hand, gods that do not exist; yet, on the other hand, gods against whom we must be on guard? The answer is not too difficult. People worship powerful forces within creation as if these were deities. They are not gods, but only so-called gods (1 Cor. 8:4–7); still, they are very real powers, able to enslave a person totally.*

We can illustrate this with the example of Baal. Who was Baal? He was the personification of the fertility of the field. Baal was the god of rain,

---

*Occasionally in the Old Testament we read expressions that give us an impression of henotheism. For example, Naomi tells Ruth that Orpah has returned to her people and to her gods (Ruth 1:15). Jephthah tells the Ammonite king: "Will you not possess whatever Chemosh your god gives you to possess? So whatever the LORD our God takes possession of before us, we will possess" (Judg. 11:24). And Saul's entourage included people who told David, "Go, serve other gods" (1 Sam. 26:19). But this is not to say that those who spoke this way were henotheists. Taking into account the fact that others believe in strange gods and that some (Ruth and Jephthah) might express themselves in the language of those others is quite different than accepting that reality oneself. Nor can a verse like Ps. 82:1 ("God stands in the congregation of the mighty; He judges among the gods") be adduced as evidence of henotheism in the Old Testament. On the basis of an analogy to Ex. 21:6; 22:8–9; 22:28; 1 Sam. 2:25; Ps. 58:1, we should interpret the "gods" in Ps. 82:1 as referring to judges. J. P. Lettinga sets forth this analysis of Ps. 82:1 more fully in his essay, "Psalm 82: The Living God and the Dying Idols," *Almanak van het Corpus Studiosorum in Academia Campensi "Fides Quadrat Intellectum"* 1988, 135–52.

thunder, and fertility. When the sun's heat scorched everything, people said that Baal was dying. When the autumn rain made everything green, people said that Baal was coming to life again. Now, Baal did not really "exist," because this idol was nothing but a human projection; however, the power of new life coming from a barren earth is real. It is just as real as the human yearning to control this life and the benefits flowing from it.

Estranged from the Creator of rain, thunder, and fertile fields, people began to worship the creature instead of the Creator. All idolatrous worship is in fact the worship of creatures like rain, sexuality, love, authority, and intellect. Everybody admits that these creatures can each exercise enormous power. If these powers remain in their rightful place assigned by the Creator, they serve people.* But when they occupy a wrong place, then they eventually master people as God surrenders fallen man to his own desires (Rom. 1:24–25). They become powers to which people ascribe divine honor.

As the years have passed, many gods have disappeared. Baal is now sleeping for good, Zeus no longer sits on Mount Olympus, and the German gods Woden and Thor have no more worshipers. But idolatry does not depend on names. The names may disappear, but the powers remain. The Bible also shows us clearly that idolatry can live apart from idol names. We read that a man's *strength* can be his god (Hab. 1:11). You can say to *gold,* "You are my confidence" (Job 31:24); *money* can be called Mammon (Matt. 6:24); and *covetousness* is explicitly called idolatry in the Bible (Col. 3:5). We can also make our *stomach* our god (Phil. 3:19).

This list could be expanded. People can make idols out of almost anything. The erotic, the desire for power, reason, nature, tradition, and conscience—each of these can be absolutized in ways both uncultured and very refined. Everyday common things can get a person in their grasp. Ancient interpreters used to speak of the three-headed idol when they quoted John's warning against worldliness: the lust of the flesh, the lust of the

---

* E. L. Smelik, *De ethiek in de verkondiging,* 3d ed. (Nijkerk, 1967), 84–85. Hendrikus Berkhof indicates that the concept of "powers" in the New Testament not only has a negative sound (as in Rom. 8:38–39; 1 Cor. 15:24; Eph. 2:1–3; Col. 2:15), but also can be used positively (as in Col. 1:15–18). "Divers human traditions, the course of earthly life as conditioned by the heavenly bodies, morality, fixed religious and ethical rules, the administration of justice and the ordering of the state—all these can be tyrants over our life, but *in themselves* they are not" (*Christ and the Powers,* trans. John H. Yoder [Scottdale, Pa., 1977], 29). The same could be said about those elements we have identified as "powers" that can enslave mankind.

eyes, and the pride of life (1 John 2:16). The heart can become addicted, we read somewhere, to anything in our homes, from attic to cellar, in cupboards and drawers, in our yards, our eating, clothing and hobbies. Everybody has something he calls his hobby, something that has hold of his heart. It is just as hard to let go of this as it was for Rachel to get rid of her father's household gods (Gen. 31:19).*

Are there other gods? The answer must be yes and no. Baal, Asherah, Chemosh, Molech, Mammon, Zeus, Neptune, Woden, and Thor do not exist. But man's yearning for prosperity, passionate love, power, and strife existed and still exist.[†] Idolatry, the Heidelberg Catechism explains lucidly, is "instead of the one true God who has revealed Himself in His Word, or besides Him, to devise or have something else on which to place our trust" (Answer 95). Idolatry can devise as much as creation holds! Images of gods may well evoke our laughter, but we must not be fooled by the outward appearance. Anyone taking idolatry seriously knows it involves passionate practices that remain relevant to this day. Elijah and Isaiah mocked the idols, but that is not the same as taking idolatry lightly. They both knew that idolaters choose for something that displeases Yahweh (see 1 Kings 16:33; Isa. 66:3–4).

The First Commandment: A Choice

Choosing for the Lord always means making a choice that excludes every other possibility. When the people of Israel had been established in Canaan, shortly before his death, Joshua summoned together in Shechem representatives from all the tribes. After explaining to the tribes of Israel in great detail how Yahweh had led them out of Egypt and had given them the land of Canaan, he concluded with his appeal: "Now therefore, fear the LORD, serve Him in sincerity and in truth, and put away the gods which your fathers served on the other side of the River and in Egypt. Serve the LORD! And if it seems evil to you to serve the LORD, choose for yourselves this day whom you will serve, whether the gods which your fa-

---

* J. Vermeer, *De Leere der Waarheid* (Nijkerk, 1857), 1:154, 173–74. Vermeer and D. Molenaar, *De Heidelbergische Catechismus* (Arnhem, 1855), 2:141, mention also the "spirit of the times" or the "god of fashion," which is "almost universally worshiped."

† Underlying these existing forces we may presume seductive, satanic spirits at work. K. J. Popma, *Levensbeschouwing* (Amsterdam, 1962), 5:216, bases this view on 1 Cor. 10:21 (the "cup of the Lord" is contrasted with the "table of demons") and Dan. 10:20–21 (where national spirits or angels can rule [in the bad sense of the word] over entire nations).

thers served that were on the other side of the River, or the gods of the Amorites, in whose land you dwell. But as for me and my house, we will serve the LORD" (Josh. 24:14–15). The entire people then made the same choice as Joshua. With a ceremony and a written testimony, the covenant between Israel and Yahweh was then renewed.

This history is instructive for more than one reason.

First of all, we are impressed once again that Joshua begins with the narrative of Yahweh's deliverance of the people, and then leads right into his appeal to choose for Yahweh. To put it in the language of the Ten Commandments: first comes the prologue and then the first commandment.

Secondly, it appears that the choice for Yahweh must be a radical choice. It is not a matter of both-and, but of either-or. You cannot choose for Yahweh and at the same time hang on to the gods of Mesopotamia or Egypt, for anyone choosing Yahweh must put away all those foreign gods (Josh. 24:14, 23). The same is true of God and Mammon: nobody can serve two masters, "for either he will hate the one and love the other, or else he will be loyal to the one and despise the other" (Matt. 6:24).

In the third place, it seems that covenant renewal is needed regularly. At Sinai the people of Israel ceremonially promised to behave according to God's words (Ex. 24:3), but in no way did that signal the immediate disappearance of idol worship (cf. Num. 25:2; Amos 5:25–26). Although Israel had been freed from Egypt, her heart was still bound by the fetters of idolatry practiced in her early history or recent past. For that reason, the choice had to be put before the people time and again (Deut. 27:11–26; 31:9–13, 24–29).

Choosing for Yahweh means *loving* Him. The intimate bond between this choosing and loving clearly underlies the so-called Shema, that confession in Deuteronomy 6:4–5 read aloud daily in the temple and synagogues along with the Ten Commandments: "Hear, O Israel: The LORD our God, the LORD is one! You shall love the LORD your God with all your heart, with all your soul, and with all your might." Later, Jesus would answer the question about the most important commandment with this Shema: the Lord is one *and* you shall love the Lord your God (Matt. 22:34–40).

Many have difficulty applying that loaded word "love" to their relationship with God. Is it not too presumptuous to apply that word to ourselves? Do we have a love relationship with God as we have with our father, mother, spouse, or child? Can we speak of God in terms of affections and emotional inclinations? It is good to talk about this for a moment, because the concept of love occupies a significant place in ethics.

First of all, we must emphasize that our love toward God does have an emotional side. For in our love, we are responding to His love toward us. The Bible talks about this very emotionally. Yahweh is a father to orphans (Ps. 68:5), pities His children like a father (Ps. 103:13), and therefore can be filled with inner tenderness and mercy (Isa. 66:13), unable to forget His people even as a woman her nursing child (Isa. 49:15). He taught Israel to walk and took them by the arms (Hos. 11:3). In the Bible, Yahweh is clearly a "He," something no feminist theology can change.* But in His expression of feelings, God is as maternal as He is paternal. His love evokes our love, so it would indeed be strange if our love would lack the emotional element. That element must come to expression, for example, in our thanksgiving and in our singing.

But love is not mere sentiment. That is our second observation. If it were, then we would have to agree with Freud, who insisted that the commandment to love our neighbors as ourselves was unpsychological. Freud argued that if a neighbor is a stranger to me, someone who cannot attract me on the basis of any intrinsic value he possesses or any significance he might have for my emotional life, then I would have a hard time loving him. In fact, I would act wrongly by loving him![1] But the Bible speaks a different language. Here, love is indeed a command; I am commanded to love even my enemy, something against which my emotions tend to rebel.

---

* The Hebrew word *elohim* can mean both "god" and "gods." Consequently, theoretically the translation of the first commandment could be, "You shall have no other god beside Me." The word *elohim* can even mean *goddess*. One could, again theoretically, translate, "You shall have no other—[namely] a *goddess*—beside Me." On this point, J. L. Koole observes that this possibility certainly lies within the first commandment: "That the God of Israel tolerated no goddess alongside Him is something extraordinary in the ancient Eastern world. The Canaanites worshiped their Baal and their Ashtoreth (Judg. 2:13). Thus, in the ancient Eastern world, the male deities were always accompanied by female deities; the opening narratives of world history always began with a pair of deities who were the ancestors of other gods and goddesses, and finally of the human world itself. But the first commandment put Israel in an exceptional position among her neighbors; Israel's God tolerated not only no other god, but also no goddess beside Him. . . . Belief in a God who is God-by-Himself and therefore not an incomplete deity, only that kind of faith leads to the deepest reverence and fullest amazement in the presence of this God, who alone needs nobody and nothing in order to be Himself " (*De Tien Geboden*, 32–33). Koole does point out (pp. 33–34) that God's "motherly" characteristics must not be neglected in our confession about God, for then we would have no defense any longer "against Mariolatry, whose view of the Virgin Mother compensates for a supposed deficiency in our view of God."

We understand more clearly exactly what love toward God really is when we *see love as a choice*. Because only Yahweh is God, Israel and we must choose for Him. *To love means to stick with your choice*. When a marriage gets into trouble, the only path to resolution is the choice to love. The emotional element in that love may be wholly or partially absent, but faithfulness must come out. Concretely, then, love means that husband and wife form no relationships with third parties, but maintain the choice they made for each other with their wedding vows. The same is true of our relationship with the Lord. He covenanted Himself to Israel, and Israel to Him. The first commandment demands a love that is faithful to the covenant. Here, too, no third party may come between them. Love cannot be shared between Yahweh and Baal, between God and Mammon. At Carmel it was confirmed that only Yahweh is God (1 Kings 18:39). We saw already that in terms of God and money, Jesus said that nobody can serve two masters (Matt. 6:24). To love is to stick with your choice, regardless of whether it feels good. Genuine love is love tried and tested.

Love must answer to yet another norm, also implicit in the Shema. When Israel is called to love Yahweh, Moses continues, "And these words which I command you today shall be in your heart; you shall teach them diligently to your children, and shall talk of them when you sit in your house, when you walk by the way, when you lie down, and when you rise up" (Deut. 6:6–7). To love the Lord means to keep His words (commandments).

In the New Testament fulfillment of the first commandment, God comes to us in Jesus Christ. As the Son of God, who by His redemptive work obtained the highest name—Jesus Christ is Lord!—all divine worship belongs to Him (Rom. 9:5; Phil. 2:9–11). The honor belonging to the Father must be given to the Son also. There is one God and one mediator between God and men, the man Christ Jesus (1 Tim. 2:5). The knees that must bow to the Father (Eph. 3:14–15) bow to Jesus Christ as well (Phil. 2:10). The choice Yahweh demands, Christ demands too: "He who loves father or mother more than Me is not worthy of Me," He tells His disciples, adding that those who follow Him must take up their *cross* (Matt. 10:37–39). You see, this kind of choice might strain rather important emotional ties! When Peter answered the Savior's question by affirming his love for the Lord three times, Jesus then showed him what that would mean: When you were younger, you clothed yourself and walked where you wished; but when you are old, you will stretch out your hands, and another will clothe you and carry you where you do not wish (John 21:18). To love Jesus means you are no longer your own boss, but as you follow

Him, you must be ready perhaps even to face a martyr's death (as in Peter's case).

In the New Testament as well, love toward God and Christ is clearly subordinated to a norm. Jesus says, "If anyone loves Me, he will keep My word" (John 14:23). We must not only hear His words, but keep them, too. In the parable of the sower, many hear the word, but do not keep it. Some hear the word, but do not understand it; others receive it at first with joy, but abandon it when persecution and oppression (the cross!) come; still others let the word gradually choke on material cares and the delusion of wealth. But other people listen well to the word and bear fruit (Matt. 13:19–23). These last ones are like Mary, who kept all the words of Jesus and pondered them in her heart (Luke 2:19). Such listeners resemble those whom Jesus pronounced blessed because they hear the word of God and keep it (Luke 11:28). God's words do not go in one ear and out the other; these listeners are not like the people Isaiah describes: "Seeing many things, but you do not observe; opening the ears, but he does not hear" (Isa. 42:20).

Earlier we mentioned that some readers may have a hard time using the loaded word "love" in connection with our relationship with God. We could say the same thing about "keeping" God's words (commandments). Already from the Shema it is clear that the Israelite was supposed to be busy with God's words at home and away from home, at dawn and at dusk. It is no different in the New Testament, where we are told throughout how important it is to keep God's words (Luke 8:15; 1 Tim. 6:20; 1 John 3:24; 5:2–3). One who keeps these words is equipped to guard against idols. This is how we abide in Christ and He in us (1 John 3:24). This summons to love God and thus to keep His words is not given to supermen. The first commandment is for ordinary Israelites and for ordinary disciples of Jesus Christ. The disciples we meet in the New Testament could be dull of understanding and slow of heart (Luke 24:25). In the Garden of Gethsemane they could not stay awake even one hour to watch with their Master (Matt. 26:40). Peter even denied Him (Matt. 26:69–75). All of them had trouble accepting the report of Christ's resurrection. But concerning *these* people, knowing their weaknesses, Jesus prayed in His high priestly prayer to the Father: "They were Yours, You gave them to Me, and *they have kept Your word*" (John 17:6). Weak, unbelieving, dozing, and rebellious men were repeatedly restored because the words of God and of Christ had received a permanent place in their hearts. They stuck with their choice, even though they were often shaken back and forth by Satan in his sieve (Luke 22:31–32) and were occasionally ensnared in the nets of idolatry.

With an Undivided Heart

The Israelite was not supposed to devote his heart to Yahweh and other gods: "You shall have no other gods *beside* Me." That little word *and* is dangerous: Yahweh *and* Baal, Yahweh *and* Molech, Yahweh *and* sorcery. We would like to return for a moment to discuss this radical choice that the Lord demands of His people. The Shema calls the Israelite to love Yahweh with all his heart, all his soul, and all his might. Of course, this cannot happen if one's love is devoted to more than one.

People are expected by the first commandment to be blameless and perfect. Words like these can generate misunderstanding, because we usually understand *perfection* to mean "without spot or wrinkle." We might stumble over difficulties similar to those mentioned in connection with loving God. Who of us can say that he serves God blamelessly, or even perfectly? Yet this is exactly what the Bible says about more than one person. Noah was a righteous and perfect man (Gen. 6:9). And if the rich young man had sold his possessions, he could have been called perfect (Matt. 19:21). Descriptions like these are neither exaggeration nor irony. If we look carefully at the Hebrew word used to indicate that Noah was perfect, then we learn that it means "wholeness." Noah's heart was completely focused on God. There was no laziness in his service of God. He walked with God, we read in the very same verse (Gen. 6:9). The story of the rich young man shows us as well that *perfection* can be understood in the same sense. The young man did much good. He obeyed the commandments relating to murder, adultery, stealing, and honoring his parents. But his heart was not wholly devoted to God. When Jesus proposed to him that he sell his possessions in order to be "perfect," he showed his halfheartedness. He could not let go of his property, for he had many possessions. He was clearly serving God *and* Mammon. For that reason, there was no wholeheartedness, no perfection, in his case. He was keeping two irons in the fire—God's law and his money—whereas Jesus was demanding his whole heart.

We find this kind of expression, then, when the Bible describes somebody as having served the Lord with a perfect heart. Yahweh says this of David (1 King 9:4), even though this king had committed grievous sins. Yet time and again he chose wholeheartedly for Yahweh. There was a single thread to David's life, which by no means denies that he stumbled very grievously. Here we learn that people who fall into serious sin can still be characterized as having walked with the Lord.

In the Sermon on the Mount, Jesus demands the same perfection of His disciples: "Therefore you shall be perfect, just as your Father in heaven is perfect" (Matt. 5:48). With this requirement Jesus is not demanding an unattainable goal, a life without mistakes, but He is asking for the same integrity of character shown by our heavenly Father. He lets His sun shine on the bad and the good and lets the rain fall on the righteous and the un-righteous. Similarly, the disciple of Jesus must show love to friend and foe alike. He may not exhibit favoritism, divided attention, by loving friend but not foe. That attitude does not correspond to the way God distributes sunshine and rain to the just and the unjust (Matt. 5:43–48).[2]

The course of our life must be determined by the first commandment. No doubleheartedness, but our whole heart for the Lord.

Sorcery and Witchcraft

Yahweh expects this same wholeness of heart in connection with a spe-cific form of idolatry. Israel was not permitted to tolerate anybody who practiced soothsaying, who was a medium, an interpreter of omens, or a sorcerer who spoke with spirits or consulted the dead. "You shall be blameless before the LORD your God," and therefore, unlike the original inhabitants of the land of Canaan, you shall not listen to sorcerers and witches. "But as for you, the LORD your God has not appointed such for you" (Deut. 18:10–14).

Exactly what we are to understand by sorcerers, witches, and soothsay-ers is not altogether clear. Even modern translations leave some doubt re-garding precisely what was being referred to in the Hebrew of Leviticus 19:31. For example: "Do not turn to mediums or seek out spiritists, for you will be defiled by them. I am the LORD your God" (NIV). Nevertheless, in spite of whatever uncertainty the translation of these terms may leave, we can still point out a few things relevant for contemporary ethics.

We must be impressed, first of all, with the fact that the Bible takes for-tunetelling (sorcery) and witchcraft seriously. We might otherwise be tempted to treat them lightly. As Shakespeare said in *Hamlet*, "There are more things in heaven and earth, than are dreamt of in your philosophy." People can manipulate secret powers and call up special phenomena, as the witch of Endor did, for example, when Saul asked her to bring up the old prophet Samuel from the dead (1 Sam. 28:11–19). Nevertheless, interpre-tations differ concerning what really happened here at Endor.* Involved

---

* The official commentary on the Dutch Statenvertaling says about the phrase "when the woman saw Samuel" (1 Sam. 28:12), "That is, an evil spirit, in the form of Samuel, which she through her devilish art had made to appear. Jesus Sirach is seriously mistaken

here is the fact that special events do occur that can exercise a great influence on people, just as, for example, King Saul was deeply affected when he received the message of Samuel's "spirit" (1 Sam. 28:20–25).

Moreover, it is clear why fortunetelling and witchcraft are forbidden. One who has given his whole heart to Yahweh cannot join the Canaanites in *listening* to sorcerers and fortunetellers. They provide a message telling people what is going to happen to them and what they must do. The fortuneteller is consulted in order to look into the future and to direct a person's life with that information. Fortunetelling, sorcery, witchcraft—these are all forms of prophecy, but of a wrong kind. Instead of placing one's life in Yahweh's hands and listening only to His words, people seek to orient their lives according to what witches tell them. But they are false prophets who mislead people (Jer. 29:8; Ezek. 13:9). The false prophet Elymas opposed the apostle Paul (Acts 13:6). Rebellion and stubbornness characterize witchcraft and idolatry (1 Sam. 15:23), while the true prophet speaks the words of Yahweh (Deut. 18:19).

When we remember that fortunetelling and witchcraft stand as false prophecy over against true prophecy (Deut. 18:10–12, 15–16), then we see clearly why consulting fortunetellers and sorcerers is so sinful. Those who consult such people are no longer trusting in the words of the Lord and are no longer expecting the certainty and safety of their future from Him. Turning to fortunetelling spirits is turning away from Him. We let go of the certainty and safety with the Lord that we *already possess* by listening in faith to His words, in order to grope after an illusory security from the sorcerer.

The warning against this applies today as well. We must not fall into spiritism and fortunetelling.* Relying on palm reading or horoscopes con-

---

when he writes that after Samuel had died, he prophesied and predicted Saul's end." W. Geesink disagrees with the opinion of these Bible commentators. He is convinced that Scripture certainly does not consider the spiritualist phenomena at Endor to be "devil's work." Geesink insists that "what the woman says to Saul is to be explained on the basis of her 'clairvoyance.' In her sleepwalking state she saw a hallucination of the old man with his mantle, whom she had seen walking Ramah's streets more than once. In this situation she spoke to Saul with the voice of Samuel, whom she, as a clairvoyant, had recognized" (*Van 's Heeren ordinantiën*, 2d ed. [Kampen, 1925], 3:330–31).

* It is difficult to distinguish spiritism, fortunetelling, and witchcraft from each other. In spiritism, people believe that survivors can contact the dead under certain circumstances. Fortunetelling can refer to any attempt to predict people's future or future events. Witchcraft is the attempt to bring about special, extraordinary effects (like healing), especially by means of incantations and ritual gestures.

flicts with showing honor to God and placing trust in Him when it comes
to directing our lives.

However, we must be careful not to see the Devil working in everything
we might call "unusual." Alongside spiritists and card readers we find
those who practice acupuncture, reflexology, yoga, and more. We would
be going too far if we put them all in the same category as Deuteronomy
18:10–11. If they are indeed false prophets who seek to predict our future
and tell us how we should arrange our lives in terms of that future, then
they certainly do belong in that category. If not, however, then although
we might still have many other reasons for criticizing acupuncture, reflexology, and the like, we should not allege that they come from "the domain
of the Devil." If a clairvoyant can help solve a murder, or if a technician
applying unorthodox treatments can ease someone's pain, then we could
view these as special abilities that can obviously be used to a good end. In
any case, these have nothing to do with false prophecy.

Of course, a wrong attitude could well be coming to expression in seeking help from these forms of treatment. You can run from one doctor to
another specialist to someone else whose unorthodox treatment is not
covered by insurance, refusing to place your life in God's hands, perhaps
refusing to face death itself. But this same attitude can be present even
when one uses recognized means of treatment.

In order to distinguish carefully in these matters, we could profit today
from an ancient distinction used by Gisbert Voetius. He spoke first of *magia bona*, referring to the art of knowing the hidden properties of natural
things. Using that knowledge, people with deeper insight into nature
could effect wonderful things. But even though they appear supernatural,
these are phenomena of nature. In terms of these *magia bona*, the Dutch
theologians W. Geesink and K. Schilder wrote appreciatively about the
phenomenon of clairvoyance, for example. No matter how much about
this phenomenon remains unexplained, we are not dealing here with the
occult in any sense of the word, argued Geesink.[*]

---

[*] K. Schilder wrote about this in *Wat is de hemel?* 2d ed. (Kampen, 1954), 128–29. There
he mentions clairvoyance and says, "Many individuals seem to have an immediate certainty
about something that happened far away, a certainty too remote and too exceptional for the
ordinary, everyday paths of knowledge. Everything in the domain of the so-called 'occult,'
insofar as it makes use of potentialities present in God's creation, is nothing more than a
very normal *employment* of what God has put in creation. In many cases the *intention* with
which people in so-called occult circles operate with such divinely given potentialities may
well be wrong, and people may well pursue those things for selfish purposes, so that for those

Next, Voetius mentioned the *magia vana*, or playful, nonverbal magic. This kind of "sorcery" is not necessarily evil, for the "sorcerer" here is a magician who understands the art of producing a trick with a sleight of hand, with agility and illusion. Not hidden forces, but manual dexterity is the power at work.

Finally, Voetius defined the *magia superstitiosa* as the superstitious sorcery that must be absolutely rejected. Involved here are the sins condemned in Deuteronomy 18 and Leviticus 19 that we discussed earlier.*

The One God and Suffering

In its explanation of the first commandment, the Heidelberg Catechism requires the Christian believer to submit with all humility and patience to God alone (Answer 94). Today these words are especially timely, for they imply that we must also accept from God's hand our *suffering*. One of the authors of the catechism, Ursinus, comments that we must obey God as we bear every adversity, not grumbling against God on account of our pain, but rather trusting that He will help us.[3] What Ursinus asserts here is vehemently rejected today. People insist that suffering does *not* come from God, and that we should therefore resist all suffering. Instead of patiently bearing our suffering, we need not put up with it any longer. Not acceptance, but rejection of suffering is the attitude recommended today.

Elsewhere we have rejected this viewpoint as absolutely unbiblical.[4] But we really should say something about this matter in connection with the first commandment as well. For if what people today are claiming

---

reasons such use and pursuits are worthy of condemnation, but we are dealing here ultimately with things that belong *to nature itself.*" Many people, Schilder continued, characterize those phenomena "because of their inherent mysteriousness, albeit fallaciously, as nothing short of the work of the devil." For Geesink's observations, see *Van 's Heeren ordinantiën*, 3:306–31.

* G. Voetius, *Disputationes selectae* (Utrecht, 1659), 3:539ff. For a brief summary of these sins, see W. Geesink, *Van 's Heeren ordinantiën*, 3:309ff. Ancient commentators viewed magic in the sense of Deut. 18 as a pact with the Devil. The connection made between magic and the Devil would have been influenced by the fact that Paul calls Elymas the magician a "son of the devil" (Acts 13:10). See Voetius, *Disputationes selectae*, 3:544. B. Bekker, "Catechisatie over den Heidelbergschen Catechismus," in *De Friesche Godgeleerdheid* (Amsterdam, 1693), 277, mentions that historically, the Greek word *nekromantes* (one who consults the dead) has been mistakenly associated with *negromantes* (black-magic practitioner). "Black magic" involves association with the Devil.

about suffering is true, then it is no longer clear how we can continue to confess that *all* things are from and through and to God, that is: from and through and to the *one* God. Alongside God, who sends forth among men only good, people set up *the Devil* as the source of sickness and other misery. Or, if the Devil no longer exists in a person's theology, then *chance* reigns alongside God. Chance means that there are things even God does not have under control. Today people assert that God subjects Himself to human suffering and undergoes the struggle against suffering, but there is no sense in which He stands above suffering as the One who sends and removes it. Alongside God is the Devil or chance, who functions in such a way that the misery each causes is not under His control.

Such a view obviously conflicts with the first commandment. Undoubtedly those holding this view do not intend to *worship* the Devil or chance alongside God. These are not idols before which people are willing to kneel, because people despise them. But even *setting up* alongside God the Devil, chance, or any other power that limits His absolute sovereignty and sway, brings us into conflict with the first commandment. At this point we are not far removed from pagan polytheism, with its gods for every time and place—a god of war and a god of peace, a god of death and a god of life.* One god strokes his worshipers; the other god strikes them. And this is the pagan solution to the problem of suffering. The sweet and the bitter simply do not come from the same source.

But Scripture teaches something quite different about God. Suffering does indeed come from God's hand. When man fell into sin, God began to execute the sentence. People were touched by *His* curse, so that trouble, hardship, and death became their portion (Gen. 2:17; 3:16–19). God established enmity between the seed of the woman and the seed of the Serpent, and *He* predicted the ultimate victory of the seed of the woman, because God Himself can decide these things (Gen. 3:15). He annihilated virtually the entire human race in the Flood and sent plagues throughout Egypt and Israel (Gen. 6:7; Ex. 3:20; Deut. 4:27; 28:20–68). But just as God sends suffering to punish sin or to test His people without necessarily punishing them (Deut. 8:6; Job; Heb. 12:6; James 1:2–4; Rev. 3:19), in the same way He can also remove suffering. He rescues His people because He is a merciful God who will neither abandon nor desert Israel, who will not forget His covenant with the fathers (Deut. 4:31).

---

* J. C. de Moor points out in *Uw God is mijn God* (Kampen, 1983), 84, that the polytheists in ancient Ugarit had separate gods of war and of peace, of death and of life.

How all of this fits together remains a riddle for us.* On the one hand, we confess that the cause of suffering and death may not be sought in God. He hates evil and death. The source of all misery cannot be found in Him. Yet, on the other hand, God does rule over evil and death. He can send both. He gives not only food, but also famine; not only life, but also disease and death (Deut. 32:24; 1 Sam. 2:5–10).† What we do not understand, we can nevertheless confess. Along with the first commandment, we believe there is one God at the beginning and end of all things, whose omnipotence we may experience as a comfort. Not chance, but God, rules—everywhere and everything.

We would do well, then, to echo the Heidelberg Catechism's excellent summary at this point. It speaks with two words: we must submit ourselves to God in *humility* and *patience*. *Humility* inclines us to speak a bit more modestly about evil and suffering, looking first not at God or chance, but at ourselves. "Therefore humble yourselves under the mighty hand of God, that He may exalt you in due time" (1 Peter 5:6). *Patience* gives us courage, for along with James we have heard how Job was patient and how the Lord blessed him after his suffering was over. God is rich in mercy and compassion (James 5:11).

The One God and the Many Religions

One more question deserves discussion because of its relevance: Do Muslims, Buddhists, Hindus, or devotees of any other religion serve a different

---

* For a more extensive discussion of this riddle, see J. Douma, *Rondom de dood,* 36–38. In her doctrinal decisions about the Trinity, the early church took care not to create a separation between a Creator-god (to whom evil could be ascribed, as Marcion did) and a Redeemer-god (of the New Testament). The relevance of the Trinity (whose *unity* we are emphasizing here) to our subject has been perceived by others as well. Although we can hardly agree with the development of his position, this observation is made by W. Harrelson in *The Ten Commandments and Human Rights* (Philadelphia, 1980), 60–61.

† So also J. C. de Moor, *Uw God is mijn God,* 84. At the conclusion of his historical-critical essay about the crisis of polytheism in the Late Bronze Age and about the gradual move toward the monotheistic confession of Yahweh, he warns against the multiplication of god-ideas: the god of the feminist movement and the god of the homosexuals, the god of Black Africa and the god of many whites in South Africa. "It is my conviction," writes de Moor, "that the church cannot tolerate all of this at once. . . . For then we would be short-changing the oneness of God's essence for the sake of the many-ness" (pp. 82–83). It seems to us difficult to find that "oneness" any longer if we join de Moor in permitting ourselves the use of a critical methodology in reconstructing biblical data.

god than the God of the Bible? That question has been posed throughout history, of course, but it obtains greater urgency when Muslims move next door and Hindus practice their religion in front of us. How many times do people not say that we are all serving the same God—some call Him God, others call him Allah, still others honor him as Shang-ti. It is just like what we do with water: English speakers call it *water*, others call it *ajer* or *tirta* or *banju*; but we are all referring to the same thing. So it is with God: the words and names are different, but we all have the same supreme being in view.[5]

We cannot agree with this conclusion. The unbridgeable gulf between the Christian faith and other religions can be identified in various ways, but in our opinion, the clearest way is by asking the central question in Scripture: "What do you think about the Christ?" (Matt. 22:42). If we see Him as one prophet among many others, one of many manifestations of the supreme being in this world, then putting Christianity on a par with other world religions is required and inevitable. Why would Jesus be unique if there is also a Mohammed who demands for himself a place alongside Abraham, Moses, and Jesus as (the highest) prophet? However, if Jesus is not a prophet standing on the same level as other prophets, but the Christ, the Son of the living God (Matt. 16:13–17), then putting Christianity alongside other religions is impossible. The same must be said of Judaism, even though it is based on the Old Testament. For those committed to Judaism deny that Jesus is the Messiah who is one with the Father in an absolutely unique way (John 1:1, 3, 14; 10:30; Rom. 9:5). This unity between the Son and the Father has consequences for reading the first commandment. We can no longer speak about Yahweh, about God, except as the Father of Jesus Christ. Their indissoluble unity makes it impossible to fill the word "God" in any other way than Christ has filled it.

For on the basis of this unity Christ can say that no one comes to the Father except through Him (John 14:2). He has made the Father known to us (John 1:18). Redemption is found in Him alone, for there is only one name given among men whereby they can be saved (Acts 4:12). If you confess this, you will not be surprised by Paul's bold declaration that before their conversion, his readers had not acknowledged Christ as God, because they had been serving gods who in essence were nothing (Gal. 4:8). The Ephesians formerly lived without God (Eph. 2:12) and were alienated from life with God, something that changed only when they came to know Christ (Eph. 4:18, 20). With all its wisdom, the world has not known God, since this knowledge depends on revelation through the Spirit of God (1 Cor. 1:21; 2:10–16). Pagans can be very religious, as Paul frankly acknowledged (Acts 17:22–28). But this does not deny that nations without Christ are walking in their own ways and can be released from their idolatry only by conversion to the living God (Acts 14:15–16).

This sharp contrast between the Christian faith and other religions would be misunderstood if people were to see it as an aversion toward non-Christians. Tacitus made this mistake when he ascribed to Christians hatred against the human race.[6] But that would conflict directly with the love required by the first commandment, as we have seen. Moreover, the gospel of Jesus Christ is designed to reach all the nations throughout the whole world.

The Christian faith is experienced as a burdensome yoke or an external compulsion or a form of discrimination only when people fail to understand that the exclusive confession entailed in the first commandment is designed to bring about *liberation*. Unfortunately, the conduct of many Christians in the course of history has failed to bear witness to this liberation. In the name of Jesus, serious injustices have been perpetrated. But all those failures do not alter the fact that the gospel brings freedom. We are led by "the kindness and the love of God our Savior toward man" out of the slavery of life without God (see Titus 3:4–7).

Liberation

That leads us to this final observation. As you listen to the first commandment, you hear in it the liberation of which the prologue to the Ten Commandments bears witness. Yahweh demands the whole person, but in this total commitment of the person to this one God, lies his greatest freedom. The one who serves Yahweh will live under His blessing, but the one who serves idols will always languish in bondage.

Let us look first at "primitive" idolatry. For the Egyptian, the Babylonian, and the Canaanite, danger lurked on every side. A tree, an animal, a rock, a river, the sea, a thunderstorm, lightning, a hostile neighbor, and more—dangerous divine powers nested everywhere and in everything. Catastrophes could occur at any moment. A wall of fear surrounded a person. Specific actions, prescribed incantations, and particular rituals were needed to neutralize the host of dangers. Magic, exorcism, and sacrifices were therefore the way to pacify the angry gods.[7]

Place over against this the confession of God as the only Creator of heaven and earth, who alone is to be worshiped and feared. Then a rock is just a rock, a tree is merely a tree, a person is only a person, and even an angel is nothing more than a servant before whom no man needs to bow (Rev. 22:8–9). For the whole world, including everything that might arouse fear, is subject to Him who wants to be our Father in Christ Jesus. And with that confession, every bondage that enslaves a person to something creaturely—no matter what it is—has been in principle broken.

Several people have made the observation that the entire development of technology would have been unimaginable apart from the Christian faith. If divine power lives in a tree, it would be hazardous to cut it down. If mother earth is a goddess, the mining industry would never have been developed. Had lightning been seen as something divine, the lightning rod would never have been invented. But these and many other possibilities all lay open before us when the world and everything in it no longer aroused fear, but became just the ordinary world that God created for us to use.[8]

We may wish to debate the theory of the Christian origin of technology.[9] But one thing is sure: the human race and the world are able to reach their full potential only when we deal with things as they are, that is, created good by God and not to be refused, as long as we use them with thanksgiving to God (1 Tim. 4:4). It must have sounded quite liberating to the Corinthians to hear from Paul that even food sacrificed to idols and sold in the markets of Corinth could be purchased and eaten, because the earth and everything in it belongs to the Lord (1 Cor. 10:25–27). Love for God casts out fear and enables genuine human development of life.

This development of the world has spread rapidly and fewer people bow down before idols anymore. But the further these Christianized nations progress, the less thanksgiving they bring to the God who gave us this world to exercise stewardship in it. The world is emancipated today; meanwhile, mankind has become enslaved to its sophisticated technology. We never get rid of idols if we are not really converted to the only true God. New forms of slavery appear. Highly developed modern man does not know where to turn anymore with the things he has invented, including his nuclear weapons. In the field of biomedical technology, he stands at the threshold of discoveries that will perhaps fill him with joy at first, only to terrorize him later.

If we idolize technology, no longer realizing what advances God's honor and our neighbor's well-being, we will learn what slavery is. We will no longer rule things, but things will rule us. This is how many a good gift of God, as soon as we misuse it, assumes the form of an idol. Gold is that kind of gift, but it chains many a person to the still powerful idol of Mammon. Government is no less a gift of God, but if power is misused, innumerable people fall prey to the totalitarian state that, like ancient Molech, never gets its fill of human sacrifices.

The young Karl Marx wrote that a person is independent only when he stands on his own feet, and he stands on his own feet only if he owes his existence to himself. A person living by the grace of another views himself as a dependent being. And I live by the grace of another, said Marx, not only if I owe to him the perpetuation of my life, but also if he has created my life—thus, when my life is not my own creation.[10]

This is the talk of a person who has fallen away from God. Often such people have a sharp eye for the idols of others. Karl Marx saw far better than Christians of his own day the unspeakable misery that can accompany, in his words, the "dance around the golden calf"—an economy driven by the pursuit of profit and power. But he failed to see the kind of slavery into which he himself would plunge large areas of the world with his atheistic self-conceit, as powerful nations followed him in the conviction that his was the path to genuine freedom.

To be free of idols you must live with God.[11] Otherwise, you remain in slavery. It makes no fundamental difference whether you kneel in terror before images of deities or stand arrogantly on your own two feet. You either glorify God or you enthrone a creature (Rom. 1:21–32). Man stands free only when he is willing to live by grace; otherwise, he stoops like a slave oppressed by the powers of this world.

Endnotes

1. Sigmund Freud, "Das Unbehagen in der Kultur," *Gesammelte Werke* (London, 1948), 14:467–68. Freud adduces Tertullian's saying *credo quia absurdum* ("I believe because it is absurd").

2. The foregoing discussion involves the Hebrew word *tamim* ("complete, undefiled") and the Hebrew expression *betom-lebab* ("in wholeness, completeness of heart"), along with the Greek word *teleios* ("perfect, complete"). For bibliographical information, see B. Holwerda, *Oudtestamentische voordrachten* (Kampen, 1971), 1:39ff. (regarding Gen. 25:27); G. Delling, "Teleios," in *Theological Dictionary of the New Testament*, ed. G. Friedrich (Grand Rapids, 1972), 7:67–78; P. J. du Plessis, *Teleios. The Idea of Perfection in the New Testament* (Kampen, 1959), esp. 168–73.

3. *The Commentary of Dr. Zacharias Ursinus on the Heidelberg Catechism*, trans. G. W. Williard (1852; reprint, Phillipsburg, N.J., n.d.), 516.

4. See J. Douma, *Rondom de dood* (Kampen, 1984), 30–38.

5. J. H. Bavinck, "Het Eerste Gebod," in *Sinaï en Ardjoeno*, ed. Th. Delleman (Aalten, 1946), 23.

6. Tacitus, *Annales* 15.44.

7. A. Maillot, *Le Décalogue* (Paris, 1976), 26–27.

8. See, for example, A. Kuyper, *Pro rege* (Kampen, 1911), 1:123–76, and A. Th. van Leeuwen, *Christianity in World History*, 4th ed. (London, 1966), 324ff., 330.

9. F. H. von Meyenfeldt, *Tien tegen een* (Hilversum, 1978), 1:78ff.; C. J. Dippel, "Halve waarheid," *Wending* 14 (1959–60): 62–63 (contra Denis de Rougemont), and J. Douma, *Christelijk ethiek, capita selecta* (Kampen, 1981), 1:25.

10. Quoted by J. M. Lochman, *Wegweisung der Freiheit* (Gütersloh, 1979), 28.

11. A. Maillot, *Le Décalogue*, 28.

The Second Commandment

You shall not make for yourself an idol—in any form whatsoever—
of anything in heaven above or in the sky, on the earth below or in
the water under the earth. You shall not bow down to them nor
worship them, for I, Yahweh your God, am a God who avenges
Himself: I punish the sins of fathers upon children, grandchildren,
and great-grandchildren, if they are unfaithful to Me; but I show
favor to the most extended generation imaginable, if they are faithful
to Me and respect My commandments. (Ex. 20:4–6)

The Unique Place of the Second Commandment

When the Decalogue proceeds with "You shall not make for yourself an idol," it is giving us another commandment. So we do not agree with the Roman Catholic and Lutheran opinion, which views this as part of the first commandment. What we understand to be two separate commandments they take as one, so that in their numbering, these two constitute the first commandment. Then, in order to come up with ten commandments, they divide the tenth commandment in two. We should not follow this line, because the division of the tenth commandment is artificial, as we will see when we discuss that commandment. Such a division is also unnecessary, since the second commandment (in our numbering) has a unique place. After the first commandment rejects all other gods, so that only Yahweh remains, the second commandment rejects every wrong form whereby people desire to worship Yahweh. The first commandment opposes foreign gods, the second opposes self-willed worship of Yahweh. If you stand with your back to idols, then you must still learn to kneel properly before the God of Israel. You can get rid of all your religious idols, but in their place you must not erect an image of Yahweh. You may serve no *other* gods; but the Lord in turn wants to be served in no other way than

35

He has commanded. In sum: the first commandment points to the true God, the second to true religion (*Gods-dienst*).

The appropriateness of this difference between the first and the second commandments is confirmed by other places in the Old Testament. We read in Deuteronomy 4:15–18 that the Israelites were not allowed to make any carved or cast images in the form of animals, birds, or fish (think of the text of the second commandment!), because when the law was proclaimed on Horeb they saw no form of *Yahweh*. When the nation of Israel erected the golden calf at the foot of Horeb, that was intended as an image of the Lord. "This is your god, O Israel, that brought you out of the land of Egypt!" (Ex. 32:4). Around this calf and the altar erected nearby, they celebrated "a feast to the LORD" (Ex. 32:5). The idea of taking a calf—or better, a yearling bull—arose from pagan idolatry. Baal was worshiped in the form of a bull, a symbol of power. But that pagan notion was used in this case to make an image of Yahweh. The Israelites were not intending to reject the Lord and go serve other gods; but they merely wanted to have Yahweh among them in a particular manner, a manner forbidden by the second commandment.

The same can be said of the new worship Jeroboam instituted at Dan and Bethel. The two golden calves (images of bulls) were to serve as images of the Lord. After the division of the kingdom, Jeroboam did not want the people traveling to the temple of Yahweh in Jerusalem. He wanted to eliminate the need for that pilgrimage to Jerusalem, by manufacturing two statues of bulls, of which he could say, "Here are your gods, O Israel, which brought you up from the land of Egypt!" (1 Kings 12:28). This was exactly the same language spoken to Israel with the golden calf at Horeb!

Later, when Ahab introduced the foreign god Baal among the Ten Tribes, that was viewed as a step further down the path of apostasy: "And it came to pass, as though it had been a trivial thing for him to walk in the sins of Jeroboam the son of Nebat, that he took as wife Jezebel the daughter of Ethbaal, king of the Sidonians; and he went and served Baal and worshiped him" (1 Kings 16:31). We could say that Ahab sank from sinning against the second commandment to sinning against the first. By following Jeroboam, he continued the self-willed service of Yahweh; but at least it remained the service of Yahweh. But by following Jezebel, he added another god, Baal. Against this vilest evil Elijah waged his great battle on Mount Carmel.

A third narrative deserves our attention as well, that of Micah during the period of the judges. Micah erected a kind of chapel on his estate to house a "carved and cast image," and for his private worship he hired a Levite to serve him as priest. Here too, it was not an idol image, but an image of Yahweh. Why else would he have been called Micah ("Who is Yahweh?")? And why else would his mother have wished him the blessing of Yahweh (Judg. 17:2)? What Micah began here obtained a central place later in the life of the tribe of Dan. This cultic worship of Yahweh obtained a still more prominent character, since priests from among descendants of Moses were hired (Judg. 18:30). The sin against the second commandment was not limited to a single incident, but infected an entire tribe in Israel. It was far from accidental that a hundred years later Jeroboam found a place for his calf worship in Dan!

Until now, archaeologists have never uncovered an image or symbol that could be seen to represent Yahweh. But you can hardly conclude from this that Israel did not continually transgress the second commandment. Archaeologists have not found images of Baal in Israelite cities either, but no one doubts the enormous spread of Baal worship within Israel.[1] Thus, alongside the worship of foreign gods, honoring images of Yahweh also exercised significant influence. Crowds paraded in front of images (1 Kings 12:30); people became devoted to such idols (Hos. 4:17) and kissed them (Hos. 13:2). All of it was intended to win Yahweh's favor. The people kept nurturing the conviction that, since they had Yahweh on their side, they could calmly await the Day of Yahweh (Amos 5:14, 18).[2]

The first and second commandments deal with different subjects, idol worship and self-willed worship of Yahweh. Thereby we do not deny the very strong connection between them. The idols were not served apart from images, and images of Yahweh inevitably became "other gods." Therefore, it is no wonder that in the Old Testament, images of Yahweh and of idols are mentioned together.[3] Think of the images Jeroboam made. They may have been intended as images of Yahweh, but Yahweh Himself views them as obtaining "other gods," with the result that they turned their backs on *Him* (1 Kings 14:9)!*

The Significance of an Image

When we reflect about the relevance of the second commandment, we inevitably face the question whether we still need to be warned against manufacturing images. When Paul walked through the city of Athens, its

---

* See also Acts 7:41 and 1 Cor. 10:7, where the history involving the golden calf narrated in Ex. 32 is described as "[offering] sacrifices to the idol" and as the behavior of "idolaters."

many images so impressed him that he proclaimed, "We ought not to think that the Divine Nature is like gold or silver or stone, something shaped by art and man's devising" (Acts 17:29). But anyone walking through our modern cities would not be able to evangelize this way, since there are no more images. They have disappeared from our parks and markets, even from our homes. If you want to see images, you will have to visit a museum. Carved and cast images belong to a bygone era, and there is no indication that this will ever change.

Nevertheless, we know that people have not changed a lot since God gave His law on Sinai. Evil runs just as deep, even though it comes to expression in different ways than formerly. So then, why cannot the second commandment point out a sin just as relevant as formerly, even though this sin manifests itself in a different way than back then? In order to get behind this, we must first be clear as to why God did not want people to make representations of Him. Which sinful inclination prompted Israel to disobey, so that Yahweh resisted it with this commandment?

We can properly understand the answer to that question only when we know the function of an image for people living in former times, or what in fact an image means to the millions of pagans in today's world. Such an image is far from a dead object of wood, stone, or gold, but a living thing, since the deity is present in it. Just as the soul dwells in the body, so the deity inhabits the image. Pagans know very well that the deity is not identical to the image. Anyone who worships sun, moon, and stars, and fashions images of them, knows of course that these "gods" dwell above. He sees his gods in the sky. When Paul performed miracles in Lystra, the crowd cried out, "The gods have *come down* to us in the likeness of men!" (Acts 14:11). Even pagans thought that their gods lived in the heavens. But while, on the one hand, the gods are far away, on the other hand, they are also nearby, in their images. The image *represents* the deity. One who has an image meets the deity himself in it. The power of the deity is collected and channeled by means of the image.

Often the comparison is made with electricity. High voltage is dangerous. So, too, is divine power. High voltage is fatal if we cannot control it. In the same way, the image of a deity functions like a transformer: treacherous high voltage is reduced so we can use it with far less risk.

That image worship involves divine *power* can be shown another way. An image of a deity is not to be compared to a portrait of similar dimensions. One might think the comparison would be valid with regard to images of deities in human form. People supposedly imagined their gods in human form, and therefore it was logical for them to represent them in images resembling people. Nevertheless, that element of human resemblance is not essential to an image of a deity. For a deity can just as well resemble a bird, an animal, or a fish. The text of the second commandment warns against making an image in any form whatsoever; the forms it mentions include creatures in the sky (sun, moon, and stars) or the air (birds), in the earth below (trees or animals), or in the water (fish). In terms of Israel's history, we might think of the images of bulls made by Aaron and Jeroboam. Neither of them thought that Yahweh possesses the form of a bull. But then their images were never intended to portray a photographic likeness, but only to control Yahweh's power. They saw a passing representation of precisely that power in the strong bull with its fertility.

We could give more examples of the same phenomenon. Extrabiblical sources point to various images of Venus, covered with multiple breasts. This indicates clearly that people intended to represent not her likeness, but her power. Recall the electricity transformer. Aaron and Jeroboam were placing within their grasp the very power of Yahweh with which He had led Israel out of Egypt; the power of fertility came within reach of Venus worshipers. Her exaggerated sexual characteristics were not intended to be photographic, but they surely represent very accurately her great power!

Without such images no pagan can live. The burning lava (to use another analogy) remains dangerous until it hardens. A similar hardening occurs when an image is crafted to enable concourse between a god and his worshipers. Without an image, people never notice a god, for the image signifies the god's presence. The reverse is also true: if people have no image of their god, then his power cannot be represented, and they are deprived of his blessings. In other words, the image is indispensable for regulating concourse between the gods and their worshipers.[*]

Naturally, handling the image and its divine power requires great care. A system of rituals and ceremonies is needed to receive the desired bless-

---

[*] H. M. Kuitert, "Het Tweede Gebod," in *De thora in de thora* (Aalten, 1967), 1:70. On the significance of the image, see also J. L. Koole, *De Tien Geboden,* 2d ed. (Kampen, 1983), 53ff., and A. Kruyswijk, *"Geen gesneden beeld,"* 28ff. Kruyswijk mentions the animal cultus prominent in Egypt, in which gods were portrayed with a human body joined to various animal heads; for example, Horus had the head of a falcon, Thot had the head of an ibis, and Anubis had the head of a jackal. "The representation of a god in the form of an animal or having only an animal's head served not as a portrait, but rather as a pictogram. Thus, whenever Anubis appeared having a jackal's head, the statement being made was: this is the deity manifested in the jackal" (p. 46).

ings from the gods. As long as these actions are performed in the proper way, people are guaranteed to get the gods on their side. The image with its related rituals renders the gods malleable!

Why No Images?

Armed with this knowledge about the image of a deity, we can easily answer the question of why the Lord prohibited making images. We would like to point out three aspects:

1. To capture Yahweh in an image is to misunderstand His *freedom*. An image attempts to make the Incomprehensible comprehensible. But in this way, the craftsman seeks to control God, when the reverse is in fact the case: Yahweh controls man and will not allow Himself to be controlled. You can use well-established rituals in front of an image to get Yahweh to do what you want, but that will never work.

A clear example of that is found in the narrative of 1 Samuel 4. The Israelites had suffered a heavy defeat at the hands of the Philistines. To rescue them from their misery, they brought the ark of the covenant into the camp. For Yahweh was enthroned upon the cherubim of the ark, and if only they had Him nearby, victory was assured. The ark arrived, along with the priests who could provide necessary instructions for taking care of the ark. The people welcomed the arrival of the ark with shouts of joy so enthusiastic that the earth shook. The Philistines became afraid: "God has come into the camp! . . . Woe to us!" (1 Sam. 4:3–8). But instead of winning a victory, Israel suffered a second defeat, and the ark was even captured as booty by the Philistines. The ark itself, made at Yahweh's command, became no more than a wooden box as soon as the Lord no longer wished to be associated with it. He sat enthroned on the cherubim of this ark as long as *He* wanted (cf. also Ezek. 1 and 10). If Israel sinned and refused to be converted as Yahweh had prescribed, then it surely was not going to work to put Him in a favorable mood by pagan manipulation.

Now, if this applied to the ark, which had been made at God's command, then it would surely be true of every image people might erect for their own cultic worship of Yahweh. For an image was simply a way to walk Yahweh around on their own leash. "Go ahead, make us a god who will lead us," the people told Aaron. Yahweh thus became an ambassador in chains, an image in fetters.[4] However, the entire Scripture shows clearly that the process is precisely the opposite. The Lord had freely chosen Israel to be His people (Deut. 7:7–8; Amos 9:7), and *He* determines the way His people must walk. He can even put the future of Israel in jeopardy when she departs from that way by making graven images (Ex. 32:8–10; Deut. 9:12–14). The Lord refuses to live that way within Israel. He is different from every other god, and that must also be evident in the manner of concourse He has established between Himself and His people.

2. To capture Yahweh in an image is to misunderstand His *majesty*. When He made His covenant known to Israel, the Lord spoke from Mount Sinai as it burned with fire "to the midst of heaven, with darkness, cloud, and thick darkness." Israel did not see any form of Yahweh; there was only a voice (Deut. 4:11–12). In contrast to such majesty stands the manufacture of images as "the work of men's hands, wood and stone, which neither see nor hear nor eat nor smell" (Deut. 4:28). An image is the creation of a craftsman, but it is no god (Hos. 8:6; 13:2; 14:4). People bow down to what their own fingers have fashioned. Even though they are made of gold and silver, on the day of judgment men will throw their images to the moles and bats, as they flee to the clefts and crags of the rocks in the face of Yahweh's terror and before the sound of His majesty (Isa. 2:20–21).

Moreover, image worship evokes ridicule and sarcasm. "To whom then will you liken God? Or what likeness will you compare to Him?" Surely it is ridiculous when craftsmen are employed to make images, nailing them down so they will not fall over (Isa. 40:18; 41:7)! Part of what people drag out of the woods they use for firewood to cook meat or warm themselves, and the rest they use for making an image to worship and entreat: "Deliver me, for you are my god" (Isa. 44:15–20)!* In contrast to these gods made

---

* G. von Rad observes: "It has been rightly asserted that the enlightened caricature in Is. XLIV in no sense squares with the earnestness of the heathen cultic practice" (*Old Testament Theology* [New York, 1962], 1:217). In other words, when you mock images, as Isaiah does here, the image worshiper would not recognize himself in such a caricature. That is surely correct, but it does not make the message of Isa. 44 a rationalistic caricature. In this connection, we recall seeing something on a German television program in 1984: Papuans from the interior of New Guinea saw white people for the first time about fifty years ago, people who had landed in their region with a wonderful "bird" (airplane). Filled with fear and trembling before their gods, they became acquainted with the traveling explorers and their technology. Fifty years later they saw video clips showing what had happened. To the same degree that they had been frightened fifty years earlier, they now laughed uncontrollably about the fear that had gripped them and their families back then. No one would argue that the laughter of these Papuans about their own past caricatured that past! When fear dissipates, there is room for humor about former folly. Exactly the same is true of the believing Israelite who allows Yahweh to instruct him. Images become dumb images (Hab. 2:18; 1 Cor. 12:2), no matter how "spiritually" these images had once been experienced by idol worshipers.

from a block of wood, stands Yahweh in His majesty as Creator of the world (Isa. 40:12–17). Nothing is comparable to Him. "Before Me there was no God formed, nor shall there be after Me. I, even I, am the Lord, and besides Me there is no savior" (Isa. 43:10–11).

In Scripture, this majesty of God is indicated by the metaphor of darkness with which He is covered (Deut. 4:11; 5:23; 1 Kings 8:12), or that of unapproachable light in which He dwells (1 Tim. 6:16). Darkness and light are thorough opposites, but here they express the same thought: God is so majestic that He cannot be brought within man's reach. How could Israel ever think to make an image of Him? The darkness surrounding Yahweh is just as impenetrable as the divine light blinding human eyes. Every human being lies open and naked before His eyes (Heb. 4:13), but the reverse is not true: God does not lie open and naked before human eyes.[5] For that reason, Israel was mocking God's majesty when she made an image of Yahweh and dared to declare of it: "This is your god who brought you out of the land of Egypt."

3. To capture Yahweh in an image is to misunderstand His *covenant*. You *may not* make images on account of Yahweh's freedom, you *cannot* make images on account of Yahweh's majesty, but you *need not* make images on account of Yahweh's covenant with Israel. The bond between Yahweh and His people does not need to be established (via images), for it has already been established. The freedom and majesty of Yahweh do not mean that He is unreachable and acts capriciously—something Israel would then have to neutralize by controlling divine power by means of an image of Yahweh. For Yahweh has covenanted Himself in faithfulness to Israel. People did not have to look far to know what He was doing. The commandment is not in heaven or even beyond the sea, so that Israel would have had to say, "Who will ascend into heaven for us and bring it to us, that we may hear it and do it?" For, "the word is very near you, in your mouth and in your heart, that you may do it" (Deut. 30:12–14; cf. Rom. 10:6–9).

Yahweh is not tangible to Israel, as the idols of the pagans are to their devotees; but on the other hand, there is no god as close to his people as Yahweh is to Israel.[6] They did not see a form, but they did hear His voice. He made His covenant known, and people could know that His commandments—obediently received—would bring prosperity to Israel (Deut. 4:12–14; 5:29; 6:24).

Thus, it is not only His majesty, but also his intimacy with Israel that makes the manufacture of images such a reproach. For that reason, the Lord will also "vindicate Himself" if the covenant between Himself and

His people is broken by serving images. The text of the second commandment puts it this way: "For I, Yahweh your God, am a God who avenges Himself." Instead of the translation "a God who avenges Himself" (*el qanna'*)some versions have the rendering "a jealous God." The element of jealousy is surely present; but that rendering is too one-sided because, in view of what follows, Yahweh is also *el qanna'* for those who keep His commandments. He is zealous toward both sides, when He punishes as well as when He shows favor. In both cases He vindicates Himself as God of the covenant. He is zealous in the sense of jealous over a people that wounds His love by making images of Him. They will see that. The sin of the fathers is visited upon the children, grandchildren, and great-grandchildren. But Yahweh is also jealous when people are faithful to Him. In their case He will vindicate Himself by showing His favor to the most extended generation imaginable.

Self-willed religion arouses the spirit of jealousy in Yahweh, much as jealousy is aroused in the husband who sees that his wife loves another man (Num. 5:14). The love that Yahweh bestows is despised. Instead of receiving life as a covenantal *gift*, people seek by means of serving images to *secure* life for themselves. Faith and obedience within the covenant are the opposite of every pagan automatism that always strives fearfully through rituals with images to remain in control.

The Spirituality of God and the Prohibition of Images

We cannot pass over in silence the fact that our explanation of the prohibition of images differs from what you will find in older commentaries on the second commandment. Briefly stated, earlier explanations come down to this: people cannot make images of God because He is nonphysical and nonmaterial. God is Spirit, and thus invisible. A spirit has no flesh and bones (Luke 24:39), so how could anyone ever make a representation of God? Earlier commentators appeal for proof of this prohibition of images straight to John 4:24 ("God is Spirit, and those who worship Him must worship in spirit and truth"), 1 Timothy 6:16 (the Lord of lords, "who alone has immortality, dwelling in unapproachable light, whom no man has seen or can see, to whom be honor and everlasting power"), and Deuteronomy 4:15 ("You saw no form when the LORD spoke to you at Horeb out of the midst of the fire").

It would be incorrect to claim that these or similar proof-texts had nothing to do with the second commandment. We ourselves have appealed to both Deuteronomy 4:15 and 1 Timothy 6:16 in our explanation above. Moreover, it would be just as incorrect to say that God may and indeed should be portrayed as physical and material. That would contradict what the church has always correctly taught about this. Man was formed from the dust of the earth (Gen. 1:7), but not God. Man has flesh and bones; that is never said of God. When we do read that the Word *became* flesh (John 1:14), or that God *revealed* Himself in the flesh (1 Tim. 3:16), then good exegesis requires us to confess that the eternal Father, Son, and Holy Spirit are nonphysical. In contrast to fathers according to the flesh, we serve the Father of spirits (Heb. 12:9). So when commentators insist that we may not portray God in an earthly, material, and physical way, the testimony of Scripture supports them.[7]

This is not contradicted when we read that God has ears, eyes, a mouth, a face, hands, arms, and feet. In fact, the point is not really whether God possesses all these organs or limbs, but that He hears, sees, manifests love or anger, creates or destroys (with His hand), draws near or departs (with his feet), and the like. What matters is not whether He has a humanlike hand, but what He does with His hand. Someone has said that in connection with Yahweh, no human organs are ever mentioned that have no external activity or function, like hair, cheeks, bones, and blood.[8] We may not ascribe to Him a body, but rather should understand these humanlike (anthropomorphic) expressions as indubitable proof of how the exalted Yahweh deals intimately with His people, whether He comes to them with His blessing or His curse. When people follow their godless practices and then say, "The LORD does not see, nor does the God of Jacob understand," then the response is, "He who planted the ear, shall He not hear? He who formed the eye, shall He not see?" (Ps. 94:7–9).

No image of Yahweh may be made because, among other reasons, no one saw any form of Him on Horeb. But He does portray Himself to make clear how seriously He takes His covenant with Israel. He can genuinely love, as when He "makes His face shine" (Num. 6:25; Ps. 31:16); He can be genuinely angry, as when He "hides [His] face" (Deut. 31:17). Anyone who realizes what ears, eyes, hands, feet, a friendly look, and an angry look can accomplish, will not easily misunderstand the anthropomorphic language of Yahweh.

But even if we can agree with earlier interpreters of the second commandment that God is not physical and therefore also cannot be portrayed, there is still reason to put a question mark alongside their one-sided explanation of the second commandment and alongside the mistaken conclusions they often draw from the spirituality of God.

Any explanation of the second commandment that rests solely upon the spirituality of God is one-sided. We have already seen clearly that image making did not always involve a human-physical representation of the deity.*

Consider the image of bulls made by Aaron and Jeroboam. They were not interested in a portrayal of Yahweh, but wanted to manipulate His power. They were not interested in making the Invisible One visible, but in making the Incomprehensible One comprehensible. This point has been properly emphasized in recent exegesis; to make images of Yahweh is to attack His freedom and His covenant. He will not permit Himself to be banished to an image, nor will He permit people to establish another path than the one He Himself established in the covenant.

In addition to the one-sidedness of earlier explanations of the second commandment, we are also struck by the mistaken conclusions so often drawn from the spirituality of God. The "spiritual" is often viewed as unique and superior, and the material viewed as inferior. What is important is not seeing, but thinking. God is spirit, and anyone who worships Him must worship Him in spirit and truth. People explain this verse from John 4 in such a way that the "spiritual" service of God consists of an inner service in contrast to an outward service. The internal efforts of the heart are more important than the external labor that can be seen with our eyes. God must be worshiped is a spiritual manner, consistent with His spiritual, nonphysical nature.

In the first place, this "spiritual" interpretation makes the second commandment something of a tautology, so self-evident that it is no longer clear just why in the Old Testament such a fierce blow is aimed at images.[9]

Second, this approach quickly leads to a dualistic view of man, in which the spiritual stands nearer to God than the physical.[10] Thought conquers sight. With the eyes of our spirit we come closer to God than with the eyes of our body. But this kind of description is mistaken. The

---

* It would be improper to argue that the longing to come up with a representation of the deity was not present at all. "You saw no form when the LORD spoke to you at Horeb" (Deut. 4:15) is not a superfluous warning at all. From extrabiblical sources as well we know of the connection between image and representation. A hymn to the Egyptian god Amun-Re goes like this: "Thou who hast appeared to us, we know not thy form. Thou showest thyself in our face, but we know not thy body. . . . Thou whose being no man knows and of whom exists no image made by craftsmen . . . the great Hidden One, whose image no man knows" (these quotations are taken from J. C. de Moor, *Uw God is mijn God* [Kampen, 1983], 18–19).

darkness surrounding Yahweh, or even the light with which He clothes Himself, makes Him unapproachable with *any* human organs. We must apply this across the entire range of revelation. The distance between Creator and creature cannot be bridged with our eyes, and neither with our understanding. Things no eye has seen, and which have not entered into the heart (understanding) of man, God has prepared for those who love Him (1 Cor. 2:9).

In the third place, the "spiritual" approach to the second commandment easily overlooks and suppresses all those Scripture passages telling us that we do in fact get to see quite a bit of God. Yahweh appeared in human form to Abraham by the terebinth trees of Mamre (Gen. 18:1). Jacob declared that at Peniel he had seen God face to face (Gen. 32:30). Moses, Aaron, Nadab, Abihu, and seventy elders of Israel beheld God, and they ate and drank (Ex. 24:11). Yahweh spoke to prophets in visions and dreams, but He spoke face to face with Moses, who was permitted to behold the form of Yahweh (Num. 12:6–8). The same is true in the New Testament. Anyone who has seen Jesus Christ has seen the Father (John 14:8–9). Christ is the image of the invisible God, the firstborn of the whole creation (Col. 1:15). Paul holds out the prospect that we shall reflect the glory of Christ, and that through Him who is Spirit we will be transformed from glory to glory (2 Cor. 3:17–18). That has to do with *seeing*—a seeing that, in terms of the context of 2 Corinthians 3:7–11, surpasses the seeing of Moses.* Now we see in part, but then we shall see face to face (1 Cor. 13:12).

Obviously, certain limits to our seeing have been established. Moses saw much, but Yahweh did say to him: "You cannot see My face; for no man shall see Me, and live." He was permitted to see only the back of Yahweh (Ex. 33:20–23).[11] A wide gap remains between Creator and creature. We shall see Him not as He sees Himself. But this kind of restriction governs not only our eyes. We shall never fathom with our understanding to the same degree that God fathoms Himself (Rom. 11:23; 1 Cor. 2:11). Both human activities have their limits, but both have also their respective promises. By our own hearing and seeing we perceive nothing unless God reveals Himself. Thought does not surpass sight, no matter how "spir-

---

* J. R. Wiskerke, "De scholastieke verminking van de aanschouwing van God," 341: "We shall see the invisible without the restriction noted in the report about Moses, who 'endured as seeing Him who is invisible' (Heb. 11:27). Thus, seeing God is much more and much different than a mere possibility; it constitutes the essence of a promise God shall certainly keep."

itual" it may appear to be. We receive much to see and to think about when first we learn what listening to God's Word means. He who hears will also see. That is true already now with respect to God's eternal power and divinity, which can be apprehended from His works, through the understanding, since the creation of the world—a wonderful combination of seeing and understanding (Rom. 1:19–21)! On the basis of promises already given, we shall, if we persevere in faith, get to see even much more, also of God Himself.

In light of this, we could say that Israel's sin lay not in wanting to see (something of) Yahweh—for even Moses wanted that—but in seeking to satisfy her longing to see and to touch, in a stubborn and disobedient manner.

In the fourth place, it is incorrect to search for the significance of God's "spirituality" in His nonphysicality alone. It is proper not to portray God physically or materially.* But this does not mean God exists as a formless Being. For we read of His "shape" or "form" (Hebrew: *temuna*). At Horeb, Israel observed no shape or form of Yahweh; but that is not to say that Yahweh has no shape or form (cf. Num. 12:8).† Aside from that, however, when we read that God is spirit, certainly that includes the message that God is *power*. In contrast to flesh as *weak* flesh, spirit indicates divine pow-

---

* N. R. Gootjes, *De geestelijkheid van God*, 187ff., disagrees with Wiskerke's remark that the confession of God's spirituality says nothing yet about the question whether God is nonphysical. On this point J. R. Wiskerke is indeed very emphatic: "In describing God as spirit, we must . . . depart radically from every definition of spiritual as nonphysical or non-material" (*De strijd om de sleutel der kennis*, 154). In our opinion, this departure is unnecessary as long as we maintain, over against the dualistic view of man, that the whole person, including his understanding, is material. In contrast to man as a material being exists the Creator, to whom the categories of matter and physicality do not apply, precisely because as Spirit He has created all of life. Therefore, we can agree with Gootjes's criticism. He understands God's spirituality to mean "that God, who bestows life as Creator and Redeemer, is non-physical" (p. 192). However, schooled by Wiskerke and others, we would elevate Gootjes's subordinate clause to a main clause: By God's spirituality we understand that God, who is not physical, bestows life as Creator and Redeemer.

† A. Kruyswijk, "*Geen gesneden beeld,*" 179; B. Holwerda, *Oudtestamentische voordracht-en: Exegese Oude Testament (Deuteronomium)* (Kampen, 1957), 3:48: Recognizing the fact and limits of anthropomorphism may "not tempt us to think of God as without form." See also Gootjes, *De geestelijkheid van God*, 203: "Our definition of God's spirituality does mean God has no body, but does not need to mean God has no form." In our judgment, Gootjes is correct in his criticism (pp. 203-4) of Kruyswijk's description of God as having a "spiritual-anthropomorphic form." Such a description still sounds too close to ascribing a *human* form to God.

er. Think of Isaiah 31:3: "Now the Egyptians are men, and not God; and their horses are flesh, and not spirit." Spirit characterizes God, just as flesh characterizes creatures. So spirit refers to the life-giving power in contrast to the weakness and mortality of the flesh. The contrast is thus not with the *physical* (as in Luke 24:39; Col. 2:5; Heb. 12:9, and elsewhere), but with what is weak and fleshly, what is transient and transitory.

This interpretation helps us discern the proper sense of John 4:24. Jesus tells the Samaritan woman, who is talking about worshiping God on Mount Gerizim and in Jerusalem, that such a time is past. God is spirit, which means that He bestows new power because the Messiah will bring an end to the ancient temple worship. The worship of God must be done "in spirit and truth," in fellowship with the Messiah's life-giving power and in fellowship with the truth that the Messiah proclaims.

So the contrast is not between a visual worship at Gerizim and in Jerusalem, and an "inner" worship that Jesus came to bring. The contrast is rather between the transitory temple ministry and the everlasting life-giving power of Christ. One who is joined to this power—or, put another way, one who is "in Christ"—can worship God anywhere in the world. That worship has just as much an external side to it as the temple worship had. Kneeling, singing, gathering in church buildings, all these are—just like the temple ministry—tangible and local.[12] But it is the re-creating power of God that in Christ lends a universal and everlasting character to worship, so that something entirely new appears.

This new and better exegesis of John 4:24 teaches us how careful we must be with conclusions regarding the "spiritual," nonexternal character of our service to Yahweh and to Christ. Of course, religion can degenerate into pure externalism. Yahweh takes no pleasure in that kind of religion (e.g., Isa. 58:3–14; Mic. 6:6–8). But this does not mean that He thereby rejects all formal worship, like bringing offerings and performing ceremonies (e.g., days of fasting)—things God Himself has instituted.

God's Own Image

Images of idols and of Yahweh may not be made. But this is not to say that Israel's worship was without images. We may understand the concept of "image" in a somewhat broader sense to include tabernacle and temple, ark, ephod, and bronze serpent. All of these occupied a divinely ordained place in Israel's history. However, their function was clearly far different from that of humanly invented images of idols. Those were designed to aid people in manipulating the power of the deity. Such use of holy buildings and objects Yahweh never permitted.

At the command of Yahweh, Moses made a bronze serpent to thwart a plague of serpents among the Israelites in the wilderness. Anyone who looked at this elevated serpent received healing from the fatal snakebite (Num. 21:6–9). There is nothing here to indicate an image devoted to cultic usage, paraded in processions or worshiped with pagan rituals. Merely looking at this bronze serpent was the simple, divinely commanded and blessed means for receiving healing. But later, when idolatry was committed with this bronze serpent, Hezekiah conducted an iconoclastic campaign against sacred stones and consecrated pillars which included breaking this bronze serpent in pieces (2 Kings 18:4). No object remains holy if it is used in a pagan manner.

We saw that already in connection with the ark, which Yahweh had chosen as His throne, but which He abandoned when Israel tried to use it as a magic box to ensure victory over the Philistines (1 Sam. 4). We can say the same with respect to the ephod. The ephod was a legitimate means that Israel used to consult the Lord (Ex. 28:29–39; 1 Sam. 2:28; 23:9–12; 30:7–8). But when Gideon or Micah made an ephod (Judg. 8:24–27; 17:5–13), theirs were both in service to idolatry. All Israel committed adulterous idolatry with Gideon's ephod (Judg. 8:27), and Micah's conduct provided an example of people in those days doing what was right in their own eyes (Judg. 17:6). Proper handling of the ephod excluded magic of every kind, and was always accompanied by *prayer* when the ephod was consulted (1 Sam. 14:41; 23:10; 30:8).[13]

Nor could one contain God in the temple. This Solomon confessed at the dedication of this sanctuary: "But will God indeed dwell on the earth? Behold, heaven and the heaven of heavens cannot contain You. How much less this temple which I have built!" (1 Kings 8:27–53). Later, when Judah confidently assumed that she would remain in her own land because she had the temple in her midst ("The temple of the LORD, the temple of the LORD, the temple of the LORD are these"), her words were but hollow sounds made by a people who perverted justice, oppressed widows and orphans, shed innocent blood, and walked after other gods (Jer. 7:3–7).

The glory of Yahweh departed from the temple when Judah broke covenant and was led into captivity (Ezek. 1 and 10). The nation might feel safe in the shadow of a sanctuary, but she would learn that Yahweh does not allow Himself to be tied down, not even to His own chosen dwelling place, if Israel became unfaithful to the covenant. The Old Testament is quite fond of ceremonies, but not of rituals assumed to guarantee salvation automatically, *ex opere operato*. At the heart of walking with Yahweh was not using the proper place or correct gestures, but practicing faith and obedience.

Man as Image of God

In this context, we should consider the significance of *man* as the image of God.* It is not easy to identify precisely what is meant by this. Numerous interpretations have been proposed, and the literature on this subject is vast. In our opinion, coming up with a good explanation of the phrase "man as the image of God" requires that we begin with what we have already learned about the meaning of an image in general. We have seen that in an image of a deity, the deity is *represented*.[14] Here we are dealing not with a good likeness, but with the presence of the *power* of the deity. Why not apply this to man as the image of God in the newly created world? He became God's representative and the gateway through which God wanted to exercise His power upon earth.

This opinion finds a parallel in the New Testament teaching about the image of God. We read that Christ is the image of God (2 Cor. 4:4; Col. 1:15). This is true in a very special sense, for in Him dwells *all* the fullness of the Godhead bodily (Col. 1:19; 2:9). That could and can be said of no mere man. The element of "indwelling" is certainly a point of comparison. References to the image of God, whether to Adam or to Christ, concern the divine power visible on earth. In both cases the reference does not mean that Adam or Christ resembles God (the Father), but that in their actions and in their authority they show forth God Himself. When Philip asks Jesus to show him the Father, he receives this answer: "Have I been with you so long, and yet you have not known Me, Philip? He who has seen Me has seen the Father" (John 14:9). From the words and works of Jesus, Philip could have concluded who the Father is!

We find an expression similar to "image of God" in the phrase "temple of God," applied to the congregation (1 Cor. 3:16), or "temple of the Holy Spirit," applied to us (our body) personally (1 Cor. 6:19). In both cases we read that the Holy Spirit dwells in us. This divine indwelling makes us into the image or temple of God. This gift is at the same time a task. If the

---

* The Hebrew word for "image" is not *pesel*, but *selem* and *demut*. The word *selem* can also mean idol-image, as in 2 Kings 11:18, for example. In the New Testament, the word used is *eikōn*, which can also refer to an idol-image, as in 1 Cor. 11:7 and Rev. 13:14.

Holy Spirit dwells in the congregation and in us personally, then He desires His power to hold sway so that we cannot live in unholiness.

It appears to me that we must relate all of this to Genesis 1:26–28, where we read about the creation of man according to the image of God. The primary and decisive significance of this, then, is that God desires to dwell within man and wants His power to radiate into this world through man. The authors of the Heidelberg Catechism have come close to the core of the matter when they use several New Testament references to fill out what it means that man is created in God's image. Man is created "in true righteousness and holiness, that he might rightly know God his Creator, heartily love Him, and live with Him in eternal blessedness to praise and glorify Him" (Lord's Day 3, Answer 6). In order for man to do that, God has created man like Himself: exalted over the animal, endowed with understanding and volition, and thereby in a position to exercise dominion over God's creation. God equipped man with various capacities (understanding, will, a unique body) he needed to function as God's image. So in these capacities we find the *conditions* for being the image of God. Without understanding, you cannot bring the world to full blossom; without understanding, you cannot praise God in a conscious, personal manner.

Nevertheless, those conditions for being the image of God are not the image of God itself. We cannot say that because man is not an animal but a rational being, he is the image of God. For we must recall what we learned earlier about tabernacle, ark, temple, ephod, and bronze serpent. What is an ark, if God no longer sits enthroned upon it? What is a temple, if God has departed from it?

We confront here the important question whether, after the fall into sin, man lost the image of God. Can we say that unbelievers are still the image of God? We must answer that question in the negative, even though our "no" is not without qualification. It is a "no, but. . . ."

First, let us say something about our "no." Since the image of God is not determined by "natural" qualities (the understanding, the potential for exercising dominion, etc.), but by the relation between man and God, man's fall into sin had serious consequences. When God's wrath rests upon man, we can hardly say that His Spirit continues to dwell within man. Being the image of God is first of all a religious matter. Just as Yahweh can withdraw from the temple, even so can He withdraw from man, who was created as His temple and as His image.

Therefore, we can also state that the image of God is *restored* in man when God shows His grace in Jesus Christ, already in Paradise. The outworking of the mother promise (Gen. 3:15) is effectual immediately. Adam, Abel, Seth, Enos, Enoch, Noah, and the rest could once again be the image of God in their walk with God. What is decisive is that man walk again in the footprints of God, so that he is, to echo the Heidelberg Catechism in its language borrowed from Ephesians 4:24 and Colossians 3:10, a *new man*, living in righteousness and holiness, thereby displaying God's righteousness and holiness in this world. Being the image of God is not a quality of humanness. Even God-fearing believers cannot say, "Once a believer, always the image of God." David prayed for a clean heart and a steadfast spirit, adding, "Do not cast me away from Your presence, and do not take Your Holy Spirit from me" (Ps. 51:11). He might also have said, "Let me remain Your image." Being the image of God is a gift with instructions. Being re-created in righteousness and holiness means: "You shall be holy, for I the LORD your God am holy" (Lev. 19:2 and parallels).*

Certainly we must add something to what we have said, to avoid one-sidedness. Is the unbeliever still the image of God? "No," the answer must be. But the "no" is not without qualification. It is a "no, but. . . ." For consider once again the ark. Even though the ark, when it was in the country of the Philistines, was no longer Yahweh's throne, that did not reduce it to a piece of firewood. Clearly the Philistines were supposed to keep their hands off the ark, since Yahweh still wanted to be connected to it. The same holds true to a far greater degree with man. Ark, tabernacle, and temple were temporary phenomena, but we cannot say the same about the relationship between God and man. The mere fact that people have fallen away from God does not mean that in their case, we cannot speak of the image of God. No matter how estranged from God and His service man becomes, he remains a temple. The temple may well be *empty*, but that does not give us the right to speak with denigration about that temple or tear it down. Scripture says something else: Whoever sheds the blood of man, his blood shall be shed by man, for God made man after His own image (Gen. 9:6). This is said after the Flood concerning man in general, or concerning men. In just as general a way, James warns against cursing other people, for they are created in the likeness of God (James 3:9).

---

* See A. Kruyswijk, "*Geen gesneden beeld*," 208: "The essence of God's image lies in the representation of God attained in manifesting a holy life, in a just and holy exercise of dominion over nature that proceeds from our relation to God as His children." He too refers to Ps. 51:12 (p. 207).

It is not always so easy to strike the proper balance in our perspective about man as the image of God. The discussions about applying various distinctions to the image of God make this doubly clear.*

Nevertheless, when we analyze various ethical issues, both the "no" and the "no, but" become important. Think of issues like abortion and euthanasia. We may say that whoever assaults human life assaults the image of God. It makes no difference whether, in the case of euthanasia, we are cooperating with killing a believer or an unbeliever. Both involve *people,* who have a very special quality, a quality that gives us a pointer for our conduct toward them. Consider, too, the arena of social ethics, a field in which our appraisal of human nature is very critical. Is man, in a collectivist sense, an impersonal cog in a large statist machine, or is he a unique creature, created in the image of God? That he might not be *functioning* as the image of God is not decisive for us; what is decisive is that God *wants* him to function as the image of God, because man was created this way and this way alone. Therefore, we do not choose a perspective about human nature that sees man as one grain in a large sandpile, even though he often behaves like one of the crowd. Similarly, we reject the liberal attraction toward the autonomous man who, in his personal development, must be left as unhindered by the community as possible. For that perspective, too, prevents us from holding to the doctrine of man as the image of God. Man is not autonomous, but is called to serve God and his neighbor, because he is created in the image of God—entirely unique, but together with other unique people in order to form a genuine *community* that is far more that the sum of its individual parts.

Once more, the reality that most people refuse to be the image of God

---

* We are thinking here of the distinction between the image of God in the broader sense (man as a creature elevated above the animal, given understanding, will, etc.) and the image of God in the narrower sense (man living before God in true knowledge, righteousness, and holiness). For an extensive analysis and an important critique of this distinction, see K. Schilder, *Heidelbergsche Catechismus* (Goes, 1947), 1:290ff. Emil Brunner distinguishes between the *formal* image of God (man is "response-able" toward God and always responds in freedom, no matter how wrong that response may be) and the *material content* of the image of God (the correct response, which man can give, however, only by the grace of Jesus Christ); for this discussion, see his *Dogmatics,* vol. 2: *The Christian Doctrine of Creation and Redemption* (Philadelphia, 1952), 55–61, 75–78. We certainly must make distinctions, but the way Brunner does it is incorrect, in our judgment. Structures that serve as conditions for being the image of God become, for Brunner, the image of God itself. With this construction, it is no surprise that man must, by definition, be unable to lose the image of God.

must not deter us from appealing to their creation in God's image and from evaluating and treating them according to that standard. The unredeemed life remains a divinely created life. Our regret about many people living as unbelievers may not inhibit our respect for them *as people*.

No Cultic Images, but Visual Arts

The second commandment forbids making images in the sense of images of gods. Israel was prohibited from bowing down before such images and from serving them, as the text of this commandment states. This language should help us understand that what is being forbidden here are cultic images and not every image that people might carve from wood or forge from metal or sculpt from clay. Jacob placed a memorial pillar on Rachel's grave (Gen. 35:20), and Samuel erected a monument to the triumph of Israel over the Philistines (1 Sam. 7:12). A memorial stone was set up to ratify a covenant as, for example, between Jacob and Laban (Gen. 31:45) or between Yahweh and Israel at Horeb, where twelve stones corresponding to the twelve tribes were set up (Ex. 24:4). In all these cases the Hebrew uses the term *masseba*. That same word is used as well for all those "sacred stones" that Israel and Judah worshiped idolatrously at their high places (see 2 Kings 17:10; 2 Chron. 14:3).* Notice, then, that images were not uniformly prohibited; it came down to the purpose behind their use.

Even the tabernacle and the temple enjoyed the benefits of the visual arts. The candlestick was decorated with flowerlike cups, buds, and blossoms (Ex. 25:31–40). Golden bells and pomegranates were attached to the high priest's garment (Ex. 28:33–34). We could also mention the cherubim. We associate them especially with the ark of the covenant (Ex. 25:18–22), but they appear apart from the ark to decorate the temple walls and doorposts (1 Kings 6:29, 32, 35). Exactly how they looked is unknown to us, although we do read of wings, feet, and faces (1 Kings 6:24–26; 2 Chron. 3:18) and of the combination of human and lion faces (Ezek. 41:18–19).

We encounter large-dimension, animal-like portrayals encircling the sea of bronze, which itself rested on twelve oxen (1 Kings 7:25, 44), and

---

* The distinction was made between commemorative *masseba*, used in connection with a memorial, military victory, and covenant ratification, and cultic *masseba*, used at the "high places" for idolatrous practices. See A. Kruyswijk, "*Geen gesneden beeld,*" 95–105.

two sculptured lions stood alongside Solomon's throne at the top of a series of six steps guarded by twelve lions that corresponded to the twelve
tribes (1 Kings 10:19–20).

Remarkably, Flavius Josephus (ca. A.D. 37–100) criticized Solomon for
permitting these animal images. Josephus pointed to the despicable conclusion of Solomon's life; but, said Josephus, long before that, Solomon
had failed to keep the law when he permitted craftsmen to carve bronze
oxen and lions to surround his throne![15] This viewpoint was certainly not
shared by all, since, according to many ancient rabbis, the portrayal of animals was indeed permissible. Nevertheless, most of the time they did not
forget to forbid portraying *people*.[16] We should notice that in the Old Testament we rarely read of making representations of people.* One effect of
the prohibition against images of deities was hesitation to portray human
beings, even for purposes other than worship. Among the nations surrounding Israel, there were any number of kings who commissioned artists
to portray their triumphs over national enemies. But nowhere do we read
that the kings of Israel and Judah did this. Instead, we are told that their
stories, including all their acts of bravery, were written down (e.g., 1 Kings
15:23; 16:5, 27).

What could be written with pen apparently could not easily be chiseled
in stone. That we can explain: it was too easy to fall into idolatry with an
image of a human being. Perhaps we can hardly imagine that, because we
find it strange that people worship images of wood, gold, and stone. But in
a world where such images exerted a powerful attraction, the line between
cultic and noncultic images was very thin indeed. The worship of cultic
images could easily be transferred to noncultic images.

However, what emerges quite clearly from all this is that the prohibition against cultic images does not apply to the visual arts. Artistry was
used in the temple and beyond (e.g., in Solomon's palace). Our information about this is scarce, leading to diverging explanations. Some have
said that Israel's artistic gift came to expression primarily in narrative and
poetic representation, closely tied to Israel's faith as the source of a unique
form and style.[17] Abraham Kuyper argued that Israel had been chosen to
be the bearer of the religion and triumph of God's kingdom, but not of its

---

* Ezek. 23:14 speaks in an allegory about "men portrayed on the wall." Perhaps we
should understand this as a reference to the Babylonian custom of decorating temples and
palaces in this way, and not to a custom appearing in Judah (see A. Noordtzij, *Ezechiël*, 2d
ed., Korte Verklaring [Kampen, 1956], 250).

art. For that reason, Hiram, king of Tyre, was enlisted to help build Solomon's temple. And this Solomon, Kuyper continues, "in whom, after
all, was found the Wisdom of God, not only knows that Israel stands behind in architecture and needs help from without, but by his action he
publicly shows that he, as the king of the Jews, is in no way ashamed of
Hiram's coming, which he realizes as a natural ordinance of God."* In his
discussion of the relationship between Christ and culture, Klaas Schilder
observes that the absence of visual artistry among the Jews must have been
a serious deficiency in the eyes of Jesus Christ, insofar as it betrayed a mistaken interpretation of the second commandment.[18]

Here is not the place to delve extensively into such wide-ranging discussions. In connection with our explanation of the second commandment, suffice it to say that no matter how scarce the visual arts may have
been in Israel—which may have resulted from a wrong interpretation of
the commandment—in any case this form of art is not condemned by the
second commandment.

Sanction and Blessing

To the second commandment are appended a sanction and a blessing.
One who gives himself over to serving images will observe the consequences among his descendants: the father's sins are punished among his
children, grandchildren, and great-grandchildren. When a person reaches
an advanced age, he receives not only children, but also grandchildren
and even great-grandchildren. That can be a genuine blessing, but also a

---

* A. Kuyper, *Lectures on Calvinism* (Grand Rapids, 1931), 161. Kuyper's opinion is governed by the notion that the "marriage between religion and art" represents "a lower stage
of religion," one that needed a subsequent phase when symbol would be replaced by worship "in spirit and in truth." In this phase, "the purely spiritual breaks through the nebula
of the symbolical" (p. 147). Notice here again how religion is spiritualized. Kuyper uses
Hiram of Tyre to illustrate his premise that Israel was unique because of her religion,
whereas other nations had received "according to God's ordination" the calling to develop
their aesthetic capacities. Hiram's contribution in connection with the bronze artistry of
the temple was significant, but notice that the gold artistry was apparently taken care of by
Israelite artisans. Moreover, Hiram's mother was an Israelite (1 Kings 7:14; 2 Chron. 2:13–
14). "Hiram inherited the technical competence of his Tyrian father and (we may safely
assume) the Israelite inclination of his mother. In this person Solomon found just the man
he needed" (C. van Gelderen, *De Boeken der Koningen*, Korte Verklaring [Kampen, 1951],
1:131). For these reasons, Kuyper's notion appears to us rather dubious. Recall as well the
Israelite artisans Bezalel and Aholiab, who built the tabernacle (Ex. 31:1–11).

very real curse. For if the head of a family turns away from Yahweh to worship images, he will observe how disastrously such disobedience influences his posterity. His entire family is swallowed up in his self-willed religion. His sin becomes their stumbling. Yahweh takes extremely seriously the evil of serving idols and worshiping images. The house of the godless will not be left standing; their name will be blotted out (Ps. 109:13). In this connection, recall kings in Israel who, from father to son, followed in the steps of Jeroboam, to the point where the Lord wiped that royal family off the face of the earth.

That is one aspect. But alongside punishment, there is also blessing, and quite a generous one at that. All the way to the most extended generation imaginable, God will show favor to those who are faithful to Him and keep His commandments. Because David honored God's commands and ordinances, his house continued for generations, even though his descendants were punished for Solomon's sins (1 Kings 11:34, 38–39). Years later, when Hezekiah became fatally ill, he received healing and could live another fifteen years, due in part to Yahweh's servant David (2 Kings 20:6). The faithfulness of the Lord to His covenant with Israel comes to expression in the blessing He bestows, long after the death of patriarchs and kings, to their descendants, even when there is every reason, on account of the sins of that posterity, to stop bestowing such blessings.* Judah's king Jehoram did what was evil in Yahweh's eyes, yet Yahweh was unwilling to destroy Judah, again, for the sake of His servant David (2 Kings 8:19).

These features help us realize that divine punishment and blessing are not automatic, such that the adage "like father, like son (and grandson)" applies automatically to their way of life from one generation to the next. It is certainly true that evil exerts a great influence. When a father turns away from Yahweh, it is surely a miracle when his son rediscovers the right path. It is rather obvious that under the father's influence, the son too would turn away from the Lord. That a sanction is appended to this particular commandment is not accidental. A father in Israel must be fully aware of the significance for him and his descendants of turning his back on Yahweh to practice idolatrous and self-willed religion. Stealing and lying are serious matters too, but someone who forsakes Yahweh is risking his own name and

---

* More than once, interpreters have connected the mass conversion of the Jews, expected on the basis of Rom. 11:24–32, with God's faithfulness to "the most extended generation imaginable." For this view, see J. van der Kemp, *De Christen geheel en al eigendom van Christus* (Rotterdam, 1737), 696; and J. Vermeer, *De Leere der Waarheid. Oefeningen over den Heidelbergschen Catechismus*, 2d ed. (Nijkerk, 1857), 2:191.

his own future. Fortunately, the reverse is also true: a good walk of life exerts a powerful influence too. God-fearing parents put a stamp on their children. Grace is certainly not inherited, but the line of God's faithfulness can be traced in Israel down through many distant generations.

So we can clearly speak of a collective working of both curse and blessing. But that does not mean they work automatically. If a father falls into sin, that does not necessary spell doom for his descendants. And if a father walks in the way of Yahweh's commandments, that is no guarantee that his children will. Pious Jehoshaphat had a godless son Jehoram (1 Kings 22:43; 2 Kings 8:16–18), and we read similarly that the God-fearing Josiah was succeeded by three godless sons and a godless grandson (2 Kings 22 and 23).

For this reason, the Lord rejected the proverb circulating in the time of Ezekiel: "The fathers have eaten sour grapes, and the children's teeth are set on edge" (Ezek. 18:2). Such a proverb was inaccurate, since the rule was: "The soul who sins shall die" (Ezek. 18:4, 20). It could happen that a righteous father has a son who murders and pillages, worships despicable images of idols, and must surely die. But this son could in turn have a son who sees the wicked conduct of his father and refuses to imitate him (Ezek. 18:5–17). The collective consequences of a father's sin, whereby he has poisoned succeeding generations of his family and brought them under the Lord's wrath, still does not eliminate the personal responsibility of children, grandchildren, and great-grandchildren.

The proverb popular among Israel in Ezekiel's day appeared to be a protest against the sanction of the second commandment: If our fathers sin, then we end up suffering for it! But history is not that deterministic. For Ezekiel had to tell Israel: If your fathers sin, you can turn away from their sin! The Lord punishes the guilty, and He takes no pleasure in the death of the wicked, but rather in their conversion (Ezek. 18:23).

So the sanction of the second commandment can never be used as an excuse by children who argue that they are suffering the judgment for what their fathers did. On the other hand, the sanction does contain a serious warning to fathers: Consider the destruction your sin can cause, not only in your own life, but also in the life of your family!

Iconoclastic Campaigns

What does the second commandment mean for today? Before proceeding to answer this question, it would be helpful to say something about the application of this commandment in the course of history.

We know of iconoclastic campaigns during the reigns of Hezekiah and Josiah in Judah (2 Kings 18:4; 23:4–20). The preaching of the prophets made a significant contribution to purifying Israel's worship, so that images virtually disappeared from the land. The lack of images in Israel's worship impressed the Romans. When Pompey conquered Jerusalem in 63 B.C. and entered the temple, he was struck by the fact that there was no image of Yahweh there. The Roman historian Tacitus wrote, "From that moment on, it was public knowledge that the temple housed no deity image and that it was an unoccupied place, an empty secret."[19]

The early Christian church also turned against the worship of images with vehemence. For the early church was embroiled in a bitter struggle against paganism and its many images. The rejection of image worship was resolute. When pagans defended this worship with the argument that they worshiped not the image, but what the image represented, Augustine found such a plea unacceptable.[20] The Synod of Elvira (ca. 306) prohibited placing images and painted murals in the churches.

But the situation changed. Christianity became the state religion, and the hatchet wielded against pagan idols and their images could be buried. Pagan *thinking*, however, had not been overcome in the least. Especially among the common people there lived the desire for Christian images to replace what they had lost when they came out of paganism. Formerly they prayed to the virgin goddess Minerva; now they could pray to the virgin Mary. Formerly the sick took refuge in Apollo; now saint Sebastian could bestow healing. Formerly the image of Pan was carried across the battlefield; now the same could be done with an image of Christ. Formerly the images of gods were kissed in the temple; now people longed to do the same in the church, with images of Christ and the saints.[21] Just as pagans used to believe, all these images were thought to be able to perform miracles. The dead were raised, the sick were healed, demons were cast out, cities were protected, and victories were guaranteed. Just as the image of Artemis had come falling from heaven (Acts 19:35), so too Christianity had obtained its images "not made by human hands" (the so-called *acheiropoiēta*).

Opposition to honoring images was not absent. The *iconoclasts* (lit., "image breakers") arose in response to the *iconodules* (lit., "image worshipers"). The edict in 726 of emperor Leo III (the Isaurian) forbade the making of religious images. His struggle against the Arabians would have influenced his perspective. The Mohammedans, who practiced a religion opposed to images, found a fertile field for proselytizing wherever the church fell into idolatry!* The Jewish voice, too, resounded in those days with the accusation that by their worship of images, Christians were despising the Old Testament.[22]

The contest between image worshipers and iconoclasts was agitated as well by the political motives that played a role. The emperor with his armies faced off against popes Gregory II and Gregory III, who enjoyed broad powers in Italy and did not share the imperial viewpoint regarding images. The Synod of Constantinople (754), called by Emperor Constantine V, once again condemned image worship; but this condemnation would not remain in force very long. Under empress Irene, widow of Leo IV and ruler before Constantine VI, the situation was completely reversed. The (second) Council of Nicaea (787) made a decision that would set its stamp on worship for centuries to come: *Veneration* was a duty with respect to representations of Christ, Mary, angels, and saints, the cross, the four Gospels, and so on, along with incense and candles, while the actual *worship* was ascribed only to God (the divine nature). Veneration (*proskunēsis*) was therefore distinguished from worship (*latreia*).[23]

But this did not resolve the struggle, either in the East, where the emperor lived, or in the West, where by this time Charles the Great ruled the territory of the Franks. The bishop of Rome did indeed participate in the Council of Nicaea, but the church of the Franks had been excluded. In his *Libri Carolini*, Charles the Great condemned the decision of Nicaea, something done also by the great Synod of Frankfurt (794). These condemnations would be nothing more than the last convulsions in the fight against image worship. From the eleventh century on, all resistance was squelched.[24]

What kinds of theological arguments did people advance in favor of image worship? We do not have the impression that people thought too deeply about it. The belief of the masses in miracle-performing images provided more impetus than theological defenses. For the theologian John of Damascus (seventh/eighth century), the incarnation of Christ served as the strongest argument for image worship. Anyone who denies the incarnation of Christ despises divinely created matter itself. The Incarnation served for John of Damascus not only to legitimate representing Christ, but also to justify the various liturgical expressions associated with Christ

---

* L. D. Terlaak Poot, *Geschiedenis van de Kerk*, 2d ed. (Kampen, 1963), 3:38. Islam rejects all direct representation of the creation. Mosques are decorated only with texts and elaborate designs (arabesque).

(Mary, the saints, and the like). Image worship is required. Seeing the Word of God is superior to hearing it; the image illumines the Word.[25]

John of Damascus extended the relation between the Father and the Son who is the Father's image to be the pattern for the relation between Christ and the image of Christ. He had the audacity to write: "I saw the image of God in human form and my soul was saved." Quite properly, his theological opponents took a different position. The Synod of Constantinople (754) declared that it was impossible for people to represent the one person of Christ in His two natures (God and man). Even saints could not properly be represented by inferior matter. The danger of falling into idolatry would be too great.* Once image worship had become completely accepted, theology came along to provide the distinction between the honor ascribed to God and the honor ascribed to the image. The familiar distinction was invented between *latreia* (worship belonging to God alone), *huperdouleia* (honor ascribed to images of Mary), and *douleia* (honor to be ascribed to images of saints).

Clearly such worship goes further than using images merely as a means of visual instruction designed for the illiterate, the laity. Concerning that view of images, one of the popes wrote to support a bishop who was resisting the worship of images. When bishop Serenus of Marseille led an iconoclastic campaign, Pope Gregory I (590–604) wrote him a letter praising Serenus for his zeal in forbidding all worship of images. However, the pope added, "We judge that you did not have to destroy the images." For a painting is permitted in the church "so that those who cannot read may, by looking at the walls, read what they cannot read in the books."[†] So here, images functioned as "books for the laity" designed not for worship, but for religious instruction.

We have seen, however, that images were not restricted to use in religious instruction, and that the image was in fact *worshiped* by kneeling be-

---

* H. G. Beck, "Geschichte der orthodoxen Kirchen im byzantinischen Reich," 74; K. D. Schmidt, *Grundriss der Kirchengeschichte*, 184, argues that the roots of the struggle against images are to be found in monophysitism, a position which insists that Christ is only divine (thus has but one nature, not a divine nature and a human nature), and therefore cannot be represented. See also H. von Campenhausen, "Die Bilderfrage als theologisches Problem der alten Kirche," *Zeitschrift für Theologie und Kirche* 49 (1952): 33ff.

† Migne, *PL* 77, 1027 (ep. 9, 105). Also 77, 1128 (ep. 11, 13): "nam quod legentibus scriptura, hoc idiotis praestat pictura" ("for what Scripture grants to those who can read, pictures grant to the laity"). We could not find the literal phrase "books for the laity," ascribed by Calvin to Gregory the Great (*Institutes*, 1.11.5, libri idiotarum), in any of Gregory's writings.

fore it, kissing it, burning incense and candles before it, carrying it around in procession, and uncovering the head in honor of the image.

Was there, then, no use for the second commandment in that period of church history? Unfortunately, this commandment received little or no attention. R. H. Charles called the second commandment a stone of stumbling for the Middle Ages. People had three options: keep the second commandment in the text of the Bible, but explain it away in a marginal note; eliminate the commandment from the text by putting it entirely in a marginal note; or simply eliminate the text of the Decalogue entirely. Charles writes that the last option became the practice of the Western church since the eleventh century.*

Perhaps this is the clearest proof of how difficult it is to reconcile image worship, in whatever "Christian" form, with the text of the second commandment.

At the time of the Reformation, renewed and expanded attention was paid to the second commandment. Unfortunately, the iconoclasts who wreaked havoc in hundreds of Roman Catholic cathedrals and other churches did not provide the most praiseworthy demonstration of that renewed attention. We can certainly understand their actions. In his exposition of the second commandment, Bastingius (1554–95) says that the iconoclastic campaign of 1566 simply had to burst forth among citizens who saw their friends, parents, children, and siblings so shamefully treated. But what they did should have been done instead by the govern-

---

* R. H. Charles, *The Decalogue*, 68, 70–71. The text of the second commandment does appear in the Catechismus Romanus (1566), a document formulated by mandate of the Council of Trent, but omitted soon thereafter in most of the booklets written for catechetical instruction. The Eastern Orthodox Church retained the text of the second commandment, and considered herself in compliance with the commandment by understanding the term *image* to refer to *carved* (stone) images, thus permitting the worship of *icons* (flat painted panels with representations of Christ and the saints). The eighth-century image controversy was preeminently a struggle against icon worship. People had in view, therefore, not so much the carved image as the painted image. The patriarch Cyril of Constantinople (Cyril Lukaris), who was very sympathetic to the Reformation, declared in his confession of 1631, with reference to the second commandment, "We should not serve the creature but only the Creator and Maker of heaven and earth and adore Him alone. From this it is clear that we do not reject painting, which is a noble and illustrious art. We even allow him who wants it, to have portraits of Christ and the saints. But we detest the adoration and worship of these, as forbidden by the Holy Spirit in Holy Scripture, in order not to ignorantly adore colours, craft and creatures instead of the Creator." For the English text of this confession, see "The Confession of Cyril Lukaris," trans. N. H. Gootjes (published privately).

ment, says Bastingius. He had to acknowledge that most of the participants in the iconoclastic campaigns had not been instructed in the truth.*
Rather, we consider the most praiseworthy demonstration of the renewed
attention being paid to the second commandment to be the uncoupling
of what for centuries had been viewed as one commandment: the first and
the second commandments.[†] Combining them enables one more easily to
neglect the second commandment, as if it were merely an appendage to
the first commandment. Distinguishing them obligates one to evaluate
critically every use of images.

It is unfortunate that Reformed and Lutheran Christians have not
stood together on this matter. We need not regret Luther's opposition to
iconoclasm in Wittenberg, but it is regrettable that he sought to maintain
images as "books for the laity." When the Heidelberg Catechism takes a
position in Lord's Day 35 against worshiping images, it is rejecting, among
other things, Roman Catholic practice. But when, in that same Lord's
Day, the catechism opposes the "books for the laity" (Answer 98), which
it finds similarly undesirable, the Heidelberg Catechism is looking in
Luther's direction.

Images Today

Is the prohibition of images still relevant today? The answer will be affirmative as long as we do not stare ourselves blind over worshiping images

---

* H. Bastingius, *Verclaringe op den catechisme der christelicker religie*, 2d ed., ed. F. L. Rutgers (Amsterdam, 1893), 506–7. In older Reformed commentaries on the second commandment, authors repeatedly mention the task of the government to remove images from
churches. Back then, people still considered that it was the task of government, just as in
the days of Hezekiah and Josiah, to intervene in the church's life for the purpose of reformation. For a more extensive discussion of this, see J. Douma, *Politieke verantwoordelijkheid*
(Kampen, 1984), 98ff.

† For the history of numbering the Ten Commandments during the time of the Reformation, see B. Reicke, *Die zehn Worte in Geschichte und Gegenwart* (Tübingen, 1973), 12ff.,
27ff. In Luther's Small Catechism and his Large Catechism you will not find the portion
of the second commandment dealing with images. The Large Catechism does treat the
sanction and blessing, but provides no separate exposition of what appears in the commandment immediately before them. The Lutheran Conrad Dieterich, in his *Institutiones
catecheticae* (1640), disagrees with the Reformed numbering of the initial commandments,
views the prohibition of images as an appendix to the first commandment, defends the
omission of this prohibition from the text of the Ten Commandments (entirely in line,
therefore, with the Middle Ages), and would retain images as "books for the laity."

of wood, stone, or gold. Our interpretation of the second commandment argued that behind image making there lies a perspective. People suppose that by means of the image they can control divine power. People imagine they can fashion the gods in images in such a way that they automatically enjoy divine favor on their own plans. So the image gives form to a *mental* image, and you cannot eradicate that mental image through an iconoclastic campaign of any kind. The difference between idolatry (worshiping images) and ideolatry (worshiping mental images) is only one letter. So there is but one little step from ancient image worship to modern self-determined worship, in which God is worshiped in a way different from what He has commanded in His Word.

But before discussing this last observation, we wish first to make a few comments about self-willed or self-determined worship that uses the more tangible and concrete form of an image.

Missionaries among pagans must still deal with this phenomenon. Hundreds of idol images have been collected and destroyed by missionaries in the course of their work. A. C. Kruyt tells how missionaries are often criticized for this. People accuse them of narrow-mindedness, shortsightedness, and silly fanaticism. After all, artifacts of human cultural history should be preserved and perhaps housed in museums. But Kruyt correctly notes that missionaries remove idols for the sake of living souls, whose welfare is far more important than that of museums. When a pagan has made the decisive step to follow Jesus, he will also want to separate himself radically from his old ways. This can happen only through fire. The convert will want to see that what he had formerly trusted is now gone. His bridges are burned; he can only move forward down the new path. The accusation of shortsightedness is unfair, for "museum directors need not complain about lack of cooperation from missionaries in helping expand their collections. Rather, the fundamental sensitivities of the converts must never be hurt or wounded."[26]

Even in the modern world, the image has not disappeared from liturgical use. For many in the Roman Catholic church, the image does not say anything anymore, but that is not yet the viewpoint of the church itself. In *The Constitution on the Sacred Liturgy*, the Second Vatican Council declared in 1963: "The practice of placing sacred images in churches so that they be venerated by the faithful is to be maintained. Nevertheless their number should be moderate and their relative positions should reflect right order. For otherwise the Christian people may find them incongruous and they may foster devotion of doubtful orthodoxy."[27] Although the quantity may change, the principle remains the same: *worshiping* the images. What the Second Council of Nicaea (787) declared was confirmed by the Council of Trent (1563)[28] and remains in force today in the Roman Catholic Church. People can make all kinds of distinctions, such as between worship (*latreia*) and adoration (*douleia*), or argue that Christ, Mary, and the saints in heaven can be honored through images. But what was true in former centuries remains true today: "Do not listen to what they are saying, but look at what they are doing."[29] Distinctions break down in practice. The question used to be asked: Why do people make pilgrimages to distant places to meet Mary, if they have statues of Mary in their own home towns?[30] We can still ask that in our own day. The number of pilgrimage destinations has decreased, but quantity is not decisive here. As long as people still hold processions and pilgrimages to show special honor to special images, they transgress the second commandment. Even though these might not be images of Yahweh, they are nonetheless images holding a special power in people's minds, providing special access to heavenly blessings.

Is the case any different for images that function merely as "books for the laity"? Undoubtedly it is improper to put all images in the same category and declare them all objectionable. Anyone with a bit of knowledge about French cathedrals, for example, will realize that particularly the extensive sculpturing on church exteriors had a clear pedagogical purpose. We find the most important stories from the Old and New Testaments carved in stone. During the Middle Ages, the masses were illiterate, but by means of the church's portraits and murals, people could still obtain a limited understanding of the Bible stories. Perhaps we could compare this to our own children, who are able to pick up quite a bit from pictures in their story Bibles.

But "laity" in the sense of unlettered people do not exist anymore. Everybody can learn to read the Bible. It is the church's task to advance, through preaching, catechesis, and other instruction, the independent reading of Holy Scripture. Illustration and image can stimulate that reading, but never be a substitute for it if we wish to avoid cultivating "laity" in the sense of immature believers. For that reason, it is improper to liken images to books for the laity and, with the purpose of instructing the laity, to make room for images either on or in the church building.

Is there absolutely no place in the church for an image? That would be going too far, since even a simple cross and an ornate stained glass window are representations. Nobody imagines that those things are to be worshiped or to be used as books for the laity. They are decorative and remind us that we are not sitting in any ordinary auditorium, but in a church building. A beautiful window, a decorative baptismal font, a fine organ (and especially fine organ playing), and other aesthetically responsible items in and on the church building can, as Kruyt has put it, "draw our thoughts upward."[31] Architect, painter, musician, glazier, and sculptor enjoy today a considerably more modest place in the church than during the Middle Ages. But we would be ungrateful, because of a misplaced fear of everything "external," if we would minimize their contribution to a liturgically and aesthetically responsible church building.

What is decisive is that the preaching of the Word and the congregation's response to that preaching continue to capture the congregation's attention. We have already mentioned several times that the living preaching can be contrasted with fixed images. An image fixates something, since that is what an image is for. A sermon does that much less.[32] What a preacher says wrongly or incompletely one Sunday he can correct the following Sunday. But if something is portrayed in glass or stone in the church, people will have to look at that for a long time to come.

The Dutch theologian H. M. Kuitert mentions in this connection the famous statue of Christ sculpted by the Danish sculptor Thorwaldsen, a statue made for a church but now housed in the Thorwaldsen Museum in Copenhagen. Kuitert has never seen a more unimpressive, more irritating statue than this smooth, polished, saccharine portrait of Christ (he holds this opinion in spite of the high market value this statue has enjoyed in the sermons of many a minister).[33] Whether or not you agree with his evaluation is unimportant. Since this kind of portrait of Christ is controversial, people should not put it in a church. Representations of Christ are numerous. You should compare the subdued portrayals of the suffering Christ with the tearful expressions so often portrayed in religious art. Nevertheless, it would be good if both remained outside the church building.

Religious art must be able to develop, but it develops best outside the walls of the church. Rembrandt was in his own way an interpreter of Scripture, but you must not make the Rembrandt Bible the pulpit Bible. Religious art reflects the history of exegesis, but that is different from the living preaching of God's Word. The argument that a sermon forms images too, and that those images will always be defective, is surely correct. One clear implication of this argument is that collections of written sermons rarely survive one generation. As the divinely commanded means to instruct Christians (Lord's Day 35, Answer 98), the living preaching of the Word always demands the correction of *our* images that must be tested in terms of *the* image that God has given of Himself and of His worship in Holy Scripture.

The arts of drawing, painting, and sculpting must be practiced in terms of that biblically governed image. To the question about what may and what may not be represented, we would answer that art may portray whatever Scripture shows us. No one has seen God as He exists in His blinding majesty. But Abraham saw Him in human form, accompanied by two angels (Gen. 18:2–16; 19:1). Ezekiel and Daniel also saw in visions "a likeness with the appearance of a man" (Ezek. 1:26) and "the Ancient of Days . . . His garment was white as snow, and the hair of His head was like pure wool" (Dan. 7:9). Artists like Dürer and Rembrandt, as well as those who illustrate (children's) Bibles, transgress no boundaries established by the second commandment when they convey their impressions of the evidences of God's presence that believers in biblical times were permitted to see. Appreciating this kind of art is different than worshiping the images it produces.

Rigid Forms

The image fixates, more so than the word that can be corrected. But even without statues or paintings in a church building, many things in church can conflict just as much with the second commandment.

Take, for example, the liturgy, which can be of such a quality as to resemble image worship. We are dealing here with extremes. Because they oppose the central place given to preaching in the liturgy, people go in search of new liturgical forms and practices designed to facilitate contact with God. The image has disappeared, but rituals and ceremonies return in order to awaken new life in an otherwise dead church. But even in a church where, in good Reformed style, people want preaching to occupy center stage, things can go awry. Only the King James Version, and no other; only Genevan tunes; no hymns; a particular style of preaching—these too can bind our concourse with God to habits that can become rigid forms. No longer are the living preaching of the Word and the corresponding faith the decisive elements of worship, but the old, habitual forms and sounds that make people feel secure. The image fixates more than the word, but that does not mean that the word and the sermon will necessarily avoid degenerating into something automatic.

By this we are not saying that worship can occur without fixed forms. We have already seen that a wrong interpretation of John 4:24 can over-spiritualize the worship of God. Hearing and seeing go together; the eye is no less important than the ear. The problem is that both eye and ear must attend to what God has said in His Word. Worship of God is not a matter simply of our internal heart, but also of our external hands and knees.

Dutch theologian J. R. Wiskerke wonders whether "our liturgical custom of kneeling only at special occasions (weddings, ordination of a minister), seen from a historical point of view, perhaps arises from an indifference toward the 'merely external,' a minimizing that can be ascribed to an unscriptural contrast between 'internal' and 'external' in worship."[34] Using forms, however, can degenerate into formalism. When that happens, something has gone wrong internally. Coming to Yahweh with burnt offerings was commanded in the Old Testament, but if Israel thought her worship was exhausted thereby, then those sacrifices became worthless. Then the people heard another message: "He has shown you, O man, what is good; and what does the LORD require of you but to do justly, to love mercy, and to walk humbly with your God?" (Mic. 6:8). Self-determined religion is often accompanied by great show: much public display (Matt. 6:5), an abundance of words (Matt. 6:7), a pile of precepts (Matt. 23:3–5; Col. 2:20–23). Behind such precepts, there was always much that was good, so that Jesus could say to His disciples: "Therefore whatever they [the Pharisees] tell you to observe, that observe and do, but do not do according to their works; for they say, and do not do" (Matt. 23:3). Religious fanaticism is often so hypocritical and powerless. The forms are empty, because the heart has drifted away from God.

In themselves, forms are not wrong, for there is no worship without forms. The Old Testament sacrificial worship has ended, but even though there is no temple, we still need church buildings with well-ordered services, worship times when everything follows a well-constructed order. Even a church order that regulates the mutual life of the churches is not a form of image worship as long as it enables the free development of the churches and does not function like a straitjacket.

Fixed forms are not wrong, fixed formulations even less. The Apostles' Creed has been around more than a thousand years, and it still serves as a brief summary of our Christian faith. Longer documents, too, born predominantly in times when the church had to give an account of what agreed and did not agree with Holy Scripture, retain their significance as confessions of faith in which the churches find their unity. Undoubtedly, a picture of the triune God emerges from such confessions. If that image corresponds to the image that God provides of Himself in His Word, then it is a good confession, even if it is a thousand years old.* Should that not

---

* Here is an altogether different question: Is it a sign of the church's strength that she does not formulate a contemporary confession, especially with a view to the church's teach-

be the case, then we must either dispose of the confession or alter it. Confessionalism is image worship, because that exalts the confession above the Scripture, and makes human writings "however holy these men may have been, of equal value with those divine Scriptures" (Belgic Confession, Article 7).

Someone has said that dogma shortchanges the freedom of God. Anyone who fixes dogma, the church's doctrines, supposedly has the audacity to say, "That is God, that is Christ, that is baptism, the Lord's Supper, the Last Judgment, and so forth," which then means we assume a certainty that does injustice to God and His secrets. Now, we must not speak with certainty where we should not, but neither may we leave vague what in God's Word is very clear. In her confessions the church has not said, "This is how God fits together, that is the image of Him we have constructed." Rather, at critical moments in her history, the church has thrown out what were, in fact, images of God. She has responded to heretics by saying, "God is not as you portray Him, for He has revealed Himself in His Word differently than you portray Him." Instead of making images of God, the church has shattered images through her pure confession. Formulating dogma is incomprehensible apart from that spiritual iconoclasm.*

Mental Images

In his *Institutes*, John Calvin stated that human understanding is a workshop where idols are continually being crafted. The fact that those idols are subsequently given form in an image of wood or stone is secondary. The spirit of man begets the idolatrous image; his hand gives it birth.† If you are interested in the relevance of the second commandment, you must

---

ing ministry? A centuries-old confessional document can echo Scripture and still be so dated in its subject matter and formulations that if we were to start over and write it afresh, we might arrange and formulate things differently. "Every confession is capable of being revised. Of course, not every three years. It is a sign of impotence that we are still unable to do that. We have clung too much to traditions and had too little opportunity for study," said Dr. Klaas Schilder in one of his theological lectures in 1942. (This comment is reported in a posthumously published account of Schilder's lectures entitled *De kerk*.)

* J. Koopmans, *De Tien Geboden* (Nijkerk, 1946), 25, sees in dogma "nothing else than the rejection of image worship, a spiritual iconoclasm," and finds in dogma a summary of "the doctrine of Scripture, so that God is believed and served *according to His Word*."

† J. Calvin, *Institutes*, 1.11.8, referring to the human mind as "idolorum fabrica," saying a bit later, "mens igitur idolum gignit, manus parit."

not restrict it to the idol images mentioned in the commandment, but ask whether, apart from materials like wood, stone, or paint, you construct wrong mental images of God. For then you are doing exactly what the image-making craftsmen were doing in the Old Testament world: fashioning God according to your own understanding.

We encounter this kind of imageless imagination already in the Old Testament. Psalm 50 provides an example of this. The people of Israel were exhausting themselves in bringing their sacrifices. There was no lack of religiosity here (Ps. 50:8)! But this religiosity was accompanied by godlessness, because people consorted with thieves, tolerated adulterers, and spread blasphemy. Apparently, people thought this was perfectly acceptable. *They imagined that God was just like them* (Ps. 50:21). Here again we are confronted squarely with the original sin against the second commandment: a person leads his own life, imagining that God bestows His approval automatically. Instead of believing that God created man after His image—so that He may demand of him a believing and holy lifestyle—man creates God in his image, ready to serve his own ambitions.

We provided examples of this earlier when we discussed improper worship and heresy. But things can go wrong beyond the walls of the church too, and heresy is not always expressed in words. We can work with a very worldly picture of God by oppressing and murdering our neighbor while we imagine that God has no eyes or ears. That is what the godless of Psalm 94 did: Yahweh does not see, the God of Jacob does not notice (Ps. 94:7). We can easily justify any sin, and if we cannot, we can always allege discrimination—as with, for example, homosexual conduct or other forms of sexual expression outside of marriage. In such cases, people use grandiloquent expressions to describe God, speaking of Him as being in solidarity with all of humanity, embracing all humanity with His love. You begin to wonder why Paul took the trouble to lead people to faith with the argument that the Lord is to be *feared* (2 Cor. 5:11)—or why another Bible writer says that it is a terrifying thing to fall into the hands of the living God (Heb. 10:31). So without using our hands, we can still make an image of God. We can imagine God to be a nice Santa Claus, who really is not all that mean toward naughty children.

We can make God out to be more friendly than He really is, but also more strict. We fashion God in our own likeness just as much when we crack the whip above people's heads, when we reach our favorite religious pitch only when we are sounding off about sin and eternal damnation. We make God in the image of Scrooge, someone who has pleasure in the death of the godless and would really prefer to see more people in hell than in heaven. We fashion an image of a god without a heart. For we no longer know Him as the Father of Jesus Christ, who is gracious, full of compassion, patient, and loving, who justifies the ungodly (Rom. 4:5) and asks simply for faith from those who seek salvation (Acts 8:37; 16:30–31).

Today the second commandment applies to us as much as the other nine. As long as human understanding serves as the workshop where images of God are crafted according to our own imagination, we are summoned by the second commandment to return to the Word of God—*the* image that will continually destroy and cast down our images of God and of His service. We must return time and again to the testimony. The sanction applies today as well, namely, that for one who does not speak according to this Word, there is no dawn (Jer. 8:20).

Endnotes

1. A. Kruyswijk, "*Geen gesneden beeld . . .*" (Franeker, 1962), 91.
2. Ibid., 142–43, 234.
3. Ibid., 67.
4. F. H. von Meyenfeldt, *Tien tegen een* (Hilversum, 1978), 1:99.
5. J. R. Wiskerke, "De scholastieke verminking van de aanschouwing van God," *De Reformatie* 41 (1965–66): 324.
6. A. Kruyswijk, "*Geen gesneden beeld,*" 230.
7. On this point, see N. H. Gootjes, *De geestelijkheid van God* (Franeker, 1984), 187ff.
8. A. Kruyswijk, "*Geen gesneden beeld,*" 166, who quotes F. Michaeli.
9. H. M. Kuitert, "Het Tweede Gebod," 67.
10. J. R. Wiskerke, *De strijd om de sleutel der kennis* (Groningen, 1978), 117ff.
11. B. Bekker, "Catechisatie over den Heidelbergschen Catechismus," in *De Friesche Godgeleerdheid* (Amsterdam, 1693), 287: God permitted Moses to apprehend the penultimate, but not the ultimate.
12. For this exegesis of John 4:24 and for a discussion of the false dilemma between internal and external (including criticism of the view held by Calvin and others), see especially Wiskerke, *De strijd om de sleutel der kennis,* 99f., 130ff.
13. A. Kruyswijk, "*Geen gesneden beeld,*" 115.
14. The idea of man as representative of God in the context of interpreting the phrase "man as image of God" has found many adherents. For bibliographical information, see C. Westermann, *Genesis* (Neukirchen, 1974), 209ff. See also K. Schilder, *Heidelbergsche Catechismus* (Goes, 1947), 1:255, 263ff.; G. C. Berkouwer, *Man: The Image of God* (Grand Rapids, 1962), 114–15; A. Kruyswijk, "*Geen gesneden beeld,*" 192ff.
15. Flavius Josephus, *Antiquities* 8.7.5.
16. See Strack-Billerbeck, *Kommentar zum Neuen Testament aus Talmud und Midrasch* (Munich, 1956), 4/1:384ff., concerning "The Attitude of the Ancient Synagogue Toward the Non-Jewish World." It was not unusual to have deep reservations about statues (p. 391).
17. G. von Rad, *Old Testament Theology,* 1:364–65.

18. K. Schilder, *Christ and Culture* (Winnipeg, 1977), 24–25.

19. Tacitus, *Historiae* 5.9 ("Inde vulgatum nulla intus deum effigie vacuam sedem et inania arcana").

20. Quoted by R. H. Charles, *The Decalogue* (Edinburgh, 1926), 39.

21. These examples come from K. D. Schmidt, *Grundriss der Kirchengeschichte*, 5th ed. (Göttingen, 1967), 29–30.

22. H. G. Beck, "Geschichte der orthodoxen Kirchen im byzantischen Reich," in *Die Kirche in ihrer Geschichte*, ed. B. Moeller (Göttingen, 1980), D1, 1:69.

23. See H. J. D. Denzinger and A. Schönmetzer, eds. *Enchiridion symbolorum*, 33d ed., no. 600ff.

24. K. Heussi, *Kompendium der Kirchengeschichte*, 10th ed. (Tübingen, 1949), 173.

25. See H. G. Beck, "Geschichte der orthodoxen Kirchen im byzantischen Reich," 73.

26. A. C. Kruyt, "Het Tweede Gebod," in *Sinaï en Ardjoeno*, ed. Th. Delleman (Aalten, 1946), 65.

27. *Vatican Council II: The Conciliar and Post-Conciliar Documents*, ed. Austin Flannery (Collegeville, Minn., 1984), 35.

28. See H. J. D. Denzinger, *Enchiridion symbolorum*, no. 984ff.

29. P. van der Hagen, *De Heydelbergsche Catechismus* (Amsterdam, 1743), 389.

30. Ibid., 389.

31. A. C. Kruyt, "Het Tweede Gebod," 69.

32. H. M. Kuitert, "Het Tweede Gebod," 80–81; see also E. L. Smelik, *De ethiek in de verkondiging*, 3d ed. (Nijkerk, 1967), 90.

33. H. M. Kuitert, "Het Tweede Gebod," 81.

34. J. R. Wiskerke, *De strijd om de sleutel der kennis*, 108.

The Third Commandment

You shall not misuse the name of Yahweh, your God,
for Yahweh will not leave unpunished those who do that
[lit., those who misuse His name]. (Ex. 20:7)

Speaking the Name

When considering the meaning of the third commandment, we would do well to remember that this prohibition against misusing God's name involves first of all *speaking* that name. The name Yahweh (Lord) must not be *spoken* without meaning or with deceitful intentions. Misusing this name means, among other things, taking it unrighteously upon our lips. On several occasions we read in the Bible that certain names are not to be named: "Make no mention of the name of other gods, nor let it be heard from your mouth" (Ex. 23:13; cf. Ps. 16:4). The names of the Baals must be removed from the mouth of Israel, "and they shall be remembered by their name no more" (Hos. 2:17).

Now, these verses are clearly talking about the names of idols. But the name of Yahweh can be used wrongly, too. An oath can properly employ the phrase "as surely as the LORD lives" (Jer. 4:2), but the name can be misused with these very same words (Jer. 5:2).

What is prohibited is not simply speaking the name of Yahweh. Nowhere in Scripture do we find any indication that the tetragrammaton—the four letters constituting the sacred name YHWH—is too sacred to take upon our lips, as orthodox Jews allege. In fact, even the names of idols like Ashtoreth, Chemosh, and Milcom are mentioned in Scripture without hesitation (e.g., 2 Kings 23:13). The only consideration is the purpose for which they are used. When a portion of history is narrated, the name of God can appear alongside names of idols, such as those of Baal and Yahweh in the story of Elijah on Mount Carmel (1 Kings 18:20–39). But what

73

is prohibited is taking the names of idols on human lips for the purpose of worshiping them. Israel also had to be careful when using the name of the true God.

We can summarize three errors that surely lead to misusing the name of Yahweh:

1. The name is misused in *sorcery*. Sorcerers invoke the Lord's name in order to summon His assistance. They call on the Lord's name in order to exercise control over Him through an incantation. Sicknesses can be driven out, enemies can be neutralized, and the future can be foretold, if people exercise control over names containing secret powers. The literature from the ancient Near East is full of such magical incantations.[1]

Surely we should notice the absence of these kinds of incantations in the Bible. Sorcerers and exorcists were not to be tolerated in Israel (Deut. 18:10–14). Evidently the danger of falling into sorcery was far from imaginary. We find a clear example of that in the New Testament. The seven sons of a man named Sceva, a Jewish chief priest, tried to drive out spirits by using the name of Jesus. They had seen how Paul had healed the sick and driven out evil spirits, undoubtedly in the name of Jesus. Without believing in Jesus' name or having been baptized in His name, these itinerant Jewish exorcists tried to do the same thing Paul was doing. They used the name of Jesus in their exorcism incantations, expecting that the mere mention of His name would unleash secret powers that they could use to cast out evil spirits. But their attempt failed. They were tackled by a man possessed by an evil spirit and forced to flee. This event made such a deep impression that fear fell on the people and the name of Jesus was magnified (Acts 19:13–17). In contrast to the fruitless misuse of this name, we find the name being exalted!

The Lord does exercise mighty powers, but He will not let people worm any secrets about their use out of Him. Using His name, they can perform miracles, but then only with His authorization. God did many mighty works through the hands of Paul, we read (Acts 19:11), whereas sorcery attempts to use God's name for selfish ambition. In contrast to Paul, who functioned under God's commission, sorcerers and exorcists are really intruders who desire to control divine forces in order to place life, death, and the future within their own power. The third commandment excludes intruders, but welcomes recipients—people willing to depend on revelation and powers bestowed from above.

2. The name is misused in *false prophecy*. False prophets declare, "Thus says the Lord," when in fact they have not been sent by Him (Deut. 18:22; 1 Kings 22:11; Jer. 14:15; Ezek. 13:6). It is not accidental that this false

prophecy is branded or categorized as divination (Jer. 29:8–9; Ezek. 13:9; cf. Ezek. 21:29). Prophecy comes with the word of Yahweh; divination comes with its own predictions and becomes false prophecy when it pretends to come in the name of Yahweh. That, too, is an empty, vain naming of the name Yahweh.

3. The name is misused in the *false oath*. Deceitful words are strengthened by mentioning the name of Yahweh in the oath formula "as truly as the Lord lives" (e.g., Jer. 5:2; Zech. 5:4). This turns the name into an instrument in service of the lie. Wicked people do not shrink from speaking the name in order to pass off a lie as if it were true. That, too, is clearly in violation of the third commandment. "And you shall not swear by My name falsely, nor shall you profane the name of your God: I am the LORD" (Lev. 19:12).

Name and Revelation

So far, we have been discussing *speaking* the name of the Lord. It is striking that the third commandment does not say, "You shall not misuse My name," whereas in both of the preceding commandments, God speaks of Himself in the first person, and not—as here in the third commandment—in the third person. Why does He use the third person here? The reason must be to focus attention on the name Yahweh. That is why the name is expressly mentioned. It is not simply, "You shall not misuse My name," but, "You shall not misuse the name of Yahweh, your God." The issue is one of misusing this precious name.

But misusing the Lord's name is surely not exhausted by an improper *speaking* of that name. We would fall far short of what Scripture says about transgressing the third commandment were we to restrict ourselves to the errors identified above. The name of the Lord can also be abused without even mentioning it.

We can easily show this to be true. Included within a person's name is his whole being. When Genesis speaks about the giants of an earlier era as "men of renown," they owed their name to their mighty power as giants (Gen. 6:4). When Solomon enjoyed a name among all the surrounding nations, his name was attributed to his unsurpassed wisdom (1 Kings 4:31). Here "name" refers not to what they *were called*, but to what they *were*. Attacking their name meant not taking seriously the power of the giants or the wisdom of Solomon. This is how Shimei attacked David's name. David too was a man of renown among Israel and beyond (1 Sam. 18:30; 2 Sam. 19:21). He was anointed by the Lord to be king

(2 Sam. 19:21). But what did Shimei do? Instead of honoring David, he went around belittling his name. He made David out to be a vigilante (on account of his efforts against the house of Saul) and a rogue, a worthless fellow. He was *cursing* David. The Hebrew uses a word here for "cursing" that contains the idea of declaring someone a nonentity and despicable.[2] According to Shimei, David should have been dealt with by the Lord (whose name Shimei would have invoked): "Come out! Come out! You bloodthirsty man, you rogue!" (2 Sam. 16:7). David's status was changed from a heavyweight to a lightweight. A similar thing occurred earlier with Abimelech, who was cursed by the citizens of Shechem. The content of that curse we can savor from the words of one of those residents: "Who is Abimelech . . . that we should serve him?" (Judg. 9:28). One's reputation is trampled underfoot. He is said to be unworthy of being held in honor.

Armed with this insight, we can now focus on the name of the Lord. Who is the Lord? What does He do? Then, what is His name or reputation? His name is His revelation in the works of creation and redemption. The poet of Psalm 8, under the impression of God's creation and man's place among the creatures, begins and ends with "O LORD, our Lord, how excellent is Your *name* in all the earth!" (Ps. 8:1, 9). Turning our gaze from the creatures to the heavens and the earth, paying special attention to man's place in the universe, one senses how weighty and significant the Lord's name really is. One also senses that attacking one of God's creatures can be an attack upon the name of the Lord. Anyone who mocks the poor insults their Maker (Prov. 17:5). You may not curse a deaf person or put a stumbling block in front of a blind person (Lev. 19:14). These actions also violate the third commandment.

Yahweh made a name for Himself as Creator; He did the same as Redeemer and Defender of His people Israel. Precisely for that reason, He has made Himself known by the name YHWH. These four letters mean "I am who I am" (Ex. 3:14)—that is, I exist as Savior and Liberator, I make real what I say, I do what I have promised. The promises I made to your ancestors I now fulfill. I will real-ize My words in deeds, as I lead My people out of Egypt and bring them into the Promised Land.

Yahweh passed before Moses on Mount Horeb as the Lord who is merciful and gracious, long-suffering and abounding in goodness and truth (Ex. 34:6). The entirety of salvation demonstrates this. "He saved them for His name's sake, that He might make His mighty power known" (Ps. 106:8). His name is His strength (Ps. 54:1); His name is declared in His wondrous works (Ps. 75:1).

On this basis, the Lord may demand that people reverence His name. Angels and men are summoned to give to the Lord the *glory* due to His name (Pss. 29:2; 66:2; 96:8). "Glory" is the English translation of the Hebrew word *kabod*, which means "weight, burden."[3] The name of the Lord is one of heavy weight. Therefore we must acknowledge His imposing power and give Him praise befitting His level of majesty.[4] The opposite would be to minimize the name of the Lord, to underestimate, despise, and scorn the name. It would be treating something weighty as though it were light. Giving "glory" would be replaced by cursing and blasphemy.

Take, for example, the son of an Israelite woman and an Egyptian father who got into a fight with an Israelite in the camp (Lev. 24:10–23). In the hand-to-hand combat that ensued, what lived inside the man came out: his Egyptian nature. He blasphemed the Name with a curse. At that point he would most likely have spoken the name "Yahweh," but there is more involved than that. He blasphemed and cursed the Name.[*] Both Hebrew words used here meant approximately the same thing. The word for "curse" is again the word we met earlier: "to declare someone to be insignificant and despicable." So angry with his Israelite opponent was this half-Egyptian, half-Israelite man, that he did not hesitate to use God's name. He did not merely say the Name, but he dragged it through the mud. He said things about God that were wildly preposterous. And in Scripture, that is precisely the character of "cursing." Bystanders watching this fight, who were shocked by such blasphemous language, brought the man to Moses. After God had been consulted, the man was stoned to death.[†] At the same time, the law was announced for both the foreigner

---

[*] Jewish exegetes insist that this episode involved *saying* the name of Yahweh, and for that reason Jews appeal to this text for the prohibition against even speaking the name. Similarly, the Septuagint (the Greek translation of the Old Testament) translates the phrase as he "named the name" (*eponomasas to onoma*), probably influenced by the Jewish exegesis mentioned above. On the basis of vv. 15–16, it is argued, then, that it is less serious to mention the name Elohim (God) than the name Yahweh. For a rebuttal of this exegesis, see the commentary on this passage by K. Piro and A. Clamer, *La Sainte Bible: Lévitique* (Paris, 1946), and see the notes that follow.

[†] The question can be asked, Why did God have to be consulted about this matter, when both the third commandment and the sanction for its transgression were already known (Ex. 20:7; cf. 21:15)? But the episode in Lev. 24 involved a *foreigner*. In addition, the subsequent instructions (regulations pertaining to manslaughter and inflicting injury) indicate that those regulations that had been in force for an Israelite were now being declared to be applicable to the foreigner as well. Cf. Lev. 24:22: "You shall have the same law for the stranger and for one from your own country; for I am the LORD your God."

and the native Israelite: "And whoever blasphemes the name of the LORD shall surely be put to death" (Lev. 24:16).*

Just as the man in Leviticus 24 despised the Lord, so too did the general of the Assyrian king, who said in the hearing of the people near the wall of Jerusalem: "Beware lest Hezekiah persuade you, saying, 'The LORD will deliver us.' Has any one of the gods of the nations delivered its land from the hand of the king of Assyria? . . . Who among all the gods of these lands have delivered their countries from my hand, that the LORD should deliver Jerusalem from my hand?" (Isa. 36:18–20). This was properly viewed as a reproach of the living God and as blasphemy (Isa. 37:4, 6). For the Lord was degraded to a second-rank deity who could accomplish no more than the gods of the surrounding nations that had earlier been trampled underfoot by Assyria.

It was not only foreigners who blasphemed and scorned the Lord; God's own people could do that, too. Even though the Lord performed many signs in the wilderness, nevertheless the people of Israel scorned Him (Num. 14:11). When the Israelites were enjoying plenty, satisfied with an abundance of food and drink, then they turned to other gods and spurned the Lord (Deut. 31:20). In times of prosperity, the godless say that there is no God—thereby scorning the Lord who, according to all appearances, is not going to require an accounting anyway (Ps. 10:3–11, 13). Riches induce one to ask lightly, Who is the Lord? But poverty can have the same effect, when poor people assault God's name on account of their poverty (Prov. 30:8–9). Blasphemy is committed by everyone who despises the word of the Lord and violates His command (Num. 15:30–31). It happens when someone who knows God's name, His revelation, who is fully aware that God has the right to prescribe the law for His people, still remains unaffected.

---

* Just before this verse, we have the words that, in agreement with exegetes such as A. Noordtzij (*Leviticus*, trans. Raymond Togtman, Bible Student's Commentary [Grand Rapids, 1982], 246; cf. footnote 36) and others, we would render as follows: "Whoever curses his god shall bear his sin" (Lev. 24:15; notice the uncapitalized "god"). That a foreigner would treat *his* god in a despicable manner would already be noteworthy. He would be showing that to him nothing is sacred. But since he would be blaspheming an idol, he would not be punishable *in Israel*. Perhaps he would be punished by "his god." But if either an Israelite or a non-Israelite blasphemed the Lord, the God of Israel, then he would deserve death. In contrast to our view, there are interpreters who understand the phrase "whoever curses his God" to refer exclusively to Israel's God (notice the capitalized "God"). In fact, this is the rendering of almost every English translation, from the King James Version to the New International Version. It is therefore surprising that these versions retain the possessive pronoun *his* in the phrase "his God."

There is a further result: when Israel scorns Yahweh, that provides reason for pagans to blaspheme the God of Israel. David's treatment of Bathsheba and Uriah gave occasion for the enemies of the Lord to heap much scorn upon Him (2 Sam. 12:14). And by being dispersed among the nations in her captivity, Israel profaned the holy name of the Lord, because the nations were saying, "These are the people of the Lord, and yet they have gone out of His land" (Ezek. 36:20–32). We might also say: He will demonstrate that He has a name, and that this name reflects who He is: "I am active as Savior and Liberator!"

From the examples given, we can see clearly enough that blaspheming and cursing the name of Yahweh are not exhausted by an improper *speaking* of that name. The issue lies much deeper; the matter is much broader than that. It is not so much that someone mentions the name of the Lord, but that he thinks, speaks, and acts disparagingly with regard to Him—that is what constitutes the essence of cursing and blasphemy.

The Name of Jesus Christ

In the New Testament, we find confirmation and an expansion of what we have found in the Old Testament. Jesus Christ has "glorified" His Father and revealed His name to those whom God gave Him out of the world (John 17:4, 6). What *kabod* represents in the Old Testament, *doxa* represents in the New: the weight, the greatness, and the honor due to the name of God. This honor Christ displayed toward His Father.

But, at the same time, Christ did much more. As the Father's Son, He revealed the name of the Father in such a way that He could say, "He who has seen Me has seen the Father" (John 14:9). In Christ, the Father Himself stands before us. For that reason, we cannot speak adequately about the name of the Lord—thus, about the third commandment—without taking into consideration the name of Jesus Christ. Christ and the Father are one (John 10:30, 38). No one comes to the Father except through Him (John 14:6). Included in the name of the Lord is the fact that He will be active as the Savior of His people. Well then, that salvation has been and is bestowed through Jesus Christ. Our salvation lies in no one else, for among men on earth there is but one name given whereby we must be saved (Acts 4:12). To Him has been given the name above every name (Phil. 2:9–11). For that reason, "glory" and honor are due to Him as well (John 1:14; 5:23; 16:5; 1 Cor. 2:8; Rev. 5:12–14).

But in addition to "glorifying" the Name, the New Testament deals also with blaspheming that Name. The beast from the sea who wages war against the saints, and the multitude in league with him, blaspheme the name of God (Rev. 13:5–9). This is an assault upon God's power and majesty. Such conduct characterizes also those who refuse to be converted, in spite of the plagues God sends upon them (Rev. 16:9, 11). But believers also can, by means of their attitude and conduct, bring discredit upon the name of God. A wicked lifestyle on the part of Christians can be the occasion for outsiders to blaspheme the word of God (Titus 2:5).

Christ Himself warned against a particular form of blasphemy, namely, blasphemy against the Holy Spirit. When Jesus healed a demon-possessed man, who was also blind and dumb, the Pharisees insisted with vehemence that this was the work of the Devil. Jesus contradicted their claim and said, "Therefore I say to you, every sin and blasphemy will be forgiven men, but the blasphemy against the Spirit will not be forgiven men. Anyone who speaks a word against the Son of man, it will be forgiven him; but whoever speaks against the Holy Spirit, it will not be forgiven him, either in this age or in the age to come" (Matt. 12:31–32).

This particular form of blasphemy must be understood, in our judgment, as *willfully* misunderstanding and branding as *devilish* what in fact comes from the Holy Spirit. With your own eyes you see the work of the Holy Spirit, so clear that you cannot miss it—but then you proceed to ascribe the work of the Holy Spirit to the Devil! God does forgive sins—even sins committed against the Son of man will be forgiven—but *this* is going too far.

We find something similar in Hebrews 10:26–31. If we would trample underfoot the Son of God, despising as unclean the very blood of the covenant by which we were sanctified, we would be spurning the Spirit of grace. Here again we see the combination of willfulness (intentionally sinning, see v. 26) and self-consciously declaring what is holy to be unclean. Again, we must notice that spurning the Spirit is related closely to the work of the Son. One spurns the Spirit of *grace*, which means the Spirit of Jesus Christ. Blasphemy against the Holy Spirit is directed against the work of the Son, both in Matthew 12 and in Hebrews 10. From this we see clearly how serious it is when the name of Jesus Christ is despised. Anyone who takes what constitutes His "glory" and drags it down by declaring it to be of the Devil or unclean, is blaspheming in a way that is unforgivable.

Modern Cursing

Let us move on to look at the meaning of the third commandment for today. We begin by pointing again to using the Name. Here we are referring not simply to using the name Yahweh, but also the names God, Jesus, or Christ, or using expressions to call down God's damnation. This kind of cursing is characteristic of our day and age. At work, on radio and television, in any number of contexts in which we deal with people, we hear profanity.

This evil is ancient. No century has passed without godly people sighing deeply over this sin. H. Bullinger observed in the days of the Reformation that virtually no government punished swearing or blasphemy. From the beginning of the world until the present, Bullinger complained, no people had so blasphemed God as the people of his day. A bit later, J. H. Alstedt observed that among all the peoples confessing the name of Christ, cries of "my God" and "my Jesus" had become commonplace. In days of old, godly church leaders complained about youngsters using language that would have made your hair stand on end. They matured from "mere" cursing to profanity, it seemed. So there is nothing new under the sun. The Christian world of an earlier time and the secular society of today have both witnessed a lot of cursing. The past and the present are matched rather evenly at this point.[5]

To form a judgment about this kind of cursing, we must realize that we are dealing here generally with something different from *biblical* examples of cursing. In the Bible, someone who cursed and blasphemed God did that from the heart. He did not just let a curse accidentally slip out, but rather, in his speaking he expressly despised the God of Israel. Something similar can indeed occur today when people blaspheme God. But then the perpetrator is self-consciously attacking the honor of God. From the point of view of civil law, a democratic society that respects freedom of religion can hardly make public blasphemy effectively punishable. That kind of ideal requires a society in which both citizens and government still publicly defend the honor of God. But when that is no longer the case, legislative regulations against blasphemy quickly become a dead letter. Of course, this does not detract from the seriousness of blaspheming God. It may well be difficult to enforce civil penalties against blasphemy, but that fact does not reduce the moral evil of the sin.

But modern profanity is not usually intended to be blasphemous. People use the name of God and of Jesus Christ as an interjection or an exclamation in circumstances of shock, surprise, and anger. People use these names to add force to their words. In this last example, we hear a faint echo—especially when people call down divine damnation—of what in the Bible is self-condemnation: "May God do so to me, and more also. . . ." This means, may He punish me with such a terrible punishment if what I say is not true, or if what I promise is not fulfilled. In ancient times that terrible punishment was symbolized when two people made a covenant together and used an oath to confirm it. We find a clear illustration of this in Jeremiah 34:18. When a covenant was ratified, a calf was cut in two. Anyone who broke such a ratified covenant would perish just like that calf, "only worse"! We see this kind of ceremony at the ratification of a covenant in Genesis 15:9–21, when God made a covenant with Abraham.

Nevertheless, modern profanity is still only an *echo* of biblical cursing. People mention God, but without really thinking about Him. In the Bible, cursing had religious significance, but today cursing is so secularized that people use the word *god* without intending to say anything about God. For most people who do this, God is dead—someone at whom nobody hurls insults anymore.

Most pagans today continue to have such fear of their gods that they do not "curse," that is, use the names of their gods as an interjection. They use the names of their gods only in their prayers, and they refrain from using them as interjections because they are too afraid of being punished by the curse threatened for the misuse of these names.[*] It is a sad thing to observe, but precisely in Christianity—rather, in a Christianity no longer *vibrant*—cursing has become customary. A Christianity that is no longer vibrant quickly becomes a *contemporary* paganism. Fear of God and Christ no longer exists. People simply keep using these names in ways ranging from familiar to coarse.

By arguing that modern cursing is something different from cursing in the Bible, we do not camouflage the evil warned against by Bullinger, or by tracts from antiblasphemy groups, or by many preachers still today. It is impossible to view such cursing as acceptable. We must indeed express our emotions, and occasionally add force to our words; but if these require cursing, then we are dealing with more than an impoverished vocabulary. We are not dealing here with a mere "peccadillo," a trivial offense "at the very edge of modern consciousness."[†] Even if modern swearing is not a self-conscious *demonstration* of

---

[*] A. C. Kruyt, "Het Derde Gebod," in *Sinaï en Ardjoeno*, ed. Th. Delleman (Aalten, 1946), 84–85. The situation is different among Mohammedans. The name of Allah has become empty through repetition. By using this name in the often endlessly repeatedly confession, "There is no god but Allah, and Mohammed is his prophet," people easily use the name of Allah flippantly in daily life (p. 85).

[†] M. Lochman, *Wegweisung der Freiheit* (Gütersloh, 1979), 49. Lochman uses a word from Luther, "Puppensünden," a word Luther obtained from his father-confessor, von

unbelief, it is nonetheless very clearly a *symptom* of unbelief. People who have turned their backs on God naturally take up using His name idly. And that is our first concern, which lies deeper than fighting against what is a mere symptom. As Christians we shudder not only at every careless summons of God's damnation, but also with any vernacular use of God's name in people's ordinary vocabulary. Their cursing does not lie at the very edge of modern consciousness, but rather prompts us with a recurring reminder to stand up for God. Not in the sense of "Why do you attack my religious convictions?" but deeper still: "Is this not the Creator of your very life whose name you use so lightly?" We are not insisting that we must respond every time with these words. Rather, the real issue is that we are willing to respond. Do we simply shrug our shoulders at the cursing of others, or do we see behind the words a person exposing his deepest emptiness through his vocabulary, and to whom we would gladly say more than simply that his profanity terribly offends us?

Various useful suggestions for beginning a conversation with somebody about his profanity include the following:

- Always speak simply, with self-control and not too emotionally, being considerate in your use of language.
- Do not criticize too quickly when somebody uses what you consider to be coarse language.
- Do not threaten someone too quickly with the punishment mentioned in the third commandment.
- You can disarm someone who is intentionally cursing, using a reaction like "If you had said the same thing in a different way, without swearing, I could have understood you just as well."
- You can stimulate the reflection of someone who, out of habit, without malicious intention, uses God's name improperly, by saying, "Would you have said that the same way if you had first written it out?"[6]

These are excellent suggestions for starting a conversation about swearing. But then we must also seize the opportunity provided to us to pene-

---

Staupitz. Von Staupitz intended this to describe those "small" sins in contrast to the weighty transgressions like cursing parents, public blasphemy, or committing adultery. "Mußt nicht mit solchem Humpelwerk und Puppensünden umgehen und aus jeglichen Bombart [noise] eine Sünde machen," said Luther (*Weimarer Ausgabe Tischreden*, no. 6669). In English we would speak of peccadillos, which are petty sins or trifling faults.

trate all the way behind the symptom of swearing to the actual ailment: the sickness of a heart estranged from God.

To this point we have been discussing outsiders, people who swear as those estranged from God and His service. But, unfortunately, swearing appears more and more today among believers—not only during fits of rage, when people lose control of themselves, but also in ordinary conversation, when people forget or perhaps do not realize that "respectable" swearing is still swearing. God's name may be used with confidence in prayer and praise and conversation, when people are really talking to or about God. But just as you wear an expensive article of clothing only for special occasions, and you take care to keep it in good condition, in the same way we must use the name of God and of Christ.[7] For that reason we must warn Christians, more so than outsiders, against misusing God's name by cursing. If we fail to use God's name sparingly, if we simply use it whether it is relevant to our conversation or not, how then will we make clear to an outsider what fearing and respecting God's name means? We must not follow the Jews who refuse to mention God's name at all. But we can learn from them that this name is not an everyday utensil, and that we should not use it like one.

First among the suggestions mentioned above is that we ourselves must be considerate in our language. Respect for God's names should incline us to shy away from coarse swearing. Those around us can figure out that we have no basis for criticizing their careless summons of God's damnation if we regularly allow the word *damn* to slip from our lips. Words like *hell* and *jeez* have the same negative effect. Please understand, we are not about to list what will and will not pass muster. We are simply trying to describe the style of our language. If you take the name of God seriously, you will do everything possible to avoid bringing discredit to that name. Sloppy language spiced with bravado makes us ill equipped to contribute toward the struggle against cursing.

Abusing God's Name with a Show of Power

Today when we speak about the third commandment, we think readily of the kind of swearing that uses the names of God and Christ in an improper way. We have just finished discussing the phenomenon of *secularized* swearing. In ancient times, pagans did not curse that way, nor do they today. Neither did the Israelites, since their fear and trembling before the God of Israel were too great. It was quite impossible for the name of the Lord to degenerate into a cliché or be used as an interjection or an exclamation. But, as we saw, there were other forms of abuse. The Name was abused in sorcery, in false prophecy, and in the false oath. To what degree do these sins exist today?

Together with the idols of wood and stone, magical incantations have disappeared from our world today. We simply smile at much of the modern abracadabra. The magician with his tricks, filling the role once filled by the sorcerer, is an innocent substitute for the ancient religious sorcerers who sought to manipulate divine powers. But just as idolatry is possible without images of wood or stone, so too sorcery is possible without sorcerers and soothsayers. Recall King Saul, who, though he had outlawed mediums and soothsayers (1 Sam. 28:3), nevertheless, when he had spared King Agag and the spoil seized from him, was severely condemned by Samuel: "For rebellion is as the sin of witchcraft, and stubbornness is as iniquity and idolatry" (1 Sam. 15:23). You can ban sorcerers from the land and still be controlled by the *spirit* of sorcery (stubbornness, defiance). Saul went his own way and clothed his conduct with piety by invoking the name of the Lord at various times in connection with this incident (1 Sam. 15:20–25).

This kind of sorcery reappears whenever we say that something is God's will, when in fact it is not. This is how we push for what *we* want, using God's name to lend force to our plans. Mentioning the Name, after all, strengthens our power. People must now follow us, for we have God on our side. Often this is accompanied by noble intentions. People imagine that they are rendering God a service, while, at the same time—witness the example of Paul—they are persecuting the church of Christ (1 Tim. 1:13; Phil. 3:6).

Crusades were organized using the slogan "It is God's will." Cruel techniques of inquisition, used during the Middle Ages and after, were clothed with the name of God. Many people have been unrighteously cast out of the church while the name of God was being invoked. Many have discovered the consequences of resisting ecclesiastical power brokers. Such resistance has always been dismissed easily with the argument that such people are opposing God. Parading power in the clothes of piety carries a lot of weight, because submission to it can appear so virtuous, like genuine Christian humility. Often—one could say: as a rule of thumb—reformation is decried as revolution. To oppose long-standing traditions is to oppose what, for most people, has acquired the glow of divine approval.

The abuse of God's name that we are identifying here occurs not only with crusades and church splits. Every believer must regularly ask himself whether he is really communicating what God wills, or whether he is simply pressing his own will and using God's name to accomplish that goal. Parents must take this into consideration when raising their children, who can easily sense the difference between genuine and pretended authority. Parents must make clear to their children who God is; parents may not protect themselves with God's name in such a way that God comes to be viewed as a bogeyman.

The show of power pretending to have God in hand can be evident in long prayers or long discourses in which the name of God is used incessantly. Jesus warned against excess verbiage, on the basis of which pagans believed they would be heard (Matt. 6:7; in older commentaries this was termed *battologia pharisaica*, the excess of words used by Pharisees in their showy prayers). What strikes us about Jesus' own teaching on prayer is the simplicity and sobriety. Reciting the rosary with the Ave Maria and the "Our Father" fifteen times adds no force to praying, just as little as the incessant use of "Lord," "God," "Father," "Almighty," and the like. Broadcasting the gospel by means of radio and television requires a sober use of God's name. It is wicked when listeners or viewers turn off the broadcast, not out of rejection (which is always still a possibility!), but out of irritation with "Jesus this" and "Jesus that." There is no depth here, and repetition turns the holy Name into a cliché, even though the one praying has the best intentions of emphasizing the joyful message for his listeners.

If you say God's name too often by falling into repetition, you are not treating it reverently. But this is not yet to say that such prayers contradict the Bible. That is different from *false prophecy*, something that occurs today just as in the days of the Old Testament. Presenting something as God's word that in fact is not, and cementing it with "Thus saith the Lord," happens no less frequently today than during the Old Testament. For example, we might well wonder what kind of prophecy we are hearing when the name of God is tied to the struggle against nuclear weapons. Ecclesiastical prophets assure us that the kingdom of peace, in which swords will be beaten into plowshares and spears into pruning hooks (Isa. 2:4; Mic. 4:3), requires that we eliminate nuclear weapons, possibly even unilaterally. Many insist that the dividing line between faith and unbelief must be drawn precisely here and nowhere else. Either we do what God demands of us (away with war, away with nuclear weapons, away with militarism), or we cooperate with the world's suicide. They are not convinced by the response that the issue of nuclear weapons is not quite that simple, for that answer is dismissed immediately as unbelief. We must strongly oppose this politicizing of the gospel (called by Dorothy Sölle "the greatest modern religious movement") and this caricature of what Scripture supposedly teaches about faith and unbelief. The slogan "It is God's will" can just as easily be an idle use of God's name when it is used *against* weapons (think of pacifism, unilateral nuclear disarmament) as when it is used *for* a cause (think of the crusades and of religious officials "blessing" military weapons).

The Oath: Meaning and Misuse

In addition to considering forms of sorcery and false prophecy, we must also look at the oath and its misuse. The oath is still common in our society, no matter how secularized it has become. Attempts to eliminate it have not yet succeeded, although since the French Revolution the oath has lost its position of supremacy. Alongside the oath, one can employ a vow or declaration that does not invoke the name of God. This kind of vow or declaration carries with it the same consequences, so that in the event of perjury the same punishments are applied as with the oath. The choice for an oath or a vow has become solely a matter of personal preference.[8]

Even though the oath is not the only tool used on ceremonial or judicial occasions, such as inauguration into office or confirming the truth in court, it still enjoys a prominent place in our society. To that degree, we can draw a line quite directly from the Old and New Testaments to today. The *forms* of oath swearing have changed. For example, we do not place our hand under the thigh of another (Gen. 24:2–9; 47:29),* nor do we raise our hand to heaven (Gen. 14:22; Rev. 10:5–7), but merely raise the right hand† and answer, "I do, so help me God."‡ But the *substance* involved in oath swearing is the same as in the Bible.

What then is an oath? The oath is swearing with appeal to the name of God, who serves as witness that a person is speaking the truth or intends to

---

* Putting ones hand under another's thigh—that is, near the organ of procreation—is mentioned only in these two passages in Genesis, both in a situation anticipating death. In his commentary on Genesis, Claus Westermann says, "The one who is facing death secures his last will by an 'oath at the source of life' (O. Procksch)" (*Genesis 12–36: A Commentary*, trans. John J. Scullion [Minneapolis, 1985], 384).

† Perhaps raising the hand with two fingers outstretched has to do with the two witnesses (God and the one making the oath). Other forms of oath taking include placing a hand on the Bible or on a cross. A Jew will often take an oath with his head covered. See W. Geesink, *Gereformeerde ethiek* (Kampen, 1931), 1:303, and the article written by P. J. Verdam on "Oaths" in *Christelijke encyclopaedie*, 2d ed. (Kampen, 1957), vol. 2.

‡ Among Germans, the usual formula was: "Hialpi mer sva Freijer [the name of some god]," whereby the deity was summoned to *help* the one swearing to tell the truth, and *not* to assist the perjurer. The word *hialpi* is the origin of our "So help me God." See W. Geesink

fulfill a vow.* Notice the double application of the oath. It is used to confirm that a person is speaking "the truth, the whole truth, and nothing but the truth," and it can assume the character of a vow, as in the oath of office. In the latter case, one confirms under oath that he will exercise his office in accordance with applicable regulations. To say it with terms derived from Latin, there are *assertory* and *promissory* oaths. We swear an assertory oath in court, to confirm the truthfulness of our statements. A promissory oath is sworn by presidents, prime ministers, congressmen and members of parliament, judges, military officers, and the like. These swear an oath of office obligating them to a careful exercise of their office or calling.

This double use of an oath we find in the Heidelberg Catechism, where Answer 101 teaches that the oath confirms "fidelity and truth." Answer 101 mentions another duality: an oath can be required by the government, but also by "necessity." The first is clear enough, but what is meant by "necessity"? A study of Calvin's *Institutes* (2.8.27) provides the answer. He distinguishes between *public* and *private* oaths. The public oath is sworn before government officials or superiors (e.g., military superiors). But oaths sworn by a private individual toward another individual can be permissible as well. Calvin gives an example. If your brother accuses you of a breach of faith, and you cannot prove your innocence, because he is unwilling to be convinced by any argument, your reputation might be endangered by his hardheaded stubbornness. In that case, you could by means of an oath appeal to God's judgment. As biblical examples of oaths between private individuals, Calvin points to Jacob and Laban (Gen. 31:53), to Boaz, who confirmed his intent under oath to marry Ruth (Ruth 3:13), and to Obadiah, to whom Elijah in the same manner confirmed that he would meet Ahab and not suddenly vanish—something that would have cost Obadiah his life (1 Kings 18:15).

A survey of these biblical examples of private oaths (which could be expanded with further examples) shows us that it is not so easy to categorize

---

Gereformeerde ethiek, 1:302. The suggestion made by some that this "help" might mean "help to die," and thus hypothetically constitutes a self-malediction (recall the biblical "May God do so to me and more if I . . ."), finds no support in dictionaries from the Middle Ages and later.

* From the time of Jerome, three criteria were formulated in Christian moral thought: (1) *veritas in mente,* which means that a person must possess a truthful spirit; (2) *ius in iurante,* which means that the person swearing must possess the capacity of discernment; thus, no children or mentally incompetent may take an oath; and (3) *iustitia in obiecto,* which means that the object or matter involved in the oath must be morally legitimate, and thus not conflict with religion or morals.

them under the concept of "necessity." These are indeed private oaths, but not always sworn in situations of necessity. These situations are not so much cases of "necessity" as of "emergency."[9] Situations can occur where, in addition to the oaths required of us by the government (Calvin calls these the safest oaths, because we are dealing here with public servants of God), oaths between private individuals may still be necessary. This kind of *emergency* can occur where, for example, in making a contract no government official exercises authority over both parties in order to register the oath.

Apparently Calvin still had a bit of difficulty with these private oaths, since in the first edition of his *Institutes* he dealt only with public oaths. Since Calvin's day, the accent has come to fall more heavily on this kind of oath. Oaths and contracts are tightly regulated today. What could earlier have been done in private (covenants, contracts, and the like) is now far more regulated by legislation.

Has this resulted in the oath between private individuals falling into disuse? We would hardly dare to make that claim, especially when we notice the example Calvin gave. It can happen even today that in the church (notice that Calvin spoke of a brother!) somebody's reputation is attacked by rumors that cannot be proved, but neither can they be disproved. The person in question can only appeal to God Himself to witness to his innocence. Suppose that this kind of situation caused a great stir within a congregation, because an accusation (that perhaps enjoyed every appearance of truthfulness) was met with a denial by the person involved; in such a situation, could it not be useful for the accused to confirm his denial under oath? Yes should be yes, and no should be no, especially in the church (Matt. 5:37); but what *should* be the case often is not, unfortunately, even in the church. Is the oath a means of binding people to their word that functions only in the world, on account of sin, confusion, and chaos? Or can it serve that function also in the church? In our opinion, the answer is yes, also in the church. If a matter that is dragging on and on can be put to rest by having the accused confirm his innocence as clearly as possible before the face of God, so that the matter may no longer be raised, then we would see that as a blessing. We would indeed insist that this kind of oath within the ecclesiastical arena may be used in situations of necessity.* Naturally, such oaths are no longer "private," since they would be sworn in the presence of the church's office-bearers.

---

* Calvin says in the *Institutes* (2.8.27) that private oaths are not to be condemned, as long as they are used "quae sobrie, sancte, reverenter *necessariis* rebus" ("soberly, with holy intent, reverently, and *in necessary circumstances*"). Notice, in necessary (and thus not just in emergency) situations.

From the preceding, we have surmised that the oath is very significant. Along with the Heidelberg Catechism, we could speak of a double purpose. One who swears uprightly honors God and advances the well-being of his neighbor.

Let us look first at the honor we give to God. One who swears an oath does so in terms of someone higher than himself, to whom he can appeal in order to end all counterargument (Heb. 6:16).* Who else could that be but God, who knows the heart with all its ruminations (Ps. 139:1–6) and who is in a position to punish us for every false oath? By swearing an oath, we are confessing our faith: God and nobody else, not even ourselves, functions as verifier of our words. For that reason, we would choose self-consciously for swearing an oath rather than making a vow or a declaration, if we were given the choice. By doing so, we are not saying that vows and declarations are worthless, but it should surely sadden us that many refuse to employ the God-given means of the oath. By appealing to Him we honor Him—with an honor that, in the days of Israel, God refused to share with any other gods (Deut. 6:13–15; Josh. 23:7–8). What was in force then is still in force today: You shall take oaths in His name; bring Him praise, for He is your God (Deut. 10:20–21).

Swearing an oath also advances the neighbor's good. We have already mentioned that the oath is a contractual tool. A society that respects the oath is not easily disrupted. In this kind of society, people still recoil from lying and expend energy in taking their office or calling seriously. An oath-bound monarch is bound by the rights of his subjects that have been established in the constitution, so that his administration does not exercise tyranny. Oath-bound physicians are committed to healing their patients. An oath-bound officer serves the preservation of the state. An oath-bound property assessor can be expected to estimate property value honestly. By means of an oath in court, witnesses are restrained from declaring the innocent to be guilty, or the guilty to be innocent. By means of the oath, we are placed before the very face of God. Reverence for God has salutary consequences for society.

---

* For this reason, those oaths in Scripture that are sworn with an appeal to people have always been difficult to interpret. For example, "By the life of Pharoah" (Gen. 42:15), sworn by Joseph to Pharoah. Others include "As your soul lives, my lord [Eli]" (1 Sam. 1:26), or "As your soul lives, O king [Saul]" (1 Sam. 17:55). Entirely in agreement with what others have written about these examples, William Perkins insisted that Joseph either sinned by swearing in this manner, or had merely used strong language that need not be taken as an oath (Alle de werken [Amsterdam, 1659], 3.1.205).

In contrast to these salutary consequences flowing from swearing oaths uprightly, consider the evil resulting from perjury or falsely swearing an oath. Scripture warns against this kind of oath because it constitutes sacrilege of God's name (Lev. 19:12). Among pagans as well, perjury was viewed as a serious misdemeanor. We find that occasionally it was seen to be of such a nature that human punishments were inadequate. Emperor Tiberius (A.D. 14–37) spoke in this connection of a crime against the gods that can be punished only by the gods. During the Middle Ages, it was the *ecclesiastical* authorities who punished perjury. As secularization set in, perjury lost its character as a serious sin against *God;* nevertheless, law codes continued to prescribe punishment for perjury as a serious form of deceit or fraud. The judge is deceived and the neighbor is defrauded. Most democratic societies impose stiff penalties for perjury, including heavy fines or in some cases even imprisonment.

Motives for perjury do not need to be self-serving. Somebody might simply be attempting to protect a family member or friend from an accusation of wrongdoing. But in such cases, perjury remains perjury. The believing Christian who raises his right hand to swear an oath must realize that such a gesture summons God as his witness. If he perjures himself he is not risking simply a prison term; he is not simply deceiving the judge or injuring only his neighbor; but he is standing first of all before God. The Heidelberg Catechism correctly confesses in Lord's Day 37 that we are calling upon God to punish us if we should swear falsely.

Moreover, it is clear that we may not swear unnecessary oaths. Such would not be the case, of course, if a judge requires us to swear an oath. But it does occur if in our daily conversation we drag God's name in for the purpose of emphasis. "Heaven help me" and "So help me God" are oath formulas designed to lend force to our words. But boosting the credibility of our words by invoking God as our witness drags God's name down. The more easily such swearing is used, the more easily lies arise. We must use the oath sparingly. The government can require an oath of us, and the arena of our work and calling can be a place for swearing an oath, but beyond these, the oath should remain something special. The exceptional and serious character of the oath corresponds to the preciousness of God's name.

Misunderstanding the Oath

The oath must remain something special. But should we not really go one step further and eliminate the oath completely? Does Scripture not point in this direction?

Well known are those groups who, throughout history, have rejected oaths altogether. In this connection we could mention the Essenes, Catharii, Albigenses, Hussites, Anabaptists, and Quakers. Our interest is occasioned by the fact that people appeal, in defense of their position, to the words of Jesus in the Sermon on the Mount and to James 5:12. Is their argument convincing, so that we should in fact avoid oaths completely? Against their position we would raise the following objections.

First, in the Sermon on the Mount, Jesus says clearly that He did not come to nullify the Law and the Prophets, but precisely to fulfill them (Matt. 5:17–20). From many different references in the Law and the Prophets we have already gathered that the Lord considered it a matter of honor when His people took oaths in His name (see in addition Isa. 45:23; Jer. 4:2; 12:16). So then, we may legitimately question whether the *upright* swearing of oaths comes under the sentence of Matthew 5 and James 5.

Second, we know that Jesus permitted Himself to be placed under oath. When Caiaphas commanded Him, "I adjure You by the living God that You tell us if You are the Christ, the Son of God," then Jesus answered him in the affirmative (Matt. 26:63–64). Moreover, both Jesus and Paul frequently employed emphatic assurances and assertions that went far beyond a simple yes or no (Matt. 5:18, 26; along with the many times Jesus used *amen*, "truly"; Rom. 1:9; 2 Cor. 1:23; 11:31; Gal. 1:20; Phil. 1:8, where Paul summons God as witness and places himself before the face of God). Furthermore, we read of an angel who, with uplifted hand, swore an oath to God (Rev. 10:5–7). To this we might add Hebrews 6:13–20, which speaks of the oath used among people (v. 16: "For men indeed swear by the greater, and an oath for confirmation is for them an end of all dispute"). All these references indicate that we can hardly interpret Jesus' criticism of oath swearing to mean a complete prohibition of every oath.

Third, the text of Matthew 5:33–37 generates one more observation that prevents us from concluding that Jesus is giving here an absolute prohibition against oath swearing. Jesus is clearly refuting both Jewish casuistry and superficial swearing. People were using oaths not in a spiritual way, but in a clever way. An oath invoking the name of Yahweh must be kept, but in order to escape the tightness of such a requirement, people swore "by heaven," "by the earth," "by Jerusalem," or "by my head." When swearing by these authorities, they did not need to be so careful about the truth, or so they imagined. It was against this deceptive use of oaths that Jesus came with His redirecting word: "Do not swear at all; when you say yes, let it be truly yes, and when you say no, let it be nothing else than no."

So when Jesus (or James) says that we must not swear *at all*, we must read this emphatic statement in its context: "Do not swear at all, neither by heaven, nor by the earth, nor by Jerusalem, nor by our heads. Every superficial oath is from the evil one." Jesus is not saying, "Do not swear at all, period." Nor is He saying, "Do not swear by God." But He is rejecting every kind of swearing that uses an oath for pulling a trick on someone.

Fourth, we must consider the difference between ecclesiastical style and civil laws. Even if it were the case that within the church the oath should never be used (a claim we cannot defend from the pages of Scripture), then it is still an open question as to what must occur in the world. Anyone making the Sermon on the Mount a law code for the world will need to institute a different court system, will never regulate divorce and will need to get rid of military service. Thus, it is not accidental that Anabaptists retreated from public life by refusing public office and military service. The laws of nonruling (Luke 22:25–26), of nonresistance, and of the simple yes and no became laws in their own ecclesiastical kingdom,[*] whereas they retreated from the world that was supposedly immersed in evil. But we must not withdraw from the world. Public office, the sword of government, and even using the name of God before the judge are all *good* things for the world. We must distinguish between worldly and spiritual polities, each of which has its own responsibilities, but both of which stand in service to God.[†]

Anyone who claims that a good society is possible without oath swearing is simply surrendering realism for idealism. In a paradise world, no oaths would be necessary; but we live in a fallen world, in which it is good that at critical moments in their lives, sinful people are confronted with the seriousness of what they are about to say (the assertory oath) or of what they are about to do (the promissory oath).

Taking Every Oath Seriously

Anyone who would claim that oaths are often taken upon the lips of ungodly people would obviously be correct. But were he to conclude that therefore we can no longer take oaths seriously, he would be mistaken. We have just observed the distinction between the ecclesiastical and the civil

---

[*] See W. Balke, *Calvin and the Radical Anabaptists*. The Anabaptists withdrew into a minichurch ("ecclesiola"), which simultaneously constituted a ministate ("imperiolum").

[†] In this connection, recall the Belgic Confession, which speaks in Article 30 about the church's polity and in Article 36 about the government and its politics.

arenas of responsibility. A civil judge cannot investigate whether someone possesses an upright faith in God and can therefore swear an oath honestly. But he certainly can remind the one under oath of the seriousness of his oath swearing and can punish him if he commits perjury.

A fine example of the meaning of an oath sworn with an appeal to idol deities is found in early commentaries on the third commandment dating from the time following the Reformation. The question arose whether a contract with people serving idols who took an oath in the name of their own gods was permissible. Take, for example, the former colonial organizations, like the United East Indies Company, that came into contact with all kinds of people and had to enter into various contracts and treaties with them. Although our colonizing ancestors took oaths before the God of the Bible, people of other nations invoked Allah or other gods. But could Christians cooperate in making such treaties or contracts? Did that not conflict with the third commandment? How can a believer participate in a treaty wherein one party invokes God and the other party an idol?

These are clear questions to which our ancestors also had a clear answer. With biblical examples they demonstrated that such treaties could indeed be made. Did not Isaac enter into covenant with Abimelech, king of the Philistines, which they had sealed with each other by means of a ceremonial vow (Gen. 26:31)? Did not Jacob do the same with Laban, even though they did not swear in the name of the same God (Gen. 31:51–54)?

However, these theologians of old did not settle for an appeal to a few Bible verses. They also indicated why entering into such treaties was necessary. Naturally, within Israel it was impermissible to swear by anyone other than the one true God. The stiffest penalties attended the invocation of foreign gods. But what was impermissible within Israel was by contrast necessary in worldly relationships. Consider what L. Danaeus wrote: We have in common with unbelievers everything belonging to this life: light, water, land, treaties, contracts, commerce and cities, war and peace.[10] If this is so, then certain matters must be regulated in common. And if you wish to legislate those matters, then an oath is necessary. If one party swears an oath in the name of his false god, then that is *his* sin, but *we* may remind him of the declarations he made under oath before his god.

Anabaptist oath avoidance does not fit with the third commandment. True, we are not of the world, but we are surely in the world. In the church we may not tolerate sexually immoral people, but in the world we must live alongside sexually immoral or avaricious people and swindlers or even *idol worshipers* (1 Cor. 5:9–11). If, in civic matters, we must take seriously an oath sworn in the name of an idol god, then surely also the oath sworn in the name of God, even if those who swear such an oath ignore God in the rest of their lives. That is *their* sin. But it is the duty of judges—believing or unbelieving—to respect, in their administration of justice, the oath and its consequences.

Difficulties with the Oath of Office

We reject the Anabaptist position that has no room for oath swearing and serving in government office. Thereby we are not denying that the oath of office sworn by the Christian can occasionally generate great difficulties.

Take the politician, for example. He pledges fidelity to the Constitution and promises under oath to fulfill his office faithfully. But both the Constitution and other laws or regulations can present him with choices that go against his Christian convictions. How should he vote regarding a Sunday law that ignores the fourth commandment? What should his position be regarding a libertine morality in the area of marriage and sexuality? Should he cooperate in subsidizing various forms of anti-Christian cultural expression? As a Christian politician, will he not inevitably become entangled in evil, so that the Anabaptist perspective is correct in wanting believers to stay out of politics?

At this point we must distinguish very carefully. When someone swears an oath to uphold the Constitution, he is not thereby declaring that he agrees at every point with the Constitution or with all the laws that have been made in terms of the Constitution. If he were, then nobody would ever be able to swear an oath or make such a promise. Any number of laws lack unanimous consent, and even with regard to a Constitution, a Christian may properly insist that the matters addressed should be formulated a different way. Within the political arena he may fight for a fundamental alteration of a system of government and for changing any number of laws. But his oath of office obligates him to *respect* the laws that are currently in force. As long as these laws are in force, he must be faithful in upholding them.

Blocking the *implementation* of such laws and ordinances would bring him into conflict with his oath of office. He may certainly employ all his efforts against *introducing* laws that, according to his convictions, conflict with God's will. That lies, in fact, entirely within the purview of his oath of office, which requires not only faithfulness to the laws, but also a faithful performance of his office. A legislator or member of parliament who votes no is also working within the purview of his oath of office. But if you vote against legalizing the sale of pornography, you may not, once the law permitting such sale goes into effect, take it upon yourself to clean out pornography stores. Not matter how morally justified such tactics may appear, there is a law forbidding them. The oath of office sworn by politicians requires them to respect bad laws too.

Difficulties generated by one's oath of office become insurmountable only when adopted laws and ordinances compel the politician to *participate* in godlessness and criminality. The oath of office obligates something other than "orders are orders, period" in the sense employed by Adolf Hitler. The oath of office does not require blind obedience, and precisely because we invoke God's name in such an oath, we realize that He is the highest and final Judge of good and evil to whom we must render absolute obedience. So we are not saying that the terms *Christian* and *politician* denote concepts that cannot really be combined. But we are saying that *occasionally* it can happen that they are no longer compatible. One can still confidently swear an oath of allegiance to the constitutions of most modern democratic states, but the oath of allegiance to Hitler became a sacrilege of God's name. It is good for us in our modern democratic societies to keep asking whether the exercise of our office still permits us to invoke God's name. Scripture teaches us clearly that we must keep oaths that we have sworn to *our* own hurt (Ps. 15:4). But we must realize that we are exempt from oaths that injure God's honor and our neighbor.* When this affects our oath of office, this would require us to resign from office.

Dishonoring God's Reputation

We have been dealing with the modern meaning of the third commandment in terms of *saying* God's name. We saw that modern cursing is a sin against the third commandment, even though the quality of this secularized cursing is different from the cursing we find in the Bible. Then we saw that the ancient sins of using God's name in sorcery, false prophecy, and perjury are as relevant today as ever. But what about that feature of cursing in the Bible where God's name is not used in the modern manner as a curse word, but is ridiculed and despised? For that lay at the heart of curs-

---

* What is at stake in this connection is the *iustitia in obiecto*, the legitimacy of that concerning which the oath is sworn. See our earlier comment regarding Jerome's three criteria for valid oaths. Herod, for example, was obligated to break his sworn promise, which led to the beheading of John the Baptist.

ing in the Bible: the name of Yahweh is very weighty, but outside of Israel or even within Israel, people did not take it seriously or mocked that name or treated it lightly.

This ancient sin is still as fresh as ever. It is no less relevant and no less frequent than the kind of cursing we discussed earlier. To understand this, each Christian must begin with himself. We would probably not use God's name as a curse word. Swearing a false oath is, in view of the infrequency of oath swearing, also not a daily occurrence in our lives. But then what value does God's name have in our lives and in our relationships with others?

We are not yet finished with this matter when we reject all kinds of theologians who dishonor God or even blaspheme Him. For example, we might object strenuously against a God-is-dead theology because such a theology dishonors God. We might also oppose those who deny God's election, since they are not giving God the honor due Him as the absolutely sovereign Giver of all grace. We might protest against the misrepresentation of our redemption through Christ's shedding of blood upon Golgotha, because in every liberal theology His name is denigrated: the Son of God is nothing more than a fine example. We might disagree completely with those who deny the resurrection of the dead and the Last Judgment, who argue that we are dealing here simply with expressions of mythical language. For these claims injure the reputation and honor of God as Creator of a new world wherein those who have followed Him upon earth will be physically present; and from Him is withheld the honor of being the Judge who will exclude many from this new paradise forever. Quite properly we reject all of these errors, and quite correctly early Reformed ethics observed that *heresy* is a transgression of the third commandment.[11] But that does not exhaust orthodoxy's concern with the third commandment! Orthodox conviction must be clothed with a Christian lifestyle preoccupied with giving honor to God.

The degree to which we fall short here can be illustrated in two ways. The Heidelberg Catechism declares that God is angry with those who, insofar as in them lies, do not oppose and forbid cursing and swearing (Answer 100). That is obvious; for if He is God, and if His name is used lightly or with sport, then He may expect His followers to defend His name. Unfortunately, we are often more afraid of our neighbor's anger that might be aroused when we bring the matter to his attention, than we are afraid of God's wrath.

A second matter that should make us modest is found in those Bible passages that speak about cursing in a holy manner. For example, Paul says, "If anyone does not love the Lord Jesus Christ, let him be accursed" (1 Cor. 16:22). Or he exclaims, "But even if we, or an angel from heaven, preach any other gospel to you than what we have preached to you, let him be accursed" (Gal. 1:8). Such crass expressions, as appear also in the so-called imprecatory psalms (Pss. 35, 109, 137), we must not take lightly upon our lips. More than one commentator warns us about this.* But that must not hinder us from inquiring into the background of such imprecations. What attitude undergirded Paul's imprecations? Was he full of hatred against certain people? The latter could not have been the case, since the same apostle wrote, "Bless those who persecute you; bless and do not curse" (Rom. 12:14). As long as *our* name and honor are involved, Paul requires us to endure much abuse. But the honor of God and of Jesus Christ is another matter altogether. The apostle can become so inflamed with passion for God's honor that he pronounces the most severe condemnation upon those who dishonor God's majesty.

This attitude of Paul and others is instructive, especially for today. Paul realized what love for one's neighbor entailed and he did far more than simply talk about it. But he refused to identify God as an extension of human cooperativeness and solidarity. God possesses a *unique* name and a *unique* honor that must remain exalted, *even when that leads to a sharp condemnation of His enemies.* That unique honor of God must remain at the center of our consciousness, not as something incidental, something useful for our private worship, but as the primary duty in Christian living. Praise and prayer are not ornaments, but constitute the foundation for exercising our task in this world.

Abraham Kuyper correctly observed that in Scripture we are seldom asked to demonstrate our gratitude to God by *doing* something, by performing any work for Him or bestowing anything upon Him. Rather, emphasis is placed upon *being* something for the Lord, namely, that we exalt, honor, praise, and glorify His name. Psalm 116 provides the melody of all

---

* For example, D. Knibbe, *De leere der Gereformeerde Kerk, volgens de order van de Heydelbergsche Catechismus* (Leiden, 1751), 578, registers four observations: (1) The imprecatory psalms proceeded not from hatred, but from zeal for God's honor. (2) The psalmists received a special revelation. (3) These are prophetic utterances. (4) They involve unconverted enemies of God and His people. In *Voetius' catechisatie van den Heidelbergschen Catechismus*, ed. A. Kuyper (Rotterdam, 1891), 2:814, the question is asked, "Why do we not pray against every papal or Islamic or pagan government?" Answer: "Because they have not all shown themselves to be sworn, absolute enemies and persecutors of the Word and the church of the Lord."

revelation: "What shall I render to the LORD for all His benefits toward me? I will take up the cup of salvation, and call upon the name of the LORD" (vv. 12–13). Religion must not be reduced to morality, Kuyper continued, and with deep conviction we would echo Kuyper today.[12] Indeed, we cannot honor God while we let our fellowman languish; but we injure His honor no less when He enters our field of vision only by way of our programs of social action.

We might also put it this way: Obedience to the third commandment requires *earnestness* in our living. The Heidelberg Catechism declares that we must use God's holy name with respect and reverence, to the end that He may be rightly confessed and worshiped by us, and be glorified in all our words and works (Answer 99). This seriousness comes to expression in our use of the Bible,* in the intensity of our praying, and also in formulating our plans. Whether we eat or drink, or whatever we do, we must do everything to the glory of God (1 Cor. 10:31). Otherwise, we do injustice to the weight of His name.

It is clear that we must personally accord to God the honor due to Him, but that is also true for the church as a body. If you survey church history, you realize that terrible things occurred that had nothing to do with honoring God's name, and everything to do with blaspheming that name. Situations can arise similar to those in Israel. Outsiders can blaspheme God's name, but sadder still are those occasions when the church herself dishonors God's reputation and puts arguments in the hands of outsiders for despising the name of God and of Jesus Christ. We have already seen that the sin against the Holy Spirit is an attack by people who have stood on holy ground and subsequently self-consciously misperceived what has proceeded from the Holy Spirit and identified it as coming from the Devil. That is a sin committed not by outsiders, but by church members. Just as

---

* We will not go into detail here, but simply mention in this note three subjects that appear in early and modern ethical commentaries on the third commandment:
  1. The *sortilegia biblica:* a person opens the Bible randomly and considers the verse that first catches the eye to be the divine answer to a problem.
  2. The *improper use of a verse:* for example, "Test all things; hold fast what is good" in terms of food and drink for daily meals.
  3. *Using Bible verses for crossword puzzles and the like:* think, for example, of the Bible Olympics held in Jerusalem in 1964, termed by someone "an Olympiad of taking the name in vain."

Superficial use of Bible verses we must condemn; but can we always forbid using the Bible for crossword puzzles and in a competitive context? If things like this deepen the knowledge of Scripture, we would like to know what principle requires their condemnation.

in those examples of cursing in the Bible, here too we must be careful in pronouncing such definitive judgments. Surely we must attempt to open the eyes of people who in their psychological confusion imagine that they have committed the sin against the Holy Spirit. Anybody who has committed the sin against the Holy Spirit is so hardened in evil that he sheds no tears about his perception of the situation and seeks no escape from his misery. But although we must be compassionate toward psychiatric patients, we must not succumb to the other extreme of identifying the sin against the Holy Spirit as a psychiatric phenomenon. The Bible warns against this sin as something that can occur in the church of God.

Speaking Is Silver, but Silence Sometimes Golden

In contrast to blasphemy stands confessing God's name. Confessing cannot occur without words. Nevertheless, there are moments when *silence* is golden. Earlier commentators speak of *confession intempestiva*, ill-timed confession, when you want to defend God's name, but at an inopportune time. These are moments when God's name could better be left unspoken because it would simply be dragged through the mud and held up to ridicule. We must not provide people, by means of our confession at an inappropriate time, an occasion for ridiculing the truth.

This wise advice is grounded in Scripture.[13] The book of Proverbs says, "He who reproves a scoffer gets shame for himself, and he who rebukes a wicked man gets himself a blemish" (Prov. 9:7). The Sermon on the Mount teaches, "Do not give what is holy to the dogs; nor cast your pearls before swine, lest they trample them under their feet, and turn and tear you in pieces" (Matt. 7:6).

Must we then not defend God's name at every opportunity? Does not Peter say that we must always be prepared to give a defense of the hope that is in us (1 Peter 3:15)? Does Paul not remind Timothy that he must preach the word, convince, and rebuke in season and out of season (2 Tim. 4:2)? Surely we need strong arguments to justify remaining silent about God's name.

Speaking is silver; but, even so, silence is sometimes golden. Consider Christ Himself, who stood silent before the high priest and before Pilate (Matt. 26:63; 27:14). There may well be occasions when we can defend God's honor by being silent. If mentioning His name might give someone a weapon for holding God and His service up to ridicule, then our silence would communicate volumes.

Today that is no less relevant than earlier. In many debates—we will mention as examples opposition to abortion and to a homosexual lifestyle—it is often difficult to get a word in edgewise. Especially when we mention God's name, resistance increases. In the secularized West, we may still think as we please about these issues, but we are permitted less and less freedom to speak or to demonstrate our convictions. Occasionally panel discussions are organized, which present you with the question: "Should I accept an invitation to participate?" Situations can arise where burning hatred is directed against you and public blasphemy is applauded. The question then becomes relevant: "Was I prudent in accepting this invitation?" That we ourselves might be accused of discrimination is not so serious; but when people start mocking God, that can shut the door for us. Speaking is silver, but silence is sometimes golden. You can encounter situations predicted by Christ. If you cast pearls before swine, such animals will turn away in irritation, for they cannot eat such food. And they will pounce on those who have put such food in front of them.

The message we must bring is precious. Confessing God's name must remain our upright intention. We must always be prepared to bring God's Word to people, regardless of whether it suits us or them. That Word matters above everything else. But occasionally we will need to ask ourselves if our speaking might be damaging for the Word of God. At that point, the issue is not what suits us or someone else, but whether it actually suits God that we would speak. We must exercise the kind of carefulness that makes us handle God's name with caution. Occasionally we will be so careful that we will not mention it.

Silence can be a matter of prudence; but, unfortunately, more often it is a matter of laziness. A silent Christian is no Christian. Speaking is silver, but silence is *sometimes* golden. We will not practice proper silence if we do not feel compelled again and again to speak. Only then is our silence no denial and our caution no cowardice.

Dice and the Third Commandment

In connection with the third commandment, we wish finally to discuss a matter that nowadays is hardly ever mentioned in this context, but which earlier was always discussed here: casting lots. This commentary would be incomplete were we to ignore this question—more so because the debates on this question have never been adequately resolved, in our opinion.

What is the issue here? Former commentators insisted that casting lots was really a form of praying. They referred to Proverbs 16:33: "The lot is cast into the lap, but its every decision is from the LORD." Anyone who cast lots, so the argument went, is asking God for a decision. We must be conscious of the seriousness of casting lots, Voetius wrote. "To bring one-self so close to the face of God—such a thing is not fitting apart from fear and trembling. In any case it is absolutely improper for people to employ such things in games. That would violate fear and reverence for God."[14] So the use of dice was condemned. Casting lots is a form of praying, and you may not do this with dice in a game of chance.

Our forefathers used to speak, in connection with casting lots, about the *immediate* providence of God. By means of His immediate providence, God rules matters that arise entirely and directly from Him, without human intervention, apart from any humanly discernible, natural, causal explanation. "Ordinary" events do not occur apart from God, but in those cases we are dealing with God's *mediate* providence. When a stone hits a window and shatters it, we can explain the shattered glass in terms of a natural cause. We threw the stone at the window, and we knew beforehand what the result could have been. But that is not true about the lot. When we roll dice, the outcome is a complete surprise to us. The outcome of rolling dice is not determined by natural causes, people used to think. Nor was the outcome dependent on human expertise. So the conclusion was obvious: if neither natural nor human causes come into play, the outcome can only proceed from God. As a Christian, you would never think of identifying an idol or the Devil as the cause of the outcome. So *if* the cause is God, then your expectation of an outcome brings you so close to His presence that the only proper attitude is one of fear and reverence. Who would then ever think of using dice in a *game?!*

Since that time, we have taken up using dice in our games without giving the matter a second thought. We can hardly imagine that people used to consider this an idle use of God's name. But then, what counterarguments against their line of reasoning do we offer? Nobody can deny that our forefathers thought seriously about issues, including the issue of play. So we should not dismiss their arguments too quickly. In our opinion, the following arguments suffice to justify a different view of using dice than that held by our Reformed ancestors:

1. The outcome of rolling dice is determined by natural laws as much as the shattering of glass. The only difference is that while we can predict the latter, we cannot predict the former. If we were in a position to account for all the factors affecting the roll of dice, we would be able to determine the outcome. We cannot do that, and from that fact arises the surprising element of every outcome. But the fact that *we* cannot account

for the outcome does not permit us to deny the natural pattern and regularity of the entire process.

In other words, when we speak of God's providence, we must not say that in the case of breaking glass, He is working mediately, and in the case of casting lots (and rolling dice), He is working immediately. The word *natural* is entirely appropriate in connection with throwing dice. In such a case we are not "closer to God" in a way that requires special fear and trembling.

2. Thinking along the lines taken by earlier commentators is also not without its dangers. Johannes à Marck, for example, claimed that no natural cause could be found for "various weather and atmospheric patterns." When a storm unleashes it fury, we should say that God's immediate providence is at work.[15] Since his day, we have the national weather service reporting about atmospheric highs and lows that account for impending stormy weather. Many things that people used to think were directed immediately by God's hand appear today to be governed by God's mediate providence. Many more things can be explained on the basis of natural causes and results than people used to think. But are rain and drought therefore further removed from God because we no longer see His hand "immediately" in these circumstances? A farmer can be thankful for weather reports, because he can arrange his work accordingly. But he should not for that reason believe that the daily leading of his life is any less in God's hand, should he? The distinction between mediate and immediate providence opens us to the danger of dividing life into two parts: at certain times you are closer to God; at other times you are farther away. We are gripped by fear and trembling when the sky is thundering, but have no trace of fear and trembling when we harvest grain with our machines, or when we employ physical laws of nature, or when we exercise our own capacities in a mental game.

3. God is involved in everything. In Him we live and move and have our being (Acts 17:28). In everything we may attempt to discover His laws and then thank Him for the blessing of a lightning rod or a polio vaccine. And what is true of serious things is equally true of the not-so-serious things. We may amuse ourselves and our children with games. But without the *surprise* provided by the element of chance, such amusement is unthinkable. For that, we need dice for board games or we need the factor of random choice in our computer games. Surprise may be a more significant factor in one game or another—it is still needed to lend excitement to playing. Various doses of the incalculable and the unpredictable provide the excitement needed for every *healthy* form of relaxation. That incalcu-

lable factor is just as "natural" as the calculable. It must be used that way too, as something entirely normal. Children are not praying, but simply playing as they go blindfolded after one of the presents dangling from a rope. They are taking the same kind of chance as when they throw dice in the air. It is just as exciting, just as natural, and just as innocent.

But What Then About Proverbs 16:33?

When we study what the Bible says about casting lots, then it becomes clear how incorrect it is to equate lots *simply* with praying. Consider Acts 1:23–26, where we are told that from the duo of Barsabas and Matthias, the latter was chosen by lot. We read, "And they prayed and said, 'You, O Lord, who know the hearts of all, show which of these two You have chosen'" (Acts 1:24). Only after the special leading of the Lord has been requested is the lot cast. In terms of the earlier Reformed viewpoint, would not that praying have been superfluous, since casting lots is already a form of praying? In terms of our viewpoint, we can say that casting lots *becomes* prayer. It is not automatically a prayer, but *through* prayer it becomes a sacred act.

What we observe in Acts 1 appears in a number of places in Scripture. Casting the lot is not in itself a sacred act, but becomes sacred through something else. Jonathan was proved innocent by means of a lot cast after a prayer by Saul (1 Sam. 14:41). We read often that the lot was cast by command of the Lord (e.g., Num. 26:52–56; 33:54; 36:2; Josh. 13:6; 21:3; Isa. 34:17; Ezek. 45:1), or "before the Lord" (e.g., Josh. 18:6–10; 1 Sam. 10:19). The lot was not just cast, because people had to "sanctify [themselves] for tomorrow," as in the case of Achan recorded in Joshua 7. Thus, we might say that in the Bible casting lots is not in itself a sacred act, but became so only when God wanted to use it and when it had been sanctified through prayer.

In the Bible, we also come across a use of the lot without reference to a *sacred* activity.[16] We might think of Proverbs 1:14 (dividing spoil) and Psalm 22:19 (dividing clothing). Both texts clearly refer to abuse of the lot, but this does not necessarily imply that the lot could not be used in a legitimate way for dividing property obtained honorably. That would then be an everyday use of the lot, similar to what we might use for dividing portions of an inheritance, without having to offer a prayer beforehand. Thus, not casting lots in itself, but the context within which it occurs, can lend a sacred character to casting lots.

But what then of Proverbs 16:33? "The lot is cast into the lap, but its every decision is from the LORD." Is not casting lots something very special? We can answer that question by taking into consideration a similar verse. Proverbs 16:1 says, "The preparations of the heart belong to man, but the answer of the tongue is from the LORD." Since the answer is from the LORD, should we characterize the preparations of the heart (similar to casting lots) as "seeking a divine testimony"? Is thinking perhaps the same as praying? And if thinking is not praying, why then is casting lots, when the outcomes of both casting lots and thinking lie with God?

Our fathers saw in Proverbs 16:33 a very special text. After having set forth our position above, we would add: precisely because casting lots is so *normal*, Proverbs 16:33 is in the Bible. Casting lots is just as normal as preparing for the battle (Prov. 21:31), thinking about what you are going to say (Prov. 16:1, 9), placing your feet upon the path (Prov. 20:24), watching grass and vegetation grow for man and animals (Ps. 104:14), seeing what is only a sparrow fall to the ground, or seeing what is merely a hair of your head fall out (Matt. 10:29–30). But even in all these normal things—including the casting of lots—we may see God's leading. His providence covers everything, *even* the outcome of rolling dice. The lot is simply cast in the lap; and especially if that act "simply" occurs in a game, you might imagine that God is not involved. But the smallest detail of our lives is in His hand. Just as without Him we cannot put one foot ahead of another, cannot speak a single syllable, and cannot swallow one bite of food, so too the outcome of the lot is of God. The Christian must not disconnect even the very ordinary details of life from God's providence.

That knowledge contains a calling: "Whether you eat or drink, or *whatever you do*, do all to the glory of God" (1 Cor. 10:31). Even when you are busy playing a game that normally employs the factor of incalculability through the use of dice, a factor that keeps the game surprising and exciting, do it as a Christian. Doing something to the glory of God does not mean, however, that one consciously thinks about Him and constantly prays to Him. When we eat or drink, drive our car, do our work with energy, or relax by playing a game, most of the time we are not thinking about God while we are acting. But everything in our lives must certainly fit within a program whose goal is the glory of God.

Not the Third, but the Tenth Commandment

Casting lots is, therefore, not a form of praying; and using dice in children's games, for dividing portions of an inheritance, and the like, cannot be forbidden on the basis of the third commandment. But in saying this, we do not deny that the lot can be misused. Thousands fall prey to greed and covetousness as they engage in activities that could not exist without gambling. We cannot separate gambling from casino games, from lotteries and grand prize drawings requiring a modest purchase. But here we are dealing with issues that must be discussed in connection with the tenth commandment, not the third. A wrong use of risk in various games of chance will be discussed when we come to the commandment, "You shall not covet."*

Endnotes

1. J. J. Stamm and M. E. Andrew, The Ten Commandments in Recent Research (London, 1967), 89.

2. Koehler-Baumgartner, Lexicon in Veteris Testamenti Libros (Grand Rapids, 1951), s.v. qalal: to be slight, trifling, be of little account; piel: to declare too trifling, of no account.

3. William L. Holladay, A Concise Hebrew and Aramaic Lexicon of the Old Testament (Grand Rapids, 1971), s.v. kabod.

4. C. Trimp, "De heerlijkheid van God (1)," De Reformatie 54 (1978–79):100.

5. H. Bullinger, Huijs-boeck (Amsterdam, 1607), 44; J. H. Alstedt, Theologia catechetica (Hannover, 1622), 566; P. van der Hagen, De Heydelbergsche Catechismus (Amsterdam, 1743), 403; B. Smytegelt, Des Christens eenige troost (reprint, Leiden, 1747), 516.

6. These suggestions, reproduced almost word for word, come from B. Roolvink, Wie vloekt verliest, a publication of the Alliance Against Cursing (Veenendaal, 1977), 23.

7. This simile comes from J. H. Alstedt, Theologia catechetica, 566, among others.

8. For the history of the oath, see J. J. de Waal Malefijt, De eed ter beslissing van het geding (Utrecht, 1907), 66ff. The philosophers Kant and Fichte, among others, considered an oath to be beneath man's dignity.

9. J. Calvin, Institutes, 2.8.27.

10. L. Danaeus, Ethice Christian (Geneva, 1577), 2:9, 161; A. Rivetus, Praelectiones in

---

* It is surprising that earlier Reformed commentators forbade casting lots, but not betting. In betting, the parties who disagree about a certain matter promise one another something that will benefit the one whose opinion proves to be correct (this is the opinion of W. Geesink, Van 's Heeren ordinantiën, 4:343). In a wager, one party can gain an advantage over the other by having superior knowledge about the matter at hand. Think, for instance, of Samson's wager with the Philistines (Judg. 14). It is precisely this display of ingenuity in a wager that made it (in contrast to casting lots) acceptable for Reformed people. Wagering would be taken too far, however, "either if the matter involved occurrences beyond human ability or knowledge, but directly dependent upon God's providence, for in such a case it would be testing God, setting limits to His holiness (Ps. 78:41); or if what had been mutually promised lost its quality as an honorable award, by one's intending to gain personal profit, by means of the loss suffered by his opponent, for that would be an illegitimate way of acquiring property" (Geesink, Van 's Heeren ordinantiën, 4:344).

cap. XX *Exodi,* in *Opera theologica* (Rotterdam, 1651), 1288ff. See also W. Amesius, *Medulla theologica* (Amsterdam, 1641), 2.10.34; B. de Moor, *Compendium* (Leiden, 1763), 2:765. We find a separate letter dealing with this question from Walaeus, *Opera* (Leiden, 1643), 2:428ff.

11. W. Geesink, *Van 's Heeren ordinantiën,* 2d ed. (Kampen, 1925), 3:393.

12. A. Kuyper, *E voto Dordraceno,* 3d ed. (Kampen, 1892–95), 3:360–61. See also J. Douma, *De onmisbaarheid van de personele ethiek,* 2d ed. (Groningen, 1971), 15ff.

13. For Alstedt's discussion, see *Theologia casuum* (Hannover, 1630), 263ff.

14. G. Voetius, *Disceptatio de lusu aleae* (Utrecht, 1660), 105. In connection with this section on casting lots and the third commandment, the interested reader may consult six articles we published in *De Reformatie* 53 (1977–78): 749ff. and 54 (1978–79): 22ff.

15. Johannes à Marck, *Het merch der Christene Got-geleertheit* (Rotterdam, 1740), 258.

16. For this see Joh. Lindblom, "Lot-casting in the Old Testament," *Vetus Testamentum,* 12 (1962): 164–78.

The Fourth Commandment

Remember the Sabbath day by keeping it holy. You have six days to labor and perform all your work, but the seventh day is a Sabbath consecrated to Yahweh your God. On it you may not perform any work—neither you, nor your son or daughter, nor your male servant or your female servant, nor your animals, not even the alien living with you. For in six days Yahweh made heaven and earth, the sea, and everything in them. But He rested on the seventh day; therefore Yahweh blessed the Sabbath day and made it holy. (Ex. 20:8–11)

Observe the Sabbath day by keeping it holy, as Yahweh your God has commanded you. You have six days to labor and perform all your work, but the seventh day is a Sabbath consecrated to Yahweh your God. On it you may not perform any work—neither you, nor your son or daughter, nor your male servant or your female servant, nor your ox, your donkey, or your other animals, not even the alien living with you. Then your male servant and your female servant can rest just as you do.

Remember that you yourself were a slave in the land of Egypt and that Yahweh your God freed you from there with a bare fist and a flexed arm; therefore Yahweh your God commanded you to keep the Sabbath day. (Deut. 5:12–15)

Difficulties

No commandment has occasioned as much controversy surrounding its interpretation as this fourth commandment. Various questions demand an answer. Here are several: When was the Sabbath instituted: at Creation (Gen. 2:2–3) or after Israel's exodus from Egypt? Is the Sabbath as a day of rest something that was characteristic for the nation of Israel, or is it valid in the same way for us today? Has Sunday come in the place of the Sabbath, or is our Sunday observance disconnected from the fourth commandment?

It would be nice if we could draw a straight line from Paradise to the present. Some interpreters insist that the Sabbath was instituted in Paradise, kept by the patriarchs, repeated as a commandment on Sinai, moved by Christ from Saturday to Sunday, and therefore observed on the basis of the fourth commandment from the very beginning of the New Testament church.*

But matters are not quite that simple. We can identify at least four difficulties with this construction.

In the first place, it is remarkable that we come across Sabbath observance in the Old Testament for the first time in Exodus 16. There are certain traces in the preceding portion of Scripture indicating familiarity with a seven-day week. For example, in the narrative about Jacob's marriage to Leah, we read of a weeklong wedding feast (Gen. 29:27–28). But this is not the same as saying that during those times the week was concluded with a Sabbath. Was there no Sabbath back then, or was the Sabbath simply unmentioned? The patriarchs lived during this long period from Paradise to Sinai. The question confronts us: Why, if we are dealing with a creation ordinance, do we read nothing about the Sabbath day during this period? Interpreters have tried to find the origin, or at least traces, of the Sabbath outside of Israel, in the land of Babylon, among the Canaanites, the Kenites, and others, but all these attempts have failed.[1]

This leads directly to the second difficulty: Is it so evident in Genesis 2:2–3 that God commanded the *observance* of the Sabbath already in Paradise? Strictly speaking, we read no more than that God rested on the seventh day, and also blessed and sanctified this day. The passage does indeed speak about rest—the rest of the Lord—but not about the Sabbath as a prescribed rest for man. Could it not have been the case that only later, at Sinai, appeal was made to what the Lord Himself did after His six days of creation work? A past event became the foundation for observing the Sabbath. In Exodus 20 that foundation is God's rest on the seventh day after His creation work. In Deuteronomy 5 that foundation is God's redemption of the people of Israel from Egypt. What Yahweh once did for Himself with regard to the seventh day (sanctified that day, i.e., gave it another character than the other days) He now mandates for Israel.

---

* Jacobus Koelman was one of many who joined the struggle for recognizing Sunday as the continuation of the Sabbath. Concerning this struggle, see H. B. Visser, *De geschiedenis van den sabbatstrijd onder de Gereformeerden in de zeventiende eeuw* (Utrecht, 1939). He discusses Koelman on page 232.

In the third place, the Sabbath is not *explicitly* maintained in the New Testament. We read nowhere that the Sabbath must be observed by the Christian church according to the fourth commandment. We do read that several times the disciples or a congregation gathered on Sunday ("the first day of the week," John 20:19, 26; Acts 20:7), and also that on this day Christians in Corinth were to set aside money for the Jerusalem congregation (1 Cor. 16:2). We know also that John received the Spirit on the island of Patmos on "the Lord's Day" (Rev. 1:10), something that leads us to think immediately of Sunday as the day of Christ's resurrection.

But does all of this mean that Sunday has come in the place of Sabbath? Is it not too strong to insist that Christ has transformed the Sabbath into Sunday, when we nowhere read of this?

What must we do with those texts in the letters of Paul that can leave the impression that we do not need to observe a special day of rest any longer? We need not esteem one day above another, Paul says (Rom. 14:5). He disapproves of the custom among the Galatians of observing "days and months and seasons and years" (Gal. 4:10). He even calls observances like a feast day, new moon or *Sabbath,* matters "which [were] a shadow of things to come, but the substance is of Christ" (Col. 2:16–17). Does all of this not indicate that the Israelite Sabbath has passed away like a shadow, since the reality of Christ has now come?

Fourth, one might argue that from the very beginning, the New Testament church observed Sunday on the basis of the fourth commandment, but there are a number of indications that the church from the very *earliest* centuries did not do this. Before the second century, we find nothing to suggest that believers rested from work on Sunday. We receive the impression, for example, that people gathered in the early morning or late evening on Sunday, while the time between was used for daily labor.[2]

Under emperor Constantine, Sunday was proclaimed a day of rest in A.D. 321. Certainly that was a momentous event, whose impact during subsequent centuries we cannot easily overestimate. But it would be a mistake to think that this decision led to a new Sabbath with strict prescriptions for resting. Constantine let the farmers work on Sunday, because Sunday was often the best day for sowing and planting. In Constantine's opinion, one should not pass up any appropriate opportunity offered by God's propitious providence![3]

Nor did the institution of Sunday as the day of rest signify for the first Christian emperor that from then on, ecclesiastical activities would be concentrated on Sunday. The Greek church historian Sozomenus tells us that as late as the fifth century, Christians in the churches of those days did not have a uniform time or manner for calling the church together. Some gathered on the Sabbath, others on Sunday.[4]

Disagreements persisted about the character of Sunday rest. The Council of Orleans (538) prescribed abstinence from agricultural labor on Sunday, but viewed regulations governing matters like traveling on Sunday, meal preparation, exertion connected with housework, or personal grooming, as belonging more to Jewish superstition than to a Christian observance of the Lord's day.[5]

As we survey church history, we see that for centuries there was no indication that Sunday was observed "on the basis of" the fourth commandment.[6] The connection between Sabbath and Sunday was certainly made here and there throughout the early centuries, but it was not until the Middle Ages that such a coupling was explicitly argued in theological writings.

In summarizing these four points, the obvious question becomes: Has the Sabbath been transformed into Sunday? Do not Sabbath and Sunday differ so greatly that we may not properly equate the two?

Celebrating the Sabbath

Before answering this question, we must first know what precisely the Sabbath was. The impression is widespread that the Sabbath was an oppressive institution, from which we fortunately have been liberated after the coming of Christ. Anyone harboring that impression must face various facts from both Old and New Testaments that point in the opposite direction. Here are several.

The Israelite was commanded to rest on the Sabbath in order to be refreshed (Ex. 23:12). He did that in imitation of God Himself, of whom it is said that after His creation work, He rested on the seventh day "and was refreshed" (Ex. 31:17). As Yahweh observed the seventh day, so too may the Israelite rest on the Sabbath day—in order to be refreshed once again.

When you read the version of the fourth commandment found in Deuteronomy, the instructions for observing the Sabbath are there based on the exodus from Egypt. Israel must recall that she was a slave in Egypt, and in contrast to that slavery must now experience the Sabbath as a day of liberation. Even the servants must be able to enjoy that rest to the fullest extent. Slaves in Israel were to enjoy the true meaning of freedom from strenuous daily labor through the kindness of their masters, who recalled how they themselves had been oppressed in Egypt. The Sabbath was a commemoration of liberation.

That comes out more strongly in the explanation of the Sabbath as a weekly recurring commemoration of the Exodus: Just as the church commemorates Christ's resurrection, not only annually on Easter, but also every Sunday, so too Israel commemorated the weekly celebration of the Exodus in addition to her annual feast of Passover.[7] The Sabbath was thus a feast commemorating liberation. That kind of commemoration could hardly have been oppressive, at least if the Sabbath was commemorated according to its original intention.

Entirely in line with this character that we have explained is the psalm bearing the title "A Song for the Sabbath day" (Ps. 92), and the description of this day as a *delight* (Isa. 58:13).

This Old Testament accent receives attention in the New Testament, too. When Jesus performed a variety of works on the Sabbath, people responded to Him with amazement and resistance. He and His disciples did things that were not permitted on the Sabbath (Mark 2:24). When His disciples were hungry on the Sabbath, Jesus allowed them to pluck grain (Matt. 12:1–8). On the Sabbath He healed a man with a withered hand (Mark 3:2–5), a stooped-over woman who had been sick for eighteen years (Luke 13:11–17), a man with dropsy (Luke 14:2–4), and someone who had been sick for thirty-eight years (John 5:5–9). All of this was forbidden by the scribes and Pharisees, but Jesus Himself found these activities entirely in accord with the fourth commandment. He accused His opponents of hypocrisy. After all, they would not hesitate to let an ox or a donkey loose on the Sabbath to give them a drink, would they? Why then could He not release a daughter of Abraham from the bonds with which Satan had been binding her for eighteen years (Luke 13:15–16)? Those religious leaders would not hesitate to rescue a sheep or an ox from a pit on the Sabbath, whereas a person is more valuable than a sheep (Matt. 12:11–12; Luke 14:5). If they were permitted to circumcise someone on the Sabbath, why then would they be angry at Jesus when He made someone entirely whole on the Sabbath (John 7:23)?

What Jesus was doing on the Sabbath was certainly in conflict with the Jewish *interpretation* of the law, even as we find it in the so-called halacha, the collection of legal precepts and rules of jurisprudence established and handed down by the scribes, which served as the authoritative interpretation and application of the law of Moses. But Jesus' actions were not in conflict with the law itself. On the contrary, what He did on the Sabbath and what He said about the Sabbath corresponded completely to that joy and restoration characterizing the Sabbath day prescribed in the Old Testament. The scribes and Pharisees, who with their hundreds of regulations had robbed the day of that character, were scolded by Jesus when He said: "The Sabbath was made for man, and not man for the Sabbath!" (Mark 2:27).

This familiar verse should not be interpreted to say that everybody is free to use or misuse the Sabbath as he thinks fit. But this saying of Jesus does make clear that the Sabbath is a gift and a blessing for man, and therefore something different from a legal regulation whose goal lies simply in a formal observance.[8] The Sabbath was not designed to put people in a straitjacket consisting of dos and don'ts, but the Sabbath was intended to be commemorated without burdensome hindrances. Just as with other commandments, Jesus blew the dust off the law, so here too in a very special way He restored the fourth commandment to its original beauty and luster.

Filling the Sabbath

This saying of Jesus, so important for our discussion, that the Sabbath was made for man and not man for the Sabbath, must not be interpreted to mean that the only purpose of the Sabbath is our relaxation. The Israelite was allowed to catch his breath, together with his employees, with the foreigner, and with his work animals. On that day he may be free and festive. But the Sabbath involves more. The Sabbath was made for man, but Yahweh also speaks about it as *His* Sabbath (Ex. 31:13; Lev. 19:3, 30; Isa. 56:4; Ezek. 20:10, and other places). The text of the fourth commandment speaks, both in Exodus and in Deuteronomy, about "a Sabbath consecrated to Yahweh your God." Clearly the Sabbath was to be a day filled with praising the Lord (Ps. 92) and exercising fellowship with Him in a special way. Extra sacrifices were brought on the Sabbath (Num. 28:9–10), and there were sacred convocations on the Sabbath (Lev. 23:7–8; cf. Isa. 1:13). Observing the Sabbath meant honoring Yahweh's sanctuary (Lev. 19:30; 26:2).

Apparently resting went together with holding sacred assemblies and praising Yahweh. Often these are mentioned in a single breath. The seventh day must be a full Sabbath: "The seventh day is a Sabbath of solemn rest, a holy convocation. You shall do no work on it; it is the Sabbath *of the* LORD in all your dwellings" (Lev. 23:3; cf. Num. 28:25).*

---

* This connection between "resting" and "gathering together" is found with other feasts, too. See all of Lev. 23 and Num. 28–29. Sacred assemblies were held also for penitential purposes (Num. 29:7), but the Sabbath clearly functioned as a symbol of joy. Notice also in connection with the beginning of the seventh month, the triad: sacred convocation, no servile labor, blowing the trumpets (Num. 29:1).

The Sabbath was a day for listening to the Word of Yahweh. When the woman of Shunem wanted to search for the man of God (Elisha) in connection with the death of her son, her husband asked her why she was going on that particular day, since it was "neither the New Moon nor the Sabbath" (2 Kings 4:23). From this we can infer that the Sabbath was a day for consulting the prophet, and, in that context, the Word of God.

Later, probably during the Exile, the synagogue came into existence as a place of worship. Thus we read that Jesus customarily went to the synagogue on the Sabbath day (Luke 4:16). We get an idea of synagogue Sabbath worship in Luke 4:16–21 and Acts 13:14–41. A portion was read from the Law and the Prophets, and thereafter opportunity was given for an extemporaneous sermon. Jesus regularly made use of these opportunities to instruct His listeners (Mark 1:21; 6:2; Luke 6:6; 13:10).

So we see that on the Sabbath, people worshiped the Lord and searched His word. Clearly it was a *holy* day. At this point, a misunderstanding can easily arise if we separate "resting" from "sanctifying" (in the sense of "keeping holy"). For example, people say that Sunday not only must be a day of rest, but also must be hallowed by going to church, and the like. Later we will answer the question whether such a claim can be made regarding Sunday; but, in any case, such a distinction does not fit the Sabbath. For keeping the Sabbath holy meant, in the first place, very simply separating the seventh day from the other six by not working. The Israelite was to keep the Sabbath holy by doing no work on that day (Jer. 17:24). The day was profaned (unsanctified) by doing work on the Sabbath (Ex. 31:14). In fact, the text of the fourth commandment itself is clear enough: Remember (observe) the Sabbath day by *hallowing* it—and then follows the prohibition against *working* on the seventh day.

Keeping the Sabbath holy obtained visible expression in resting, although we must immediately concede that it was a resting on the day consecrated to Yahweh, as the commandment says. Keeping the Sabbath day holy meant thinking not only about oneself. The Sabbath is a joy for man, but man finds his deepest joy in the Lord.

Distorting the Sabbath

How was it possible, then, that Sabbath observance was experienced by many Israelites as a burden, and that in Jesus' time various conflicts arose between Him and the scribes? The answer to this question involves both a gross distortion and a refined distortion of the Sabbath.

First the gross distortion. For many people, it was extremely difficult to abstain from their work one day per week in order to consecrate it specially to God. In the days of Amos the merchants complained, saying, "When will the New Moon be past, that we may sell grain? And the Sabbath, that we may trade our wheat? Making the ephah small and the shekel large, falsifying the balances by deceit . . . ?" (Amos 8:5). People out for profit could hardly rest on the Sabbath. They trampled the Sabbath underfoot as they went about their business on God's holy day, and would not hesitate to exploit their laborers on these and similar days (Isa. 58:3), even though that did not correspond to what the fourth commandment demands with a view to the resting of employees.

In the days of Nehemiah the situation was no different. People worked on the Sabbath in the winepress and carried sacks of grain and various goods into Jerusalem, while the salesmen and merchants stood at the city gates all night long, itching to get into the city on the Sabbath (Neh. 13:15–22).

This kind of transgressor will naturally come into conflict not only with the fourth commandment, but with other commandments as well. Those who chase after profit come into conflict just as much with the eighth and the tenth commandments as with the fourth commandment. There is no reason for saying that the fourth commandment demanded a lot from the Israelite, so that transgression of this commandment was more obvious than transgression of other commandments. The entire law is the law of *liberty*. But the law is not experienced that way by people with a slave mentality, people who look out for their own well-being, but not for the honor of God and the advantage of their neighbor.

Nevertheless, transgression of the fourth commandment did bear a special character. We must be impressed with the fact that the Lord attached great significance to obeying *this* particular commandment (e.g., Ex. 35:1–3; Isa. 58:13–14). This should not surprise us, because the Sabbath is called a *sign* of the covenant between Yahweh and His people (Ex. 31:12–17; Ezek. 20:20). One could discern from the Sabbath that there was a covenant between the Lord and Israel.

The Sabbath clearly expressed the blessing that Yahweh had bestowed upon Israel. Just as God had rested after His work of creation, so too He now permitted Israel to rest, liberated as she was from the slavery of Egypt. The Sabbath day showed who Israel was: a people chosen and liberated by Yahweh, who could be assured of His providential sustenance of her life, sustenance that did not depend on her laborious exertion.

This comes more sharply into focus when we consider the so-called sabbatical year and the Year of Jubilee. Every seven years the land was supposed to rest, meaning that the field was not sown and the vineyard was not pruned (Lev. 25:1–7). In every fiftieth year (the year after seven times seven), not only was the land to enjoy rest, but also the liberty lost by any inhabitant in Israel was to be restored, so that the slave with his family could return to his possessions and to the inheritance of his ancestors (Lev. 25:8–19). Here we see again how closely Sabbath is related to liberty!

Observing the Sabbath, along with all the consequences of observing sabbatical years and Years of Jubilee, appeared to be a weighty mandate. For observing the Sabbath was clearly the proof of the pudding: Would God's people keep the reins in their own hands, or would they confidently entrust their lives to the Lord? Someone who wants to keep control of his own affairs would experience the interruption of business on the Sabbath day as a hindrance. Observing the Sabbath day requires faith. Where faith is destroyed, the Sabbath is destroyed along with it. One who violates the Sabbath violates the covenant. For that reason, it is understandable that Sabbath violation could even be identified as the reason why Israel suffered calamity (Neh. 13:18; Ezek. 20:13).

One More Distortion

There is one other, more refined way of distorting the Sabbath. This distortion clothes itself in the garments of piety. We are thinking of the distortion of the Sabbath found among the Pharisees.

The brief reference in the fourth commandment, "You may not perform any work," was far too vague, according to the interpretation of the Pharisees. What exactly is "work" and how can someone be sure that he is not guilty of doing any work on the Sabbath?

In the Mishnah, which contains the oral traditions and "precepts of the ancients" since the Babylonian captivity, we come across no fewer than thirty-nine kinds of forbidden work. The Mishnah dates from the first half of the second century after Christ; but on the basis of what we know from the Gospels, we can confidently assume that Jesus and His disciples lived in a Sabbath atmosphere much like the one described for us in the Mishnah. With great precision, the writers disentangle questions relating to sowing, plowing, harvesting, threshing, weaving, and spinning, not to mention weaving two threads, sewing two stitches, writing two letters of the alphabet, extinguishing a fire and igniting a fire, carrying an object from one place to another, and still more forms of work. Working on the Sabbath was forbidden; but one who wove only one strand, sewed only one stitch, and wrote but one alphabet letter, was not yet working. In Jewish literature we can find permission to kill a louse on the Sabbath, but not a flea, since the flea is a kind of predator.*

Without a doubt, underlying the extensive work of the scribes was a deep-seated respect for the Sabbath. We can well imagine that they wanted to provide clear guidelines, so that the unique character of the Jewish people would find expression in a lifestyle consistent with the law of Moses. How easy it was, in the Hellenistic society surrounding the Jews after the Babylonian captivity, where they had already lost their political independence, to lose their spiritual identity as well! So it was understandable that the *sign* of the covenant between Yahweh and Israel—the Sabbath—received close scrutiny.

But we know the disastrous consequences. Not Scripture, but the tradition of the "ancients," functioned authoritatively. Within a detailed casuistry, it is no longer possible to quiet one's hunger on the Sabbath by plucking heads of grain in a grain field. For whoever picks a head of grain is busy harvesting, and whoever rubs that head of grain between his fingers is busy threshing. Someone who healed a man with a withered hand on the Sabbath, as Jesus did, was performing work that could have waited until the following day. Someone who picked up his mattress and walked away with it, after he had been healed, was making himself guilty of Sabbath desecration because he was carrying a burden on the Sabbath from one place to another (John 5:9–10).

We have already seen how Jesus condemned this casuistry.[9] Although it can be dressed in the clothes of piety, it can nonetheless be a form of hypocrisy. What people withhold from others (permission to work, for example) they grant to themselves. And what else can you expect? Legalism always lives in tension with the normal development of life and sooner or later will shipwreck on the realistic and wholesome demands of practicality. The Sabbath was made for man, not man for the Sabbath. Jeremiah's prohibition in the Lord's name against carrying a burden into the city gates of Jerusalem (Jer. 17:19–22), this prohibition of *daily* labor, is quite different from prohibiting the carrying away of a sleeping mattress which the man who had been healed by Jesus could roll up with great joy! Those

---

* This casuistry involving the louse and the flea has often been attributed to the Reformed theologian Gisbert Voetius and his followers, although it comes from the Jewish Talmud. See H. B. Visser, *De geschiedenis van den sabbatsstrijd onder de Gereformeerden in de zeventiende eeuw*, 157–58.

Pharisees who forbade that activity were destroying the festivity of the Sabbath. Their attitude robbed the Sabbath of its characteristic gratitude for liberation. Gratitude had to make way for precisionist obedience, freedom was replaced with a new bondage, and relaxation was ruined by a perpetually plagued conscience.

Nor must we argue that such a legalistic interpretation was rooted "somewhere" in the law of Moses with all of its "strict" regulations allegedly characteristic of the old covenant. The Mosaic law did require a careful observance of the Sabbath, but knew nothing of an expanded casuistry. It speaks clearly of laying aside all *daily* work. Construction of the tabernacle had to be stopped (Ex. 31:13–17). Plowing and harvesting were forbidden, even during the prime days for these activities (Ex. 34:21); commerce and transport of goods likewise were forbidden (Amos 8:4–6; Jer. 17:21). No household was permitted to start a fire for cooking or baking (Ex. 35:3), and gathering firewood was also forbidden (Num. 15:32–36).*

Moreover, there was a difference between rest on the Sabbath and the rest commanded for the other feast days. The seventh day was a *complete* Sabbath, a day on which "no work at all" might be performed, whereas the rest on other feast days was limited in terms of "doing no *servile* labor" (compare Lev. 23:3 with 23:7–8, 21, 25, 35). In connection with the institution of the Passover, we read that on the first and the seventh days of the Feast of Unleavened Bread, "no manner of work" might be done, except to prepare what would be eaten by the Passover participants (Ex. 12:16). But even this work of preparing food was forbidden on the Sabbath (recall the prohibition against starting a fire). The phrase "no *servile* labor of any kind" apparently permitted a bit more on certain feast days, such as preparing food and drink. So the category "no work of any kind" included all work in one's occupation *and in one's house,* work such as

---

* Some interpreters insist that the prohibition against lighting a fire pertained only to fires needed for daily occupations involving forging, and not for cooking purposes. (See, for example, Joh. van der Kemp, *De Christen geheel en al het eigendom van Christus in leven en sterven,* 10th ed. [Amsterdam, 1737], 736–37.) This view then ties the prohibition in Ex. 35:3 to the following passage describing the building of the tabernacle. An absolute prohibition against any and every fire could hardly have been the point, Van der Kemp argues, since the children and the infirm had to be kept warm in winter.

In our judgment, this latter purpose was not forbidden in Ex. 35:3 either. Restricting the prohibition against lighting a fire strikes us as similarly fanciful. The important thing to remember is that back in those days, because of the *efforts* connected with lighting a fire and keeping it going, the whole enterprise involved quite a bit more than using a stove or a microwave oven today!

plowing, harvesting, preparing food, lighting a fire, and gathering firewood, whereas the category of "no servile labor of any kind" pertained
only to one's occupational labor outside of the house.

With these two categories we have summarized all the regulations
found in the law of Moses. Even from all this data we still do not receive
the impression that Sabbath activities were like living in a straitjacket,
governed always by what the people of Israel were not allowed to do. On
the contrary, we can well imagine that the Sabbath was something very
positive for the life of the Israelite,* and in no way bore the character of
the later Jewish Sabbath.

Here are two more proofs confirming the fact that in the Old Testament, people did not spend the day with their hands folded. On one Sabbath, Joshua led Israel around Jericho seven times, after which this city
collapsed (Josh. 6:15–20). Apparently the Shunammite woman was ac-
customed, as we have seen, to visiting the man of God on the Sabbath (2
Kings 4:23); that trip required her to travel more than twenty miles! The
prohibition in Exodus 16:29 that forbade Israel, en route to Canaan, from
going outside the camp on the Sabbath was apparently not a perpetual
regulation later requiring Israelites to stay at home. Pharisees later may
have occupied themselves with the proper length of a "Sabbath journey,"
but you will find no basis for that in the Old Testament. Finally, we would
mention that Jehoiada the priest did not hesitate to carry out his plot
against queen Athaliah on the Sabbath, since this day provided the greatest chance of success (2 Kings 11; 2 Chron. 22:10–23:15).

Preliminary Assessment

Let us pause at this point to make a preliminary assessment. We began by
summarizing various arguments that make it difficult to equate the Sab-

---

* We could mention in this connection Ezek. 20:18–30, where Yahweh speaks about
ordinances *and Sabbaths* that were good for Israel—"which, if a man does, he shall live by
them" (v. 21). But when Israel transgressed Yahweh's commandments, He gave them laws
that were *not* good and in terms of which they could *not* live (v. 25). The "giving" of these
laws that were not good must be interpreted in the same sense as God "surrendering" people
to their self-willed desires and godlessness, spoken of in Acts 7:42 and Rom. 1:24 (including child sacrifices in the days of Ezekiel). For a presentation of this view, see A. Noordtzij,
Ezechiël, 2d ed. (Kampen, 1956), 1:222. In any case, these laws cannot be equated with the
"burdensome ceremonial laws" that some interpreters might understand to include the
Sabbath.

bath of the fourth commandment and our modern Sunday. Next, we tried to make clear what Scripture says about the commemoration, the observance, and the violation of the Sabbath. On the basis of these comments, we believe we are correct in drawing the conclusion that there is a fundamental correspondence between Sabbath and Sunday. The following points of agreement between these two days seem obvious.

Both days possess a special character. The Sabbath was connected either to God's rest after His six-day work of creation, or to Israel's exodus from Egypt. Sunday is called the Lord's Day, recalling the resurrection of the Lord Jesus Christ.

Both days are feast days, since there is salvation to be commemorated. Deliverance from the slavery of Egypt, commemorated on the Sabbath, finds its extension and expansion in deliverance from the slavery of sin accomplished by the resurrection of Christ, commemorated on Sunday.

On both days, worship occupies an important place. The "holy assemblies" and the gatherings in the synagogue from former times are comparable to our modern church worship gatherings.

Just as the Sabbath was made for man, in order to rest up and to celebrate a feast, so too Sunday was made for man. The rest we may enjoy on Sunday and the liberation through Christ that we may commemorate are just as essential for the character of this day as they used to be for the Sabbath. Old Testament rest was not disconnected from worship, and New Testament worship is not disconnected from rest. The accents may differ (about which, see below), but as far as the essential elements are concerned, there is surprising similarity.

There is similarity also in terms of the violation of Sabbath and Sunday. In every age there have been people enslaved to their work, people who cannot lay their work aside for a feast day. Whether we are talking about violating the Sabbath or violating Sunday, it makes no difference. Anyone unable to rejoice in God's laws because he cannot surrender his own preoccupations has as much trouble with Sunday as with the Sabbath.

The distortion of the Sabbath given in the casuistry of the Pharisees finds its mirror image in various casuistries related to what we may and may not do on Sunday. Every gospel—whether concerning the exodus from Egypt or concerning Christ's redemption—can be made into a law. Therefore, when Sunday was repeatedly wrapped and bound with the chains of casuistry, that happened not because the church observed Sunday "on the basis of the fourth commandment," and was *thereby* compelled to reason along the lines of "Old Testament" casuistry. Rather, this Sunday casuistry came about because the church no longer grasped the gospel of the fourth commandment. And this, after Christ's own instruction about the Sabbath, is even more blameworthy.

We must still deal with the four difficulties we began with. But the things we have already said about the commemoration, observance, and violation of Sabbath and Sunday enable us to avoid a still greater difficulty: if we *cannot* commemorate Sunday on the basis of the fourth commandment, because it is supposedly merely an institution authorized by the church (after Constantine the Great), and because its character supposedly differs *radically* from the Sabbath, then are we not actually dealing today with nine instead of ten commandments? We have elsewhere defended our conviction that the Ten Commandments retain their validity also for the church of Christ.[10] We do not need to surrender that starting point now when we are dealing with the fourth commandment, if Sabbath and Sunday resemble each other as closely as we have explained above.

One Day or Every Day?

We can provide a bit more dimension and depth to our discussion by comparing our view with what *John Calvin* offers concerning the Sabbath/Sunday question. According to him, the Sabbath was given for three reasons: (1) to depict spiritual rest, (2) to preserve ecclesiastical order, and (3) to provide relief to workers.

This sequence is already quite revealing! One would have thought that Calvin's third reason would have been listed first, not only because workers were to enjoy rest, but because everybody was. The Sabbath was given so both servants and masters could catch their breath, just as Yahweh Himself did after six days of work. That emphasis is primary in the fourth commandment and corresponds to Jesus' saying about the Sabbath being made for man.

But Calvin emphasizes something else in the fourth commandment. According to him, resting on the seventh day depicts spiritual rest, the rest from their "evil" works that believers enjoy in order to allow God to work in them.

Calvin sees the Sabbath as a sign teaching Israel that God was Israel's sanctifier: "If our sanctification consists in mortifying our own will, then a very close correspondence appears between the outward sign and the inward reality."[11] Just as Israel was to observe "externally" a complete rest on the seventh day, so we should rest "inwardly," says Calvin, by putting to death our own will and by allowing God to work in us. For Calvin, the Sabbath was not primarily something outward, an external sign, a figure or shadow that passed away with the coming of Christ. After all, Christ is the body, the substance, the full reality, and with His appearance an end has come to those Old Testament shadows (Col. 2:16–17). Christ is no longer satisfied with one day, but with nothing less than the full span of our lives. "Christians ought therefore to shun completely the superstitious observance of days."[12]

Does this mean that Calvin opposed observing any special day of rest? No, since Calvin mentions *three* reasons why the Sabbath was given. And according to Calvin, we cannot restrict the last two reasons to the former dispensation of shadows. Anyone claiming that the Sabbath has passed away, says Calvin, does not have a full grasp of the matter. For we must also remember that God decreed a certain day for Israel to assemble together to hear the law and to perform the ceremonial rituals. Moreover, workers were supposed to receive rest from their labors.

When it comes to working out the implications of all this, we are again struck by Calvin's difficulty with the fact that only one day is reserved for worship. If someone should ask him why we do not rather assemble daily "to remove all distinction of days," Calvin replies: "If only this had been given us! Spiritual wisdom truly deserved to have some portion of time set apart for it each day. But if the *weakness* of many made it impossible for daily meetings to be held, and the rule of love does not allow more to be required of them, why should we not obey the order we see laid upon us by God's will?"[13]

We have put the word "weakness" in italics. Calvin used this term elsewhere when he wrote about Sunday. For example, he wrote in his *Catechism* of 1545 that due to our weakness, God ordained but one day for our meditation upon His works. Actually, God should have assigned more than one, but due to our weakness, and especially due to the weakness of public society, we have but one day.* This is the reason why, in his *Insti-*

---

* You will find Calvin's sermon on Deut. 5:12–14 (*Sermons on Deuteronomy* [reprint, Carlisle, Pa., 1987]) instructive in terms of his emphasis on our weakness. We find a similar line of reasoning with Luther, in his Large Catechism: a Sabbath is necessary really only for the simple and for the greater society ("der gemeine Haufen"), not for the educated and learned Christian. The public needs a free day for physical reasons and especially for taking time out for worship. However, worship should by rights occur every day, but since the larger part of society has no time for it, we must reserve at least one day. This emphasis on human weakness (and therefore only one Sabbath day per week) reappears in discussions of the fourth commandment, as in J. Bastingius (*Verclaringe op een catechisme der Christelicker religie* [Amsterdam, 1892; reprint of the 1549 edition], 542; J. H. Alsted, *Theologia catechetica* [Hannover, 1622], 572; F. Turretin, *Institutes of Elenctic Theology*, trans. George Musgrave Giger, ed. James T. Dennison, Jr. (Phillipsburg, N.J., 1994), 2:90.

tutes, Calvin writes that he is not bound to the number seven. People may certainly assemble together more than one day per week.*

But on this particular point we must disagree with Calvin. Repeatedly when he discusses the Sabbath, in the *Institutes*, in his *Catechism*, and even in his sermon on the Deuteronomy passage, this element of our weakness comes up: we have but one Sabbath, one Sunday, per week— but really there should be more. We are led to ask this question: What does the fact that there is only one day reserved in each week have to do with our weakness? How can we insist upon this point so strongly if we re- call that God Himself also rested but one day and gave this to Israel as an example for her? We would not argue that already in Paradise mankind observed the Sabbath (see above); but if we take Calvin's position, then in Paradise the human race—at that point without sin or weakness— would have had to observe *every* day as a Sabbath! After all, does not Calvin's argument depend on the connection between our sinful weak- ness and the Sabbath being "only" one day per week and not every day of our lives?

In our opinion, we are dealing here with a *spiritualizing* of the Sabbath. This spiritualizing approach is not satisfied with the "external" feature of the Sabbath and moves quickly from the one day of "ordinary" rest to the seven days of rest from all our "evil" works. The ordinary rest that we may enjoy in order to catch our breath is of secondary or even tertiary impor- tance (as with Calvin). Only when we tie it in with going to church do we then speak of our weakness as the reason for having one day per week.

---

* "I shall not condemn churches that have other solemn days for their meetings, pro- vided there be no superstition" (*Institutes*, 2.8.34). People have understood Calvin to be saying also that one day in ten could be observed as "Sunday." But that is incorrect. Com- mentators from various quarters have pointed to Calvin's sermon on Deut. 5:12–14, in which he says that we must "observe the same order of having some day in the week, be it one or be it two, for that is left to the free choice of Christians" (*Sermons on Deuteronomy*, 205). In other words, we must reserve *at least* one day per week for church worship gather- ings. Thus, according to Calvin, we could commemorate Sunday once every four days, too. This interpretation corresponds fully with his view that on account of our weakness we ac- tually have too few days for worship.

On this question, see P. Visser, *Zondagsrust en zondagsheiliging* (Kampen, 1959), 39–40, and J. Primus, "Calvin and the Puritan Sabbath: A Comparative Study," *Exploring the Her- itage of John Calvin*, ed. D. E. Holwerda (Grand Rapids, 1976), 64–65. Abraham Kuyper (*Tractaat van den sabbath* [Amsterdam, 1890], 57) would probably not have attributed to Calvin a "ridiculous sentiment" if he (and they) had read the disputed passage in the *Insti- tutes* (2.8.34) in the light of Calvin's sermon on Deut. 5:12–14!

Now, there is no objection to seeking a broader meaning in the fourth commandment. We do that with the other commandments, too, imitating Christ's own instruction in the Sermon on the Mount. So why not talk about all the other days of our lives when this commandment deals with our use of one day? But our point is this: when we understand the external rest on the Sabbath *merely* as a depiction of inner rest, then we fail to grasp the full meaning of the fourth commandment. That "ordinary" physical rest, whereby we catch our breath and make room for praising God, is in itself already a spiritual enjoyment. The spiritual essence does not lie somewhere beyond our physical rest, but within it. Resting from your daily work, and generously allowing your employees to rest as you do, is already putting to death your own will and allowing God to work in you. This kind of Sabbath is a delight and not simply an external depiction of delight.

Moreover, if every day is really supposed to be a Sabbath or a Sunday, that would eliminate the special texture God has given to the weekdays. We have six days to labor and do all our work, and that too is serving Yahweh. The Sabbath is not the only peak where people enjoy communion with God, in an otherwise flat existence. Each day has its own fullness, its own delight for the person who knows he is working in God's service. There simply are no feast days without ordinary days—days that are certainly different, but not for that reason "weaker" days! This varied texture found in ordinary and extraordinary days is a result not of our sinful weakness, but of a creation designed by God.*

Ceremonial and/or Moral?

What Calvin said about the external Sabbath and the inner mortifying of our will is rooted in an earlier theological tradition. In this tradition, the distinction was made between the *literal* and the *allegorical* meaning of biblical expressions. When Rahab hung a scarlet cord from the window of her house on the wall of Jericho (Josh. 2:21), the red color was thought to be very significant because it pointed to Christ's shedding of blood. When Scripture speaks of Abraham's 318 servants (Gen. 14:14), that number

---

* Many theologians, following Calvin, have connected the observance of one day with human weakness. All the more remarkable, then, is the view of Joshua le Vasseur, explained in his *Thesaurus disputationum theologicarum in Alma Sednaensis Academia* (Geneva, 1661), 1066: Even if mankind had not fallen, he still would have had to free up a *special* time divinely set aside for reflecting upon God's works and for honoring His name.

was thought to have no other purpose than to convey a special message. The ordinary language of a Bible narrative really has a deeper, spiritual intention and therefore must be interpreted not literally, but allegorically (figuratively).

It is true that Calvin did not follow this allegorical approach to Scripture. His interpretation was sober, because he followed the text closely without surrendering to the numerous speculations bound to ensnare the kind of exegesis seeking the text's deeper meaning. But when it came to the Sabbath, Calvin continued the earlier tradition, as we can easily demonstrate.

That line of interpretation brings us back to Augustine, for example. We observe the other nine commandments, says Augustine, in the ordinary sense with which they are commanded; but we must interpret the fourth commandment figuratively. The external rest on the Sabbath really signifies the spiritual rest identified by Jesus with the words: "Come to Me, all you who labor and are heavy laden, and I will give you rest" (Matt. 11:28). Our Sabbath is internal, in our heart, said Augustine.[14]

Somewhat different is the interpretation offered by the great medieval thinkers Peter Lombard and Thomas Aquinas, who understood the Sabbath rest to signify not only the rest of our soul, but also Christ's rest in the grave (on the Saturday after His crucifixion). This interpretation easily leads to viewing the Old Testament rest as passing away, since Christ has risen from the rest experienced in the grave.

This nonliteral significance had the great advantage of permitting people to erect a wall of principle between observing the Jewish Sabbath and commemorating Sunday and other Christian festival days. Judaism continued to exist alongside Christianity, making it necessary time and again to explain how the Jewish Sabbath differed from the days of rest and festivity known to the Christian church.*

But here is the question: Was it not the allegorical interpretation that led to the disappearance of the fourth commandment from the consciousness of the Christian church? If all that matters is the soul's rest, then how

---

* The way the Jews celebrated their Sabbaths was often portrayed negatively. They might rest in their physical members, said Augustine, but never with their conscience. For the Jews, Sabbath observance remained an outward exercise. No wicked person can really observe the Sabbath. The Jews observed their Sabbath rest in a "lazy, frivolous, and licentious manner." "Our freedom is a freedom from evil works; their freedom is freedom from good works. Still, it is better to plow than to dance," Augustine argued (W. Rordorf, *Sabbat und Sonntag in der Alten Kirche*, 117–18). This means something like: working on Sunday is better than sinning on Sunday!

significant is resting from daily work? Is the fourth commandment still binding? This kind of question arises naturally when we hear Augustine assert that the other nine commandments apply in their natural sense, whereas that approach is no longer valid for the fourth commandment.

Nevertheless, the church has never made this claim about the fourth commandment. After widespread uncertainty in the first centuries, the church coupled Sunday observance to the fourth commandment. In that connection, another distinction came into use alongside (actually, within) the distinction between literal and figurative; this was the distinction between *moral* and *ceremonial*. These terms have not always had the same meaning throughout church history, but in terms of practical consequences these words mean basically this: the term *moral* is understood to refer to everything in the fourth commandment that remains binding, while *ceremonial* refers to what belongs to the Old Testament aspect of the fourth commandment and therefore is no longer binding today.

Especially the distinctions employed by Thomas Aquinas were very influential in later centuries. He distinguished four meanings of the fourth commandment:

1. The *literal* meaning, further classified as moral and ceremonial: The *moral* consists in the fact that the fourth commandment prescribes a day for resting from our physical and mental activities. What we are taught in the fourth commandment is taught us already by "natural reason." *Ceremonial* refers to the fact that the rest prescribed in the fourth commandment fell on Saturday.

2. The *allegorical* meaning, which likewise bore a ceremonial character: The rest on the Sabbath pointed to Christ's rest in the grave.

3. The *moral* meaning: Once again the concept of "moral" is used, this time in a deeper sense: we must cease our sins and rest in God with our spirit. Involved here is not "external" rest, but resting from our sins and our spiritual rest in God.

4. The *anagogical* meaning, which again bore a ceremonial character: Sabbath rest prefigures something future, namely, tasting and enjoying God (the "fruitio Dei") in our fatherland, heaven.[*]

These distinctions employed by Aquinas are not altogether clear. What

---

[*] Thomas Aquinas, *Summa theologica*, II/II, qu. 122, art. 4. P. W. J. van den Berg correctly observed (in *De viering van den zondag en de feestdagen in Nederland vóór de Hervorming* [Amersfoort, 1914], 61) that every distinction and uncertainty involving the Sabbath question had been unraveled by medieval theologians long before the struggles broke out over this issue in the Netherlands and in England during the seventeenth century.

precisely is meant by "ceremonial"? In the short section devoted by Aquinas to this matter, the concept surfaces with at least three meanings.

First, the fact that the Sabbath fell on Saturday is called ceremonial. This means simply: that is how it was in the Old Testament, but that is no longer how it is now. But a few sentences later, the Sabbath is called ceremonial because it was a shadow of Christ's rest in the grave. Here, "ceremonial" has a meaning similar to that quality we ascribe to blood, to priests, and to sacrifices in the Old Testament: they constituted a shadow of Christ's blood, His priesthood, and His sacrifice. But that is quite different than describing the Saturday observance of the Sabbath as ceremonial. The fact that the Sabbath fell on Saturday did not point Israel forward to the coming of Christ, but backward to God's creation work (and the Exodus). Moreover, what did observing the Sabbath have to do with Christ's resting in the grave? How can the joy of the Sabbath have been an example of Christ's "humiliation"?[15]

Still different again is the shade given the term *ceremonial* when Aquinas speaks of the anagogical meaning. In this context, the Sabbath points ahead to our heavenly rest and to the prospect of enjoying life with God. But why must that be termed ceremonial? In a similar way, Sunday points forward to heavenly rest. Yet, surely that anticipation is no reason for describing either Sabbath or Sunday as ceremonial. *

The term *ceremonial* is, therefore, anything but clear. For that reason, we would propose substituting for the terms *moral* and *ceremonial* a simpler pair of concepts, namely, *provisional* and *permanent*. With these terms, we could then properly say that the observance of the Sabbath (on Saturday) was provisional, because after Christ came, the church began observing another day. At the same time, we can say that the fourth commandment contains permanent elements, which are as binding on the New Testament church as they were on Old Testament Israel. We will return to this proposed distinction below.

---

* W. à Brakel, in *The Christian's Reasonable Service*, 151–52, properly wonders what the term *ceremonial* means precisely. If it means that the use of the Sabbath was a shadow of Christ, then he would reply that the fourth commandment contained no shadow of Christ. But if the term *ceremonial* means simply that something was an external circumstance that could be altered while the essence of the matter continued, then he would say that the Sabbath (now altered to Sunday) was ceremonial. À Brakel and others often translated the term *ceremonial* with the phrase "ecclesiastical duty" ("kerk-plicht"), referring to an external circumstance, deed, action, or transaction, occurring not only under the old covenant, but also in the new covenant.

Hebrews 4

Before addressing the difficulties that we identified at the beginning of this chapter, we should first discuss Hebrews 4—a chapter quoted often to show how the Old Testament Sabbath was provisional. Regardless of how significant this chapter became for what Aquinas called the "anagogical meaning of the Sabbath," this passage provides us no definite answer concerning the Sabbath and Sunday.

Hebrews 4 tells us of God's rest on the seventh day. That rest had fundamental significance, for it seemed to contain a promise for mankind. Man was allowed to *enter* that rest. But the proclamation of this good news had no effect if it was not received in faith. Recall the Israelites in the wilderness. Because of their disobedience, they failed to enter the place of rest, the land of Canaan. Hebrews 4 quotes Psalm 95:11 concerning that failure, where Yahweh said, "So I swore in My wrath, 'They shall not enter My rest.' "

But God did not leave the matter there, for in view of the fact that others were expected to enter that divine rest later, God once again fixed a day, when He spoke through David many years later, "*Today,* if you will hear His [Yahweh's] voice, 'Do not harden your hearts' " (Ps. 95:7–8). If Joshua had brought them into the rest consisting of the land of Canaan, God would not have spoken of a later day, as the writer to the Hebrews concludes: "There remains therefore a rest [Greek: *sabbatismos*] for the people of God. For he who has entered His rest has himself also ceased from his works as God did from His" (Heb. 4:9–10).

From the progress of the argument, we see clearly that the rest spoken of earlier was but a provisional rest. The people of God were awaiting the real Sabbath rest. The fulfillment of that rest did not become a reality in Israel's day. And just as Israel forfeited the rest through her disobedience, the same result will befall those addressed in Hebrews if, by following Israel's example of disobedience, they fail to seek entrance to that rest (Heb. 4:11).

The question of the Sabbath day is only indirectly present in this passage. In view are Sabbath places, more so than Sabbath days. Often we could translate the word "rest" simply by "resting *place.*" This refers to Canaan and to heaven. When we read that God once again fixed a day (Heb. 4:7), what is in view is not another day of rest, but another rest. Instead of the rest brought by Joshua, another, heavenly rest would be bestowed upon God's people.

Aquinas and others quite properly assigned an "anagogical" meaning to the Sabbath. For that we may appeal to Hebrews 4. Resting on the Sabbath pointed forward to the heavenly rest as the definitive rest. Their mistake, however, was that on the basis of this correct observation they improperly termed the resting on the Sabbath a ceremonial rest, as though this forward-looking quality was something specifically Old Testament. For Sunday also points forward to entering the resting place of God, just as bread and wine point forward to the meal we will soon enjoy with Christ. But this feature says nothing at all about whether the Sabbath day and the fourth commandment remain binding.

Once More: the Difficulties

In the preliminary assessment made above, we concluded that there is no difference in principle between the Sabbath and Sunday. If that is correct, then we may commemorate Sunday in terms of the fourth commandment. Whatever may have changed in the transition from the Sabbath to Sunday, the fourth commandment continues, along with the other nine commandments, to be valid for the church today *as a commandment*.

We must now defend that claim against those objections outlined at the beginning of this chapter. We mentioned four difficulties.

The *first* difficulty involved the institution of the Sabbath. Before Exodus 16 (with its narrative about manna and the Sabbath), we read nothing about observing the Sabbath. This fits well with what we read in Ezra 20:10–12, namely, that Yahweh gave His precepts and ordinances to Israel *in the wilderness,* with this particular addition: "Moreover I also gave them My Sabbaths, to be a sign between them and Me" (Ezek. 20:12). We read similarly in Nehemiah, which mentions the giving of the law at Sinai this way: "You made known to them Your holy Sabbath, and commanded them precepts, statutes and laws, by the hand of Moses Your servant" (Neh. 9:14).

Putting it this way does not imply that the Sabbath was unknown to Israel before Exodus 16. When you read this Bible passage, you soon get the impression in some of the verses (for example, v. 29, "See! For the LORD has given you the Sabbath") that the Sabbath was well known by this time. In our opinion, we will not solve this completely by means of exegesis. Nevertheless, taking into account all the data, it seems correct to speak of a Sabbath given *to Israel,* and incorrect to view it as a universal human institution, given in the beginning (after the Creation), which then later became an observance limited to Israel. The Sabbath is described for us as a sign of the covenant between Yahweh and *Israel* (Ex. 31:12–17; Ezek. 20:20).

But even if this is correct, so that at its inception the Sabbath was not a universally known and prescribed day of rest, this does not yet mean that therefore we are free from the fourth commandment. *For not everything beginning with Israel ended with her*. In Abraham all the families of the earth were blessed. Why, then, cannot also the gift of the Ten Commandments, including the day of rest given to Israel, benefit all humanity?

Occasionally people suggest that the Ten Commandments applied already from the beginning of Creation. What was proclaimed from Sinai is viewed merely as a repetition of what man knew in his heart immediately at Creation. We would suggest that this argument does not help us very much. Were there ten commandments before the Fall, or could we better say that before the Fall (as well as thereafter) there was one great command: love God and love our neighbors as ourselves? The latter is more accurate, so that we should understand that the one command was unfolded in numerous precepts. For example, consider the prohibition in Paradise against eating of the tree of the knowledge of good and evil. At Sinai this prohibition was unfolded in the Ten Commandments.

But it would be strange if before Sinai there was nothing reminding us of the fourth commandment. That commandment, just like the other commandments, deals with an aspect of the great commandment. Surely this aspect was present in a particular form from the very beginning, was it not? People set aside time to call upon God and to bring sacrifices to Him. Early on we read that people began to call on the name of the Lord (Gen. 4:26). The worship referred to in the fourth commandment was present from the very beginning.

But this does not require us to insist that the form of worship prescribed at Sinai by Yahweh for His people was the same as before. The essence of the fourth commandment is permanent, but its expression we learn from Sinai onward. Mankind always had to set aside time for worshiping God, but on the basis of biblical information it is not certain that mankind had to observe a *sabbath*. Of that we read clearly for the first time in Exodus 16.

Although it is therefore probable that we can speak of people beginning to observe the Sabbath in the Sinai period, that claim in no way restricts the validity of the fourth commandment to the nation of Israel. Surely a requirement need not have been proclaimed at the time of Creation in order to apply to all times and peoples, need it?

For that reason, we are not troubled by the *second* difficulty that is indissolubly connected with the first. Naturally, it is true than Genesis 2:2–3 does not clearly indicate that God commanded Sabbath observance already in Paradise. We do read that Yahweh rested on the seventh day and that He blessed and sanctified that day. Nor is it a strange leap of logic to connect this divine "sanctifying" of the seventh day to the *human* conduct of sanctifying the Sabbath. But such a connection is not necessarily required.*

Regarding Yahweh's activity, we can say that He not only blessed the seventh day, but also sanctified it *for Himself,* and thus differentiated the seventh day from the six preceding creation days as a day special to Him. "The work is finished! This creation is all there is. We are not still waiting for any science-fiction universe inhabited by strange beings with bizarre capacities." God rested from *His* work. For the first man, "it was, in our opinion, no day of rest. At that point had he worked six days already? Of course not, he had just arrived on the scene to have a look around. And immediately he could profit from the finished work of his Creator."[16]

God set the seventh day apart from the other days, for Himself. *To sanctify* means "to set apart." And what God did then, He later directed the Israelites to do, so that they too set apart the Sabbath day.

Genesis 2 does indeed discuss the Sabbath as God's rest, but not the Sabbath day for mankind. This permits us to maintain the position we argued in connection with the first difficulty.

Nor does the text of the fourth commandment say that the Sabbath was instituted at Creation. It declares simply that the Sabbath is *grounded* in God's resting after His creation work. Nor can we argue that the "remembering" of the Sabbath must be a thinking back to what had been instituted at creation. This is so because the word for "remember" is precisely the same word used in Deuteronomy for Israel's "remembering" that she was a slave in Egypt. Therefore, the institution of the Sabbath need not have occurred in the distant past of Creation.

If the Sabbath was not instituted at Creation, the fourth commandment is not therefore just a typical Jewish custom whose validity is restricted to ancient Israel. In order to defend the universal significance of the fourth commandment for the church and the world, we must not try

---

* B. Smytegelt once exclaimed in a sermon on the Heidelberg Catechism, Lord's Day 38, dealing with the fourth commandment: Even if someone came from the land of Barbaria, from an unknown culture, never having heard that there had been an argument about the issue of when the Sabbath was instituted, would he not, if he read Genesis 2:2–3, "be sweetened in disposition to know that God instituted the Sabbath at that time, the Sabbath spoken of in the fourth commandment?" (*Des Christens eenige troost* [reprint, Leiden, 1747], 534). But before forming an accurate opinion, the man from Barbaria would surely have had to read Ex. 16, Neh. 9, and Ezek. 20, first.

to invoke the help of "natural reason." On the basis of this reason, some have argued that all people have innate knowledge regarding the need for an occasional day of rest. For example, Abraham Kuyper came up with an argument about "the ebb and flow of the sacred number seven," in which "the stream of time breaks forth before us, since the feature of harmony between the rhythm of divine life in and after creation is maintained especially in this manner." Of this sacred rhythm that God supposedly created in human nature we know precious little, and among Assyrians and Babylonians, who "lived nearest to the cradle of our human race," we observe less of this than Kuyper presumably knew.[17] Scientific investigation has uncovered nothing suggesting a kind of creational Sabbath known to all men, if only they had thought carefully about it.

Once again we would insist that we need not depend on this kind of argument in order to view the fourth commandment as having universal validity. Why could not a gift and a mandate that originated at a later time, given to the people of Abraham, become so universally significant that it embraces our Sunday?

Texts from Paul's Epistles

Here we come to the *third* difficulty: in the New Testament, the fourth commandment is not expressly maintained. Moreover, in Paul's epistles we find texts that could give the impression that the obligation to observe special days (thus also a day of rest according to the fourth commandment) has expired.

People on all sides of the question will have to admit the presence of several exegetical difficulties in these verses, problems that have led to continuing disagreement about the matter of the Sabbath and Sunday. But on the basis of what is clear in both the Old and New Testaments, we would offer the following reply to objections raised against the connection between Sunday and the fourth commandment on the basis of Pauline texts.

In the first place, it might well be true that in the New Testament the fourth commandment is nowhere *explicitly* maintained, but the reverse is even less true. Earlier we referred to the strange situation where only nine of the ten commandments would still be valid, where only the fourth commandment would have a spiritual significance for the New Testament church.

In the second place, we have seen how Jesus resisted the pharisaical perversion of the Sabbath, but He did not turn against the fourth com-

mandment itself. On the contrary, He bound Himself to that commandment and made very clear that it was a commandment for us to enjoy.
From His declaration that the Sabbath was made for man and not man for
the Sabbath, we can conclude that the Sabbath must have been something more that a purely *cultic* (worship-oriented) command. That is what
the Jews had made of it. They viewed it not in terms of the enjoyment of
freedom for people, but in terms of "rest" as a purely religious act, with
meritorious consequences if one held closely to the multiple rules that
safeguarded Sabbath observance. But the Sabbath Jesus explained looks
quite different. Would this Sabbath—a *gift*, a day in which refreshment
and praising God go hand in hand—have been designed for the old and
not the new dispensation?

In the third place, we must determine whom Paul is opposing when he
makes relativizing, or even denigrating, remarks about observing particular days. Just as it was important for us to ask about the view of the Sabbath
that Jesus was opposing, so too here with the interpretation of Paul's
words. Against whom and about what is Paul contending? Let us look
more closely at three passages.

1. The first passage is Romans 14:5: "One person esteems one day above
another; another esteems every day alike." Does this involve the Sabbath
as we know it from the fourth commandment?

The context (Rom. 14:1–4) discusses eating or not eating, and along
with that apparently speaks about days on which people either fasted or
did not fast. Paul considers this a subordinate matter. Difference of opinion exists in the congregation at Rome regarding days of fasting. Some
members distinguish one day from another, while other members equate
all the days. In such a matter they must not condemn one another, Paul
says. "He who observes the day, observes it to the Lord; and he who does
not observe the day, to the Lord he does not observe it. He who eats, eats
to the Lord, for he gives God thanks; and he who does not eat, to the Lord
he does not eat, and gives God thanks" (Rom. 14:6).

Because eating and not eating are bound so closely to *days*, we should understand the difference of opinion in the church at Rome to be about days
of fasting. But that is a view completely different from understanding Paul
to be making a pronouncement here about a Sabbath day which, at least in
its proper meaning, was not to be a day of fasting, but a day of feasting.

Moreover, we would ask whether, if we observe Sunday as a separate,
special day, we are thereby honoring that day above all the others? In the
New Testament, we read about Sunday as "the Lord's Day." That points
to something special, something that may be commemorated. But must

such a day be seen, on that account, as surpassing other days? We can say that in Christ all days are holy, while Sunday is still a special feast day for celebrating everything that we possess in Christ.[18]

2. In his letter to the Galatians, Paul's judgment concerning the observance of days, months, seasons, and years is much sharper than in his epistle to the Romans (see Gal. 4:10). Here the apostle's tone is no longer mild, as if each one is free to choose, as in the matter of fasting discussed in Romans 14.

In view of the sequence "days and months and seasons and years," the term "days" must surely refer to the weekly Sabbath day. In addition, Paul speaks of the "months" (for example, the new moon festivals, Num. 10:10; 28:11–13), the "seasons" (the great feasts of Passover, Pentecost, and Booths), and finally, the "years," (referring to the sabbatical years and the Years of Jubilee). Here Paul is apparently discussing more than simply the observance of days of fasting, as in Romans 14. Whereas in that matter Paul was quite mild, since there was nothing against observing such days, here Paul is much more firm. The gospel of Jesus Christ is at stake. The Galatians were threatened by a Judaizing doctrine requiring circumcision and the observance of the entire Jewish ritual system of days, months, seasons, and years.

It would certainly have been strange if the Sabbath had not been mentioned in this context! For the Sabbath *as here described* was an indissoluble link in the heresy of the Judaizers, since they refused to part with what in fact had expired. Paul is not rendering an isolated judgment here about the Sabbath (or the fourth commandment), but is discussing the Sabbath in the context of matters like circumcision and the entire Jewish annual festival cycle. This cycle, with all its accompanying ritual, was established by the Judaizers as an indispensable condition for sharing in the salvation of Jesus the Messiah. This kind of salvation rested on the law, interpreted in a Judaizing sense, and not upon the righteousness that comes through faith (Gal. 3:10–14).* This opinion of the Judaizers would have been fatal for the Christian church. It had to be radically and completely abandoned.

---

* Here Paul is contrasting "faith" to "law." He qualifies the law as "whoever keeps it shall live by it." This is a citation from Lev. 18:5, but we must remember that such a text was interpreted by the Judaizers not in an evangelical way, but in a pharisaical manner. Elsewhere (Rom. 7:10–13), Paul could say that the commandment (the law) is holy, righteous, and good, and aims at leading unto life. But through our *sin*, the law brings us *death*. Involved here is the proper understanding of the law, so that its bond with the gospel remains intact. See Rom. 10:5–9, where Paul cites from the "law" (Deut. 30:11–14) in connection with righteousness through faith.

In practice, this signified an end to observing the Sabbath as a weekly day of rest in the Jewish sense. What Paul says to the Galatians seems to us a sufficient declaration that the Jewish Sabbath has ceased.

But does this give us the right to say farewell to the fourth commandment insofar as it speaks of a weekly day of rest? Decisive for answering that question is the basis underlying the "Lord's Day." If that basis is really the day of Christ and His justification through faith, then Sunday lies *within the parameters* of the fourth commandment and that day signifies a *break* with the kind of Sabbath that Paul is arguing against in his epistle to the Galatians.

3. The situation of the Colossians was a bit different again. Here Paul was embroiled in a struggle with false teachers who had established ascetic Jewish requirements. "Do not touch, do not taste, do not handle," they commanded (Col. 2:21). In that context, they came not only with demands about eating and drinking, but also about "a festival or a new moon or sabbaths." Their error resembled that of the Judaizers, but in what follows in Colossians 2, elements are mentioned that are not easily explained from a Jewish context (especially the worship of angels in 2:18). We are probably dealing here with a legalistic-ascetic religiosity of a Jewish-pagan brand.

Here too the Sabbath is mentioned. Nobody may continue condemning church members "in food or in drink, or regarding a festival or a new moon or sabbaths, which are a shadow of things to come, but the substance is of Christ" (Col. 2:16–17). The plural "sabbaths" is possible, and makes no difference for our point. Paul could be thinking of the entire cluster of sabbaths (including, therefore, the sabbatical year and the Year of Jubilee); in any case, there is no reason for excluding reference to the weekly Sabbath here.

Just as in Galatians 4:10, there can be no doubt that Paul is here rejecting the demand for observing the Sabbath. The Sabbath is included when he describes fasts and feasts as "a shadow of things to come," whereas Christ is the "substance."

This term "shadow" does not refer primarily to "a differentiated messianic typology in connection with Old Testament prescriptions."[*] Rather,

---

[*] Here we differ with Herman Ridderbos (in his *Aan de Colossenzen*, Commentaar op het Nieuwe Testament [Kampen, 1960], 190–91), who insists that Paul's argument about the Sabbath proves that for Paul, the fourth commandment had no continuing significance. Surely that is a hasty conclusion, similar to the mistake of Smytegelt. The man from Barbaria would be easily misled if all he had read was Genesis 2. Ridderbos is easily misled when he isolates Pauline texts.

the expression is intended generally to mean this: What we find in Israel in terms of religious activities and prescriptions portrayed in the most vague of outlines what Christ would bestow upon His church. The "shadow" is indeed related to the "substance": just as the shadow indicates the outline of the reality, so Christ was already visible in the precepts and commandments of the Old Testament. But now that He has come, it is no longer possible to travel the old paths of circumcision and Sabbath observance, and even less to establish these as conditions for determining genuine and true religion.

Christ is the fulfillment of circumcision. That shadow has disappeared; but precisely for this reason, something else could replace the Old Testament sacrament, something which, just like circumcision, signifies and seals the covenant: baptism. Christ is the fulfillment of the Sabbath. That shadow too has disappeared, but in its place something else could arise which, just like the Sabbath, commemorates liberation. Anybody wanting to maintain the fourth commandment without keeping time with the clock of redemptive history, must stick with the *Jewish* Sabbath. But then such a person will catch no glimpse of the true, liberating intention of the fourth commandment. For that liberation presupposes a different Sabbath after Christ than before Christ.

A shadow of "things to come" disappears when those things to come have become reality. The "substance" (Christ) has appeared, so that the shadows have faded.*

Days of feasting and fasting were known in the New Testament church, too. But these were no longer shadows of something still to come, but rather signs of what had come. The shadows of circumcision, Passover, and Sabbath made room for the signs of baptism, Lord's Supper, and Sunday.

---

* For this reason, we cannot agree with the opinion of the Seventh-Day Adventist S. Bacchiocchi, who argues that we must observe Saturday as the New Testament Sabbath. We agree heartily with what he writes in his superb study, *From Sabbath to Sunday*, about the nonlegalistic character of the Old Testament Sabbath and about Jesus' explanation of the Sabbath. We agree with him also when he states, concerning Paul's criticism of the Sabbath, "It is a *perversion* and not a *precept* that is condemned" (p. 368). We can all learn from Bacchiocchi that, as long as it is understood properly, the Sabbath was not a *dark* shadow of the substance (Christ). But we cannot go along with his insistence that we may maintain "shadows" as long as they *remain* shadows, that is, as long as they are not presented as the reality (the "substance" or the "Head," Col. 2:17, 19) (p. 357).

From Sabbath to Sunday

It took a long time before the Sabbath was replaced by Sunday throughout the Christian church. For that reason, we must still comment on the *fourth* difficulty mentioned at the beginning of this chapter: If the Christian church, during the first centuries of her existence, did not connect her observance of Sunday with the fourth commandment, does that not suggest that we should do the same? Is it not better to say that we observe Sunday as an *ecclesiastical* ordinance rather than a *divine* ordinance?

In our opinion, we should not overestimate the difficulties connected with this historical development. It is true that the observance of Sunday was not instituted by Christ personally or by His apostles. In that respect it is not a divine ordinance, since Sunday observance obtained public validity by means of regulations promulgated by church and state.

Sunday observance is thus an ecclesiastical ordinance. But then, it was surely an ordinance that was inevitable on account of the Spirit of Christ, who has led the church into all truth. The claim exerted upon Christian life and thought by Christ's resurrection simply implied that believers would most naturally use Sunday to commemorate Christ's resurrection. The transition from the Sabbath to Sunday was not arbitrary, but flowed from the authority of the One who called Himself Lord of the Sabbath and who was the fulfillment of the Sabbath. For this reason, the treasure of the fourth commandment could not possibly remain tied to the Jewish Sabbath, but required the celebration of another day, namely, the Lord's Day.

Therefore, the institution of Sunday observance cannot be rejected as *merely* an ecclesiastical ordinance that just happened to arise from historical considerations. There is no specific verse in the New Testament clarifying for us the transition from Sabbath to Sunday. But only biblicism, with its desire to have a verse for everything, makes an issue out of that. There are more issues that lack a particular and specific Bible verse, like infant baptism, but they nevertheless enjoy biblical warrant. Frequently the parallel is drawn to fixing the canon of the Bible. The church did not acknowledge right away all those books that make up our Bible. But eventually she did, and then not "merely" on the basis of her own authority, but by virtue of the testimony of the books themselves, through the work of the Holy Spirit.

On the basis of New Testament teaching, we can say that from the very beginning, Sunday was held in honor among believers. It was the day of Christ's resurrection, and for that reason was self-consciously called "the Lord's Day" (Rev. 1:10). From the earliest period, Christian writers followed this form of expression. We might mention here the *Didache* (ca. A.D. 100) and a still more convincing witness, Ignatius, who wrote in his *Letter to the Magnesians* that Christians "no longer observe the Sabbath, but direct their lives toward the Lord's day, on which our life is refreshed by Him and by His death." We read for the first time in Justin Martyr (ca. 150) of the term *Sunday* being used in reference to the day when everybody in the cities and the countryside gathered together in the same place. Dionysius of Corinth (ca. 170) speaks of the *holy* Lord's Day. Tertullian (ca. 200) informs us that for Christians, Sunday is a day of joy. In another place he says that pagans would not celebrate the Lord's Day or Pentecost for fear that they might be mistaken for Christians.

Such expressions clearly indicate that Sunday observance among Christians must have been rather widespread! In Tertullian's day, Sunday observance was a distinguishing mark of Christians.[19]

It is true that in these and similar documents, we rarely read that Christians laid aside their daily work. Only from Tertullian do we read a remark about laying aside (daily) business on Sunday.[20]

The conclusion is obvious that where Sunday observance is mentioned, this naturally put a stamp on the entire day. "Observing" the *day* included more than attending a church meeting between periods of daily work. This fits entirely with what the Council of Laodicea (ca. 360) prescribed: Christians must not live according to Jewish patterns, and therefore they perform work on Saturday; but they must respect Sunday and as Christians they should quit their work, if possible.[21]

In early Christian writings, where the matter of Sunday is discussed, authors (such as Papias, Marcion, and Eusebius) frequently distinguished it from the Jewish Sabbath.[22] So Sunday was viewed as having been instituted *over against* the Sabbath. Interestingly, these authors omitted any suggestion that Sunday observance was *in accordance with* the fourth commandment. Why this omission?

We think there are at least two reasons for this—explanations that we have already suggested. First, the sharp opposition between Christians and Jews throughout this period resulted in an aversion toward connecting Sunday observance with a precept from the "Jewish" law. Christians broke radically from Judaism, and that left little room for the distinction between the Jewish Sabbath and the permanent validity of the fourth commandment.

A second reason—one that only strengthens the first—lies in the allegorical interpretation of the Old Testament: the letter of the fourth commandment must give way to the spiritual meaning thought to lie behind the letter. That view was held by more than Augustine (see above), for we encounter it throughout the literature of the early centuries: after Christ's first coming we must rest in a spiritual sense, all our days, from our evil works; resting on the Sabbath day was a shadow of Christ's resting in the grave. Everything that could provide the fourth commandment with a deeper meaning was put into words during the first centuries of the Christian church.[*]

We should not follow earlier Christian writers in this direction, as we have tried to show. Inquiring into the deeper meaning is legitimate, but permitting the interpretation and application of the fourth commandment to be *limited* to this deeper meaning is incorrect. Fortunately, the church later reflected upon the fourth commandment with more nuance, so that alongside the provisional also the permanent aspect received attention.

Even though the early church did not initially adopt a very solid view regarding the fourth commandment, on one point of cardinal importance the church was definitely correct: she received Sunday as a day of joy, exactly like the original intention of the Sabbath. Later the church realized that this joyful commemoration required freedom from daily work, entirely in line with the fourth commandment, something wholly unrelated to "Judaizing" the faith.

We do not need to look down our nose at the early church.[†] After the break with Judaism, she had to construct much that was new. She lived in a world where, as the oppressed minority, she was not in a position to proclaim Sunday as a day of rest. The Jews had their Sabbath, but Christians still had to earn their Sunday as a day off. Only when Christian emperors came to power could a social measure like this be effected. Just as in Egypt, Israel could not observe the Sabbath, even if she had been acquainted with Sabbath observance back then, so too the church could hardly ob-

---

* W. Rordorf, *Sabbat und Sonntag in der Alten Kirche*, 37, 99 (Justinian and the *Apostolic Constitutions*: rest all our days), 45, 59, 67ff., 79ff. (Ptolemeus, Tertullian, Origen, Eusebius: rest in a spiritual sense, from our evil works), 101, 111 (Augustine, the *Apostolic Constitutions*: the Sabbath as a shadow of Christ's rest in the grave).

† W. Geesink goes too far when he calls the lack of insight in the ancient church "an error no less serious than that of Judaism" (*Van 's Heeren ordinantiën* [Kampen, 1925], 3:508). Because the church observed Sunday with fervent Christian joy ("die solis laetitiam curare," said Tertullian, which means "devoting oneself on Sunday to joy" [W. Rordorf, *Sabbat und Sonntag in der Alten Kirche*, 152]), this comparison is unfair. The church's deficient understanding regarding Sunday could be augmented, something that could not be done for Judaism. For the latter, conversion, not augmentation, was required.

serve Sunday as a complete day of rest during those first centuries, even if she had possessed proper insight into the Scripture.

The Provisional and the Permanent

As promised earlier, we must still say something about the provisional and the permanent, especially in terms of the transition from the Sabbath day to Sunday.

The terms *provisional* and *permanent* seem to us better than *ceremonial* and *moral*. We would like to say a bit more by way of explanation.

We may certainly say that Christ is the fulfillment of the Sabbath, and as a commemoration of liberation from Egypt, the Sabbath was a "shadow" of what we now possess in Christ, who is its "substance." Our Passover lamb, Christ, has been slain (1 Cor. 5:7), and therefore the Sabbath as an institution looking back to the Exodus from Egypt has passed away. Our looking back on Sunday focuses on Christ's resurrection from the grave.

We also find much that is permanent in both the Sabbath and Sunday. The Sabbath was also a looking back to God's resting at the end of His creation work. That applies to Sunday as well, as one day of rest every seven days.

Moreover, we may say, especially in view of Hebrews 4, that the weekly Sabbath was a sign of the eternal Sabbath. That feature applies just as well to Sunday. The definitive rest from our works, similar to God's rest from His work, is not yet within our reach (Heb. 4:9–10). *Both* the Sabbath and Sunday are a sign pointing to that truth. *

Among those provisional elements that have lost their place after the coming of Christ, we would identify the following:

1. Observing the Sabbath on Saturday, as we have already explained.

2. Observing the entire sabbatical cycle (with sabbatical years and Years of Jubilee), which was so interwoven with the existence of Israel as a separate theocratic nation, that the disappearance of Israel meant also the end of the practical feasibility of this legislation (with its regulations pertaining to working the land, releasing land and houses, releasing slaves,

---

* Some popularize the difference between the Sabbath and Sunday this way: The Sabbath conveys the message: first work and only then rest, *in contrast to* Sunday with its "evangelical" message: first rest and out of that rest go to work. But the popularized explanation shortchanges the evangelical character of the Sabbath. The fourth commandment in its former application (to the Sabbath on Saturday) was unimaginable without the gospel of God's redemption. Remember the prologue to the Ten Commandments!

and so forth). The text of the fourth commandment speaks only of the weekly day of rest, something that obtained a typological, theocratic-Israelite expansion in the Sabbath cycle.*

3. The sanction of capital punishment tied to the transgression of the Sabbath commandment (Num. 15:32–36, the narrative of the man who picked up sticks on the Sabbath). This sanction also brings us within the sphere of a separate people, wholly dedicated to Yahweh, a nation in which "ecclesiastical" and "civil" discipline still completely coincided. That no longer applies today.[23] We shall return to this point below.

4. Several concretizations regarding things not permitted on the Sabbath. We have already seen that the number of regulations in the Mosaic legislation covering the Sabbath is small. Nevertheless, those we do possess lead us to think more readily of the Old Testament as a period of immaturity during which carefully formulated prohibitions were fitting, whereas the New Testament is characterized as a period of freedom (Gal. 4:1–5).

Not Overestimating Confessional Differences

Before discussing our observance and commemoration of Sunday, we would like to consider several differences existing among Christians regarding the matter of the Sabbath and Sunday. These differences can be surmised simply by reading two closely related confessions. Let us compare what two Reformed Confessions, the Westminster Larger Catechism (1648) and the Heidelberg Catechism (1563), say about Sunday.

We read in the Westminster Larger Catechism (Answer 117),

> The Sabbath or Lord's day is to be sanctified by an holy resting all the day, not only from such works as are at all times sinful, but even from such worldly employments and recreations as are on other days lawful; and making it our delight to spend the whole time (except so much of it as is to be taken up in works of necessity and mercy) in the public and private exercises of God's wor-

---

* Here we take issue with C. Vonk, who asserts in *De voorzeide leer*, vol. 1b (Barendrecht, 1963), 695, that the church has taken her scissors and snipped the embroidery threads of the special Sabbaths from the garment of the weekly Sabbath days. "The measly remnant of her vandalism—the garment of the weekly Sabbath days—she mended for a Sunday dress." If everything had indeed been interwoven like a piece of embroidery, why then does not the fourth commandment say, "Remember the Sabbath days"?!

ship: and, to that end, we are to prepare our hearts, and with such foresight, diligence, and moderation, to dispose and seasonably dispatch our worldly business, that we may be the more free and fit for the duties of that day.*

The Heidelberg Catechism gives an answer in Lord's Day 38 to the question about what God commands us in the fourth commandment:

First, that the ministry of the gospel and the schools be maintained, and that I, especially on the Sabbath, that is, the day of rest, diligently attend the church of God, to learn God's word, to use the sacraments, to call publicly upon the Lord, and to give Christian alms. Second, that all the days of my life I rest from my evil works, let the Lord work in me by His Holy Spirit, and thus begin in this life the eternal Sabbath.†

The differences are striking. The Westminster Larger Catechism focuses on resting from our daily work, even as the text of the fourth commandment does. The Heidelberg Catechism is silent concerning this resting, but rather focuses attention on something that must occur each day: the "spiritual" resting, namely, from our evil works. This constitutes an interpretation of the fourth commandment wholly in line with the nonliteral exegesis of Calvin that we discussed earlier. What lies at the center of the Heidelberg Catechism is not resting from ordinary labor

---

* The Westminster standards (the doctrinal standards of the Orthodox Presbyterian Church and the Presbyterian Church in America), reprinted in *Ecumenical and Reformed Creeds and Confessions: Classroom Edition* (Orange City, Ia.: Mid-America Reformed Seminary, 1991). The Westminster Confession (1647) also mentions the Sabbath and calls it a "law of nature" that a specific period of time must be set aside for worship. In His Word, God has provided a positive, moral command that has permanent validity for all men in every age, whereby He designated one day in seven as a Sabbath. From the beginning of the world until the resurrection of Christ, this was the last day of the week, whereas thereafter it became the first day of the week, called in the Scripture the "day of the Lord," which until the end of the world will be the Christian Sabbath (21.7; notice that the Westminster Larger Catechism in Answer 116 discusses this same thing, but without mentioning the "lex naturae").

† The Heidelberg Catechism, reprinted in *Ecumenical and Reformed Creeds and Confessions: Classroom Edition* . The words "especially on the Sabbath, that is, the day of rest," do not appear in the original German and Latin version of Lord's Day 38, but appear for the first time in the Dutch edition of Dathenus.

(even though that rest is covered by the phrase "the day of rest," which explains the word "Sabbath"), but going to church.

People have summarized the difference between these catechisms this way: the rest from daily work is in the Westminster Larger Catechism a religious end in itself, while in the Heidelberg Catechism it is merely a means to the religious goal of going to church. But this characterization strikes us as not altogether accurate, for the Westminster Larger Catechism also views rest as a means: we must employ "the whole time" for "public and private exercises of God's worship"! Therefore, we could better say that the Westminster Larger Catechism devotes attention to both rest and exercises of worship, and that the Heidelberg Catechism directs its attention to Sunday church attendance and our "spiritual" rest.

Throughout European, British, and American Protestantism, rather sharp polemics have been waged about the Sabbath question, so sharp that at times a church split appeared inevitable.[*] Many followed the English Puritan stream (for example, the Dutch theologians Walaeus and Voetius). They believed that Sabbath rest continued in Sunday rest. Others (like Gomarus and later Cocceius, with even more vehemence) emphasized the Jewish and provisional character of the Sabbath, whereby Sabbath rest came to be viewed differently than Sunday rest.

Nevertheless, ecclesiastical divisions were avoided, in large part because the various viewpoints approached one another more closely than would appear from the discussions, especially when it came to the *practice* of Sunday observance. Arranging Sunday church services was difficult apart from resting on Sunday, no matter which theological view one adopted. Even those who did not agree that both rest and worship were principled extensions of the fourth commandment nevertheless found rest and worship united in practice. Where people set aside a *day* for worship (in church and at home), ordinary labor had to be interrupted.

Church divisions in the Netherlands were avoided because the Synod of Dort made a moderating decision about this issue. The English theologians at this synod had complained about the neglect of Sunday, even as they could witness with their own eyes in the city of Dordrecht. Still, the synod did not come up with a strictly Puritan pronouncement. Actually,

---

[*] We must also take into account that Sunday observance was at a low in the the Netherlands after the Reformation. See especially S. D. van Veen, *Zondagsrust en zondagsheiliging in de zeventiende eeuw* (Nijkerk, 1889), and T. de Vries, *Overheid en zondagsviering*, 236ff.

it made no pronouncement, but agreed to a compromise statement forged with the help of professors attending the synod from churches in the province of Zeeland who were arguing the matter at the time.*

An ecclesiastical split was thwarted even more by the wording of Lord's Day 38 of the Heidelberg Catechism. For both parties could properly appeal to it! Those who, in the spirit of the Puritans, fought for Sunday rest could point to the reference to Sunday as the Sabbath and day of rest; those defending strongly the ceremonial character of the rest required by the fourth commandment could with similar justification quote the passage about the New Testament "resting" from our evil works.

Educated by the past, we must be careful today to avoid exaggerating the differences involving the Sabbath and Sunday. One might hold the view (as we do) that Lord's Day 38 of the Heidelberg Catechism evidences a certain gap at this point, because its formulation echoes the fourth commandment too weakly. The "ceremonial" stands out more sharply in this Lord's Day than the "moral," to use those unfortunate terms once more. It does not speak directly about resting from daily labor. On the other hand, the Westminster Larger Catechism also shows weaknesses. This catechism is in fact quite negative toward activities of relaxation, because the *whole* day must be used for public and private worship, with the exception of time needed for works of necessity and mercy. In this way, the day is certainly "spiritually" full, so much so that there is little opportunity left

---

* H. H. Kuyper, *De post-acta of nahandelingen van de nationale synode van Dordrecht* (Amsterdam, 1899), 191. The following points were decided:

1. In the fourth commandment, there is a ceremonial and a moral element.
2. The rest on the seventh day after the Creation and the strict observance of this day assigned to the Jewish nation in particular were ceremonial.
3. That a definite and appointed day is set aside for worship, and along with it as much rest as is necessary for worship and for holy meditation, belongs to the moral element.
4. Now that the Sabbath of the Jews is set aside, Christians are duty bound to hallow the day of Sunday solemnly.
5. This day has always been kept since the time of the apostles in the early church.
6. This day must be so consecrated to worship that on it men rest from all servile labor (except those required by charity and present necessities), and likewise from all such recreations as prevent the worship of God.

So no pronouncement was made about various theological points of contention (When was the Sabbath instituted? Is the transition from Sabbath to Sunday based on divine authority or ecclesiastical decision? Is Sunday rest of the same nature as the ancient Sabbath rest?). What is certainly clear is what Sunday observance must look like: Sunday is a *day* that must be consecrated to worship, something impossible without rest from daily labor.

for doing what is also characteristic for Sunday: catching our breath through genuine physical rest.

Nevertheless, there is no sensational difference between these two catechisms. Both start with the abiding validity of the fourth commandment. The matter becomes much more serious as soon as people declare the fourth commandment to have been *set aside*, severing the connection between Sunday and the fourth commandment. Never has a struggle broken out over the differences between these two catechisms. These differences were far too small for that to happen, involving no more than variety in emphasis in their interpretations of the fourth commandment.

Something similar can be said regarding the polemic between Gomarus and Walaeus, involving several points of difference *within* the context of their shared agreement that the fourth commandment remains valid for today. But that was not the case in the struggle between Cocceius and Hoornbeek. Cocceius rejected the continuing validity of the fourth commandment, which he declared to be entirely ceremonial.[24]

That the fourth commandment has retained its validity is the correct confessional starting point. But with regard to the way in which the Sabbath and Sunday are connected, and the consequences of that for our Sunday observance, differences will likely continue indefinitely.

Celebrating Sunday

Years ago, the Dutch theologian A. van Selms wrote that, on average, ten thousand families in the Netherlands alone were affected by serious quarreling about what was and was not permissible on Sunday. By his calculations, that made for half a million quarrels per year; statisticians might be able to tell us how many nervous disorders are traceable to that number. Perhaps by now that number has decreased, since reflecting about the special character of Sunday occupies the attention of fewer people today than when van Selms wrote his booklet. But we can rest assured that even today, quarrels break out when families discuss what may and may not be done on Sunday.

In our view, there are much less important questions that occasion quarrels. We quarrel about big questions like faith in God and in Jesus Christ, loving our neighbor, marriage and sexuality, peace and security. Why not about Sunday observance? We might lay the blame for this quarrel at the feet of the Puritans, whose view of Sabbath observance supposedly wounds children and alienates them from the church when they grow older. But that is not honest. Many quarrels arise because *enjoying* Sunday in a biblical sense is not so easy. "Res severa est verum gaudium"—"True joy is a serious business."

Enjoying Sunday according to the tone of the fourth commandment presupposes a few important realities.

Enjoyment presupposes that we are able to let go of our ordinary daily concerns. This involves not only our occupational labor, but all labor, including that connected with organizing our free time outside the working hours of a five-day workweek. Thousands of church members have trouble already at this point. Involved here is the way we celebrate our freedom. We must not be enslaved to our work or to our hobbies, but too often we are.

Enjoyment presupposes also that we can enjoy other people. When the Sabbath was properly celebrated, everybody was equal: *everybody* rested—family members, slaves, work animals, and the foreigner. The freemen were not allowed to have their slaves do their work, and, as an extension of the Sabbath, the Year of Jubilee was a time for liberating all the slaves. Nowhere in the Ten Commandments is it clearer that there may be no social discrimination. Sunday must be a reflection of that, too. Enjoyment is not an individual activity, but requires the communal celebration of our liberation through Christ Jesus. This too is far from easy on Sunday, namely, being and acting like a *communion* of saints.

Enjoyment presupposes that we devote Sunday to God. Sunday, just like the Sabbath, is for man. But at the same time, it is the Lord's Day, a day for doing things that we cannot do or can do less easily on the other days, namely, go to church, pray together as families, sing, and discuss the service our risen Lord asks from us.

All these activities make Sunday different in character than, for example, a Saturday off from work. We can enjoy our holidays and vacations because they help us catch our breath, similar to Sunday. But by means of the *combination* of "rest" and "consecration," we enjoy Sunday differently than any other holiday. This special enjoyment involves problems, of course. Each of us knows from experience that self-denial requires us to devote Sunday to *God,* for then we are not busy with ourselves.

On the basis of all these observations, it should be clear that besides being a divine gift, enjoyment of Sunday is also a divine mandate. This leads us to the question regarding how we fill our Sunday. How do we spend the day? Can we determine what may and may not be done on Sunday, or are all forms of casuistry forbidden here?

Filling Our Sunday

In his *Church Dogmatics*, Karl Barth has written some excellent things about Sunday as a feast day. On Sunday we celebrate the fact that we are free from ourselves because we are free for God. We may experience the day as an exercise in faith wherein we deny ourselves. However, even though Barth uses the word *exercise*, he is dead scared of any Sunday casuistry. He cites William Ames, who forbade any walking (except to and from church). Barth also criticized the arbitrariness with which Ames determined what were permissible "works of necessity" on Sunday. A physician may work on behalf of his fellow man, as may civil servants and military personnel, whose job is national security. But a farmer may not use Sunday for harvesting hay or crops, even if his entire harvest is threatened by bad weather.[25]

Without agreeing with Ames when it comes to the *outworking* of what may and may not be done on Sunday, we think that Barth's comments at this point are unfair. He condemns making distinctions and providing guidelines regarding what may and may not be done on Sunday. But he himself also provides guidelines. Celebrating Sunday as a day for God, he says, calls for avoiding all sorts of Sunday work and any number of all-too-programmed (and by that fact improper) Sunday activities.[26]

Why may Barth permit himself this guideline and forbid others the privilege of making their own sentiments concrete? With his remark about all sorts of Sunday work, Barth is actually arguing for the same principle as Ames and others who use the distinction between necessary and unnecessary work. For deciding what kinds of relaxation are permissible on Sunday, Barth explains concretely what he means: To celebrate Sunday as the Lord's Day, you cannot sleep late on Sunday morning or take a walk in the woods.

Barth's concern is understandable. Concretizations of principles may not become a burdensome yoke, because Sunday is a feast day. Moreover, you have not yet *celebrated* Sunday if you have merely done what "may" be done and avoided doing what "may not" be done. We must not do to Sunday what the Pharisees did to the Sabbath.

Barth saw an infallible proof that one was keeping the commandment about Sunday in this: whether and how sincerely we are in a position to celebrate Sunday as a true day of joy.[27] We can agree wholeheartedly with what Barth says here. It is God who ultimately judges our Sunday observance; we see only the outward appearance. Moreover, outward appearances can vary. Not everyone does things the same way on Sunday, although in spite of such differences, we may still speak of the same "spiritual" celebration of Sunday.

We have no uniform Sunday observance, and we need not strive for that either. If we would pursue such uniformity, we would soon fall into excessive casuistry like that of Ames and many others.* For today, this could mean that on Sunday we would not be permitted to take a walk or a drive, to knit or do needlework, to watch television, and so forth. Fair is fair. What goes for one goes for the other—especially to avoid giving offense, as people say. Now that is certainly a good biblical principle (Rom. 14:13), and occasionally it may be necessary to refrain from an otherwise innocent activity for the sake of the neighbors. But then we are doing that on account of their weakness and not their strength.

The same Paul who wrote about "not giving offense" warned against immaturity (Gal. 4:1–11) and against a plethora of precepts of the quality "Do not touch, do not taste, do not handle" (Col. 2:21). We too must be worried about this danger, for otherwise we will restrict Christian liberty that permits different ways of spending our Sunday.

However, even though there is no *uniform* celebration of Sunday, there is nonetheless *uniformity* to this degree, that we all seek to obey the same commandment. A number of observations will make this clear.

Sunday cannot be a workday, for the commandment clearly requires us to cease our daily labor. This communal resting in itself lends a degree of uniformity to all Sunday observance.

Because we are celebrating *Sunday*, our resting from daily labor includes ceasing from various leisure activities. For many people, sprucing up the house or the yard is a form of relaxation enjoyed on a day off, but this can hardly be considered a way to spend our Sunday.

Going to church is another way Christians display uniform behavior on Sunday. Following the principle that we should not forsake the assembling of ourselves together (Heb. 10:25) will give clear shape to our Sun-

---

* On the whole, churches have stayed away from casuistic minutiae, even when requested to provide it. One of the most extreme examples we have come across was of a Reformed church in Urk (a fishing community in the Netherlands) that wanted to censure church members "who fish on Sunday by setting their nets, snares and traps in the sea on Saturday and retrieving them on Monday"! In the record of official synodical proceedings (1899), you will read that this synod refused to enter into the matter, praying "that it may please the Lord to lead the brothers of Urk by His Holy Spirit in this sensitive and weighty matter."

day. This is especially true when this principle involves going to church twice each Sunday.

If we are celebrating the day of Christ, then our sincere celebration will exclude putting other things on our calendar, such as sporting events, school assignments, making long trips for recreation, and the like. We need not take out a yardstick to measure the distances we travel on Sunday. After celebrating Sunday with family, one might be required to travel quite a distance back home in order to start work early Monday morning. But it seems rather self-evident that in order to concentrate on worshiping God in church, we are going to need sufficient rest, so that the kind of travel we might enjoy on Saturday would not fit our schedule for Sunday.

We will want to spend Sundays as much as possible among brothers and sisters in the faith. Sunday is a feast day that keeps us away from the company of those who do not celebrate the feast with us. This is why it is unthinkable for someone to celebrate Sunday and at the same time voluntarily mingle in public among those who are strangers to God, as in a football stadium or on the beach or in a shopping mall. Sunday is a day for the communion of the saints, and for that reason we avoid situations where we would feel isolated as a believer. By acting this way, we are not separating ourselves from the world (remember, the next day is Monday), but we are celebrating a feast that is not available to us every other day. It fits with the festive atmosphere of Sunday that we spend our time with fellow festival participants and not with those who do not care to participate.

We would be dragged too far into moral casuistry if we were to discuss when *precisely* our observance of Sunday begins and when it ends. From midnight Saturday to midnight Sunday? From dawn to dusk? From Saturday evening to Sunday evening (thus in the line of the Jewish Sabbath)? A lot of ink has been spilled in the past to answer these and similar questions, without arriving at a consensus.

Nevertheless, it is helpful to reflect on the fact that Sunday is a special *day*. For every other feast day in our life experience, we prepare ourselves and get things ready ahead of time. We should do that for Sunday, too. For that reason we begin already on Saturday to prepare for Sunday, so that we can sit in church well rested and ready. Spending our Sundays properly requires more than getting ready for church once or twice. Between and after the services it is still Sunday, so that we may properly ask whether spending the entire Sunday afternoon or evening watching television really fits with celebrating Sunday aright. We will leave aside for now the question about how profitable watching television may be on other afternoons or evenings, but what kind of Sunday celebration are we pursuing when we expect television broadcasters to provide it for us? We have already said that it is incorrect to prohibit watching television on Sunday. But for that reason we would suggest that it would still be a matter of style to enhance our Sunday celebration by following the general practice of not turning on the television. This would be a good exercise in self-denying faith, to use once more Barth's characterization of Sunday!

Sunday is a day of consecration *and* rest. This rest does not exist for the sake of something else, namely, going to church, praying, singing, family devotions, and everything else connected with the "spiritual." Unfortunately, an overly spiritual observance of Sunday has brought about widespread damage, especially among children and young people who were doomed to doing nothing except those activities consistent with the kind of "resting" expected of them.

Think, for example, of the specific activities prescribed by Richard Baxter: rise early on Sunday morning; pray in private; have family devotions; go to church (and do not sleep in church); after returning home, while the noon meal is being prepared, pray in private and review everything said in church; enjoy a festive meal with conversation about the love of our Redeemer or something fitting for Sunday; after the meal, gather as family for a psalm or for singing and instruction; go to church once more; come home and gather as family to call upon God in prayer and song and to rehearse the sermon; thereafter eat, but not too much, just as at noon; after the evening meal, question the children and servants about what they had learned during the day; sing a psalm and conclude with prayer; and end the day with holy thoughts!*

Earlier we mentioned the busy "spiritual" program prescribed by the Westminster Larger Catechism. We find in Baxter an outworking of that. But let us remember that earlier, people did not have as many opportunities for educating their children as we have in our Western culture. In those days, children received on Sundays what many of our children learn in school during the week. Nevertheless, we still observe today in some countries that Sunday functions as a day of education to compensate for

---

* Richard Baxter, *The Practical Works of Richard Baxter* (reprint, Ligonier, Pa., 1990), 1:472–73. For a similar arrangement of the day, see G. Voetius, *Catechisatie over den Heidelbergschen Catechismus* (republished by A. Kuyper, Rotterdam, 1891), 871–72. People should go to church twice on Sunday; but what should they do between and after services, "for the day is long"? Voetius mentions catechetical instruction and retelling the sermon. If there is time left, then visit the sick and elderly or others in distress, to comfort, strengthen, and warn them.

the lack of Christian day schools. But even if we view our modern practice to be a reduction in terms of Baxter's suggestions, the program he prescribed is too intense for a day that is supposed to be a feast day for young and old alike.

The man-directed element of catching one's breath on the Sabbath—very simply to stretch our legs and relax a bit—is missing in Baxter's system. Sunday must be a feast. But where is the feasting when the day is filled with endless discussions without breaks and snacks, especially for children?

Precisely *how* we use this element of pleasure in spending our Sundays is again a matter of Christian liberty, where we may not prescribe uniformity. The unfortunate fact that many people are bored on Sunday is in large part probably due to the inability of many families to celebrate Sunday *together*.

Thus, our rest on Sunday may have a recreational dimension, too. Remember, we should not view our resting "merely" as a necessary means for staying awake during church services. Without intending to do so, people who have this view of rest contribute to the secularization of Sunday. As long as we get enough rest in order to go to church, why do we need to distinguish the rest of the day from an ordinary workday or a day off? Rather, just like going to church, light recreational activity on Sunday is a good exercise in self-denying faith: are we willing to spend our time off in a style that permits the entire day to be the Lord's Day?

Working on Sunday

Sunday is a day of rest, but not for everybody. A police officer is on duty; so is a nurse; and Sunday is the minister's busy day. These three examples correspond to a distinction that has been used for a long time: on the day of rest, the only works permitted are those of *necessity*, of *mercy*, and of *religion*.*

---

* The Latin expression is *opera necessitatis, charitatis, et pietatis*. Various biblical examples are used to illustrate each of these, such as letting animals drink, Luke 13:15, and pulling an ox out of a pit, Luke 14:5 (works of necessity); healing, Mark 2:31 (works of mercy); performing temple service, as the priests in the temple who "profane the Sabbath, and are blameless," Matt. 12:5 (works of worship).

In contrast to these activities permitted on Sunday were the impermissible activities, often distinguished as *opera servilia* (daily labor), *opera forensia* (public courts, markets, assemblies, and the like), *opera liberalia* (activities for developing the spirit that required exertion, such as studying and teaching).

From the examples given, it appears that the boundaries are flexible. For example, the work of a nurse can be categorized just as well a work of necessity as a work of mercy. The familiar triad is useful as a rule of thumb, but we must not assign it any more value than that.

Everyone is convinced that some work must be performed on Sunday. Society and the needy may not be left without help. The police and fire departments must be prepared for duty. We visit family members and friends in hospitals and other institutions. And it is obvious that on Sunday not only the minister and church custodian, but many more people as well must work hard to make Sunday truly a day of worship.

It gets more difficult when we have to identify which work is really necessary on Sunday. Even in an agricultural society, that could be problematic. Emperor Constantine proclaimed Sunday as a day of rest for his whole empire, but he permitted farmers to work when they needed to sow and plant their crops. There have been Reformed theologians who appealed to this law to justify (occasional) field work on Sunday.*

Problems arise also in an agrarian society. May farmers bale hay or harvest crops that would otherwise be destroyed by bad weather? May businessmen cover outdoor plants to protect them from unexpected frost? Why may we extinguish a fire, something called by early Reformed casuists a work of necessity, and why cannot the same be said of saving what harvest can be saved when there is a threat of loss?

Still more complicated is our modern society with various services running on Sunday. Utility companies require effort from many people, on Sunday too. Public transportation can be restricted, but it cannot be halted. Especially in industries dealing with chemicals there are processes that must be continued over Sunday, or else they would be so expensive that people would be forced out of competition with other businesses and nations.

Two observations must be made at this point. First, secularization of society brings with it an increase in Sunday work. In various sectors of the economy, a larger portion of Sunday rest could well be implemented, but why would people push for that if they already ignored Sunday observance anyway? Many things that did not happen on Sunday thirty years ago have become commonplace nowadays; this is not because society has become

---

* L. Danaeus appealed to this law of Emperor Constantine to justify his opinion that field work was occasionally permissible (*Ethices christianae* [Geneva, 1577], 169). On this point he was opposed by Voetius, though it is not entirely clear whether Voetius rejected field work on Sunday in *all* circumstances. See C. Steenblok, *Voetius en de sabbat* (Hoorn, 1941), 117ff. For Voetius's opinion, see his *Selectae disputationes* (Utrecht, 1659), 3:1262–1263.

more complex, but because maintaining Sunday as a day of rest does not interest the majority of citizens any longer. Especially the recreational sector has become labor intensive on Sunday, compared to former times. We can certainly say that much Sunday work, also in our modern, complex society, conflicts with the fourth commandment.

A second observation: It is far from obvious that many work activities need not be done on Sunday. Perhaps we can say that a given activity did not have to be done thirty years ago; we might assume that even today something is not strictly necessary, or that we could suffice with doing only part of the job on Sunday. Anyone who works in the airline industry would perhaps need to work less if air traffic were restricted on Sunday. We might question the need for many services in the public sector. Even in modern hospitals we see, in addition to "works of mercy," various procedures performed for economic reasons (maintaining full capacity, non-emergency operations), something we might surely question. A hospital can easily become a nonstop business, where Sunday is no different from any other day.[28]

Here we would speak of a gray area, of work not easily evaluated in terms of the criterion of necessity. Here it is important to be careful in our judgment. The comment of William Ames about the household subordinates named in the fourth commandment (male servants, female servants) is instructive. They could not always judge whether a particular task assigned by their master was necessary. Therefore they must, according to Ames, consider as necessary those tasks that *might* be necessary.[29] Along this same line, we would say that our complex modern labor structures are not always transparent to us—again, something that warns us to be modest in our judgments.

Naturally, a technologically well-developed society wanting to listen to God's Word will make Sunday as work-free as possible. But now that we are seeing a totally different development, it is not always possible for someone in this gray area to avoid Sunday work.

We can employ the following distinctions: There are

1. people who work in the health care sector (for example, doctors, nurses, ambulance personnel);
2. people in the safety and service sectors (such as police officers, firemen, emergency rescue personnel, postal workers, telephone operators, utilities servicemen); and
3. people working for larger industrial concerns with round-the-clock shifts, or working in long-distance hauling.[30]

Many tasks in the first and second categories belong to the gray area. The example we gave was of a hospital keeping a full staff on Sunday in order to remain as profitable as possible. But on that basis, a Christian cannot refuse for that reason to work Sundays in that kind of hospital. Patients admitted on Sunday must be cared for, even though it may be that they are not being admitted on Sunday on account of their serious situation, but because it is more economically advantageous for the hospital.

But the tasks performed in the third category are different. For example, there are truckers who leave on Sunday with a load in order to be on the road as early as possible. Shipping especially consumer and perishable goods requires early arrival and unloading. In order to remain competitive, drivers must work on Sunday so businesses can be ready to open on Monday.

All of this is understandable, but still in conflict with the fourth commandment. Those elements of "necessity" and "mercy" disappear from view here, replaced by "economic productivity" and "profit."

There is some Sunday work that we cannot claim to be necessary. A Christian must not pursue that work, and if it happens to be his occupation, he must look for another job. That is more easily said than done in a society where unemployment is a reality and the majority of the populace cares nothing about the fourth commandment. But a Christian knows that one who keeps the commandment keeps his soul (Prov. 19:16), even though it costs him a good job.

Therefore, it is very important already when one chooses an occupation to pay attention to whether or not it will require working on Sunday. A Christian may become a police officer or a nurse, even though those occupations involve working on Sunday. Even then we must remain alert and work hard (as much as in us lies) to keep that Sunday work to a minimum. The story is told of an army officer who refused to attend receptions organized by his superiors on Sunday. One might well say that such a duty belonged to his job. Once you join, you're in all the way. But this army officer refused to draw such consequences, and with success. A colonel who had called him to task for his objections said afterward, "This officer has a high sense of duty."[31] Fortunately, a consistent position in terms of Sunday observance will often still command respect.

Some occupations are or can become so problematic on account of Sunday work that one must reflect carefully whether his choice for such an occupation is responsible.[32]

We need to *exert ourselves* to defend and expand the Sunday rest still permitted. We are inclined quickly to put certain jobs in the gray area, when perhaps we could attain greater success along the route of a well-grounded and communally organized protest.[33]

Take, for example, working in shifts, where many employers would like to include Sunday in the rotation. At that point we must dare to say no, on the basis of our convictions and our familiarity with business operations.

A simple appeal to our obedience to the fourth commandment is stronger than various subjective arguments (for example, Sunday work disrupts the family). Such arguments may well have value, but they fail to resonate with the fact that our struggle for Sunday involves our faith.

Moreover, our arguments must demonstrate familiarity with business and manufacturing practices. If you can demonstrate that a different division of labor need not result in loss of productivity, you will be in a stronger position than someone who suffices with the statement that he has conscientious objections against working on Sunday. The former approach appeals to the society in a way that leads people to see in the fourth commandment not an idiosyncrasy of Christians, but a healthful regulation for society itself. Sunday is for man, who may not and need not be a slave to his work.

A Few More Comments

We conclude with a few comments occasioned by questions raised occasionally in connection with our subject.

1. *Does the fourth commandment require us to work six days?*

An answer was given to this question long before a five-day workweek could have generated such a query. It has been correctly observed that the fourth commandment gives a command, not to work, but to rest. So it is improper to say that we *must* work six days. It is just as improper as saying that we should work *six* days rather than four or five. The fourth commandment simply says that we must perform our work within six days.[*]

---

[*] A. Maillot, *Le Décalogue* (Paris, 1976), 76ff., sees the Sabbath commandment also as a commandment to work. In that connection, he distinguishes between the optimistic view of labor underlying the version found in Ex. 20 (six days of work, culminating in the Sabbath feast) and the pessimistic view of labor supposedly found in Deut. 5 (work reminds Israel of slave labor in Egypt). We view this distinction as untenable; our discussion of it appears in J. Douma, *Vrede in de maatschappij*, 2d ed. (Kampen, 1986), 39–71, where we deal with the subject of work.

Recall the translation, "You have six days to labor and perform all your work"! This does not require that all six days be spent working.

Others have also correctly observed that the matter of laziness or sloth belongs under the eighth commandment, not the fourth. Consider the interpretation of the eighth commandment given by the Heidelberg Catechism (Answer 111), insisting that we must labor faithfully.

2. Can we use the term Sunday observance? *Does this phrase not suggest putting one day above another, in an Old Testament fashion, whereas all days are really equal?*

The answer must be that a day whose character is different does not need to be exalted above other days. We serve Christ every day. To say that we hallow or sanctify or observe Sunday is really to say nothing more than that we spend this day in a special way prescribed by God.

Earlier we observed that resting on the Sabbath and keeping the Sabbath holy were one and the same thing. It was precisely by resting that the faithful Israelite kept the Sabbath holy. Likewise, our terminology relating to Sunday does not need the distinction between resting on Sunday (not working) and keeping Sunday holy (going to church). We keep Sunday holy according to the fourth commandment by both resting and going to church.

3. Is transgression of the fourth commandment to be considered as weighty as transgression of the sixth commandment, for example?

In the Old Testament period, capital punishment was applied to violating the Sabbath as well as to murder. Nevertheless, we could draw mistaken conclusions for today from that fact. Israel was a theocracy in which the Sabbath, just like circumcision, was a sign of the covenant between Yahweh and Israel. Anyone who was not circumcised or who violated the Sabbath was to be put to death. But our modern society is not a theocracy. Church and society no longer coincide as they did for Israel in the land of Canaan. Therefore, anybody who today pleads for the same degree of punishment for violating Sunday rest as for committing murder is forgetting which world he is living in. Moreover, our society is so secularized that the majority of the populace no longer knows what the fourth commandment contains.

The same thing could be said about the sins of idolatry (first and second commandment) or about the misuse of God's name (third commandment). Thus we observe that for maintaining society, there are various degrees of weight among the commandments. No nation would tolerate murder and robbery as being commonplace, since no society can survive without opposing these evils. But any number of nations exist with a government like that of Paul's day, one that serves strange gods, that refuses to honor God, and that is unacquainted with Sunday observance. It is the patience of God Himself that makes it possible for nations and governments to reject the Ten Commandments and yet enjoy a tolerable life as a society.

Saying this does not automatically mean that *therefore* the Ten Commandments are not valid for all people. They are indeed valid for all people, even though they might not be enforceable among all people. A politician who strives to defend and/or restore Sunday observance does so to God's honor and for the blessing that such observance brings to an entire nation.

It is self-evident that the situation within the church is different than in civil society. In her exercise of discipline, the church will punish those who transgress the fourth commandment. For transgressing this commandment is just as much an expression of unbelief as murder, adultery, and robbery.

4. Must we not resist observing (other) Christian feast days if we want to maintain Sunday with its unique significance?

It is understandable why many people, during and after the Reformation, when they had to break with the multitude of Roman Catholic feast days, became so radical as to reject every feast day except Sunday. In Geneva, John Calvin was not very sympathetic to celebrating feast days; in Scotland, John Knox even less. But other forces were at work here, such as governments that wanted to give the people and themselves a measure of enjoyment. This in turn led the church rather to tolerate feast days and call for worship services on these days in order to spend them in a Christian and honorable way.[34]

Arguing about this now is foolish. The number of Christian feast days is limited, and practice shows that the church can spend these days meaningfully, especially by preaching the great redemptive acts of her Lord. Celebrating feast days only in terms of going out, eating and drinking, but not in terms of Christ and His salvation, is not proper. But the same is true for Sunday. And the fact that relaxation occupies a larger place during these feast days than on Sunday will disappoint only those who, when all is said and done, really want to treat such days like Sunday.

Endnotes

1. For an overview of various hypotheses, see Joh. Francke, *Van sabbat naar zondag* (Amsterdam, 1973), 33ff.

2. See W. Rordorf, *Sabbat und Sonntag in der Alten Kirche* (Zürich, 1972), 18, 137 including the letter from Pliny the Younger regarding an early morning gathering and (probably) an evening meeting.

3. T. de Vries, *Overheid en zondagsviering* (Leiden, 1899), 133, 139. This old, but still useful study provides a collection of civil laws pertaining to Sunday observance since the time of Constantine.

4. S. Bacchiocchi, *From Sabbath to Sunday* (Rome, 1977), 196–97.

5. T. de Vries, *Overheid en zondagsviering*, 169, 175.

6. W. Geesink observes that appeal to the very words of the fourth commandment was made for the first time in the law of King Dagobert (ca. 630) (see *Gereformeerde ethiek* [Kampen, 1931], 357). For the text of the law, see de Vries, *Overheid en zondagsviering*, 168.

7. For this insight we are gratefully indebted to J. P. Lettinga, who follows the interpretation of J. L. Koole.

8. D. A. Carson, "Jesus and the Sabbath in the Four Gospels," in *From Sabbath to Lord's Day*, ed. D. A. Carson (Grand Rapids, 1982), 65.

9. Regarding casuistry, which need not always be wrong, we have written extensively in *Christian Morals and Ethics* (Winnipeg, 1981), 91–96.

10. See J. Douma, *Christian Morals and Ethics*, 39–42.

11. J. Calvin, *Institutes of the Christian Religion*, ed. John T. McNeill, trans. Ford Lewis Battles, The Library of Christian Classics, vol. 20 (Philadelphia, 1960), 2.8.29.

12. Ibid., 2.8.31.

13. Ibid., 2.8.32 (emphasis added).

14. For this quotation, see W. Rordorf, *Sabbat und Sonntag in der Alten Kirche*, 117.

15. This was correctly observed by W. à Brakel, *The Christian's Reasonable Service*, trans. Bartel Elshout (Pittsburgh, 1994), 3:150–51.

16. H. M. Ohmann, *In het licht van Genesis*, ed. A. P. Wisse (Barneveld, 1986), 108.

17. A. Kuyper, *Tractaat van den Sabbath*, 17, 152.

18. J. A. Heyns, *Theologiese etiek* (Pretoria, 1982), 1:323.

19. For all these quotations and references, see W. Rordorf, *Sabbat und Sonntag in der Alten Kirche*, 135–55.

20. Ibid., 89.

21. Ibid.

22. Ibid., 27ff. (Papias), 33 (Marcion), 83 (Eusebius).

23. See J. Douma, *Politieke verantwoordelijkheid* (Kampen, 1984), 98ff.

24. For a discussion of this conflict, see H. B. Visser, *De geschiedenis van den sabbatsstrijd onder de Gereformeerden in de zeventiende eeuw*, 115ff., 135.

25. Karl Barth, *Church Dogmatics* (Edinburgh, 1961), 3/4:65–66 (concerning Ames).

26. Ibid., 3/4:67.

27. Ibid., 3/4:68–69.

28. See the position paper *Werken op zondag*, published by the Reformed Social Union (Zwolle, 1986), 7.

29. William Ames, *De conscientia*, 2d ed. (Franeker, 1635), 4.33.12.

30. D. Koole, in *De wekker* (publication of the Christelijke Gereformeerde Kerken), 9 May 1986.

31. Reported in J. de Bruyn and G. Puchinger, *Briefwisseling Kuyper-Idenburg* (Franeker, 1985), 16.

32. See D. Koole, in *De wekker*, 9 May 1986.

33. For what follows, see the position paper *Werken op zondag*, 16ff., which mentions possibilities provided by current Dutch labor laws for employees to follow their convictions regarding Sunday rest.

34. H. H. Kuyper, *De post-acta of nahandelingen van de Nationale Synode van Dordrecht*, 151ff.

The Fifth Commandment

Honor your father and your mother. Then you will have a long life in the land Yahweh your God is giving you. (Ex. 20:12)

Honor your father and your mother, as Yahweh your God commanded you. Then you will have a long life and it will go well with you in the land Yahweh your God is giving you. (Deut. 5:16)

Both Father and Mother

Many issues come into view as we now discuss the fifth commandment. It is legitimate, for example, to bring up, besides the matter of honoring parents, also the matter of honoring others in authority. The church has always understood this commandment to require respect for the authority of the state, for example. We will discuss that subject as well, but first things first. We should start with the text of the fifth commandment by discussing the honor due to father and mother.

Children must honor their "father and mother." The Old Testament Hebrew mentions father and mother very specifically. We do not have here a kind of summary word or phrase like our term "parents." Such a term does appear in New Testament Greek. We read of the "parents" of Jesus who brought Him to the temple shortly after His birth, and took Him along to Jerusalem when He was twelve years old (Luke 2:27, 41, 43). Concerning a certain man born blind, the disciples asked Jesus who had sinned, this man or his "parents" (John 9:2–3). Children are not supposed to save for their "parents," but "parents" for their children, says Paul (2 Cor. 12:14).*

---

* Prov. 19:14 says that a prudent wife comes from the Lord, whereas houses and riches are an inheritance from *fathers*. This is how the King James Version renders the verse, but

161

There is no substantive difference between the more specific phrase "father and mother" and the more general term "parents." Paul begins by saying, "Children, obey your *parents*," and follows immediately with the fifth commandment, *"Honor your father and mother"* (Eph. 6:1–2). The deliberate mention of the mother is significant. At one point, the Bible even mentions the mother before the father: "Every one of you shall revere his mother and his father" (Lev. 19:3).

Mentioning the mother is no afterthought, for she deserves to be treated with as much respect as the father. Practice demonstrates that children can easily misuse the fact that a mother's physical condition often renders her less able to enforce her word. She is physically the weaker parent. But the fifth commandment clearly requires respect for both father and mother. Children must honor their mother even when she is physically and physiologically declining: "Do not despise your mother when she is old" (Prov. 23:22).

The Bible presents a relationship of authority between husband and wife where the husband takes the lead. But children must show *equal* honor to both mother and father.

The Role of Parents

Why do we have the fifth commandment? People offer biological and sociological explanations like these: Cultural development was possible only because parents passed on to their offspring the knowledge they had acquired. What could the succeeding generation have done without the knowledge of the former generation? So children had to respect their parents in order to win in their struggle for survival. In this world, nobody builds on nothing; everybody builds on tradition. Children walk in the footsteps of their parents. In earlier centuries, this was evident in the occupational choices people made. If a father was a baker, saddle maker, or blacksmith, his son followed him in that occupation.

So, back then it was important for his development that a child submit-

---

the New International Version renders the verse to say that houses and wealth are an inheritance from *parents*. This latter translation does not seem compelling to us, no more so than the New International Version of Prov. 17:6: "Children's children are a crown to the aged, and *parents* [orig.: *fathers*] are the pride of their children." The only text we must translate with the term "parents" is Heb. 11:23. The original Greek text says that Moses had been hidden for three months by his *pateres*, his *fathers*. Both the King James Version and the New International Version render this by the term *parents*.

ted to his parents' guidance. Obviously, according to this theory, that need gave rise to a command: "Honor your father and your mother." Obedience was required from children with a view to their own best interests. You need not command parents to love their children, since that happens automatically. But inexperienced children, who do not yet know what is good for their own future, need to be commanded to love their parents, since often that is not automatic. In order to put teeth into that command, appeal was made to higher, invisible powers (e.g., Yahweh). What was needed for guaranteeing the children's future received divine sanction.

However, since these ancient times many things have changed. Thanks to the invention of the printed word and other forms of modern communication, older people, including parents, are less indispensable than earlier. It used to be that parents passed on stories orally, but now you can read them in books. According to some, this is one of the factors that can explain why youngsters no longer respect older people and their own parents. They need their parents for instruction, for occupational preparation, and for future direction far less today than young people did in previous centuries.

We find this theory, as we have sketched it above, impossible to accept. The claim that *people* invented the fifth commandment is an evolutionist, not a biblical, explanation. Supposedly after the fact, people added a divine sanction to the command in order to lend it an aura of authority in the ears of the youth. But this view is upside down. We believe that God gave this commandment; it is not a product of a necessary, evolutionary process. Even less do we accept the argument that the fifth commandment has lost some of its original value because of cultural development (e.g., the fact that everyone can now read and consult books).

Nevertheless, the theory we have sketched does contain an element that we can profitably use, an element found also in the Bible. When we speak of parents, we may confidently add in the very same breath that they are called to provide *teaching*. But then this instruction is of a particular kind. We are thinking here of Deuteronomy 6, where parents are told to make known to their children the commandments of God: "And these words which I command you today shall be in your heart; you shall teach them diligently to your children, and shall talk of them when you sit in your house, when you walk by the way, when you lie down, and when you rise up" (Deut. 6:6–7).

This role given to parents is so dominant that the relationship between the instruction-provider and the instruction-receiver is very often characterized in terms of the relation between father and son. The author speaking in Proverbs, who instructs the youth in practical wisdom for living, calls himself "father," while addressing his pupil as "son" (Prov. 1:10; 2:1; 3:1, etc.). In his instruction, he confronts the "son" with his obligation to listen to the discipline of his (own) father and not to reject the teaching of his mother (Prov. 1:8–9).

This close connection between parenthood and instruction appears elsewhere when the Bible speaks, as it does in the fifth commandment, about receiving a long life: "My son, do not forget my law, but let your heart keep my commands; for length of days and long life and peace they will add to you" (Prov. 3:1–2). The son must accept the words of his father, so that "the years of your life will be many" (Prov. 4:10). In other words, honoring *parents* in order to receive a long life is coupled with respecting the *teaching* of parents.

What we find in the Old Testament is confirmed by similar teaching in the New Testament. Fatherhood involves instruction. The unmarried apostle Paul can tell the Corinthians that he is their father, because he has "begotten [them] through the gospel" (1 Cor. 4:15). For the same reason, he calls Timothy, Titus, and Onesimus his children (1 Cor. 4:17; 1 Tim. 1:2; Titus 1:4; Philem. 10).

We might also recall what Jesus taught in a more general way about family relationships. The woman who pronounced a beatitude upon the mother of Jesus, who carried Him in her womb and nursed Him at her breasts, heard from Jesus that the *genuine* family relationship is characterized by listening to God's word: "Blessed are those who hear the word of God and keep it!" (Luke 11:27–28). Jesus said something similar to those who told Him that His mother and brothers were standing outside and wanted to speak to Him. Pointing to His disciples, He said: "Here are My mother and My brothers! For whoever does the will of My Father in heaven is My brother and sister and mother" (Matt. 12:46–50).*

We are reminded of the role of "tradition" in the theory we explained earlier, the duty of passing on from one generation to the next the knowledge attained by parents. We might put it this way: In Israel parenthood functioned properly when parents preserved God's word in their own hearts and handed it on to their children.

Biological, physical parenthood obtained its value from the parents instructing their children in the commandments, ordinances, and precepts commanded by the Lord (Deut. 6:1). That view of tradition goes much

---

* Karl Barth quite correctly identifies this connection between the fifth commandment and instruction in his *Church Dogmatics*, 3/4: 253–55.

deeper than the theory we set forth above. It is surely true that parents (still) play an important role in transmitting knowledge and skills that render an inexperienced child competent to function in the world. In every generation people must make their own history part of their identity in order to move ahead into the future. And drawing that connection between the past and the future makes having parents very important. But that is not yet the core of parenthood according to Scripture. For the Bible talks about imprinting knowledge that is decisively important for the *quality* of life. The Bible talks about living *with* God. Of course, that includes nurture, instruction, choice of occupation, and providing children with direction in this world, but it includes far more. This living encompasses a relationship with God. The fear of Yahweh is the beginning of knowledge (Prov. 1:7). "Seek the LORD and live" (Amos 5:6). It can even be said: "Your lovingkindness is *better* than life" (Ps. 63:3; cf. 73:26; Hab. 3:17–19).

By drawing a connection between parenthood and instruction, we are not saying that instruction is exclusively the task of parents. That was not the case in Israel. We read of guardians and governesses who brought up children (Num. 11:12; Isa. 49:23; 2 Kings 10:1, 5; Est. 2:7), whose task we may properly consider to have been primarily instruction. Priests and Levites taught the Scriptures. The book of Proverbs is a demonstration of how someone other than the father performed the role of father in giving instruction. Later the rabbinic schools would become centers of instruction. We must be careful not to assign a low standard to the level of education in the ancient Near East, including instruction in various skills. In Egypt, Moses received an excellent education—"learned in all the wisdom of the Egyptians" (Acts 7:22)—and even an ordinary fellow from Succoth could apparently read and write (Judg. 8:14).

Developments leading to institutionalizing most education outside the family have continued. It would be foolish to ignore these developments and to insist that education should fall entirely to the parents. But it would be just as wrong to deny the significance in our modern world of parents as teachers of their children. Ultimately it is *the parents* who are responsible for their children's instruction, even if it can and occasionally must be given by others.

The early years of a child's life are very important, for these are the years when it is almost exclusively the parents who nurture their children. Also important is the child's early learning of Bible stories and songs and prayers, most of it obtained at home. Parents must think carefully about which school they will use for their children's education. Just as important is the atmosphere children encounter at home, where often they sense clearly whether what they are hearing from the Bible is being put into practice.

Parenthood and Freedom

What we have been saying thus far helps us understand better that the fifth commandment involves *freedom*, as formulated in the prologue of the Ten Commandments: "I am Yahweh your God, who brought you out of Egypt, out of the house of slavery."

We can illustrate the connection between the fifth commandment and freedom quite well from Deuteronomy 6. Israel received the mandate to impress deeply upon her sons (children) all of Yahweh's commandments. Those commands arouse questions from the children: "What is the meaning of the testimonies, the statutes, and the judgments which the LORD our God has commanded you?" they might ask their father (Deut. 6:20). The answer given was to be an indirect answer, not a direct one. *First* the father would tell the story of Israel's bondage in Egypt and of the Lord's deliverance from Egypt. *Then* the story would be concluded: "And the LORD commanded us to observe all these statutes, to fear the LORD our God, for our good always, that He might preserve us alive, as it is this day" (Deut. 6:24). First came the gospel of liberation; then the avenue for *staying* liberated was explained. Israel's well-being was connected with listening to and obeying God's commandments. But then it becomes clear how important instruction in God's commandments was. Israel retained her freedom in the Promised Land when her sons and daughters obeyed their parent-teachers.

The Commandment with a Promise

We should understand the promise added to the fifth commandment in that light.* Yahweh rewards children who honor their parents who have

---

* Eph. 6:2 calls the command to "honor your father and mother" (according to the most common translation) the *first* commandment with a promise. Often interpreters will observe that the second commandment also contains a promise: "I show favor to the most extended generation imaginable, if they are faithful to me and respect my commandments." The common explanation is that the second commandment supposedly contains a *general* promise that applies not simply to one commandment, but to the entire service of God and to all the commandments (thus Calvin, *Institutes*, 2.8.37). The fifth commandment was understood, then, to be the first one with a *special* promise.

But interpreters are making the matter more difficult than it really is. The translation passed on to them His commandments. Such children will enjoy a long life in the Promised Land (Ex. 20:12), and it will go well for them there (Deut. 5:16).

We should not absolutize this promise, but neither should we downplay it. It is not a rule without exceptions, not even among Israel. Abijah, the sick son of Jeroboam, died young, even though he was the only one in Jeroboam's family in whom any good was found. Not a long life, but an honorable burial was his portion, in contrast to others in Jeroboam's family who did not enjoy even that dignity (1 Kings 14:13). Death can even be a blessing, since it spares people much misery, as in the case of King Josiah (2 Kings 22:20).

So it may "go well" with someone (Deut. 5:16) even though they die. People like Abraham, Isaac, and Job died at a time when they were *full* of living (Gen. 25:8; 35:29; Job 42:17). A long life is not always a blessing. Someone who is strong might live to be eighty, but—the psalmist adds—everything still bears the mark of transiency, of trouble and sorrow (Ps. 90:10).

Life leaves a lot unexplained. People in Israel knew that just as well as we do. Why do the godless get to keep on living, growing old and going peacefully to the grave (Job 21:7, 13)? The oppressed shed tears because they have no comforter, while their oppressors enjoy power and strength. So the Preacher praises the dead above the living (Eccl. 4:1–2). God does settle accounts with the godless (Ps. 73:17; 92:8), but not always in the sense that *they* get to live only a short time and the *righteous* get to live long.

For that reason, the promise attached to the fifth commandment can never be understood in an absolute sense. We echo earlier commentators on this commandment: A long life is a demonstration of His grace for those who fear the Lord, but His own glory or the salvation of the elect could make a short life advisable, too.* Moreover, in the New Testament

---

of Eph. 6:2 need not be, "It is the *first* commandment with a promise." Just as permissible is the rendering, "It is a commandment of the *greatest importance*, with the promise attached." The Greek word *prōtos* can mean "first, foremost, most important, most prominent" (see Walter Bauer, *A Greek-English Lexicon of the New Testament and Other Early Christian Literature*, trans. W. F. Arndt and F. Wilbur Gingrich, rev. Frederick W. Danker [Chicago, 1979], s.v.).

 * See, for example, J. H. Alstedt, *Theologica catechetica* (Hannover, 1622), 587. See also Calvin, *Institutes*, 2.8.37: We are promised long life insofar as it is a blessing of God, and it is a blessing only insofar as it is an evidence of God's favor. But He can testify of His grace far more richly and substantially through death.

era we realize that we are citizens of a commonwealth in heaven (Phil. 3:20) and not of an earthly Canaan. Therefore, the promise of the fifth commandment remains valid. Otherwise Paul would not have mentioned it in Ephesians 6:2. But this kind of promise obtains a deeper and broader reach through the work of Christ. The earthly Canaan makes way for the kingdom of heaven, and our still all-too-brief life on earth lies under the promise of eternal life in heaven and on the new earth.

On the other hand, we must be careful not to downplay the promise and make the exception (a short life here on earth) the rule! For the rule remains valid: Anyone who honors his parents (and thus accepts God's commandments through them) will receive benefit from doing so, not only in a life after this life, but also already here and now. That was true for Israel in the Promised Land, but applies just as well today in the New Testament dispensation, when the connection to the land of Canaan has fallen away. Now too we may say that godliness is profitable for all things, because it holds promise for life, both for *today* and for the future (1 Tim. 4:8).

We should apply that very concretely to our parent-child relationships. Children are inexperienced, and for that reason are accident-prone, not only when they are small, but also when they grow older en route to adulthood. The book of Proverbs provides an excellent illustration of that. Why does the "father" teach his "son"? Because his son must learn wisdom, which gives long life (Prov. 3:16). That wisdom is very practical. Various warnings against a sinful and dangerous life are given to the son. He must not hang around robbers who lie in wait to commit violence, because that will cost him his life (Prov. 1:10–16). He must avoid the seductive net of an immoral woman, because her house will lead to death (Prov. 2:16–18; 7:26–27). Foolishness—otherwise translated *stupidity*—leads a person to the house of a prostitute. Such a fool will die, because he lacks discipline; he strays because of his great stupidity (Prov. 5:23). The same thing happens when you are lazy. Laziness is your destruction. The desires of the lazy man are his death; he refuses to use his hands (Prov. 6:15; 21:25).

Fools die through lack of understanding, whereas its opposite, the good use of understanding, is a fountain of life (Prov. 10:21; 16:22). The way of sin leads to death (Prov. 12:28), but righteousness rescues a man from death (Prov. 10:2; 11:4). The upright will dwell in the land, but the unfaithful will be uprooted from it (Prov. 2:21–22).

So there is a very direct connection between instruction and life, between despising instruction and death. Receiving a long life is a gift from the Lord, but quite understandably this gift is tied to the fifth commandment. Very young children must be warned about poisonous containers, about fire, and about cars on the street. A few years later, they learn from their parents and others the teaching that God gives in His law—how dangerous it is to have bad friends, to use drugs, to play with sex, or to marry the wrong person. Wisdom, drawn from the law of God, guarantees long life; stupidity ends in death. Gaining wisdom is thus not only a spiritual matter, but also a physical attainment of great benefit.

Parenthood and Discipline

In light of what we have been learning, it is not surprising that *discipline* is so important. Discipline is not designed for fathers to let off steam. If that needs to happen, then it is not discipline that is called for. We must discipline our children in wisdom, not by impulse. Chastisement is a bitter pill that must be coated with wisdom and dispensed with love; otherwise, the pill will be spit out.[1] Discipline applied at just the right moment is effective medicine. One who shrinks from discipline does not love his child, but one who loves his child disciplines him while he is young (cf. Prov. 13:24). A child will not die from a spanking. He might hurt for a while, but . . . his soul is saved from hell (Prov. 13:13–14). Here again is the familiar theme: discipline is lifesaving.

As parents, we might use strong expressions like "You had better not try it!" or "Keep your hands off!" or "Don't even think about it!" But they become empty threats if they are not supported by discipline—possibly in the form of a whack on the backside. If they will not listen, they had better feel it. Eli was guilty of permitting his sons, who were priests, various forms of godless behavior and refusing to punish them (1 Sam. 3:13). That seems strange, especially when we read earlier that he had spoken to his sons about the nasty rumors he had heard about their conduct (2:23–25). Eli was undoubtedly a pious man who was grieved by his sons' actions, but he never got around to punishing them by using all the means at his disposal as father, priest, and leader of Israel. Even righteous people can be too soft, with far-reaching consequences, as we learn from the history of Israel in the time of Eli.

At the time it is given, punishment is anything but pleasurable, but one who has allowed parental discipline to do its work will later pick the fruit (Heb. 12:11). How much crooked growth could have been prevented among children if, during their childhood years, they had not been spoiled and had received a stricter upbringing! One commentator observed concerning the mission field where he had labored that, just as clearly happens among us, the attitude of "I don't want to" turns little children into little tyrants who can always win by force and perseverance.[2]

It is a serious fallacy to think that we must permit our children to make important life choices on their own. "You should give them plenty of freedom" sounds very open-minded, but is really very naive. All children grow up in a particular setting where choices are made that leave them no longer free. For example, limiting ourselves to the area of religious nurture, if parents do not take the family to church, a choice is already being made for the children. If at home children never hear people talking about God and His service, nobody should claim that these children are being "left free" to choose regarding faith in God. During the childhood years, very significant decisions with lifelong consequences are being made *for* the children and not *by* the children.

Naturally this applies as well to nurture in a Christian family. There, too, a lot has been decided for the children while they are en route to adulthood, before they begin making their own choices. If you want to talk about freedom in this context, that's fine, but then in an entirely different sense than "You should give them plenty of freedom." Recall what we have said earlier about the fifth commandment and freedom. A person is truly free when he loves God and keeps His commandments. Children raised this way get what is coming to them, on the basis of the covenant God made with believers *and* their children.

Quite properly, parents commit themselves to this kind of child rearing when they present their child for baptism. With John they can say, "I have no greater joy than to hear that my children walk in truth" (3 John 4).[*]

This kind of verse presupposes that things could go differently. Children can follow a wrong path, in spite of their good upbringing by their parents. Parents are deeply grieved when their children leave the good path and do not fear God. No matter how right it is for parents to nurture their children in a particular direction, they cannot force faith, for faith is a gift of God (Eph. 2:8). Grace is an inheritance. Nobody is saved *because*

---

* The apostle John is using the word "children" not to mean "children according to the flesh," but, more broadly, in the sense of "children begotten by the gospel." But parents can still find in this verse an expression of their feelings toward their believing children. In the same spirit the apocryphal book Sirach says, "Whoever honors his father will live long, and whoever obeys the Lord will bring rest to his mother" (3:6). Here "rest" can refer to dying in peace. See the commentary on this passage by A. van den Born, *Wijsheid van Jezus Sirach* (Roermond, 1968), who refers to other passages in Jesus Sirach (22:11; 39:15). If children walk in the right path, parents can lay their heads down with quiet confidence.

his or her parents were believers, no matter how important for proper nurture it is that parents are believers.

The choice for God and for the church must be the child's own choice. Parents can warn children to make the right choice, even when these children are adults, but you cannot force them to make the right choice. Discipline has stages and limits. You cannot treat a fifteen-year-old lad as if he were a little boy, and when legally he is an adult, his parents can still advise a course of action, but can no longer compel him to follow it.

Moreover, the arm of parents does not reach as far in our modern world as in theocratic Israel. A rebellious son who was a glutton and a drunkard, who would "not obey the voice of his father or the voice of his mother, and who, when they have chastened him, [would] not heed them," had to be separated from the community by death through stoning (Deut. 21:18–21). A son who went to serve other gods was not to be pitied, but to be put to death. His own father had to throw the first stone (Deut. 13:6–11). The thing that impresses us here again is how *freedom* was at stake: "And you shall stone him with stones until he dies, because he sought to entice you away from the LORD your God, who brought you out of the land of Egypt, from the house of bondage" (Deut. 13:10). That deliverance from Egypt was not to be endangered, which would have happened if the worship of other gods had gained a foothold in Israel.

However, even though this kind of capital punishment is no longer possible today, the underlying principle does remain valid. Anyone who despises the freedom granted only in covenant with God is committing a serious sin. He is playing with his life. Even though our life is no longer being lived in Canaan, we do serve the same God and are obligated to keep the same commandment. No less than in the Old Testament, it is stupid and foolish to disobey parents when they point us in the way of life, the way of faith in Jesus Christ.

Honoring Parents

Children are called to *honor* their parents, according to the fifth commandment. We discussed this word earlier, when we treated the third commandment. In Hebrew, the word used for "honor" is one whose basic meaning is "heavy." Someone who must be honored is someone of weight. That is true also of parents. They are placed by God over their children and they share some of the *kabod*, the glory or the honor belonging to God. In this connection, we might think of what Paul wrote about bowing his knees before the Father, from whom every "fatherhood" (as it says literally) in heaven and on earth is named (Eph. 3:14–19). For that reason, fathers and mothers may demand respect for their office as parents.

The opposite of respect is disrespect. Something weighty is treated as if it were light. That comes to expression quite clearly in Hebrew usage. Frequently a warning is given against "cursing" father and mother (Ex. 21:17; Lev. 20:9; Prov. 20:20; 30:11), where a word is used whose basic meaning refers to something indecent or despicable. Figuratively speaking, a child sticks his tongue out at his parents, which means he views them as nothings.

We have seen how serious this wickedness is, even if it involves aged parents. Their "glory" remains, even though they are beyond the prime of life. Even when parents can no longer *function* (see above), we must still continue to respect them. The fifth commandment is relevant also to the question of euthanasia. If euthanasia becomes legalized, it will be easier to dispose of any life thought to be without dignity. But the fifth commandment requires us to honor our parents, even if they become (to all appearances) useless and a burden to society. "My child, support your father in his old age, do not grieve him during his life. Even if his mind should fail, show him sympathy, do not despise him in your health and strength" (Sirach 3:12–13).*

Honoring parents involves several aspects. Naturally the notion of honor means that children will *take to heart* the *instruction* given by their parents. In this way they submit to the "good instruction" of their parents, as the Heidelberg Catechism puts it (Lord's Day 39). To honor is to listen, to hear-ken (hear carefully) to their instruction. Further, to honor is to *show deference toward* parents, because they are placed over children and therefore deserve respect. This deference can be expressed in various ways. Rachel addressed her father with the phrase "my lord" (Gen. 31:35), and Solomon bowed down before his mother when he went to visit her, although by that time he had become king (1 Kings 2:19). Among us things are not so formal, but we may still expect children to show deference to their parents by their language and forms of address. Children must let their parents speak first, answer respectfully, be quiet when parents are speaking to them, say "thank you" when they receive something from them, and the like.

Using good manners shows respect for those relationships in which we cannot simply "let ourselves go." Manners are the brakes that conscience

---

* This deuterocanonical book is also known as Ecclesiasticus; our rendering is that of *The New Jerusalem Bible* (Garden City, 1985), 1082.

provides to slow us down in thinking only about ourselves and our own pleasure. This is why etiquette is such an important part of a moral disposition. The primary and most decisive schooling in this subject that we will receive for our entire lives happens in the home. What we learn (or fail to learn) there will have good (or bad) repercussions in other relationships across the entire range of the social order.

Honoring parents also includes *loving* them, even though the Bible nowhere explicitly says that children must love their parents. But this is self-evident; if the general rule of loving our neighbor as ourselves is binding, surely this applies as well to children loving their parents.

Parental love for their children is a universal phenomenon. Children are their flesh and blood, their pride and their future. Parents will endure trouble and poverty so that their children can have it good. People say, and rightly so, that many parents bend over backwards for their children. The reverse is far more difficult, namely, that children bend over backwards for their parents. In this context, love is especially a form of gratitude, a way of giving back something to our parents for all they have meant and still mean to us. Love takes us beyond the obvious truth that parents are for children and not children for parents. When we ourselves become members of the "middle" generation and observe how our own children are no different than we were at their age, suddenly the deficiencies in our love toward mother and father hit us with force.

Honoring involves also *being faithful*. Children must put this into practice especially when their parents become old and invalid. Financial provision may be less of a concern now than in former times, due to various retirement and insurance benefits. However, Christians do object to programs of government social insurance that tend to remove the stimulus for children to provide financially for their needy parents.

Without doubt, children must honor their parents here too, in the matter of helping out where there is financial need (Matt. 15:4–9; 1 Tim. 5:4). But needy parents need have no qualms of conscience about accepting the kind of financial help to which the laws of the land give them access.[3] In such circumstances, the task of children is far more one of spiritual support, visiting parents and easing their loneliness, which so easily comes along with becoming an invalid or growing old. Nobody will die from poverty nowadays, since in many of our countries welfare programs have virtually eliminated poverty, or at least should have done so. But in many of these same countries we are now facing a growing demand for euthanasia by people who, though provided for financially, are nonetheless languishing in loneliness. It would be truly sad if among Christians—beginning in the family and among friends—the faithfulness toward parents, required by the fifth commandment, would disappear.

Honoring Parents and Choosing a Spouse

There is one aspect to "honoring parents" that we would like to isolate for special attention. If you consult older commentaries on the fifth commandment, you will discover repeated discussion about the task of parents with respect to their children's courtship and choice of a marriage partner.

Often conflicts arise between parents and children regarding dating and marriage plans. That is understandable, since along with the dating partner comes an entirely different family and context altogether, something that can cause friction if parents fear that their son or daughter is walking down a wrong spiritual path.

In former times, the influence of parents in the whole matter of their children's choice of a marriage partner was far greater than today. We see this in the Bible when, for example, in 1 Corinthians 7:25–40 (especially v. 38) we read that a father was free to give or not to give his daughter in marriage. That is not done today, and children whose parents chose a marriage partner for them would properly view this as wrong.

Nevertheless, parents do have a say about such a serious decision in their child's life. It is more than a friendly gesture toward their parents when children state on their wedding invitations that "the parents of so-and-so" are pleased to announce the upcoming marriage of their son or daughter. Older wedding forms used to speak of marrying "with the knowledge and consent of parents or guardians." This is the usual custom.

Children are not honoring their parents by treating courtship and marriage as strictly private matters beyond parental control. Serious dating means the son or daughter is preparing to "leave his father and mother" (Gen. 2:24), and parents should be able to talk with their children about this departure. Think of it this way: "For twenty years or so these parents have been providing for their child with a lot of effort and enthusiasm; now the child begins to date, but considers it inane to have to discuss the matter with his or her parents. After all, it's none of their business, right? You can see why these parents would be deeply hurt and disappointed!"[4]

Nowadays parents do not choose marriage partners for their children. But they still have a right to be involved in the choice. That right becomes all the stronger if they see their son or daughter taking a wrong spiritual turn in dating. We are thinking here of "mixed dating," which often leads to "mixed marriages," where one partner is a member of another denomination or of no church at all. Of course, just because the two are from the same denomination does not *by itself* justify getting married. Unfortunately, sometimes church members live like the unchurched. So when parents see their child making some wrong choices, it is their responsibility to warn against those choices and (if it is still within their power) to forbid their child from beginning that kind of dating relationship. Children honor their parents by accepting this kind of correction.

The opposite can also occur, namely, that the child makes a good choice which the parents either have not fully accepted or wrongly oppose. That situation, too, calls for respecting one's parents, *not* by giving up the guy or gal for the sake of peace in the family, but by discussing courtship and marriage plans openly and honestly, and by being as patient as possible. If love should grow between the couple, and they become convinced that God Himself has brought them together, no parental force may or can impede such a marriage. If the children have done all they can to persuade their parents, but without success, they may get married with a clear conscience without parental permission, using the legal rights afforded them by civil law.

The Limits and Style of Obedience

There are limits to the obedience that children should render to their parents. Giving respect is different from worshiping. Over the parents stands God Himself, and it can be necessary for children to choose for Him and against their parents.

This becomes clear by considering once more the function assigned to parents. Theirs is the task of teaching children about God and His service. But when parents do the exact opposite, children (who know better) are not obligated to follow the instruction of their parents. They might have to act without their parents. Abraham's life became significant at that point when he left "his father's house." Ruth came to occupy an important position among the women of Israel when she left her parents and her country behind. Hezekiah radically rejected the upbringing of his godless father Ahaz and instead followed the path of his "father" David (2 Kings 18:3).[5]

Calvin formulates the matter clearly.

> For they [parents] sit in that place to which they have been advanced by the Lord, who shares with them a part of his honor. Therefore, the submission paid to them ought to be a step toward

honoring that highest Father. Hence, if they spur us to transgress the law, we have a perfect right to regard them not as parents, but as strangers who are trying to lead us away from obedience to our true Father. . . . It is unworthy and absurd for their eminence so to prevail as to pull down the loftiness of God. On the contrary, their eminence depends upon God's loftiness and ought to lead us to it.[6]

That is put rather strongly: view one's parents as strangers. But this can happen if their course goes against choosing for Christ. In the kingdom of heaven, it can be necessary to forego burying one's own father in order to follow Jesus (Luke 9:59–60). Anyone who loves father or mother more than Me, said Jesus, is not worthy of Me (Matt. 10:37). Anyone who is unable to hate father and mother cannot be His disciple (Luke 14:26).

This is a bold saying, especially when we recall that the words used in the Bible for "hate" can have the softer meaning of "neglect." If it comes down to a choice between God or one's parents, children must choose against their parents and for God. That would be a sad situation for parents and a serious difficulty in the life of the children, who would prefer that it could be otherwise. But the honor due to parents always bears a creaturely character and can never be paid at the cost of the honor we owe to the triune God. Giving honor to the creature is different than worship and can come into conflict with our duty to obey God rather than man (Acts 4:29).

Obviously, one must not seize too quickly the possibility of denying obedience to one's parents. Saying no to them at one point, no matter how serious that point, does not imply total rejection of one's parents. When a grown child's lifestyle differs quite radically from what he was raised with, he must take care not to be at fault for growing apart from his parents. This kind of situation is quite possible if a child comes to faith in Christ and thereby becomes estranged from the context within which he grew up.

Paul found it possible for an unbeliever and a believer to stay together in a marriage (1 Cor. 7:12–16). In the same way, surely, children of unbelieving parents must remember that a spiritual rift does not yet entail or require cutting all natural ties.

Faith and unbelief do not always need to be positioned as radical opponents, for then serious difficulties can arise between parents and children. Moving from one denomination to another through marriage can generate problems. For example, someone who grew up Roman Catholic who becomes a member of a Reformed church will readily see how deeply the differences permeate life, down to the smallest detail. Wisdom is required, therefore, in order to be honest in expressing one's faith-convictions while seeking at the same time to maintain family relationships. If family bonds are broken in spite of efforts to preserve them, the obligation remains to seek to restore broken relationships wherever possible.

It goes without saying that parents may not do with their children as they please. Children may be punished, but not abused. Tyrannical parents who drive their children like slaves forfeit their right to be called parents. Abusing their children sexually or letting them be sexually abused is wicked. Incest occurs even in Christian circles. Anyone who knows anything about incest realizes how much courage it takes for a girl who has been sexually abused by her father to confide in *anybody*. For most children, the parental home is a place of security, but for some it is the place where they are destroyed for life.

Naturally, problems between parents and children are rarely of the kind where a choice "for or against Christ" is required. Parents have weaknesses and inadequacies, which children must deal with patiently. Often children cannot find the patience needed, and sometimes it is very hard to exercise patience. Children can make life miserable for their parents, but parents can do the same for their children. "Fathers, do not provoke your children, lest they become discouraged" (Col. 3:21). Always ordering children around, always carping and finding fault, will anger and exasperate them. They might obey without back talk, but a grudge will begin to grow and will eventually explode.

Children easily sense when their parents' talk and walk do not match. Outsiders may think so-and-so are happily married and have such a nice family, but the children know what happens inside the home. They know it so well that they soon begin making plans so that, when *they* get married and have children, they will do things differently than their parents are now doing.

That intention is fine, since it often arises from a clear understanding of the sins and faults that children have spotted in their parents. But children often lack self-knowledge. When they have their own families, they soon realize that *all* parents are sinners. For that reason, the family must be a classroom for learning patience and for realizing that parents too have serious faults. Children must learn resilience, even the kind that can accept punishment that is not always administered fairly.

When they learn to do this, they begin to show in their own lives what obedience "in the Lord (Jesus Christ)" really is. These words, encountered especially in Paul's epistles, provide an excellent description of the limit and style of obedience.

We have already discussed the *limit* of obedience. We might describe that limit this way: Children must obey their parents only "in the Lord" (Eph. 6:1; Col. 3:20). Obedience is no longer proper if, out of respect for their parents, they choose *against* the Lord.

And what about the *style* of obedience? The phrase "in the Lord" also indicates that we must obey as the Lord Jesus Himself obeyed. As a child, He could spot the sins and faults of His own parents better than we can see those of our parents. Moreover, Christ must have suffered under His parents more than we suffer under ours! As young as He was, He did not shrink from mentioning something about this (Luke 2:49). But if we look at the style with which He treated His parents, then we read that He "was subject to them" (Luke 2:51).

To obey "in the Lord" means, then, that our parents must be doing things quite wrong before we refuse to obey. Christ exercised patience, so that Peter could tell slaves to obey their masters not only when they were kind and gentle, but also when they were harsh, because Christ had suffered much while He lived on earth (1 Peter 2:18–24).

Times change, and, along with them, so does the way children relate to parents and servants to masters. But the style of our obedience must remain Christian, which means: it must correspond to what Christ did. Honoring those who are over us requires, then, that we must be ready to endure a lot.

Other Forms of Authority

The fifth commandment covers other forms of authority as well. Is it exegetically warranted to extend honoring "father and mother" to include the honor due to "all in authority over me" (Heidelberg Catechism, Lord's Day 39), so that this commandment envisions also the government official, the elder, and the school teacher?

That seems entirely justified when we investigate the broad sense in which the Bible speaks of fatherhood. There is many a "father" to whom appropriate honor and obedience are due.

Fathers could become tribal heads, like Shem (Gen. 10:21) and Abraham, who became "a father of many nations" (Gen. 17:4). The distinction was rather fluid between one's "elders" (meaning parents) and those with authority who are the oldest.* Heads of families and elders exercised au-

---

* *Translator's note:* The original reads, "Tussen 'ouder' en 'oudste' is de grens vloeiend."

thority in society (Ex. 12:21; Deut. 5:23). Elders sat by the city gate to administer justice (Deut. 22:15; Job 29:7). Paternal authority flowed naturally from the household and family to the court and the state.

Thus, the king is called "father," as David addressed Saul (1 Sam. 24:12). That applied to other preeminent persons as well. Naaman's servants called their military leader "father" (2 Kings 5:13). The name Abimelech (literally, "father is king") combines the terms father and king.* Just as a king could be called "father," so too a woman like Deborah could refer to herself as "a mother in Israel" (Judg. 5:7).

Clearly, the source of royal authority must be seen to lie in the fatherhood of God. Solomon's throne is established as long as Yahweh was his father and he was Yahweh's son (2 Sam. 7:13–16).

In these relationships of authority, the concept of fatherhood indicates the possession of wisdom and insight. Joseph was appointed to be Pharaoh's father, a position in which he became advisor to the ruler and enjoyed wide influence (Gen. 45:8). Solomon could assume his royal duties because he had received wisdom in answer to his prayer (1 Kings 3:9–12).

Earlier we saw that instruction created a father-son relationship between, for example, the "son" and the one instructing him in wisdom (Proverbs). Elisha called Elijah his father (2 Kings 2:12), influenced as he was by this great prophet.

The honor due to father and mother must therefore be given to all those other "fathers" and "mothers." A child stood up when his mother entered the room, as King Solomon did (1 Kings 2:19). People were to stand up out of respect for "gray hair": "You shall rise before the gray headed and honor the presence of an old man, and fear your God: I am the LORD" (Lev. 19:32). People showed honor to kings (Dan. 2:37; 5:18), before whom they bowed (2 Sam. 18:28; 1 Kings 1:23).

The king was to be shown deference and not to be despised (cursed). "Do not curse the king, even in your thought" (Eccl. 10:20). Gaal did precisely that, quite openly, when he cursed Abimelech of Shechem. The text shows us clearly what that meant. This king was being mocked: "Who is Abimelech, . . . that we should serve him?" (Judg. 9:27–29). Someone

---

* Some suggest that the name Abimelech was not a personal name, but an official title. Comparison is made between 1 Sam. 21:11 and the title above Ps. 34. Achish, prince of Gath, is thought to be the same as the Abimelech mentioned in the title of Ps. 34. Thus, "Abimelech" would have been a title similar to "Pharaoh," a title used for Egyptian kings. See W. C. Kaiser, Jr., "Abimelech," in *Zondervan Pictorial Encyclopedia of the Bible* (Grand Rapids, 1975), 1:15–16.

whose eminence is "weighty" is treated as if he were a featherweight. The same thing was done to David by Nabal (1 Sam. 25:10) and by Shimei. This latter called the king a "rogue," which means something like a "bum" or a "clod" (2 Sam. 16:7). This kind of attitude is a far cry from what Peter commands: "Fear God. Honor the king" (1 Peter 2:17).

The honor due to parents, the elderly, judges, princes, and teachers includes the duty to obey. Paul instructs children on the basis of the fifth commandment to obey. Immediately thereafter, he writes about the obedience that slaves owe to their masters (Eph. 6:1–3, 5–8). Even the husband-wife relationship, in which the wife is obligated to obey her husband, appears in the same series of instructions (Eph. 5:24, 33). Later on in the New Testament we read that leaders in the church must be obeyed (Heb. 13:17), or more generally that the younger men in the church must be subject to the older (oldest) ones (1 Peter 5:5).

Very clearly, obedience is required toward governments (Rom. 13:1–7; Titus 3:1; 1 Peter 2:13–17).

A survey of all this information makes it difficult to deny that dealing with the specific relationship between children and parents involves authority relationships in general. It is certainly true that in earlier times authority functioned in a much more *patriarchal* fashion than now.* The Ten Commandments are clothed in the robes of ancient Israel, with its strongly family-oriented authority structures. Dynastic royalty, something we still have today, is a remnant of the connection (much stronger in ancient times) between blood and authority.

Today the face of authority looks far less patriarchal than in earlier times. We no longer refer to those who exercise authority beyond the family circle as "father." But the same issue is involved today as back then: authority,† honor, obedience. Analyzing this in

---

* This word *patriarchal* in fact nicely expresses the connection between paternal authority and other forms of authority. The father exercises authority within a wide circle.

† Von Meyenfeldt, *Tien tegen een*, 42, insists that the Bible never mentions authority as such. The Bible does speak about people exercising power, but not about authority. This claim is all the more remarkable in view of the many different words used in the Old and New Testaments for "power," "authority," "authorization," and the like. It becomes still more incredible when Von Meyenfeldt seeks to back it up by insisting that in the Bible, "rendering obedience to someone" ordinarily rests on the fact that "this someone is stronger than the rest or more clever, or part of a ruling family or anointed by a prophet." We find such a claim hard to defend, since the Bible describes for us people who were to render obedience *in the Lord* within various authority relationships. Why else would the phrases "fear God" and "honor the king" be spoken in the same breath by Peter (1 Peter 2:17)?

light of Scripture requires the luminescence of the fifth commandment.*

Different Forms, Different Words

Even though we are discussing the same issues that occupied earlier
commentators, nevertheless many authority relationships now have a different look. The husband-wife relationship is not as it used to be. Back in
1918, Herman Bavinck mentioned the objection women were leveling
against the marital promise to be "submissive to their own husbands, as
Sarah obeyed Abraham, calling him lord" (1 Peter 3:5-6).[7]

This passage appeared in the liturgical form used for weddings in the
Reformed Churches of the Netherlands before 1933, but was later removed by the general synod. Nevertheless, the synod retained the duty of
the wife to obey her husband in all things right and fair, honoring him as
"lord." Since then, the word "lord" has also disappeared, and in the most
recent wedding form included in the *Reformed Book of Worship* (1986), we
read simply that the wife must follow her husband's leading "obediently."
The bride's vow in this wedding form lacks the word "obey," and the bride
promises to follow her husband "in love."

The term "follow" contains the notion of a certain rank and authority
relationship. After all, the Bible does teach that the (married) man is
the head of the (married) woman, and that this relationship rests on the
fact that Adam was created first, and then Eve (1 Cor. 11:3; 1 Tim.
2:13). But even though the fundamental structure abides, cultural
changes can necessitate choosing other words than those used in earlier
wedding ceremonies.

A similar change has occurred in the master-servant relationship. Servants are no longer slaves, serfs, or chattel property, but free citizens who
voluntarily enter into contract with an employer. Their employer no
longer has his personnel at his disposal, as could have happened in former
centuries. Such developments change the texture of authority, without

---

* B. de Moor, *Commentarius perpetuus in Johannis Marckii compendium* (Leiden, 1763),
2:838, mentions that the Remonstrants were of the opinion that others besides parents
who were in authority *could* have been in view in the fifth commandment, and have *come
to be* discussed in connection with the fifth commandment, but that this does not mean
their authority flows forth from the fifth commandment. However, if you accept the patriarchal origin of various forms of authority, you need not restrict the breadth of the fifth
commandment so narrowly.

causing the *concept* of authority to disappear from the employer-employee relationship.[*]

Authority relationships in the political sphere, once very strong in certain parts of the world, are also changing. In particular, the introduction of democratic elections has broadened the exercise of political influence, so that it flows not only from the top down, but also from the bottom up, especially through political parties. Many political dynasties have disappeared, and where they continue, their power bears a limited and representative character. Not the king, but the president, premier, or prime minister has become responsible for political administration.

Nevertheless, it would not be correct to suggest that governmental authority no longer exists today. The word *democracy* (literally, "rule by the people") does not mean the absence of government over the people, but rather that such a government has been chosen by the people.[†] Once a government democratically chosen by the people is in power, the instructions of Romans 13 apply to such a government just as much as to any other government.

So we may argue that *authority* relationships remain, even though these relationships look a lot different than they used to. Occasionally this might mean that our description of this authority will employ different language than formerly. In the Bible, the same word is used for "obey" in the relationships between parents and children, husband and wife, masters and servants, as well as government and citizens (Luke 2:51; Col. 3:18; Titus 2:9; Rom. 13:1).[‡] This kind of usage indicates that similar relationships were put on the same level in earlier times and probably treated in that way as well. But now that is no longer the case. Authority and subjection, said Herman Bavinck, can never be destroyed in principle, because without authority and subjection an ordered society cannot exist. Nevertheless, authority and subjection no longer have the same

---

[*] For further discussion of the authority relationship between employer and employee, see J. Douma, *Vrede in de maatschappij* (Kampen, 1986), 170–78.

[†] "Democracy" is not a phenomenon appearing for the first time after the French Revolution. John Calvin, for example, was acquainted with the word and the concept. See his *Institutes*, 4.20.8 (French edition). According to Calvin, monarchy, aristocracy, and democracy are all worthy of consideration, although he preferred a mixture of aristocracy and democracy.

[‡] We have in mind the Greek word *hupotassō*, found not only in the texts already mentioned, but also in 1 Peter 5:5 (older men and younger men) and 1 Cor. 15:20 (God and all people).

kind of adversarial quality they used to have. "They have come closer to one another and have reached a kind of equilibrium."[8]

All of this means that we should take these changes into account in our usage. The subjection rendered by children to their parents we now distinguish from that rendered by a wife to her husband. *Both* cases involve authority exercised by one party over the other, according to God's ordination. But although we can use terms like "subjection" and "subservience" to describe what children owe their parents, these are out-of-date for describing the attitude of a wife toward her husband. Instead of a wife "rendering obedience to" her husband we have come to speak of a wife "following her husband's leading." This latter expression harvests the good fruit both of modern emancipation movements and of the scripturally described relationship between husband and wife.

The same applies to the employer-employee relationship. Whereas children must obey their parents, employees must conform to the policies of their superiors. The "obedience" of former slaves has given way to accepting policy directives on the basis of contractual obligations which are voluntarily assumed and can also be voluntarily relinquished.

Authority and Power

Any consideration of authority, whether of parents, employers, government officials, or anyone else, must include attention to the nature of *power*. We can easily perceive that the concepts of authority and power are not identical. A person can possess authority without having the power needed for carrying out his authority. Think, for example, of the Dutch government during World War II, seated temporarily in London, but without the power needed to exercise its authority in the Netherlands. Queen Wilhelmina possessed authority, but Hitler had the power.* So legitimate authority can in fact be quite powerless. This applies to situations where parents have little power over their children or where teachers are unable to keep order and for that reason cannot exercise any supremacy (power) over their pupils.

---

* See B. Holwerda, *De crisis van het gezag* (Groningen, 1947), 10–11, where he distinguishes between *exousia* as commission or mandate, and *dunamis* as power. His opinion that Scripture keeps these concepts distinct is debatable. More than once *exousia* means "power," as for example in Matt. 9:8; Acts 26:18; Rev. 9:19; 13:12.

The reverse also occurs. We often say that a certain individual is cut out to be a pastor or a military officer or a politician. They exude a kind of "power" in the sense of having a particular presence, a special bearing characteristic of a particular profession. But one cannot be a pastor without the call of a congregation, or an officer without taking an oath, or a politician without a party behind him. Perhaps there is somewhere a businessman who can command a platoon of soldiers far better than many an officer, but he lacks the commission, and thereby the authority.[9]

Let us say something first about "power." This word quickly arouses negative associations because it is often associated with "raw" power, with grasping or craving for power.

But in itself power is something good and indispensable. Herman Dooyeweerd called power the great engine behind cultural development. Everything that needs to be developed requires power. Dooyeweerd used a nice example to illustrate his claim. The story is told about Leonardo da Vinci (1452–1519) that early on he had constructed an airplane. But this invention was buried with the inventor and thus remained his private property. That would have been different if da Vinci had won the human race over to his side. But as experience shows, to win people over you must exude power.

Power can be abused, but power *in itself* is never brutal or demonic.[10] A few examples will make this clear. We might speak of the power of the *word*. You can have ideas that are ever so nice, but what do they mean to anybody else if you are unable to put them into words? The Bible calls a man like Moses *powerful* or *mighty* in words and works (Acts 7:22).

We can also speak of the power of *love*. We see from 1 Corinthians 13 how powerful and mighty love really is. Power and love do not contradict each other. Paul tells us in 1 Corinthians 13 that without love, we are "nothing" (13:1–2), which means also that we possess no power.

We could also mention the power of *numbers*. In order to bring something about in various contexts, the majority of people must be won over. Many legislative bodies require a majority, or one half plus one of all members, in order to implement a political agenda and to enact laws. The tyranny of the minority is prevented by means of this democratic form of government.

Consequently, consolidating power is not in itself a questionable undertaking, but rather is necessary and wholesome for the proper development of society. In a very general way, we might define power as the ability to *do* something. In our sin-affected society, life does not proceed quite as easily as our definition might suggest. Somebody with musical talent has the "power" to develop that talent. Give her a flute, violin, or piano, and she "does" it. But for exercising political power, more is needed. Politics deals with conflicting interests and with enacting legislation that cannot be transgressed with impunity. The state bears the sword and exercises political power to enforce adopted laws by means of judges and policemen. This sense of power we might define as the ability to *compel* compliance. Someone possessing this kind of power is in a position to impose his will on others and to enforce it, even in the face of possible opposition.

If we were to compose a definition of *authority*, we would suggest this: Authority is the authorization for the (appropriate) use of power.[*]

Consider first this idea of "appropriate" use. It is beneficial to show in our definition that authority has a *serving* character. God gives nobody authority for self-indulgence. It must be used for the honor of God and service of the neighbor. Shepherds are to care for the flock and not feed themselves (Ezek. 34:2). Parents must use their authority to serve their children, and governments must use theirs for the sake of the citizenry. Even if the state bears the sword, this may not be done indiscriminately, for the sword must serve to prevent murder, as the Heidelberg Catechism so nicely puts it (Lord's Day 40). A good government uses its power appropriately and in that way combats criminality in society so that human life can develop in a peaceful context.

In earlier expositions of various catechisms, you will repeatedly discover two sides being illuminated. Naturally, children and others subject to authority are supposed to obey parents, governments, and those in authority. But the other side of the coin is also mentioned: all those in authority have the mandate, in their respective authorizations, to use their authority appropriately.[11] Nowhere do we read: Authority is authority, period. The idea that authority—to say it in modern terms—must be *functional* is quite old.

So authority is the authorization for the (appropriate) use of power, for authority must be functional. In this way we have opted for a definition of authority indicating how authority ought to be used.

But that confronts us with a problem. If in a given situation authority does *not* function appropriately, does it cease being authority? If in the

---

[*] *Translator's note:* The original reads: "Gezag is de bevoegdheid tot het (doelmatig) aanwenden van macht." The Dutch word *bevoegdheid* means "commission" or "entitlement," hence our rendering, "authorization."

nurture of their children, parents fall far short, are they thereby no longer parents? If the state enacts unfair laws, do we then have the right to disobey such laws? If a teacher is unable to teach, must the pupils still respect him as their instructor?

The definition we are using must be read carefully. It does not say that authority is the appropriate use of power. If that were the case, everybody in a situation of inappropriate use of power could say, "I no longer acknowledge you as being in authority." But we have intentionally placed the word "appropriate" within parentheses, because in our view that is not the decisive element for acknowledging authority. The decisive element is the *authorization* for using power. Naturally, such power must be used in a proper, goal-oriented manner, but when that does not occur, the authorization for using power does not thereby disappear. Parents do not become ex-parents if they raise their children inappropriately. A government under bad administration is still a government and must be honored as such, as long as it remains in power.

No earthly power is ever absolute. Parents can be stripped of their parental power, ministers and elders can be deposed from office, and there is the right of revolution against tyrannical governments. Nevertheless, one form of authority is more lasting than another. That depends on the way authority came into existence and could possibly be terminated. Parents have authority over their children even though the children had no say about the origin of this authority. Along with receiving children comes parental authority over these children. Christians confess that this authority—just as the children themselves—is entrusted by God to those parents. A person may not declare himself to be the father of another's child. Perhaps he is able to raise that child more appropriately than the child's own parents, but he lacks the authorization for that. A lot of things need to happen before parents can be stripped of their power.

Removing people from power happens more easily with members of congress or parliament. In a democratic society, they can exercise power only because they have been chosen and appointed. If they do not do their work well—that is to say, if in the judgment of the citizenry or the electorate they use their power inappropriately—then either a government will collapse, or, after an election, it will be unseated from power.

In this case, one form of authority (that of the voters) limits another form of authority, something that is good. Authority must not only function appropriately, but also continue to be limited by its purpose. An employee is under the authority of his employer, but then only during working hours. A meeting is led by an elected chairman, but his authority is limited to the duration of the meeting and to the circle within which it is supposed to function. At a subsequent board election, this authority can be taken away. The more restricted the nature and scope of authority happens to be, the less significant it is. Parental and governmental authority is far more significant than the authority of an organization's board. When conflicts arise, this kind of board must be very careful not to maintain its own position by an appeal to the fifth commandment. Many boards are merely boards; if they no longer enjoy sufficient confidence, they must be prepared to surrender their mandate. In this situation, a wise board does not seek to protect its authority, but opens itself to outside arbitration rendered by a committee of competent advisors.

We can well understand why the notion expressed by the phrase "sphere sovereignty" is of such interest. There may well be justifiable criticisms of the phrase and of certain applications made by Abraham Kuyper, but those criticisms do not render the basic idea underlying the phrase invalid.* Authority is always *limited* authority and is bordered by other spheres of authority. This notion is helpful especially with respect to the authority of the state, which should not seek to pull everything within its sphere of authority.

Even if we confess that all authority comes from God, that is not to say that it is thereby untouchable. Authority comes in various kinds, of wide and narrow scope, of long or short duration. We must not overlook clear developments in authority relationships. Slavery used to be possible, but it could not continue. Colonialism could not endure. Especially after World War II, we saw the often violent end of colonial regimes. That an end had to come to these regimes was obvious to anyone who was keeping up with the developments of history. The time was past for nations, no matter how primitive in their development, to continue being tied to the apron strings of colonial powers. They developed and desired self-government. Colonial authority in modern form maintains itself principally through the oppressive exercise of power. The same must be said of every form of minority rule forcing its will on an unwilling majority of the population. Authority relationships in this kind of situation will need to change fundamentally, if peace is to be preserved in a multicultural population.

---

* See J. Douma, *Politieke verantwoordelijkheid* (Kampen, 1984), 119–35, 149–51, where we suggest an improvement, namely, that we speak of "sphere authority (authorization)," in order to avoid the (too absolutistic) word *sovereignty*.

Nevertheless, we must still respect authority, no matter where and in what form it is exercised. To the question, Why must we obey someone in authority? or Why must we accept his leadership? or Why must we follow him? (or some similar formulation), the answer is this: On the basis of the authority bestowed upon him and *not* merely if his "power" is obvious or if he uses that power appropriately. Pupils in school must have respect for their teacher, even if he cannot maintain order and he might better quit teaching. He possesses authority, although it should stimulate him to reflect on his inability to use his power (namely, the knowledge of the subject he is teaching) appropriately. But that does not give his students the right to take his authority lightly. Political subjects must respect their prince on account of the authority bestowed upon him, *even* if it must be said, "Woe to you, O land, when your king is a child, and your princes feast in the morning!" (Eccl. 10:16). It would be a blessing if such a king, along with his officials, were willing to step aside for the sake of better government. But citizens are still obligated to respect and obey the king as long as he is in power. That applied to ancient Israel, but that applies just as much today, even where people live under oppressive or minority governments.

Max Weber (1864–1920) introduced a distinction between charismatic, traditional, and legal authority.[12] *Charismatic* (or gracious) authority characterizes the prophet, the war hero, and the leader who speaks to the heart of the people. We could mention as well the teacher who has everything at his fingertips so that he can manipulate both his material and his class. There is a strong emotional bond between those who exercise charismatic authority and their disciples and subordinates. The pupil often raves about his teacher.

Respecting this kind of authority is easy. Rarely do problems arise, because obedience seems automatic. Notice, we said "seems"—for charismatic leaders can plunge the world into deep misery, as Hitler did, after he had gotten all of Germany behind him.

In addition to charismatic authority, there is *traditional* authority. This authority rests upon "sacred" traditions. Think of patriarchal authority, or of the authority of caste and of office. It is not so much emotion as longstanding tradition that sustains this kind of authority. Often we are tied to customs whose roots go deep into the past, a feature that legitimizes them as "untouchable."

It is not always easy to conform to traditional authority. Traditional authority can be very oppressive, as, for example, in a family business where the people at the top seem unable to run the business the same way the family founder or his heirs did.

Then there is *legal* authority, characterized by laws and bureaucratic institutions. We conform to laws enacted by legislators who themselves are subject to those laws. The person disappears behind his office. You could say that this kind of authority has no face. We do not submit ourselves to this kind of authority on the basis of emotion or tradition; rather, it is rationality, objectivity, and discipline that lead us to obey this modern form of authority.

All of us deal with this form of authority. For example, consider filling out our tax returns. This exercise shows us immediately that it is not quite as easy to obey laws bearing a more impersonal form of authority. Nobody looks over our shoulder threateningly as we are filling out our tax returns. Criticism of unrighteous legislation (the government just "does what it wants") leads many people not to be very scrupulous when it comes to taxes.

The distinction Weber makes between kinds of authority can be very enlightening. His is a sociological approach to forms of authority and of respect for authority. But Weber does not help us from a normative point of view. The real basis for respecting authority does not flow from deep emotions, respectable traditions, or rationality. If you review the material we gathered from the Scriptures, you will conclude that we must respect authority because it comes from God and people are clothed with authority by God.

So it makes no difference whether the forms of authority are traditional or modern. Undoubtedly, many changes have come about. We view the president and prime minister, a member of congress or parliament, a minister and a boss at work, differently than people did before World War II. The distance between superior and inferior has decreased. To say it in Bavinck's words, authority and submission are approaching one another and reaching a compromise. We should welcome that. Those in authority are people, and we can talk about their authority in a matter-of-fact way. Through the votes of ordinary citizens, government officials obtain their high positions.

But this matter-of-fact observation hardly makes respect and obedience unnecessary. In numerous relationships, we are *under* other people and we can say that they have been appointed by God to be over us, even when those put in higher positions have us to thank (in part) for their elevated position.

No matter what form (or mixed form) the exercise of authority takes, with a little or a lot of power, functioning well or badly, accepted easily or with great difficulty—as long as it is legitimate (legal) authority, we must submit to it. Paul's remark about governments can be generalized: We must respect authority not only out of fear of punishment, but also for the sake of a clear conscience (Rom. 13:5). Obedience must be rendered not out of compulsion, but voluntarily, out of respect for God and for Christ, to whom all power and all authority have been given (Matt. 28:18).

Crisis of Authority and Handling Suffering

It is remarkable how the influence of and respect for authority have declined in recent decades. Children have become much more forward toward parents. Already as small children they argue their opinions. Underage children can more easily leave home and find a place where others will lend an ear to their complaints about their parents.

Shared administration is popular today in businesses, universities, and schools, as a form of distributing power. Petrified authority structures must be dismantled. The reach of the director, professor, and many others in high positions must be shortened. Everybody in every field should be a co-pilot. Sometimes it seems that only fearful psyches are troubled by chaotic situations resulting from inexperienced administration. Apparently order is supposed to arise spontaneously out of disorder, since many believe the alchemy lies not in authority but in freedom, which supposedly makes all things new.

Acts of civil disobedience are designed to draw the political process into the street. People protest and conduct sit-ins as frightened victims of bureaucracy or fiscal cutbacks or nuclear buildup. The voice of "the" people is no longer heard in the majority votes of the electoral process, but through opinion polls.

We are describing the situation in general terms. Not every change should be condemned. Developments toward sharing administration in various sectors of society can be good.[13]

But even the factors of fairness and various needed modifications in social relationships do not completely explain the cry for change. A different view of authority is exercising strong influence in society today.

We mentioned earlier the contemporary emphasis on describing authority as *functional*. We have no objection to this term in itself. But we surely object to the interpretation of authority that leaves little room for *authorization*, a view that sees authority solely as the appropriate use of power. Where that appropriateness is absent, authority does not exist. In this way, authority is mere functionality, something we unequivocally reject.

Let us imagine the consequences of the view that authority is mere functionality. Those consequences are drawn clearly enough by defenders of this view. For example, someone has argued that we can speak of real authority only where those under authority "go along" with authority. Once we accept and thereby legitimate a use of power, then authority is said to exist. Authority proceeds from the person, specifically from those under authority who consolidate to form a civil order. The Heidelberg Catechism does say that we must show all respect, honor, and love to all those in authority over us, because it pleases God to rule us by their hand; but according to this new interpretation of authority, this is "a dangerous summons to accept the existing power relationships." It is more honest and realistic to say not that God bestows authority, but at most that God provides the means that could lead to the exercise of power. We who are under authority are the people who determine whether authority functions and thus whether it can be legitimated. If we come to a negative judgment, then authority no longer exists. If that occurs, "then the person in authority must change his administration or move aside for another person who knows how to obtain the endorsement of those under authority."[14]

Now, if we were to apply this in all spheres of authority, then children could dismiss their parents, pupils their teachers, and employees their employers. For as soon as those who are to be subject to authority discover that existing authority no longer functions, since it fails to meet the objectives established by *them*, that will be the end of authority. Such authority has nothing left to *say*. And this last observation applies in two senses: (1) such authority no longer has any say-so (according to those who are supposed to be subject to authority), and (2) the right to exercise authority no longer exists.

But the second does not follow automatically from the first, as we have explained earlier. If those called to be subject to authority can terminate badly functioning authority, because they possess legitimate means to do that (voting rights, veto power, and the like), they must certainly make use of those means. But as long as those in authority retain their authorization to use their power, they must be respected as those in authority, no matter how difficult that might be(come) for us. Otherwise, society would degenerate into chaos. We cannot refuse obedience whenever *we* determine that those in authority are no longer functioning.

Often the question is asked, How can we explain the drastic lowering of respect for authority? It is not easy to analyze clearly the time we are now living in. This kind of analysis remains incomplete. Nevertheless, our current situation does have a few observable characteristics.

We begin with the observation that there is not much new under the sun. The matter of respect for authority has always been a problem. Both deference and despising, often toward the same persons, have appeared in every era. Those in authority are merely ordinary persons, but how do they fancy themselves? Miriam and Aaron had problems with the authority of their famous brother Moses: "Has the LORD indeed spoken only through Moses? Has He not spoken through us also?" (Num. 12:2). Gaal knew the ancestry of King Abimelech, leading him to ask, "Who is Abimelech, and who is Shechem, that we should serve him?" (Judg. 9:28). It has always been hard to accept inequality and to avoid jealousy toward people with more power and (often for that reason also) greater prosperity.*

Moreover, there is always tension between freedom and limits, so that people do not often see why *defective* authority is always better for society than unbridled freedom, where everybody does what is right in his own eyes. We have already seen that the fifth commandment comes to us in the context of freedom, which, in order to *remain* freedom, requires respect for law. It is a naive notion that anarchy (a situation without authority, where each may do as he or she pleases) leads to true freedom. An unrestrained people inevitably produces sooner or later a strong leader who brings order . . . and tyranny. So the result is not freedom, but its opposite. It is good to share and distribute authority, but it is absolutely disastrous when authority and respect for authority are absent.

These issues that have plagued mankind for centuries are clearly relevant today. Secularism has conquered territory within Christian circles where "respect for authority" used to reign. You soon discover that authority may no longer be viewed as divine, but must instead be humane (as if that is a contradiction). Away with the halo of divinity surrounding authority! The respect for authority of a former era is now ridiculed as the servility of a slave mentality. Back then, people had to obey authority because it supposedly came from God. Just look at history: was it not precisely this view of authority that brought Hitler to power and enabled white minority governments to oppress the black majority?

The entire "capitalist" system and its authority structures, especially those of marriage and family, are endangered today. It is no wonder that, with all this criticism, the climate has soured when it comes to standing up for power and authority.

Along with this, we find people preoccupied today with their own in-

---

* For a more extensive discussion of inequality among people (something just as fundamental as their equality), see J. Douma, *Vrede in de maatschappij*, 22ff.

dividual rights, but forgetting about their responsibilities. Individualism is fueled by stories of the right to self-determination, creating an appetite for as much independence as possible. Authority restricts a person, and where a person experiences this restriction as injurious to his own development, he is sure to protest. Solidarity with others weakens, as does the readiness to accept regulations designed for the community and not directly for the individual.

We would mention one more factor. The expansion of public assistance has been accompanied by a decline in willingness to endure *pain*. People used to say that in our pain we could see God's hand.[15] Where pain and suffering could be overcome, that was done (for example, with the sick). But often they could not be overcome. That applied to the fifth commandment, too. Keeping this commandment meant that you were supposed to obey your parents and others in authority, and you were supposed to have patience with their weaknesses and faults. Many a young lady spent the best years of her life caring for an aged (and sometimes cranky) father or mother. Many a worker has had to clench his teeth to keep from cursing his boss for paying him starvation wages.*

Today things are much easier. For our aging parents we have rest homes, and the master-servant relationship has become one of employer-employee. Much of the pain and suffering is gone today, fortunately.

But other kinds of pain are still around. Obeying the fifth commandment will always involve problems. Even though we have written very positively about authority, we are aware that tremendous pain can arise because of authority. But then we can go one of two ways: we can deal with the pain and suffering occasioned by authority in a Christian manner, with respect for the fifth commandment, or we can protest against our pain and suffering with means both ancient and modern, like insults, reviling, strikes, civil disobedience, and similar revolutionary actions. For a Christian, the choice is not difficult, even though implementing that choice can sometimes be very difficult. Recall what we wrote earlier under the heading "The Limit and Style of Obedience."

Notice how, in our moral reflection, many things seem interrelated. An analysis of the modern crisis of authority leads us directly into the issue of

---

* Notice in Eccl. 7:21–22 the matter-of-factness with which the Preacher evaluates cursing: "Do not pay attention to every word people say, or you may hear your servant cursing you—for you know in your heart that many times you yourself have cursed others" (NIV).

euthanasia, for example. Our view of authority is integrally related to our total worldview.

The Authority of the State

Many commentaries on the fifth commandment—especially catechism expositions from Lutheran or Reformed confessional circles—devote special attention to the authority of the civil government. These commentaries exhibit differences at some points, but demonstrate overall agreement on the main issues. Those main issues include the following:

Scripture clearly teaches that there must be civil government, and that a Christian may be a civil servant. The Anabaptists denied the latter claim with the argument the only Christ rules and we may not exercise authority over others; but that view is incorrect and cannot be maintained consistently. The Anabaptists recognized the husband's headship over his wife, the parents' authority over their children, and the teacher's authority over her pupils. Romans 13 and other passages clearly show the importance of the authority of government. Cornelius the centurion was never told that as a Christian he could no longer be a centurion (Acts 10), and the apostle Paul made use of the authority of the civil government more than once.

Political power is not absolute. Government itself is subject to divine justice and to the laws of the land. If government officials fail to follow these, then certain qualified and authorized persons (lower magistrates, representatives of the people) can, in cases of extreme emergency, oppose tyranny and assume power. We have seen that happen among the Spanish, French, British, Scots, Danes, Swedes, Germans, Swiss, Dutch, and Americans. The right of revolution must be used very cautiously. It does *not* belong to every citizen or subject, but to those who themselves possess political power.

The state also has power to bear the sword, both to punish domestic wrongdoers and to wage war against another nation if necessary.

But is there no calling to bear the cross in every circumstance and to suffer rather than to offer resistance? Certainly, but what may be valid for one person may not necessarily be valid for the other. Preachers and church members may not defend Christian teaching with physical force, but should suffer, if necessary, as the martyrs did. But that does not contradict the calling of the state and its agents (therefore possibly even Christian civil servants) to employ force in defending or restoring public order. And even this still does not give the state a free hand for arbitrarily controlling the lives, property, and freedom of its citizens. That happens frequently (cf. 1 Sam. 8:11–17), but that is definitely not God's desire.[16]

The picture given by the earlier catechism expositions concerning the task and limits of governmental authority agrees completely with scriptural teaching, in our opinion.

Let us recall once again the definition of authority we offered earlier: authority is the authorization for the (appropriate) use of power. The authorization of the state is sketched for us in an unmistakable way in Romans 13, as is our duty to obey civil authority: "Let every soul be subject to the governing authorities. For there is no authority except from God, and the authorities that exist are appointed by God. Therefore whoever resists the authority resists the ordinance of God, and those who resist will bring judgment on themselves" (Rom. 13:1–2).

We would observe also that the lamp of Scripture illumines the meaning of *appropriate* use of civil power: those who do good receive praise, those who do evil receive punishment, and the sword functions for the latter (Rom. 13:3–4). This shows us that civil power apparently can function well and need not be treated with suspicion.

Christians in the past have generally operated with a favorable view of government. Often, people view politics through the eyes of Machiavelli (1469–1529), and it looks something like this:

> In politics you cannot love the least significant, cannot let the other go first, cannot forgive and begin again (unless that gives you power), cannot think the other more excellent than yourself (at least, you can never say that), for those who do that sort of thing give away power which they never get back. In politics you must show how good you are, walk at the front of demonstrations, love meetings, see yourself (and praise yourself) as being far better than others. In politics you give your opponent a push if he almost falls rather than helping him; you do not let anything go his way, you seize what you can in order to put the other party in a bad light.*

---

* H. M. Kuitert, *Everything Is Politics, but Politics Is Not Everything: A Theological Perspective on Faith and Politics*, trans. John Bowden (Grand Rapids, 1986), 149. Kuitert is here describing *his* understanding of politics as well, and he contrasts politics (as his portrait already suggests) to the demands of the Sermon on the Mount. With this portrayal Kuitert does not intend to speak *disapprovingly* of politics. He is making the observation that this is simply the way politics works, but also that this is the way politics usually works. This is characteristic of politics, whether we like it or not. The climate in which the Sermon on the Mount must and can be heard (within the church) is different than that of politics.

This picture corresponds well to the political contests we see on television during the weeks prior to a national election. It also corresponds to the multitude of situations we could use to illustrate Machiavellian politics. But that is not to say that politics *per se* has a Machiavellian character and therefore a morality completely governed by the desires of those in power. Politics—that is to say, the public arena—includes politicians, officials, diplomats, commissioners, mayors, aldermen, policemen, judges, and others, of whom we could give hundreds of examples of impartiality, of unimpeachable and objective performance of their tasks so significant to society. From the point of view of morality, political power is not a suspicious matter, even though that power may often be abused. As far as abuse of power is concerned, we can find plenty of that outside of politics, even in the church.

Politicians are constantly getting their hands dirty, people say. That is true. The question is simply this: Is politics *so thoroughly stained* that there is no possibility of resisting dirty compromise?

Those of an earlier era who "respected authority" viewed politics favorably. They too were aware of abuses of power, and they warned against such abuses; they certainly never favored the attitude of "authority is authority, period." That is how some of their descendants have caricatured political power, some of whom even appeal to the example of Hitler to illustrate what kind of disaster can befall the world when people follow the line of Calvin and others who used to submit so meekly to authority. But, as followers of Calvin, our ancestors insisted that both parents and governments can become *strangers* to us, so that we may need to cease obeying them. They devoted many pages to discussing the servant character of governmental authority, and did not side with tyrants. However, they did assert—as we too have asserted already—that as long as authorization exists, there must be respect for that authorization, even when it is tyrants who control that authorization. It is no small thing to overthrow a government, in the light of Romans 13:1! But if it must be done, and if God provides leaders for such a revolution, then it is done with respect for authority.

Must We Read Romans 13 Differently?

Although we would like to conclude our discussion at this point, we need to respond to those who today are saying that the church has misunderstood Romans 13. What the church has drawn out of that chapter, they claim, is not really there. The traditional interpretation of Romans 13, with that key word "obey," no longer fits our situation and merely stimulates Christians to adopt a submissive attitude toward the state. And this posture is unacceptable.

Therefore, we need to devote some attention to more recent interpretations of Romans 13, although it is difficult for us—we might as well admit it up front—to see these interpretations as credible in light of the text. As one example, we choose the argument of a writer who is well known in the Netherlands as an "evangelical Christian."[17] He clearly wants to avoid a theology of revolution, which is why it might be valuable to hear what he has to say. Further, he has summarized a lot of material that he has gathered from other interpreters who have propagated explanations of Romans 13 similar to his own. We will mention a few important points from his arguments.

Romans 13:1 says that each person must submit to the powers that are over him. The Greek word used (*hupotassein*) means something other than to obey (*hupakouein*).

Using a word with the same stem, the apostle Paul describes the position of the government. The powers that exist have been ordained (*tetagmenai*) by God. But the phrase "by God" must be understood—so the argument goes—to mean "under God." God provides the state a place in His order. The state functions within the limits that God has ordained. The entire arena of politics always and everywhere exists *under* God.

That should lend a soberness to our thinking about the authority of the state. Between God and the state exists an absolute distinction of position. These are not two parties of a covenant to which the citizens need simply to conform. Peter correctly observed that the government is a *human* ordinance (1 Peter 2:13). God never created, installed, or appointed human governments, but only *ordered* them and put them *under* Himself. The state bears all the characteristics of the provisional and the passing. The state is not eliminated, but made subservient. In this Scripture passage, Christ is nowhere mentioned. Jesus never permitted Himself to be directly involved with political activities.

The state bears the sword, but this passage nowhere states that the use of force is "good." Nor does it claim that the use of force occurs on the basis of a divinely given commission. For that reason, terms like "the right of the sword" and "the power of the sword" are misleading. The sword is certainly employed, but Paul is merely *observing* that fact, as a sign of the provisional character of this world's order. The sword is a sign of the order that is passing away, and so its use cannot be theologically justified.

The "good" that Christians must perform, according to Romans 13, has nothing to do with living life according to the laws of the land, but refers to the "good" actions of Christians mentioned in Romans 12. And the "evil" must not be identified with violations of law, such as tax laws, for example, but with transgressing the commandments and precepts of God. The law of the state is not in view here.

Romans 13:1–7 is written to warn against anarchy. A Christian must avoid participating in anarchy. But this passage also calls (indirectly) for a critical attitude. We are obligated not only to loyalty, but simultaneously to resistance.[18]

There you have a sample of contemporary interpretation of Romans 13. When we first read this explanation, we wondered how much *loyalty* toward the state was actually left. True enough, "living out of the new reality in Christ obligates the church to acknowledge that God permits the state to perform a task and a function."[19] But as soon as the concrete reality comes into view, and as soon as we begin discussing the laws of the land, the sword, and taxation, all of these are placed outside of the "good" discussed in Romans 13:3. Romans 13 begins by saying that each person must submit himself to the powers that are over him; but, it seems, in this new view, that the message is precisely the opposite, namely, that the *state* must submit to God and that in numerous situations *we* should *not* submit to the state.

The claim that Romans 13 does not summon people to obedience is exegetically untenable. The Greek word employed here for "submit" (which supposedly means something other than "be in subjection to" or "obey") presupposes simply an attitude of obedience. The word appears elsewhere in the New Testament. Slaves must be in subjection to their masters, "with all fear," not only to the good and friendly masters, but also to the oppressive ones (1 Peter 2:18). Young people must "submit" to older people, with an attitude of humility (1 Peter 5:5). These things are written by the same Peter who—precisely as Paul in Romans 13—summons believers to "submit" to every human ordinance (1 Peter 2:13). The fact that these are *human* ordinances functions in no way to reduce obedience!*

All of this is the same with Paul. Slaves must "be obedient to" their masters "in all things" (Titus 2:9), and church members must be reminded by Titus that they must "be subject to" rulers and authorities, "to obey, to be ready for every good work" (Titus 3:1).† Why would "being subject to" exclude "being

---

* Here the word "human" can simply mean that these ordinances have been instituted for human society. But the authority exercised can still come from God.

† For "obey," the same word is used as in Acts 5:29, "We ought to obey God rather than men."

obedient to," when we find the same word used to describe people being in subjection to God (James 4:7), or to the Father of spirits, just as we have been subject to our fathers according to the flesh (Heb. 12:9)?

Returning to Romans 13 with all these observations, we may confidently continue doing what our ancestors did—just read what is in the text, without imposing the view that it is talking about being in subjection, but not about rendering obedience. To "be subject to" (v. 1) and to render "honor" and "fear" (v. 7) belong to the obedience that is contrasted to the forms of disobedience adopted by those who "resist the ordinance of God" (v. 2).

Why must we render obedience? Because governments are ordained *by* God.[*] It is self-evident that since governments are ordained by God, they also exist *under* God. That appears clearly from what follows: the government exists *in the service of* God (v. 4), and the state is a *minister* of God precisely at that point where it is maintained through taxation (v. 6). But the fact that the state is *God's* servant highlights its exalted position. Since it is the servant of no one less than God Himself, refusing to obey the government is not a ready option.

The theme of Romans 13:1–7 is that since governments are ordained by God, *we* must live *under* them. Romans 13 is not about the *government* being in subjection, but about *us* being in subjection. The exhortation to remember that the government too lives "under" God would render the word *for* in the middle of Romans 13:1 quite meaningless, whereas this little word is very important for the proper interpretation of the passage. Each one must be subject to the government over him, *for* its authority comes from God Himself. Resisting the government is nothing short of resisting the ordinance of God.[†]

---

[*] Some manuscripts read "of God" (*apo theou*) instead of "by God" (*hupo theou*). According to Herman Ridderbos (*Aan de Romeinen* [Kampen, 1959], 291), "by God" refers more to God's active involvement with the particular government in existence, "of God" more to the source of that government.

[†] Compare the interpretation of Herman Ridderbos, *Aan de Romeinen*, 291: *Tetagmenai* "denotes being ordained by God, which is to say: assigned to a particular *order* in terms of which the state's authority will have to answer. Nevertheless, Paul provides no criteria for obedience to the state. He speaks unconditionally and generally, in terms of the need present in the church in Rome and without entering into all sorts of related situations. . . . But by making such a close connection between the government and God, the apostle not only provides the most powerful motive possible for obeying the state, but he also connects this obedience not to government personnel (in a fatalistic or deistic manner), but to God."

If this is true, we can simply continue to say that the government has been instituted by God. No authority *exists* except that which God has established, says Romans 13:1. To that is then added: The authorities that do exist have been ordained and established by God, namely, to be His servants. God ordains His own personnel, and to these high-placed officials we must render obedience.

It is good to know that the state, with its sword and its force, bears the characteristics of the provisional and the passing. But then it is indeed strange to hear someone say that as "signs" of the order that is passing away, the sword and the use of force cannot be theologically justified. Marriage is also a "sign" of an order that is passing away, for the time is coming when marriage will no longer exist (Matt. 22:30). But does that prospect mean that we cannot justify marriage theologically?

There is a more important question: Who gives us the right to say that the sword and the use of force, which are servants of God (and thus within His mandate), can never be called "good"? There is much abuse of power, something God would never approve. But Romans 13 discusses the use of power, by means of the sword and more, for punishing those who commit evil. Why is that not something "good"? Paul is not merely *observing* that the state uses the sword; he is also saying that the state does not bear the sword in vain, because the state functions as a wrathful avenger in service to God (v. 4).*

Christians must do "what is good," Paul says (v. 3). But the view that says this "good" cannot refer to obeying the laws of the land is surely foreign to the text. We agree that it is permissible to understand the "good" to refer also to what Paul has said in Romans 12:9–21 (sharing with God's people who are in need, blessing those who persecute us, not repaying evil for evil, as far as possible living at peace with all men, and so forth). But that for which the *state* is responsible as a servant of God is, among other things, the paying of taxes (v. 6). We receive praise from the state when we do the "good" (v. 3). That will

---

* In his commentary on Rom. 13:2, Calvin mentions that government is of God, but not in the same sense as pestilence, famine, and war, all of which God sends as punishment upon the world. Modern interpretations of Rom. 13 could easily lead to the view that government comes from God in the same sense as these other things. But Calvin contrasts the state with those catastrophes that can befall the world, because God has instituted the state to guide the world in justice and uprightness. You cannot call punishments divine ordinances, but you can call the state a divine ordinance that God intentionally instituted to preserve the lawful order. See the following footnote as well.

occur especially when we demonstrate our loyalty toward the state by honoring its tax laws!

We have assembled enough arguments at this point to justify our rejection of the new view of Romans 13. Just one question remains: How do people actually arrive at this new interpretation? It cannot possibly be found in Romans 13, so then where does it come from?

It seems to us that the dominant motif in this new interpretation of Romans 13 is to be found in something already mentioned when we set forth this view.* Interpreters insist that Jesus never allowed Himself to be directly involved with political activities. Years ago, the Anabaptists said this, too. For them, Jesus Christ kept the business of worldly politics at arm's length. Today they have a grateful following.

Moreover, these modern disciples of Anabaptism paint a remarkable portrait of the power of God and Christ. The power of God and of Christ is their infinite capacity to *suffer;* their power consists in their capacity to tolerate everything. If you believe that, then it becomes very difficult to talk very positively about the power and the sword lying in the hands of the state. Any positive evaluation of political power is paltry at best.

What is indeed remarkable is that in spite of their image of a suffering God, many nevertheless end up with a theology of revolution. But that is not something new. Both quiet and boisterous representatives of the Anabaptist viewpoint have always been around. The quiet ones are willing to

---

* Whether influenced by or independent of this motif—we will leave that undetermined—we have the exegesis of Oscar Cullmann (in, among other works, *Der Staat im Neuen Testament,* 2d ed. [Tübingen, 1961], especially 68ff.), who understands the "powers" of Rom. 13:1 to refer to evil powers appointed by Christ to His service. This interpretation enjoyed a wide measure of support, since Barth and others subscribed to it, but has since been abandoned by most scholars.

Nevertheless, Cullmann's exegesis has influenced people's view of government negatively. The angelic powers that function in the background behind earthly governments could at any time become *pernicious* powers, and then quickly come to resemble what we read about in Rev. 13 concerning the anti-Christian power of the beast from the sea and from the earth! What happened under Hitler no doubt strengthened popular suspicion of the state's authority.

Nowadays, people can hardly find a theological discussion about the state that does not use Rev. 13 to supplement the picture of Rom. 13. We would simply observe that even Rev. 13 does not contain an appeal for resisting anti-Christian governments. Instead, we receive the distinct impression that believers were tolerating the suffering done to them. Their *perseverance* (in suffering) is mentioned with admiration (Rev. 13:9–10).

tolerate and to suffer, imitating their Lord. The boisterous ones are willing to write off a world lying in the grip of evil. The good must arise, evil must vanish. People can swear off using the sword, but then again they really need it to usher in the new and more just order.

In contrast to these views, we must hold fast to the message of Romans 13. This Scripture passage does not condemn the state as something negative, since it was instituted by God Himself in the world in order to reward good and to punish evil. Yes, governments do abuse their power. Samuel warned Israel of this when that nation craved a king (1 Sam. 8:11–18). In the prophecy of Amos, directed against the surrounding nations, but also against Israel herself, we read how governments misbehave toward each other and how they snare and plunder their own subjects (Amos 1–3; 5:7–13). Even Paul experienced the pain of governments that persecute the good instead of rewarding it. The governor of King Aretas wanted to capture Paul in Damascus (2 Cor. 11:32). More than once Paul was imprisoned or whipped. He did not hesitate to protest vigorously when he was publicly flogged or imprisoned without due process (Acts 16:37–39). Paul would never have listened to an order to cease preaching Christ. Even less would he ever have spoken the confession "Caesar is Lord."[20]

But all the knowledge that Paul had of the wicked and anti-Christian conduct of governments did not prevent him from writing about the state as positively as he did in Romans 13. Throughout her history, Israel had wicked rulers, but she also had rulers who honored the law for royalty set forth in Deuteronomy 17:14–20. One of these latter was David, who, in spite of all his faults, was a man after God's heart (1 Sam. 13:14; Acts 13:22). There were and are also pagan rulers who did and do what God mandated, whose rule corresponds not to the portrait of the anti-Christian state found in Revelation 13, but to the picture of the good state Paul gives in Romans 13.

For that reason, kings will one day bring the glory and honor of the nations into the new Jerusalem (Rev. 21:24). For that same reason, it is not at all unusual that Jesus Christ can be called King of kings (1 Tim. 6:15), or that *all power* has been given to Him (Matt. 28:18). This power is the power of His love, but it is also the power of the rod of iron with which He rules the nations (Rev. 12:5). The Lamb that has been slain is also the Lion from the tribe of Judah (Rev. 5:5, 12). Jesus Christ and politics— these two can be combined, even though His name is not mentioned in Romans 13.[21]

The Right of Revolution

The fifth commandment, therefore, requires us to respect political authority. Romans 13 teaches us what that obedience looks like. We are not to view the state negatively, as if we are always facing the choice between being loyal or resisting. The key word to describe our attitude is "obey." Resistance is permissible only in emergency situations.

But such situations have occurred and remain a possibility. Since we have dealt elsewhere with the right of revolution, we can be brief here and simply set forth our conclusions.[22]

Situations do arise in which we must obey God rather than man (Acts 5:29). The midwives refused to obey the Egyptian decree to kill the baby boys of Israel (Ex. 1:17). The soldiers in Saul's guard refused to follow orders when the king commanded them to put the priests of Yahweh from Nob to death (1 Sam. 22:17). Nevertheless, those actions did not represent revolution against the government. The history of Christianity has seen many martyrs whose refusal to worship the emperor, for example, cost them their lives. But they did not organize a revolution against the existing government.

Religious persecution can be the basis for justifying revolution. But then usually other factors come into play as well. Consider the American revolution, or the Dutch revolution against Spain in the Eighty Years War. Freedom of religion was one of the goals, but that was only one *component* of the rights being defended and sought.

For alongside freedom of religion, there are other rights that can provide the spark for a legitimate struggle against a government. When a government continually and brutally violates or even suspends the elementary, codified rights of its citizens, such a government should not be surprised to find its citizenry in open rebellion. The government has the same obligation as its citizens to keep the law.

It is necessary that a revolution against the state be conducted by people with political authority. As we said earlier, the one authority is asserting itself against the other. Lesser governments, or people who are recognized as leaders by the general populace, are the ones who should lead such a revolution. Someone like Lech Walesa in Poland can serve as an example. Although he had no political function, everybody considered him a leader in Poland when serious problems arose between the people and the communist regime there.

The example of Walesa is instructive for another reason. The situation in Poland did not escalate into a revolution, because there was virtually no probability of success. The Russians would have crushed any revolution, as they had done earlier in Hungary and in Czechoslovakia. No matter how bitter the situation is, if the costs of revolution are going to be very high, it may be necessary to abandon that alternative.

In summary, we would identify three conditions that must be met in order for the *right* of revolution to exist:

1. Elementary rights belonging to citizens are brutally and continually violated by the government.

2. Persons who may be considered to represent the people are the ones leading the revolution.

3. The probability of success for such a revolution must be high, so that possible bloodshed remains limited.

Civil Disobedience

The subject of civil disobedience is not very old. We have written elsewhere about this matter as well, so that again a brief summary will suffice.[23]

We understand the phrase *civil disobedience* to refer to publicly visible conduct that consciously violates the law in order to change a law or government regulation by means of what is intended to be nonviolent compulsion.

This form of violating the law does not occur in secret (for example, by means of tax evasion), but bears a public character. It applies the force of moral compulsion. Civil disobedience is different from a protest march; it can take the form of sit-ins, blockades, and the like. The intention is nonviolent acts, since otherwise it would not be civil disobedience any longer, but sabotage, guerrilla resistance, or revolution.

How must we evaluate civil disobedience? In practice, it rarely succeeds in remaining nonviolent, even though that is how it starts. Even if it occurs without violence, civil disobedience can nevertheless contain a very refined form of violence. For example, boycotting a chain of stores can put merchants out of business. Perhaps they might prefer a good beating rather than this form of attack.

Another objection against civil disobedience is that it undermines parliamentary democracy. People go around their elected representatives to extort decisions. What "the people" want is played off against what the lawmakers are (or are not) doing.

A Christian must stay far away from such activities. For this kind of behavior has little in common with the good *style* required from us toward those in authority. Each of us has the right and the duty to use every legal means at our disposal (assembly, protest marches, petitions, exercising influence upon and through our elected representatives, and the like) in order to fight against regulations and laws that we consider unjust. But we take the law into our own hands when we walk outside the fence of the law and try to force our will upon others.

Disobedience to the government can be necessary; but *civil* disobedience, in terms of both its definition and its well-known practice, looks entirely different from the disobedience commanded for Christians in extreme situations.

Endnotes

1. J. Koelman, *De pligten der ouders, in kinderen voor God op te voeden* (Middelburg, 1838), 63.

2. H. van den Brink, "Het Vijfde Gebod," in *Sinaï en Ardjoeno*, ed. Th. Delleman (Aalten, 1946), 117.

3. For a more extensive discussion of this question, see J. Douma, *Vrede in de maatschappij* (Kampen, 1985), 183ff.

4. J. Hoek and A. B. F. Hoek-van Kooten, *Man en vrouw in Gods weg* (Kampen, 1985), 29.

5. F. H. von Meyenfeldt, *Tien tegen een* (Goes, 1980), 3:22.

6. J. Calvin, *Institutes*, 2.8.38.

7. H. Bavinck, *De vrouw in de hedendaagsche maatschappij* (Kampen, 1918), 75.

8. Ibid., 77.

9. The example is from S. U. Zuidema, *Van geloof tot geloof* (Franeker, 1952), 106, where he is speaking particularly about the authority of office in the church.

10. H. Dooyeweerd, *Vernieuwing en bezinning* (Zutphen, 1959), 63ff.; cf. also *A New Critique of Theoretical Thought* (Amsterdam, 1955), 2:68–69.

11. Of the many expositions, we would mention two, that of Gisbert Voetius, *Catechisatie over den Heidelbergschen Catechismus*, ed. A. Kuyper (Rotterdam, 1891), 2:969ff., and that of B. Bekker in *De Friesche Godgeleerdheid* (Amsterdam, 1693), 312ff.

12. M. Weber, *Economy and Society*, 3d ed. (Tübingen, 1947), 1:16ff., 122ff. He briefly describes the three "Typen der legitimen Herrschaft" (types of legitimate authority) in *Preussische Jahrbücher*, 187:1ff. In both works, Weber describes these types in the reverse order that we are treating them. We are doing nothing more than identifying these types, occasionally choosing our own examples.

13. For further discussion of shared administration, see J. Douma, *Vrede in de maatschappij*, 163ff.

14. H. J. van Zuthem, *Gezag en zeggenschap* (Kampen, 1968), 72ff., 79.

15. We discussed this earlier, in connection with the first commandment, under the heading "The One God and Suffering"; see also J. Douma, *Rondom de dood* (Kampen, 1984), 30ff.

16. We are mentioning a number of points similar to those made by Voetius in *Catechisatie over den Heidelbergschen Catechismus*, 975ff.

17. E. W. van der Poll, *Op gespannen voet: Geschiedenis en aktualiteit van Romeinen 13 en Openbaring 13* (Kampen, 1985).

18. See ibid., 26–27, 38–41, 60–63, 69, 73–74, 76–77, 85. For arguments similar to those of van der Poll, the reader is referred to J. Douma, *Politieke verantwoordelijkheid*, 186–87.

19. Van der Poll, *Op gespannen voet*, 41.

20. W. Schrage, *The Ethics of the New Testament*, trans. David E. Green (Philadelphia, 1988), 238.

21. For further discussion of this, see J. Douma, *Politieke verantwoordelijkheid*, 77–86, 125–26, and 144–51.

22. Ibid., 193–203.

23. See ibid., 177–93.

The Sixth Commandment

You shall not kill unlawfully. (Ex. 20:13)

Respect for Living Things

Clearly the sixth commandment is directed against killing people. Its formulation is very general: do not kill—without specifying who or what is not to be killed. But obviously this commandment is directed at the protection of human life. Just as the subsequent commandments treat marriage, property, and the reputation of others, here too the command envisions the lives of *other people*.

Nevertheless, when discussing the sixth commandment, it is helpful to begin more generally by making some observations about plant and animal life before moving on to discuss human life.

Why may we not simply decide to kill a person? Is it because a person is a creature of God? But plants and animals are also creatures of God, over which we have just as little say. The fact that we have any say at all with respect to the life of plants and animals does not arise from "nature," but rather is a kind of sovereignty *bestowed* upon us. To mankind in Paradise God gave permission to eat the plants of the field and the fruit of the trees (Gen. 1:29–30). Concerning animals, we read that after the Flood God gave man permission to eat their meat (Gen. 9:3).

The farmer harvests grain and the butcher slaughters animals not because these activities are self-evidently permissible and "natural," but because the Creator of all life has granted mankind permission to do these things.

God cares for every living thing. Animals and plants receive their food and drink from God (Ps. 104:11–30; Matt. 6:26–30). They receive His separate attention, alongside the care He devotes to mankind. God clothes flowers, even ordinary flowers of the field, with a grandeur that surpasses human grandeur, a fashion with which even Solomon's richly colored robes cannot compete (Matt. 6:29). God supplies animals with a strength and cleverness that should make men modest. Are not the crocodile and elephant imposing creatures of God (Job 40:15–24)? Does not the wild donkey laugh at all the urban commotion, roaming as he does across the mountains, not listening to a driver's shout (Job 39:5–12)? Do not the ants show a zeal that can serve as an example for the slothful person, something to make him wise (Prov. 6:6–8)?

The important place animals occupy is expressed also by the fact that from Israel God accepted animals as sacrifices in exchange for human life. In the case of an animal not offered to God but used by men for food, the blood was not to be eaten, since the blood was seen as the source of life (Gen. 9:4; Lev. 3:17; Deut. 12:23). The life of the animal belongs to Yahweh, and for that reason the blood could be sacrificed to Him, but not used or enjoyed as food for people (Lev. 17:10–14).*

No matter how much the life of plants and animals is intertwined with human life, we can still talk of a distinct plant and animal kingdom, a resource we are not permitted simply to use for our own purposes. Plants and animals exist first of all for the glory of God, and only then for human benefit. "O LORD, how manifold are Your works! In wisdom You have made them all. The earth is full of Your possessions" (Ps. 104:24), such that this creation causes Him to rejoice (v. 30).

It should not escape our notice that the coming kingdom of peace will include animals and plants, too (Isa. 11:6–8; Rev. 22:2). Not only man, but the rest of creation, too, sighs now under its bondage to mortality, whereas the time is coming when the rest of creation will share in the liberty of the children of God (Rom. 8:21). Once man has reached his final destination, the other creatures will, too.

These observations are sufficient to teach us that we must respect liv-

---

* The prohibition against drinking blood was related to the pagan practices where people drank blood in order to obtain divine powers, to increase their own vital powers. See A. C. Kruyt, "Het Zesde Gebod," in *Sinaï en Ardjoeno*, ed. Th. Delleman (Aalten, 1946), 163ff., and D. K. Wielenga, "Sanctorum Communio," in *Almanak fides quadrat intellectum* (Kampen, 1971), 73. The latter essay deals with Acts 15:29 and the use of "blood" and "things strangled." One need not object on the basis of principle against blood transfusions or against eating food containing blood (e.g., sausage), precisely because these practices no longer form part of idolatrous superstition about increasing vital powers. Otherwise, it is commendable to abstain from using blood for consumptive purposes, out of respect for animal life.

ing things. Jonah's expectation that Nineveh would be destroyed was different from God's, who took thought for the 120,000 people and the animals living in that city (Jonah 4:11). Man must care for animals. Animal abuse is, from the Bible's viewpoint, an abomination. Even when your enemy's donkey stumbles under its load, you may not stand by watching (Ex. 23:5). The righteous man knows what his livestock needs (Prov. 12:10). He knows also that an animal must be able to rest on the Sabbath (Ex. 20:10; 23:12), and that a threshing ox may not be muzzled (Deut. 25:4).

Nor was Israel permitted to do whatever she wanted to the trees, since when she besieged an enemy's town, she was not allowed to destroy the groves around the town. "Are the trees of the field people, that you should besiege them?" (Deut. 20:19 NIV).

The issue of *environmental stewardship* has rather forcefully compelled us to deal more wisely with our plants and animals. Numerous species of plants and animals have become extinct, or will become extinct if we fail to take remedial measures. Deforestation and overplanting have made extensive regions infertile. Hundreds of thousands of acres of forests in Europe and North America are dying from poisonous gases that go up into the atmosphere and come down as acid rain.

The livestock industry, with its enormous concentration of thousands of pigs and cattle and chickens, results in a surplus of manure that in no small way contributes to air and ground pollution. The term livestock *industry* is already significant: animals are raised in the smallest possible space, with methods developed for mass production, removed entirely from the natural environment in which animals used to be raised.

The chemical industry pollutes rivers and lakes, affecting the fish population as well as the drinking water. One serious accident in a Russian nuclear plant at Chernobyl in 1986 made it necessary to relocate cattle a thousand miles away. And we still do not really know what to do with the radioactive waste from nuclear plants.

We do not intend to discuss environmental issues here, since we have treated this subject elsewhere.[1] Here we simply wish to mention a few of these problems to show that our analysis of environmental issues involves our perspective regarding what *life* is. If we think that man is the center of everything, then we will easily ignore the land, plants, and animals. We will surely see the consequences of that neglect, for God will not leave us unpunished if we let the balance in His creation be destroyed.

Our view of ecological balance involves our faith. Are all living things subject to us as our slaves, to be treated as arbitrarily as we wish—

or are they creatures of God, just as we are, to be treated with respect? On the one hand, it is true that man has received authority and dominion over plants and animals. We must avoid reacting against the misuse of creation by putting other creatures on a pedestal, elevating them as our brothers and sisters, just as valuable in God's sight as people. In the future, despite environmental disasters, trees may be cut and animals may be slaughtered.

For this reason there is no biblical basis for *vegetarianism*, especially when this lifestyle is propagated out of "reverence for life" or "love for animals."* Even less acceptable is the attempt to use Scripture to oppose *animal experimentation*. Medical remedies, research techniques, and modern surgery would never have reached their modern effectiveness without experimentation on live animals. Animals may serve our needs, both for our food and for our health.

On the other hand, our permissible use of plants and animals may not degenerate into abuse. We must protect the environment, and therefore we may not neglect or mistreat animals, cause them unnecessary suffering, or kill them unnecessarily. *Animal protection societies* and other organizations seeking to protect our environment can perform a needed service. Stripped of their possibly unbiblical ideologies, various projects on behalf of our environment can be heartily supported by Christians.

Respect for Human Life

If we should respect everything that lives, then surely that applies to human life. Plants and animals are called creatures of God, but only people have been created in the image of God (Gen. 1:26–27).

When we discussed the second commandment, we explained the significance of this expression. Here is a summary of that discussion: Among all God's creatures, people are unique. They represent God on earth. God wants to live in them and have His own power radiate through them in this world. Man was destined to be God's temple. He is in a position to fulfill his exalted task since he received the gifts of understanding and vo-

---

* Some vegetarians defend using organic food and avoiding meat products out of a conviction that these will improve civilization and increase humaneness, health, and happiness. As it functions within this ideological context, the vegetarian lifestyle is alien to Holy Scripture. But it is another matter altogether when people are vegetarians because they are convinced that a vegetarian diet is more healthy than a nonvegetarian diet.

lition. These extraordinary gifts elevate him above the animal and enable him to exercise dominion over God's creation.

What we are saying here about people in general has consequences for our attitude toward individuals in particular. "Whoever sheds man's blood, by man his blood shall be shed; for in the image of God He made man" (Gen. 9:6). It is just as wrong for us to curse other people, for we must always remember in such cases that they have been created in the image of God (James 3:9).

These directives are stated very generally. Apparently it makes no difference whether someone is *behaving* as the image of God; his unique status and special calling should be enough to keep us from attacking his life and from cursing him. In both instances, we would be acting as if a person's life and reputation are of little or no value. Anybody who curses another person despises him as being an insignificant nobody (as we saw earlier in connection with honoring parents), whereas a person is valuable and significant precisely because he is the image of God! Someone may kill an animal that ranks lower than a human being, and we have already seen that even this must be done with careful thought. But among people there exists a fundamental equality that renders it entirely impossible to dispose of human life thoughtlessly and carelessly.

A ruler like King David experienced this when he thought he could get rid of Uriah. A king can easily suppose that he controls the lives of his subjects. David killed Uriah so that he could have the dead man's wife, Bathsheba. But even David fell under the law of Genesis 9:6. The Lord's sentence was clear: David killed Uriah by the sword, so the sword would never depart from David's family (2 Sam. 12:9–10). Later, the same thing would happen to King Ahab, who, at the advice of Jezebel, killed Naboth so that he could annex Naboth's vineyard to the rest of his estate. At the very place where the dogs licked up the blood of Naboth, they would also lick up Ahab's blood (1 Kings 21:19).

So even kings do not have the right to treat people as if they were less than human. Seen from another vantage point, even kings are "merely" the image of God, and in that respect are equal to every other person. They are the image of God, but not God Himself, who alone has control over life and death. You shall not elevate yourself to be as God, putting yourself over your neighbor's life or wife or property. David and Ahab knew that! Confessing man as the image of God should make us think highly of (the life of) our neighbor and, in comparison, think modestly of ourselves and our own life.

Freedom, Life, and Praise

It is good to remember that the sixth commandment, like all the others, comes after the prologue to the Ten Commandments: "I am Yahweh your God, who has *freed* you from Egypt, the house of slavery." The prohibition against killing obtains more depth once we read it against the background of Israel's history in Egypt.

There too the king appropriated to himself the right to dispose of human life. At Pharaoh's command, all Israelite baby boys were to be put to death at birth. Had his plan succeeded, the nation of Israel would have gradually died out. Then Egypt would have been more than a house of slavery; it would have been a house of death. By liberating Israel from Egypt, Yahweh made life itself a sign for the people of His grace. Therefore, anyone who failed to respect the life of another person, while owing his own life to Yahweh's work of liberation from Egypt, would really be attacking Yahweh's grace.[2]

So we see that for Israel, life *originated* in Yahweh's grace, whereby He freed His people from Egypt. But this life had a very clear *purpose*. Dutch theologian J. L. Koole has pointed out the relationship between living and praising. Living is really for praising. After being freed from hostile power, the one who enjoys new life sings: "I shall not die, but live, and declare the works of the LORD" (Ps. 118:17). God's name is glorious throughout the earth, but it is man who can speak that name in praise (Ps. 8). With a view especially to this relationship, the psalmist dares to ask God for restoration from a fatal illness. For what would it profit God were he to die and descend to the grave? "Will the dust praise You? Will it declare Your truth?" (Ps. 30:9).[3] A human being is not only spiritual, but is involved with his entire body as well in that praise of God. "All my bones shall say, 'LORD, who is like You . . . ?'" (Ps. 35:10). In a prayer composing part of the Jewish liturgy for the Sabbath morning, we find this text explained as follows:

> Therefore shall our bodily organs, which You have prepared for us, and the spirit and the breath, which You have breathed into our nostrils, and the tongue that You have placed in our mouth, behold, they shall magnify and adore and praise and exalt and lift up and fear and sanctify and declare before kings Your name, our King. For every mouth will confess You, every tongue shall praise You, every knee shall bow before You and every heart shall fear You and every internal organ shall sing Your name, as it is written: "All my bones shall say, 'Yahweh, who is like You?'"[4]

If man receives life for that purpose, clearly the Bible nowhere permits a vitalistic or humanistic justification for the sixth commandment. "A person may not be killed for this reason, that he is, either actually or potentially, someone who declares God's praise, and therefore anybody who kills another person thereby robs God."[5]

We wish to emphasize (as Koole also indicates) that what must be respected is not only the life of someone who *actually* praises God. Even if a person does not praise God, we are still dealing with someone who, as the image of God, has the calling to praise God. In any case, *we* do not have the right to cut such a life short.

Reverence for Life?

The fact that life is a gift of God bestowed upon us for a specific purpose implies a limitation. Human life is not a goal in and of itself, but is designed for service to God and neighbor. One poet put it well: Living is not life's greatest good![6] Life is something we receive, something we can lose, and sometimes something we may even need to give up entirely.

Therefore, we must be careful with the expression "reverence for life," especially if that involves having *absolute* reverence for life. We have already observed that such absoluteness does not apply to animal and plant life, since we have received permission to use both for our needs. But neither does human life have absolute value. True, it is of higher value than plant and animal life—but that does not justify absolutizing human life. We shall see in a moment that situations occur where one person does have the right to take another person's life. That would be nearly impossible if everybody's life possessed absolute value.

Occasionally we speak of an immortal soul and of an eternal value that every person possesses; but even with these expressions we must always remember that immortality is *bestowed* upon man. Immortality is not simply a natural property embedded in our humanness. For only God possesses immortality (1 Tim. 6:16), whereas we must be *clothed* with immortality by God (1 Cor. 15:53–54).

We can leave this "eternal perspective" for what it is, since the expression "reverence for life" is intended to generate respect for human life in its earthly form.

Now, it may be possible to use this expression profitably, because reverence literally means nothing more than offering or showing honor. Honor is owed to God, to our parents, and to others who are in positions of authority. For all these ways of showing honor, we can use the word "reverence." Nevertheless, this word easily obtains a religious nuance, such that we would prefer to reserve it for describing the honor due to God and use the word "respect" for those other cases.

Certainly, where people speak of reverence for life—very generally and abstractly—we need to sound a warning note. Reverence for life gives the impression that life is sacred. Albert Schweitzer viewed reverence for life as the highest norm for ethics. Life in itself was for him something sacred, so that we should not so much as pluck a leaf from a tree or pick a flower or kill a fly. Schweitzer advised people of his day (before air-conditioning!) that if someone were to work indoors on a summer evening, it would be better to keep the windows closed and breathe stale air than to watch insect after insect fall to their death with wings singed by the candlelight![7]

We cannot share this perspective, since we prefer to speak of reverence for God rather than reverence for life. Where God demands respect for life, we may not cut life short. If God gives us the animals for food, then we may put animals to death. If God entrusts the sword to the state, the state receives along with the sword the right to curtail the life of those who act unlawfully, that is, the right to kill. "Reverence for life" is therefore a maxim that is far too broad, one that separates life from the relationships in which God has put it and from the task for which God has created it.

No Unlawful Killing

The text of the sixth commandment can make clear for us that not every killing is forbidden out of "reverence for life." The Hebrew text indicates that this commandment is dealing with *unlawful* killing, that is to say, with killing that violates justice. The word used here (*rasah*) never appears in contexts involving God putting someone to death or putting to death an enemy in wartime. Nor does this command prohibit a killing that has been ordered by the court. The sixth commandment is speaking about a very specific kind of killing, one that does not *serve* society, but rather violates society.

Why not then translate the commandment this way: "You shall not murder"? Perhaps at first glance this seems correct, but this translation would still be too restrictive. "Unlawful killing" includes far more than what we usually mean by "murder." We can clarify this by explaining various forms of killing fellow human beings that are distinguished in modern jurisprudence.

If somebody kills another person intentionally and with premeditation, then he commits *murder*. Premeditation means that the killer intended to take the life of his victim. He committed the deed with calculation and in cold blood.

If somebody kills another person intentionally, but without premeditation, then we speak of *voluntary manslaughter* rather than murder. Somebody might take the life of another person in a fit of rage. In that case we would not say the deed was committed in cold blood (as with murder), but in hot-blooded passion. Voluntary manslaughter does involve intention, but the decision is made under the impulse of strong emotions. Consider an exchange of words that leads someone to grab a knife to kill another person.

Or somebody can kill another person by recklessness. A driver who runs a red light is not intending to kill another person, let alone premeditating that act. But the way he drives can certainly result in someone's death, so that he is charged with *reckless homicide* or *involuntary manslaughter*.

Manslaughter occurs wherever death results from carelessness. A nurse who—perhaps very understandably—misreads a label and administers the wrong medicine can cause the death of a patient. It is very distressing to punish an otherwise excellent nurse on account of what appears at first glance to be no more than a foolish mistake, but the result of this mistake was still the death of a patient. In most cases of this kind, the punishment would be rather light. We would not call the perpetrator a murderer, but we would still call the act involuntary manslaughter.

A fourth kind of situation occurs in which there is no culpability. Somebody swings an ax to fell a tree, but the ax head flies off the handle and kills someone. This example we have borrowed from Scripture (Deut. 19:5), but something similar can easily happen today. In such a case, one could say that this is certainly a grievous action, but not one that subjects the perpetrator to criminal punishment.

Now, if we were to ask, "To which of these situations was the sixth commandment applied in Scripture?" then we would have to answer, "To all of these." The sixth commandment encompasses more than a condemnation of murder alone, so that the translation "You shall not murder" would be inaccurate and incorrect. Scripture is unaware of our modern legal distinctions, although we do encounter nuances that resemble our contemporary legal categories.*

Killing a person was such a serious matter that *even* if it happened accidentally, special measures were needed for the Israelite to avoid the impo-

---

* In times past, criminal law viewed the objective outcome and not the subjective attitude as decisive. This was more a jurisprudence of *conduct* than of *guilt*. The objective outcome was decisive for the punishment of the crime. However, the fact that Mosaic legislation took into account also the attitude of the perpetrator is evident from the institution of cities of refuge. The presence or absence of hatred played a role (see the following note).

sition of the sentence commanded in Genesis 9:6 ("Whoever sheds man's blood, by man his blood shall be shed"). Israelite society was familiar with the vendetta or family feud, whereby the closest relative of the victim had the right to avenge the killing. But the Mosaic legislation regulated the family feud in such a way that if the death had occurred accidentally,* the perpetrator was permitted to flee to the altar of Yahweh (Ex. 21:13; see 1 Kings 2:28) or to one of the cities of refuge. There he was able and obligated to be protected against the avenger, but he would have to remain there until the death of the high priest in office at the time of the accidental death (Num. 35:9–29; Deut. 19:1–12).

Here there is no culpability for crime; rather, the required (temporary) exile of the perpetrator shows us how seriously we must take every form of killing. Fortunately, the family feud is a thing of the past, but this should not prevent us from being shocked today whenever someone is killed, whether intentionally or accidentally.

In biblical times, people were also familiar with the phenomenon of negligent homicide. Someone trying to reduce building costs by not installing a railing around the perimeter of his roof terrace could be held liable for the death of anyone who fell from his roof (Deut. 22:8). If an ox's owner knew his animal was dangerous and nevertheless failed to take the necessary steps to protect his neighbor from the animal, that could cost the life of both ox† and owner (Ex. 21:29).

Examples of other forms of killing abound in Scripture. Jacob condemned his sons Simeon and Levi for their hot-tempered slaughter of the men of Shechem (Gen. 34:25; 49:6). They were guilty of manslaughter, just as we could say that David and Ahab intentionally and with premeditation got rid of Uriah and Naboth, respectively.

"You shall not kill unlawfully"—that can include: murder in cold blood, manslaughter with passionate rage, negligent homicide resulting from recklessness or carelessness, and so on. All these kinds of killing are condemned by the sixth commandment.

---

* Ex. 21:13: "But if he did not lie in wait, but God delivered him into his hand . . ."; Deut. 19:4: "Whoever kills his neighbor unintentionally, not having hated him in time past . . ."

† An animal that killed a man had to be killed (see Gen. 9:5 and Ex. 19:13). The meat of that animal was not supposed to be eaten. "An animal's life was *permitted* to be taken whenever it served human need. It was *required* to be taken whenever it endangered human life" (J. L. Koole, *De Tien Geboden*, 97; emphasis added). Well into the Middle Ages, in Europe, animals that caused human death were killed.

Abortion

In 1973, German theologian Bo Reicke observed that the prohibition against murder was the only element of the Ten Commandments that still functioned in our secularized world.[8] In our opinion, this claim becomes dubious when we look around at one country after another where abortion is being legalized. Something that formerly had been branded as murder is nowadays legally permissible, though with certain restrictions.

We could well speak of a clear turning point in history, because the Christian church—and, in her footsteps, social legislation—has always condemned abortion. The turning point we are talking about is quite abrupt. Within the space of a few years Christian ethicists turned from condemning abortion as murder to defending it. In so doing, they left their ecclesiastical heritage and came up with pronouncements resembling what had been argued already in the classical Roman period, namely: "An unborn child cannot legitimately be called a person," or, "Before a child is born it is part of the mother, that is, part of her intestines."* These same voices are resounding today among modern defenders of abortion, voices claiming that the unborn embryo in its first stages is really nothing more than a collection of cells, a lump of tissue, formative life, or something similar. The embryo is nothing but a part of the woman's body, and since she is "boss of her own body," she has free reign to do as she wishes.[9]

From the very beginning, the church has judged differently. She did so on the basis of what the Bible says about a child being knit together by God's hands in his mother's womb (Ps. 129; Job 10:8–12).† Something in the process of becoming a human being is already a human being, Tertul-

---

* From pre-Christian times we hear other voices as well. Consider the well-known Hippocratic oath (ca. 460–377 B.C.). There we read, in part: "I will give no deadly medicine to anyone if asked, nor suggest any such counsel; furthermore, I will not give to a woman an instrument [pessarium] to produce abortion. With purity and with holiness I will pass my life and practice my art." This pessarium must have referred to a vaginal suppository, consisting of a piece of woolen or linen cloth soaked in something that would induce abortion.

By contrast, the story is told that this same Hippocrates prescribed for a ballet dancer, whose pregnancy threatened her with the loss of her elegant style, some gymnastic jumping exercises designed to cause a miscarriage. See B. Schöpf, *Das Tötungsrecht bei den früchristlichen Schriftstellern* (Regensburg, 1958), 115.

† The Bible says very little about abortion itself. See J. Douma, *Abortus*, chap. 2, especially the treatment of Ex. 21:22–25, which deals with men who, while fighting, injure a pregnant woman who is trying to stop them, resulting in a miscarriage.

lian wrote. Already before his time, Christian authors had branded abortionists as "destroyers of God's image."

There has always been something of a difficulty in determining the moment when a human embryo receives a soul. Often it was customary to say that a boy received a soul on the fortieth day and a girl on the eightieth. But even this kind of speculation never led people to declare the time period before these particular days an open season for destroying life in the womb. Both Rome and the Reformation condemned abortion with equal severity. Consider these clear words of Calvin (in commenting on Exodus 21:22):

> . . . for the *foetus*, though enclosed in the womb of its mother, is already a human being, (*homo*), and it is almost a monstrous crime to rob it of the life which it has not yet begun to enjoy. If it seems more horrible to kill a man in his own house than in a field, because a man's house is his place of most secure refuge, it ought surely to be deemed more atrocious to destroy a *foetus* in the womb before it has come to light.[10]

Consider as well the papal encyclical *Humanae vitae* (1968), in which Pope Paul VI affirmed the centuries-long rejection of abortion.

Unborn life deserves the protection afforded to human life. Undoubtedly, differences in value between one or another form of human life do exist. A person travels through various stages of life. An embryo that is but a few weeks old is viewed differently than a newborn child. The loss of a newborn baby is more grievous than that of a two-month-old embryo. The "value" of someone who has his whole life ahead of him is greater than when he has become old and senile. Why may we not talk about inequality among people in terms of differences in value? Many more physicians care for the health of the president of the United States when he falls ill, than for the health of an "ordinary" patient who gets sick. But all these differences in *valuation* do not exclude equality in *the right to protection*.*

---

* We wonder whether the distinction H. de Jong makes in *Opbouw* 30 (1986): 116 between "human life" (the unborn embryo) and "person" (after birth) can be supported with biblical evidence, as de Jong thinks it can. Recall the time when the child John leaped in Elizabeth's womb (Luke 1:41, 44), where the same word is used that later describes the child Jesus in the manger. Still more questions arise from the consequence that de Jong draws from his distinction: Since unborn life has less value than an independent human being, abortion could be permissible in certain (exceptional) cases. But being of "less value" is far from equivalent to being "not worthy of protection."

May we insist, then, that no argument justifies abortion? No, we may not, for the so-called *medical* argument can be a justification. In countries with a well-developed health care program, the situation hardly ever occurs where a mother suffers from a disease that either does or would endanger her life if her pregnancy were to continue. In cases involving the choice to save one life or the other, we may legitimately decide to save the mother's life, and the abortion would be justifiable.

But that same verdict can hardly apply to other arguments for abortion, if at all. The *psychological* argument comes very close to the medical argument. A woman's psychological health can be severely threatened if she were to continue her pregnancy to its full term. Whether her pregnancy is really *life*-threatening is obviously more difficult to determine than on the basis of a strictly medical diagnosis. But this should not preclude a psychiatric assessment as a possible legitimate basis for an abortion.

The *eugenic* argument rests on the claim that the unborn embryo would be born either probably or certainly with a handicap. Any degree of probability means, however, that the aborted child could have been born healthy. Even if that were the case, however, we are still dealing with a human life. We are not allowed to dispose of that life arbitrarily—whether or not the child is handicapped. Whoever performs that kind of abortion perhaps does so legally, in the sense of "with legal permission," but nevertheless does so unlawfully, in the sense of "against God's law." In many cases, a handicapped child constitutes a ponderous testing for the parents of such a child; but we should consider transgressing God's law a far more ponderous burden.

In connection with the eugenic argument, we must be careful about submitting to prenatal tests like amniocentesis or other available tests done on the amniotic fluid. Whenever the consequence of abortion is linked to a negative or presumably negative outcome of such tests, Christians should not cooperate with this kind of research.

Another argument for abortion is the *judicial* or *ethical* argument, used to defend terminating a pregnancy resulting from a criminal act like rape, incest, or sexual intercourse with a minor. Surely here too we can feel the trauma associated with carrying a child conceived through rape or incest. We can brand as an aggressor not only the brutal rapist, but also the father who impregnates his daughter or the man who makes someone else's minor child pregnant. But is the resulting embryo of such a nature that we may legitimately kill this human life out of "self-defense"? Is this not a new and independent life that ought to receive protection? A society in which these unborn children are accepted with love by their mothers, and/or by others who can offer a helping hand if the mothers cannot nurture their children after birth, has a highly developed morality.

In practice, the psychological argument is frequently linked to the *social* argument. The social argument defends abortion when the woman would suffer severe social difficulties were she to carry the child to full term, even though she could cope well enough without psychological trauma. Rather, she might consider her accommodations too cramped, her income too strained, or the completion of her studies too important, so that she decides to have an abortion.

Difficulties of a psychological or social nature confront us with the demand to search for solutions. It will not always be possible for the mother to continue caring for her child. But then *adoption* is often a legitimate solution. However, the problem is solved brutally when the unborn child becomes the victim of abortion. In such situations, those responsible are sinning against the sixth commandment.

In lending help to women in need, it may be wise not to use the term "murder" to describe abortion, even though abortion is surely an intentional premeditated killing. But "murder" is a word freighted with *emotion*, a word that calls to mind the murderer who kills his victim in cold blood, whereas many women in distress do not attack their unborn children with *that* attitude. Utterly miserable hopelessness, for example, at the prospect that the pregnancy will not be accepted by family members or others, can lead a woman to abortion. If we use caution in our choice of terms when we seek to dissuade mothers (and fathers!) from having an abortion, or even when we seek to help those guilty of having had an abortion, we will not be minimizing the seriousness of the evil of abortion.

In addition, there is no reason to ignore the doctor who performs abortions. By allowing himself to become an accomplice of death, he has become unfaithful to his medical calling, which must be directed toward healing, restoring, and rescuing. Judges in a secularized nation where abortion has been legalized might be unable to treat him this way, but in the light of the sixth commandment, he is a murderer.

Euthanasia

Little or no attention was devoted to abortion and euthanasia by older commentators on the sixth commandment. Universal opinion, whether Christian or non-Christian, rejected both, making long essays about these subjects unnecessary. Today the situation is quite different, as we have already indicated with regard to abortion and now observe with regard to euthanasia. Although euthanasia has made fewer legislative advances than abortion, it is nevertheless becoming widely accepted.

For this brief discussion,[11] we would like to distinguish between two forms of euthanasia. The *first* form of euthanasia involves an intentional life-ending act without the consent of the person affected. Somebody ends the life of another because that is thought to be in the best interests of the person affected or of others involved. We have in view here euthanasia of newborns who come into the world with severe handicaps or of older persons who suffer senility.

Often it is indeed very difficult to assign value to such lives. What kind of future awaits children who will never take care of themselves, will never set foot out of bed, and perhaps never be able to communicate with anybody? And the life of people who become senile—what value does it have for these people themselves or those around them?

Nevertheless, we are not following in the steps of Jesus Christ if we terminate such lives that appear so meaningless to us. He provided a place in His kingdom for demon-possessed, lunatics, paralyzed, lepers, the blind, and the deaf. In our concourse with others, we naturally employ a scale of values, something not wrong in itself. We can view the dying of a worn-out body as a liberation, for the one who dies and for us. Moreover, unanswerable questions confront us when we reflect on the value and meaning of the lives of the severely handicapped. But all of this together should not tempt us to equate *our* scale of values with God's, so that we end up sitting in the judge's seat. We must try to bear the incomprehensibilities of life without resorting to killing.

The *second* form of euthanasia involves an intentional life-ending act at the request of the person affected. Here another person is not determining the course of events for the patient, but the one who wishes to die requests termination of life.

Many who cannot agree with the first form of euthanasia, because that involves people determining somebody else's life or death, nevertheless find this second form of euthanasia acceptable, since it rests upon the right of *self*-determination.

The concept of self-determination can be employed profitably in various contexts. Nations oppressed by external powers properly strive for self-determination. In various personal matters I myself must and may "determine" my own choices, and another person should not cramp my exercise of that liberty.

Nevertheless, the concept of self-determination is unacceptable if it functions as part of a worldview. It sounds very bizarre to insist upon self-determination when we reflect on the great influence that hundreds of people exert on our conduct! Surely, in the dying stages, most people are hardly in a position to exercise self-determination regarding what should or should not happen to them. As long as they receive the loving care they need, it is a good thing that others exercise determination over them in the good sense of the word.

But there is something more important for the Christian: When we live and die in God's presence, we do not exercise self-determination over ourselves. When God says that we may not kill, then we must not proceed stubbornly to put an end to our own lives. The wish for death can be a Christian desire, even outside of the dying stage of life (see Phil. 1:23). We may even pray for that; but that kind of praying itself presupposes that we must leave the realization thereof to God Himself.

Nowadays people say that praying for a "natural" death is a form of self-deception. Modern health care is of such a nature that nobody lives a natural life anymore and nobody dies a natural death. Here, too, everything is a product of cultural development. We have brought life to a higher level, we have lengthened life, and so why should we not be allowed to shorten it, too?

We would reply that a difference still remains between nature and culture, even when the human race holds in its hands power over virtually everything. Groves of trees dotting the horizon throughout the Midwest belong to nature, even though they are relatively young (since the 1930s) and were planted entirely by human hands. We even call such cultivated ("cultured") groves "natural," something we would not say about works displayed in an art museum. The boundaries shift somewhat, for a cultivated grove of trees is not as "natural" as a primeval forest. But life is not a human product, though a museum painting certainly is.

Similarly, it makes a difference whether someone dies from cancer or from an act of euthanasia. In the latter case, the cause of death is not the fatal illness, but the fatal human act. Why then would we not be justified in calling the former a natural cause of death and the latter an unnatural cause of death? Either we die when our physical and psychological powers are depleted, no matter how artificially those powers may have been sustained through proper diet, hygiene, and medical procedures—or we die because we are killed. Therefore, the question returns: who gives us the right to terminate human life?

In arguing this way, we are not saying that prolonging life is always a good thing and shortening life always wrong. Perhaps someone living in an otherwise hopeless situation might live a bit longer if he submitted to yet one more operation or one more treatment. But in that situation, he could legitimately refuse further treatment if it promises no real relief and would only further his misery and extend his suffering. In such a case, we observe once again how important it is to avoid the phrase *absolute* "reverence" for human life.* We must respect human life. If we can expect a medical procedure to extend life for a meaningful time, then we have an indication that such a treatment is desirable. But if not, then we have an indication that our task here on earth is finished. Life can be prolonged, but need not be stretched.

For this reason it is important to distinguish between terminating *life* and terminating *treatment*. Perhaps death will follow quickly after a treatment has been terminated, although that is by no means always the case. If a patient undergoes no further medical treatment, he must still be fed and cared for. That is not killing him, but giving him up. For this reason, the phrase "passive euthanasia" is less accurate than the phrase "termination of treatment." Someone who lets another die is not committing euthanasia, not even passive euthanasia. Moreover, terminating treatment is not so passive, since it consists of a well-considered decision to "do nothing more" for a patient.

In what we have written to this point, we have given merely general observations. Every reader must realize that in practice, very difficult situations arise, even the kind in which medical treatment is difficult to distinguish from active euthanasia. For example, life support cannot simply be terminated by (as the saying goes) "pulling the plug." If that were done, a patient could very well suffocate; to prevent that from happening, it is occasionally necessary to administer an injection, after which the life-support system is disconnected.

But in that kind of situation, too, the intention behind the medical procedure is important: Administering an injection so that the patient will fall asleep, never to awaken, is *here* indissolubly connected to discontinuation of *treatment*.

Suicide

The distinction between patient-requested euthanasia and suicide can be formulated very generally this way: Suicide occurs when the victim takes his own

---

* The Genevan Declaration, accepted by the World Medical Association (1948), reads in its *Dutch* version: "Ik zal absolute eerbied bewaren voor het menselijk leven vanaf de bevruchting" ("I will maintain *absolute* respect for human life from the time of conception"). The *English* version seems to us a bit broader (and therefore better): "I will maintain the *utmost* respect for human life from the time of conception."

life, while euthanasia requires the help of another person (most often a doctor). Moreover, suicide usually involves discontinuation of *life* and euthanasia the discontinuation of life's *final stage*. In specific situations, it can be quite difficult to see how these distinctions function, but usually they do.[12]

Just as with abortion and euthanasia, from the very beginning the church has condemned suicide. Occasionally opinion was divided regarding specific instances. Suicide by girls and women in order to preserve their sexual purity was approved by Ambrose but condemned by Augustine. Not the defilement of the body but the corruption of the soul is what must be feared, said Augustine.

Church councils of a later period decided that a church burial would not be permitted to those who died by suicide. One who committed suicide had acted contrary to nature. Had not the apostle Paul written that no one ever hates his own flesh (Eph. 5:29)? One who committed suicide had failed to fulfill his obligations toward the society of which he was a member. But above all he had sinned against God. He was viewed as a coward, who lacked the courage to endure his suffering.

In the Bible we read of six men who took their own lives: Samson (Judg. 16:23–31), Saul and his armorbearer (1 Sam. 31:3–5), Ahithophel, who had taken the side of Absalom in his struggle against David (2 Sam. 17:23), the Israelite king Zimri (1 Kings 16:18–19), and Judas Iscariot, after he had betrayed Jesus (Matt. 27:3–5). Nothing either good or bad is said about their actions. Saul is said to have fallen on his own sword, but later it is also said that the *Lord* killed him (1 Chron. 10:4, 14).

Biblical condemnation of those who took their own lives is possible only by taking into account their *entire* lives. Naturally, the suicides of Saul, Ahithophel, Zimri, and Judas were condemned, but in the case of Samson the matter is far more difficult. For in Hebrews 11 (vv. 32 and 39) he is mentioned as one of the heroes of faith. For this reason, Augustine thought the Spirit of God must have directed Samson to commit this act; otherwise, it would have to be condemned.

We do not get very far if we are limited to a few stories as the basis for our evaluation of suicide. It would be more appropriate to take as our starting point the sixth commandment with its prohibition against unlawful killing. Why not evaluate self-killing in terms of this commandment? We may not kill our neighbor because he is created in the image of God. But this applies to us as well.* We may not destroy the image of God that we

---

* In many older treatises against suicide, the argument was used that we are neighbors of ourselves. According to a Latin proverb, we are even "closest to ourselves" ("proximus

ourselves are. With Christian style, we must try to bear up under those troubles that can pressure us to consider suicide as a way out.

Nevertheless, we must be careful in our judgment of people who have taken their own lives. Remember that a relatively small percentage of suicide victims take their lives after cool and calm consideration. The kind of suicide where the victim has considered all the pros and cons and all the foreseeable consequences occurs less frequently than the suicide resulting from pathological behavior.

What people used to call cowardice is often mustering the courage of despair in order simply to escape the misery the victim is experiencing or expecting.* Numerous *suicidal gestures*† are nothing but cries for help arising from the depths of loneliness.

In the past, people were somewhat aware that psychological problems and depression could lead to suicide, but that awareness was not sufficiently developed. People used to say that the person who committed suicide sinned against society, but only recently has it dawned on us that the reverse is also possible: society may be offering no security to its psychologically weaker members.

Many of us know of believing Christians in our own communities who nonetheless took their own lives. Notes that they may have left behind leave us speechless. If we do speak about guilt, we are more inclined to ask ourselves what *we* could have done to prevent this tragedy.

Nevertheless, the fact that we have gained a deeper awareness of what leads people to commit suicide does not keep us from listening to the sixth commandment also when it talks about suicide. In a certain sense, we might well understand why a particular person committed suicide; but we can never justify suicide *ethically*. We cannot say that suicide is ever a permissible way out of the struggles of life. This applies first of all to ourselves,

---

est sibi quisque"). But, in our opinion, this is neither a biblical expression nor a biblical idea. This notion leads easily to overestimating the element of self-love.

* This is why the author Menno Ter Braak killed himself when the Germans invaded the Netherlands in 1940. Fellow writer Anton van Duinkerken commented: "He banned Hitler from the light of his eyes. He no longer desired life. Perhaps you would call this cowardice, but committing this act does require courage. I myself would choose psalms over rat poison" (quoted by G. Th. Rothuizen in *De thora in de thora*, 2:46).

†*Translator's note:* The terminology used in the original reflects categories found in *The Merck Manual* (Rahway, N.J., 1977), 1548. It may be more useful to distinguish as follows: *attempted suicide* is an intentional, though unsuccessful and nonfatal, attempt to kill oneself; *suicidal gestures* are chosen for their high probability of failure and are predominantly a means of communication, thus, a cry for help.

but this must also be the church's message, especially in response to arguments seeking to justify both euthanasia and suicide on the basis of the supposed right of self-determination.

But then we need to add immediately: Suicide is not necessary, either. Dietrich Bonhoeffer and others have pointed to the truth that in Jesus Christ there is refuge and hope for those who are most desperate. He is sovereign, not we. He makes of our lives what He wants; we do not decide that. He directs our lives toward their goal; it does not depend on our efforts. In this evangelical manner, we can counsel all who are psychologically distressed, all who feel it is senseless to go on living.

Suicide can also include cases of *self-sacrifice*. Besides selfish suicide there is permissible suicide. We read that no one demonstrates greater love than the one who lays down his life for his friends (John 15:13).

One can give up his life for wicked or for noble purposes. Samson took his own life, but not to put an end to his miserable situation. His final deed belonged to his life calling that he had pursued up to that point: opposing the Philistines as enemies of God's people. One can give up one's life for one's country by not allowing oneself to fall into enemy hands. This is why some have blown up their own ships, knowing that they would die in the process. Evaluations of this kind of act differ. What is clear, however, is that the motive for self-sacrifice differs from the motive behind suicide where the victim desires an end to his own personal misery. For that reason, from an ethical point of view, it is easier to show a measure of understanding for self-sacrifice.

Negligent Homicide

We mentioned earlier that it is possible to be responsible for someone's death through our own recklessness or negligence. The Israelite was supposed to build a railing around his roof terrace to prevent accidents; there are various situations in which we too must be aware of the danger that others (and we ourselves) could be exposed to because of our conduct. Loose scaffolding, exposed wiring, slippery sidewalks, containers with dangerous contents accessible to children—these and many other examples deserve mention.

An example on an international level would be the pollution caused by nuclear plants and the disposal of nuclear waste. All the coal mines together have exacted thousands of victims, often because of inadequate safety measures. But if ever there were an accident at a nuclear plant, the consequences could well be far more terrible. The nuclear accident at

Chernobyl demonstrated clearly how cosmic the consequences of but one nuclear accident at one nuclear plant can be. The life and health of millions of people depend on enforcing proper safety measures.

Here we can see that the sixth commandment extends far and wide into our daily lives. The number of murders and killings mentioned in our daily newspapers is small compared to the number of people who are liable for the death of others through their irresponsible behavior.

A couple of matters deserve our attention. Consider first our vehicle *traffic*, which daily claims life upon life. Some have even identified "sicknesses" associated with driving, like being in a constant hurry, driving aggressively, reacting emotionally to the driving behavior of others, driving while overly tired, or driving under the influence of alcohol. Sicknesses associated with driving which cause injury and death are more than sicknesses—they are sins. Being in a hurry is no excuse for dangerous passing or exceeding the speed limit. These tactics simply demonstrate how in reality we think everything should revolve around our needs. As a pair of Dutch ethicists have put it, "In principle and in practice the egocentric person wants to have nothing or as little as possible to do with his fellowman. He follows traffic laws only with reluctance, considers them to be a limitation of his freedom and obeys them only when the policeman is nearby and he might get stopped."[13]

Should we then say that in view of the large number of traffic accidents, anyone using an automobile is really endangering the safety of others? Such a claim would be unrealistic. Every form of travel involves some risk. Even when walking, we do not always follow the safety rules. The story is told that when Pierre Curie, the French physicist and Nobel Prize winner (1859–1906), was killed as a pedestrian, the news of his death reached his father, who reportedly exclaimed, "Wonder what he was thinking about this time?"[14] Traveling by airplane is not without risk. But in past centuries more people died in storms at sea than die now in much more congested air traffic.

The person who wants to avoid all risk will never travel, but that would paralyze life. The warning of the sixth commandment is not designed to frustrate living life, with all the risks connected with that living.* Using a

---

* Risks can be reduced through better safety precautions, but risks can be increased by other factors, such as higher traffic speeds. Still, this latter can perhaps be acceptable. Here is a good example: In 1937 a bus driver who had hit a horse and wagon was sent to prison. He should have been prepared for that horse and wagon crossing the street. Today, because of higher speeds, a driver would have difficulty avoiding such a collision. See Noyon and Langemeijer, *Het wetboek van strafrecht*, Introduction, 65.

car involves inherent risks, but that is no reason to view a car as a coffin on wheels. Many things go faster than before, but that also accounts for lives being saved that previously would have been lost (ambulances, for example). We cannot eliminate the automobile anymore, but at most restrict its use. Evil lies not in the automobile, but in people who misuse this good invention.

It is not possible to avoid every danger. Explorers, mountain climbers, and other pioneers of a former era exposed themselves to quite some dangers, but that does not mean that they *recklessly endangered* themselves—something the Heidelberg Catechism, in Lord's Day 40, properly condemns. If you have no sense of adventure, you had best not go exploring, and if you have a fear of heights, do not go mountain climbing. But what one person cannot do and therefore should not do, another certainly may do. It would be narrow-minded to force everybody to fit the mold of the average person.

In the areas of *sport and entertainment,* as soon as risks are taken that endanger someone's health or perhaps his very life, then the line is being crossed. We have in mind sports such as automobile and motorbike racing, boxing, and the like. Acrobatic performances at the circus or on tour provide enormous thrills to millions of spectators, but if they put human lives at risk, then we are no longer enjoying a healthy sport or form of entertainment.

We can also undermine our health by becoming addicted to *drugs* or by excessive use of *alcohol* or *tobacco.* No single drug is without danger, and the surroundings in which the drug user ends up often lead him from one step to another, not stopping at the use of soft drugs, but finally becoming addicted to hard drugs. Many young people have landed in this make-believe world of happiness with fatal consequences. Without reserve, we must say no to drug use.

Addiction to *smoking* does not seem to affect the mind to the same degree as addiction to other drugs. This makes it look safer. But if cigarette packages are required to inform people that smoking poses a health hazard, that should be enough to make us realize we should quit smoking. But people do not always do what should be done. There is something a bit hypocritical in all the hue and cry about drug abuse if we continue to tolerate the habit of smoking.

There is much good that can be said about *alcohol,* since wine makes the heart glad (Ps. 104:15) and the fruit of the vine will be enjoyed in the kingdom of God (Matt. 26:29). The teetotaler deserves our respect if, in protest against alcohol abuse, he abstains from all use of alcoholic beverages. But he should not try to press this upon others as a demand of Scripture. There is a wholesome use of alcohol, one that does not debase life, but rather rejuvenates it.

We are certainly aware of the reality that alcohol abuse can destroy a person just as terribly as drug addiction. The Bible warns us clearly enough against this abuse. Wine can bite like a snake and sting like a viper (Prov. 23:32). Moderation in drinking is a requirement that applies to everybody.

Our health is a priceless possession that must be protected wherever possible. We denounce the drunkard and the drug addict, but someone who strays from his prescribed diet is guilty, too. We must use moderation in eating and drinking.

Preventive measures are part of the caution required in the context of the sixth commandment, with a view to protecting our own lives. We cannot keep suffering out of our lives, but there are kinds of suffering that we can either eliminate or prevent. Consider, for example, the matter of *vaccination* as a preventive measure against various infectious diseases. Unfortunately, there are still many people who consider vaccination to be forbidden by the Bible. As a result of their arguments, sometimes publicly advanced and defended, thousands of children have fallen victim to diseases preventable by modern medical means.[15] The Mosaic laws prescribed measures to prevent the spread or outbreak of leprosy (Lev. 14:33–57). We may get out of the way of approaching danger. "A prudent man sees danger and takes refuge, but the simple keep going and suffer for it" (Prov. 22:3 niv).

Getting to the Heart of the Matter

The Heidelberg Catechism confesses in Lord's Day 40 that we are not to belittle, insult, hate, or kill our neighbor by thought, word, look, or gesture. God's commandment penetrates to the human heart, since He hates the *root* of all murder: envy, hatred, anger, and vindictiveness.

But even this does not yet penetrate to the essence of the sixth commandment. For, as Lord's Day 40 teaches, when God forbids envy, hatred, anger, and vindictiveness, He *commands* us to love our neighbors as ourselves; to be patient, peace-loving, gentle, merciful, and friendly toward him; to protect him from harm as much as possible—and even to do good to our enemies.

The duties that the Heidelberg Catechism connects to the sixth commandment do indeed fit. In the Sermon on the Mount, Jesus Himself taught clearly that we need to go beyond what "was said to [or, by] those of old, 'You shall not murder,' and whoever murders will be in danger of the judgment" (Matt. 5:21). For someone who is merely angry with another person without a cause, or calls him stupid or an idiot, will have to answer to the Sanhedrin and "shall be in danger of hell fire" (Matt. 5:22). Jesus uses these provocative statements to indicate clearly that *every* sin against the sixth commandment is serious, no matter how trivial it may seem. We should look behind the dramatic act of murder to consider everything that can lead up to it.

We can dishonor another person without laying a finger on him. Nabal and Shimei used "mere" words when they mocked David (1 Sam. 25:10; 2 Sam. 16:7–8), yet their language was full of deadly venom. "Reckless words pierce like a sword" (Prov. 12:18 NIV). Many people have been robbed of their honor and have watched their futures disintegrate because of slander and backbiting. That too is destruction of life.

It does not require a lengthy discussion to show that hatred, anger, envy, and vindictiveness are forms of killing. Someone who hates another person is really thinking, "I wish he were dead." In fact, "whoever hates his brother is a murderer" (1 John 3:15).

Compared with hatred, anger is more of a momentary explosion of rage, and in that way it is a far more direct display of the disgust we feel toward another person. We hurl angry words in another person's face and our eyes betray what we would really like to do. Yes, looks can kill, too.

Envy means wanting to steal a piece of good fortune that we do not have. Envy is not only a way of attacking another person, but also a way of destroying ourselves (Prov. 14:30).

A vindictive person wants to enforce a punishment against another person without the right to do so. Vindictiveness is just as unlawful as other forms of killing. We may not avenge ourselves, but should leave room for wrath, which means, we must let God be the judge, so that He can enforce His wrath by avenging evil (Rom. 12:19).

So, then, hatred, anger, envy, and vindictiveness are rejected. Still, all four of these can be expressed in legitimate ways. "Do I not hate them, O LORD, who hate You? And do I not loathe those who rise up against You?" the poet asks (Ps. 139:21). We may not casually dismiss the so-called imprecatory psalms (Pss. 69, 109, and 137) by labeling their content Old Testament and therefore out-of-date. There is also a kind of jealousy where a husband does not look kindly on his wife chasing another man, just as Yahweh shows His jealousy when Israel chases other gods (Num. 5:11–31; Deut. 32:21).

There is room for righteous anger and a holy vengeance, both of which desire the honor and justice of God and our neighbor. In such situations we may get really angry. A person without the capacity for vengeance is a person without a sense of justice, someone has observed.*

The story comes to mind of the man interviewed by the Americans after their soldiers had liberated a concentration camp where hundreds of thousands of Jews and others had been murdered. The man declared that if he had to watch the Americans shoot, one by one, the brutes guilty of these murders, he would not blink an eye. That kind of person is not necessarily being vindictive. He is simply giving expression to the kind of hatred that human beings *must* demonstrate whenever others are tortured and murdered in such a godless and inhuman way. He simply wanted to watch *justice* take its course.

Obviously, the situation is not made easier when unrighteous anger is mixed with righteous anger. After all, we are inclined to justify our own impulses of anger and feelings of hatred by insisting that we are looking out for God's honor, when in fact we are simply pursuing our self-interest. If you dig more deeply into what the sixth commandment requires, you will always end up at the point of self-examination. Honesty with ourselves requires us to check carefully whether we are really pursuing God's honor in our anger and our cries for justice. We must pray that God will test us and examine us to see if we are walking down a wicked path (Ps. 139:23–24).

The sixth commandment penetrates down to the root of all killing, and thereby forbids any wrong attitude of heart. It unmasks not only wrong actions, but wrong attitudes as well. But we must take one more step, for otherwise we would be stopping with the negative. Saying *no* to death means saying *yes* to life. And this yes is just as radical as our no. We have not arrived if we simply avoid killing or hating our neighbor, for the opposite of these is that we must *love* our neighbor.

This too Jesus taught in the Sermon on the Mount. If someone slaps us on the right cheek, then we should offer him the left one (Matt. 5:39). If someone compels us to go one mile with him, offer to go two

---

* A. F. C. Villmar, quoted by W. Geesink, *Gereformeerde ethiek* (Kampen, 1931), 1:396. To this Geesink adds his criticism of a passive and philosophical acquiescence to whatever happens, as well as the kind of unquestioning acceptance found in Buddhism and Hinduism, or any weakening of the sense of justice, or the attitude of "tout savoir c'est tout pardonner," along with a false peaceableness and lack of courage to make a moral judgment— all of these being ethically indefensible.

miles (Matt. 5:41). We must love not only our neighbor, but even our enemy (Matt. 5:44). Later, Paul wrote that we should give our hungry enemy food and our thirsty enemy drink, thereby heaping coals of fire on his head (Rom. 12:20–21).

The tone of the entire Sermon on the Mount is not that we spare our neighbor the worst, but that we give him the best.[16] And that best we should bestow even upon our enemies. Right here the deepest significance of the sixth commandment comes to light.

The Commandment's Long Reach: "Your Neighbor"

At the same time, the widest significance of the sixth commandment comes to the surface. If we are to love our enemies, then surely in principle nobody is excluded from that love. Showing love toward our enemies broadens the notion of "neighbor" to include all people.

The story is told of an old Toradja tribal member who agreed enthusiastically that it was bad to kill anyone. But by "anyone" he meant another member of his own tribe. Anybody not belonging to this tribal clan could be killed.[17]

So the term "neighbor" applied only to one's fellow countryman. This was also the view of "those of old" whom Jesus mentioned several times in the Sermon on the Mount: "You shall love your neighbor [meaning, your fellow countryman] and hate your enemy" (Matt. 5:43). That restriction of the term "neighbor" to "fellow countryman" we find also in Leviticus 19:18: " 'You shall not take vengeance, nor bear any grudge against the children of your people, but you shall love your neighbor as yourself: I am the Lord." Loving one's enemy was commanded already in the Old Testament, but that applied only to enemies among one's fellow citizens. The Israelite who found his enemy's lost donkey or ox was supposed to return it to its owner. He was also supposed to help ease the load on his enemy's donkey who would otherwise have collapsed under its burden (Ex. 23:4–5). No Israelite was permitted to gloat over the misfortune of his enemy (Prov. 24:17). The enemy suffering hunger or thirst was to be given food and drink (Prov. 25:21). In spite of all these exhortations, the field of vision including friend and foe remained limited to one's own countrymen, occasionally going beyond to include the resident foreigner who was to be loved in view of the fact that Israel herself had once been a foreigner in Egypt (Lev. 19:34).

In the New Testament, the circle expands. There the neighbor includes not only one's fellow countryman, but also the stranger beyond the national border. Quite appropriately, the parable of the good Samaritan has been called a parable of worldwide historical significance.[18] In the gospel of Christ, the term "neighbor" has lost its limits. If every nation is to be discipled for Christ (Matt. 28:19), then for a Christian no single nation can remain a *foreign* nation outside the circle of those who are our neighbors (see Eph. 2:11–13).

But saying this is not to insist that everyone is our neighbor in the same sense. Indiscriminate love of humanity is cheap love. Nobody is ever tempted to hate an unknown faraway Mexican or Oriental. But things become more difficult when a Mexican or an Oriental is put in our pathway. For it is when they stand *in our path* that we begin to notice how soon they get *in our way*.

In that connection, we are called first not to love those living farthest away, but those who live nearest to us. This means those people who cross our path, just as in the parable mentioned earlier. Have you ever been struck by the fact that no fewer than three times it is said—of the priest, the Levite, and the Samaritan—that they *saw* the half-dead man lying alongside the path? By seeing *and* doing, the Samaritan became a neighbor to the man who needed help. We do not have to look far in our search to discover whom we should love. We cannot love four billion people, but we have our hands full with those people whom *God* has put in our path:* family members, brothers and sisters in the church, fellow citizens and foreigners, friends and enemies. Although not in practice, certainly in principle, any person in the world could belong to these circles. Like all the others, the sixth commandment too has come to fulfillment in Christ. We must love life to the farthest ends of the earth.

---

* Abraham Kuyper rejected the notion of a universal love for humanity. God puts people—including our enemy—in our path. "That person does not stand there by mistake. It is not by accident or divine oversight that he treats you the way he does." Kuyper goes further to identify the difference between Reformed and Pelagian ethics. The contrast can be reduced to this: "We on our part deduce every relationship from God's sovereign rule and for that reason either perform or omit performing everything *for the sake of God's will*, measuring everything according to His precepts. Pelagian ethics, by contrast, simply views people as sovereign individuals, without a higher power binding them together, and therefore finds no other motive for moral consciousness, moral values and inclinations, than a sovereign human will to choose. But precisely at the point of loving one's enemy, Pelagian ethics is fatally flawed, because this ethical system can never naturally climb upward from the platform of a sovereign choice of the human will to reach the pinnacle of loving someone who is an enemy" (*E voto Dordraceno*, 3d ed. [Kampen, 1892–95], 4:96ff.).

Self-Defense

"You shall not kill unlawfully," says the sixth commandment. Someone can be killed by another person, however, without that killing being *unlawful*. With this topic we are nearing the end of this chapter. For what reasons and under what circumstances is it permissible to kill another person?

We think first of *self-defense*. This refers to defending ourselves against someone who is attacking our person or property. Recall the biblical example of an intruder: If a thief caught breaking and entering received a fatal blow, that would not be considered a culpable killing (Ex. 22:2).

What is remarkable is that culpability is involved when such an intruder is killed in broad daylight (Ex. 22:3). In the darkness of night, the situation is confused. Is the intruder armed? Is there only one, or are there more? If the owner (properly) refuses to let the intruder simply rob him, a fight could well break out at the cost of the intruder's life. But during the daytime the situation is clearer, and then everything must be done to prevent bloodshed. From this twofold regulation we see how precious human life is. Even when someone is busy robbing another, care must still be taken with his life. In our modern criminal law this distinction about self-defense operates too. If the government and its agencies are unable to provide the necessary protection when it is urgently and immediately needed, then *self-defense* is permissible.[*] We have a right to resist unrighteousness.[19]

Capital Punishment

We have seen that respect for human life forbids a person to kill another human being, so that even in cases of self-defense the greatest care should be exercised. If all this is true, is there any room for capital punishment where in fact the life of one person is taken by another?

The answer must be positive. What is clear in Scripture is the basis for capital punishment, namely, *respect* for human life: "Whoever sheds man's blood, by man his blood shall be shed; *for* in the image of God He made man" (Gen. 9:6). Because a human being is so precious, the shedding of human blood must[†] be paid for with the blood of the killer.

---

[*] By "self-defense" we mean securing justice for oneself without the intervention of an officer of the law.

[†] It is incorrect to construe Gen. 9:6 as merely an *observation*, in the line of: Experience teaches us that murder inevitably leads to murder, and that one who raises his hand to kill

Thus, respect for human life means also that a person may not be killed with impunity. Rather, because human life is so precious, it deserves *protection*. We can see this clearly in the fact that the government possesses the sword. The government is called to use that sword in service to God, as an avenger to execute wrath on him who practices evil (Rom. 13:4). So evil must be punished and requited. But at the same time the sword serves to *prevent* murder, as the Heidelberg Catechism properly confesses in Lord's Day 40. This sword exists not only to strike, but also to prevent another from striking. Government exists to forcefully punish law-breaking citizens; but, at the same time, by this means the government constructs a protective wall around the life of law-abiding citizens.

It is important to underscore this positive aspect. The sword can serve life. For that very reason, God gave it to the government. If you understand this, then you have an effective argument against those who talk in a pacifist sense about "reverence for life." Their "reverence" is not deep enough, for it leads eventually to leaving human life unprotected.[20]

God constructs barriers in this world for the protection of human life. All of us are murderers, measured by the deepest meaning of the sixth commandment. But there are certain obstacles that prevent us from moving from one stage to the next. Everything we think, we dare not say. And everything we say, we dare not carry out. Even though a straight line ran from Cain's angry glance to his murder of his brother Abel, fortunately most people never take that next step.

Various factors could be mentioned, factors that function to prevent us from going that far. Undoubtedly among them is our fear of retribution. To say it with a term from Romans 13 (v. 5), the *wrath* of the government restrains people from doing what deep down in their hearts they would like to do.

The sword has been entrusted to the government, and therefore not to every individual. In Romans 12, Paul says to believers: Take no revenge, but let God be the judge (Rom. 12:19). But in Romans 13 he says that the *government* may exercise, on God's behalf, the vengeance due those who practice evil (Rom. 13:4). We are forbidden to take vengeance, but obviously the government is not. What we may not do, the government may

---

another will himself ultimately fall victim to the same fate. This interpretation blunts the point of Gen. 9:6. Precisely *because* man is created in God's image, there is a justifiable, divinely willed connection between murder and the bloody *retribution* for murder. This verse is not simply making an observation about capital punishment (carried out at that time through personal vengeance); rather, this text is giving us a command.

do. In God's name, the government may use the sword, whereas we as individuals must keep our hands off.

Using the sword to avenge murder was the prerogative, in former times, of the victim's family. We see already in the Bible that this right was somewhat restricted. Cities of refuge were built to provide safety for people who killed unintentionally. One single witness was insufficient to sentence a killer to death (Num. 35:30). The elders of the city (Deut. 19:12; Josh. 20:4) and even an "assembly" (Num. 35:12; Josh. 20:6), most likely a higher court, became involved. The trial clearly investigated the defendant's intention. Did the death occur unintentionally, or did it involve hatred (Deut. 19:4)?

The meticulousness of this investigation is striking, because we read of nothing similar in connection with other offenses that received the death penalty. Their number was not small, for some thirty crimes received the death penalty, such as idolatry, Sabbath desecration, rebellion against parents, adultery, and homosexual conduct.

Naturally, in all these cases the trial proceedings would not have been sloppy. But it is quite significant that in no other case was such a careful investigation prescribed as when the death penalty was going to be administered for murder.[21]

In our opinion, this is an indication of the transition from private vengeance by family members to adjudication by government agencies—a fortunate development that brought an end to indulging in vendettas and feuds.

So we can draw a line from the vengeance executed by family members to the authority for exercising capital punishment, an authority that has come to rest in the hands of official judicatories.

But should we not take the next step of eliminating capital punishment altogether? Can we in this day and age defend capital punishment?

Many Christians believe that capital punishment should no longer be exercised. In addition to objections of a more general nature,* we encounter one particular objection that deserves separate discussion. This objection argues that after the death of Jesus Christ, there is no place for the death penalty. This is what Karl Barth argued when he insisted that Christ was put to death for the sins of all men and through His death the judicial

---

* Such as: (1) capital punishment has no deterrent effect; (2) the exercise of capital punishment is irrevocable, and therefore, in view of possible judicial error, it is irresponsible; (3) any rehabilitation of the criminal is impossible; and (4) reverence for life must always be the most important consideration.

basis underlying the death penalty was satisfied. If God is reconciled to all men, we can no longer deal retributively by enforcing a criminal code that includes capital punishment. At most, the death penalty may be used in certain boundary situations, such as high treason in a time of war.[22]

In a separate volume in this series, we discuss capital punishment more extensively.[23] Here we suffice with several summary remarks.

If Christ's death is the basis for eliminating the death penalty altogether, does not the death of Christ (as Barth understands it) also require eliminating any and all retribution from our *criminal* punishments? But clearly this conclusion does not agree with what the New Testament teaches us. The gospel does not exclude retribution. God is going to reward each man according to his deeds (Matt. 16:27; Rom. 2:7). Even though *we* may not personally avenge evil, for that reason God does avenge evil (Rom. 12:17; 1 Thess. 5:15; 1 Peter 3:9, along with Rom. 12:19; 2 Thess. 1:6; 2 Tim. 4:14; Heb. 10:30). The testimony of Scripture—not just the Old Testament, but the New Testament as well—is so clear that we cannot follow Barth down the path he has chosen, the path of universal reconciliation. It was not Christ's intention that sin and evil be, as it were, pushed aside and paid for by His cross, apart from any consideration of whether people received His message or not.[24]

As we have already seen, God places responsibility for avenging crimes in the hands of the government. The government does not possess the sword "in vain" (Rom. 13:4)—which means, not for nothing. The apostles had no problem with this. Characteristic of their attitude was the fact that Paul would not have opposed a death sentence if he had committed a capital crime, as we read in Acts 25:11.

Moreover, in our opinion it is difficult to defend with consistency Barth's claim that a traitor or war criminal may be punished with death, but not someone who murders in peacetime. Experience also shows that the general public has a hard time understanding this distinction. As soon as terrorists commit violence or when criminals attack children, the public cries out for reinstating the death penalty. Of course, for us this is not a strong argument for capital punishment, but it does nonetheless show just how strange it is to ban the death penalty altogether, only to reinstate it for punishing only certain murderers. Someone who believes that all people have been reconciled to God through Christ will have a difficult time showing why then certain people may still need to be executed.

For the reason that God has provided the right to avenge through capital punishment (and only for that reason), we continue to insist that there is room also in our modern age for capital punishment. The question is appropriate whether we should push for reinstating the death penalty now that a secularized society no longer accepts the only legitimate *foundation* for capital punishment (the command of God to punish all attacks against man as the image of God).

If we do, we must certainly take into account the fact that we cannot simply use the death penalty in the same way Israel used it. We no longer enforce the death penalty for crimes like Sabbath desecration, adultery, and homosexuality. In so doing, we take into account that Israel was God's people and was supposed to live holy before Him. The civil and the spiritual were intertwined, something not true (or in any case, something that does not have to be true) of the ecclesiastical and civil governments as we know them today.

Capital punishment for murder is different from those cases just mentioned. This death penalty applied in the context of avenging wrongdoing: life for life, eye for eye, tooth for tooth, and the like (Ex. 21:23–25). The basic idea underlying this regulation is applied in the criminal codes of all nations, no matter how much these applications differ from those among Israel. After all, this regulation aims at fair and controlled retribution.*

Criminal justice systems in Western societies are organized differently than that of an ancient Eastern nation, something that will always have implications for the subject of capital punishment. For example, our judicial system employs imprisonment, a phenomenon that appears nowhere in the Mosaic legislation. Alongside the *retributive* element of punishment, incarceration provides Western societies with greater possibility for benefiting from the *preventive* character of punishment. Locking up a criminal bans him from society and protects the public from him.† So even in secularized societies that no longer enforce the death penalty, if capital

---

* Lamech killed a man for wounding him and a young man for injuring him (Gen. 4:25). Here the injury and the punishment were not at all proportionate. But the outcome is different with the so-called *ius talionis*, the law of retaliation or right of retribution found in Ex. 21:24. There we read about proportionality. One who destroys the eye of another person must pay with the loss of his own eye, but not with the loss of his life. Modern criminal justice cannot function without a concept of proportionality. A fruit grower who protects his orchards by installing an electric fence carrying a dangerous voltage is not exercising proportionality. See Hazewinkel-Suringa, *Inleiding tot de studie van het Nederlandse strafrecht*, 213ff.

† The retributive and preventive elements are not mutually exclusive, but rather complementary. For that reason, we need not choose between punishing "quia peccatum" (because crime has occurred, punishment must follow) and "ne peccatur" (so that crime will not be committed again). Both have a legitimate place.

punishment were to be reinstated, it would definitely be administered far less frequently than in biblical times. We have already seen how meticulous the judicial procedure prescribed for Israel really was. If the death penalty were reinstated, the reputation of a judge would not be tainted if, in cases of intentional homicide, he very seldom prescribed death and instead regularly sentenced such criminals to prison.

Destruction of man as the image of God is avenged with other punishments as well. We do not believe it is correct to say that *every* illegitimate killing should be punished with only the death penalty. That position is too narrow[*] and fails to recognize developments in the area of jurisprudence and refinements in penology (in comparison with, for example, the Mosaic legislation, in which prison sentences were unknown).

War

The sword given to the government may be used not only against evildoers from within, but also against invaders from without. The right of a government to wage war cannot be rejected, when defending national territory or assisting threatened allies.[25] The best example is the last world war. The regime of Adolf Hitler was destroyed, putting an end to mass murder (especially of Jews) and returning freedom to many nations.

Only on the basis of pacifism could anybody oppose that kind of war of liberation. Surely the Bible is not pacifist. Numerous wars were fought at God's command or with His approval (Num. 21:14; Deut. 20:16–18; Rev. 19:11, and more), so that we can hardly characterize war with the generalization that it is *sin*. God does require restraint in deciding to wage war or in waging war, as we are taught by the laws of war in Deuteronomy 20. Partially on this basis, the concept of "just war" developed in history. Generally stated, a just war must be waged (1) by a legitimate government, (2) for a legitimate cause, (3) with a legitimate purpose, (4) with consideration of benefits and costs, (5) with means proportionate to the offense, and (6) recognizing the difference between civilians and soldiers.

War is an abnormal business, also in the Bible. Although Scripture presents no prohibition against waging war, the Bible does make clear that

---

[*] That narrow position cannot be maintained even on biblical grounds. For example, Cain was spared by God after he murdered Abel (Gen. 4:13–15), and both David and Ahab were punished on account of their murder of Uriah and Naboth, respectively, but not with the death sentence (1 Kings 12:13; 21:29).

war and bloodshed must never be accepted as normal phenomena (Josh. 1:13; Isa. 2:2–4; Mic. 4:1–5). King David was not allowed to build a temple for God because he had waged war and had shed blood (1 Chron. 28:3). The goal of war must always be peace, and any program of armament must be pursued in the context of preserving peace.

But is the sword of the government still acceptable when it is a *nuclear* sword? Are not nuclear weapons like the sword of Damocles that hangs over the world with the threat of total destruction? Is it still permissible to manufacture these weapons? Should we not become *nuclear* pacifists in view of the demonic character of these weapons?

Fear of nuclear weapons is very understandable, but must not drive us to do stupid things. We may well sloganeer that nuclear weapons should be banned; but what if unilateral disarmament results in the other side seizing the opportunity to employ its nuclear weapons? We are responsible also for the conduct of the other insofar as we may entice him to react.

We realize, of course, that this line of reasoning does not help if making nuclear weapons and using them as a deterrent would lead *inevitably* to using them offensively. But reality teaches us something else. Precisely the horrifying awfulness of these weapons and the realistic threat of their use has resulted in the emergence of a new phenomenon. Until now, new weapons were always quickly introduced in battle to gain an advantage over the enemy. But with nuclear weapons, this has remained restricted to the use of two bombs in the war against Japan (dropped on Hiroshima and Nagasaki). When not only America, but also the Soviet Union, and, later, still other countries, had nuclear weapons at their disposal, that spelled the end of their use. The effects of nuclear weapons are so horrible that any government that tries to attack another with such weapons will itself be annihilated by a counterattack.

To that extent, nuclear weapons are effective as a *deterrent* that until now could not be used effectively in *combat*. For that reason, nuclear weapons function to preserve the balance of power in the modern world.

Someone has said: "The tactic of preserving peace by threatening one another with mutual destruction belongs to the kind of moral and political system that deserves our deepest moral indignation." But we would formulate the matter differently: "The tactic of preserving peace by restraining one another from that mutual destruction belongs to the kind of moral and political system that unquestionably deserves our moral approval."[26]

Without a doubt, we are confronted here with ethical difficulties. On the one hand, a government must *be willing* to use nuclear weapons in an emergency, so that they *will never be used* by an opponent or by the government itself. Otherwise, the deterrence is implausible. A government with nuclear weapons at its disposal that never threatens to use them will become easy prey for its enemy. On the other hand, we know that nuclear weapons actually *may* not be used, because the danger is far too great that (part of) the world will be plunged into unimaginable misery. We need not study those six conditions of a "just war" very long to realize that a nuclear war could never be a just war!

This brings us to a final comment. Nuclear weapons expose the deep misery into which man has plunged himself. He cannot get rid of these weapons anymore.* He cannot live without them. And he cannot use them.

In obedience to the sixth commandment, we must do everything possible to prevent nuclear catastrophe from occurring, by means of discussions and decisions carried out on a global level. At the same time, we look forward to the return of Jesus Christ, because only He will be in a position to remove the sword of Damocles hanging over our heads. What the sixth commandment demands, He alone can ultimately provide, He who said of Himself: I am the way, the truth, and the *life* (John 14:6).

Endnotes

1. See J. Douma, *Milieu en manipulatie*, 2d ed. (Kampen, 1988).
2. See P. W. Marais, *Die tien woorde van God* (Pretoria, 1978), 170; J. A. Heyns, *Teologiese etiek* (Pretoria, 1982), 1:330.
3. J. L. Koole, *De Tien Geboden*, 2d ed. (Kampen, 1983), 97.
4. Cited by M. A. Beek, "God loven met het lichaam," in *Loven en geloven: Opstellen van collega's en medewerkers aangeboden aan Prof. Dr. Nic. H. Ridderbos* (Amsterdam, 1975), 202.
5. J. L. Koole, *De Tien Geboden*, 97.
6. Cited by W. J. Aalders, *De Tien Geboden* (Zeist, 1932), 39.
7. See A. Schweitzer, *Kultur und Ethik*, 7th ed. (Munich, 1948), 241. For an evaluation of Schweitzer's perspective, see K. Barth, *Church Dogmatics*, 3/4:324, 326, 349–51.
8. B. Reicke, *Die zehn Worte in Geschichte und Gegenwart* (Tübingen, 1973), 59.
9. See J. Douma, *Abortus*, 5th ed. (Kampen, 1984), 39, 55–56.
10. John Calvin, *Commentaries on the Four Last Books of Moses arranged in the Form of a Harmony*, trans. Charles William Bingham (reprint, Grand Rapids, 1981), 3:41–42.
11. For a more extensive discussion, see J. Douma, *Rondom de dood* (Kampen, 1984).

---

* Even if we were to collect every nuclear weapon, the secret for annihilating millions of people in one fell swoop has been discovered. We had better learn to live with the fact that nuclear weapons will become increasingly easier to manufacture.

12. The interested reader will find a more extensive discussion of this subject, along with the bibliography for the information that appears here, in ibid., 61ff.

13. E. L. Smelik and M. van Witsen, *Ethiek van het verkeer* (Nijkerk, 1964), 39. For their discussion of "driving sicknesses," see 36ff.

14. Ibid., 41.

15. For a review of this issue, including a broad discussion of the arguments advanced from the Bible against vaccination, see J. Douma and W. H. Velema, *Polio: Afwachten of afweren?* (Amsterdam, 1979).

16. See J. van Bruggen, *The Sermon on the Mount: A Travel Guide for Christians* (Winnipeg, 1986), 32–33.

17. A. C. Kruyt, "Het Zesde Gebod," in *Sinaï en Ardjoeno*, 154–55.

18. W. Geesink, *Van 's Heeren ordinantiën* (Kampen, 1925), 3:151.

19. See Hazewinkel-Suringa, *Inleiding tot de studie van het Nederlandse strafrecht*, 6th ed., ed. J. Remmelink (Groningen, 1973), 216–17.

20. See G. Th. Rothuizen, in *De thora in de thora*, 2:28.

21. See J. L. Koole, *De Tien Geboden*, 99.

22. Karl Barth, *Church Dogmatics*, 3/4:437–50. Concerning this entire subject, see W. H. Velema, *De rechtvaardiging van de straf* (Amsterdam, 1978), 121ff.

23. See J. Douma, *Recht en straf.*

24. W. H. Velema, *De rechtvaardiging van de straf*, 127.

25. We offer an extensive discussion of the entire subject of war in J. Douma, *Gewapende vrede*, vol. 14 in the series *Ethische bezinning* (Kampen, 1988).

26. The first statement came from the Inter-Church Peace Conference (in a speech by Ben ter Veer); the second remark is ours, made in a speech entitled "Bergrede en kernwapens" ("The Sermon on the Mount and Nuclear Weapons"), contained in *Vrede in vrijheid (Peace in Liberty)*, a collection of addresses given on 24 September 1983 in Congress Hall at The Hague (published by the Foundation for a Politics of Peace).

The Seventh Commandment

You shall not commit adultery. (Ex. 20:14)

A Crime Against Property?

The Hebrew word used in the Bible for "to commit adultery" (or for "marital infidelity") indicates that a man who is either married or unmarried has sexual intercourse with a married woman. He thereby destroys the troth (the marriage) of his neighbor. He takes into his possession the woman who belongs to another man. Even if this woman is not officially married, but merely engaged to be married, the same verdict applies: the adulterer has violated his neighbor's wife (Deut. 22:24).

If a man had sexual relations with a woman who was neither married nor engaged, at least in Israel that would not have been called adultery. The decisive factor was the woman's status: did *she* belong to another or not? The fact that the *man himself* was married would lead us, but not necessarily an Israelite, to speak of adultery. For in Israel a man could have more than one wife. Bigamy and polygamy were practiced, and having sexual relations with yet other kinds of women would frequently not have been considered adultery.

An illustration of this is the conduct of Judah with Tamar (Gen. 38). Initially, Tamar was charged with adultery on account of her behavior, but Judah was not. The reason was that he had had sexual intercourse with a woman he thought belonged to no other man.

It seems as if in Israel adultery was in fact a *crime against property*. Just as people were forbidden to violate the life or possessions of another (the sixth and eighth commandments), so too they were forbidden to do this to a neighbor's wife (seventh commandment). She was the property of that neighbor, and for this reason every other man was supposed to keep his hands off.

243

But we would not be doing justice to the teaching of the Old Testament if we evaluated adultery simply as a question of property. A man's wife was more than an expensive piece of chattel property. This becomes evident when we consider the distinction made in the Mosaic law between sexual intercourse with a married woman and sexual intercourse with a neighbor's slave girl. The law viewed intercourse with a *slave girl* not as adultery, but as a violation of the property of her owner. A special fine was assessed (Lev. 19:20–21)—something impossible in a case of adultery, which required the death penalty by means of fire (Gen. 38:24) or stoning (Deut. 22:23–24).

This degree of punishment, completely different from any fine assessed for stealing, shows that we are dealing with something other than stealing property.

The seventh commandment is clearly more than a variation of the eighth commandment ("You shall not steal"), in the sense of "Keep your hands off another woman, because she is part of your neighbor's property." The seventh commandment goes much further, because the man who violates his neighbor's wife violates that neighbor's *honor*.[1] "For jealousy is a husband's fury; therefore he will not spare in the day of vengeance. He will accept no recompense, nor will he be appeased though you give many gifts" (Prov. 6:34–35).

The uniqueness of the seventh commandment appears even more clearly when we consider what the Old Testament says about Yahweh's relationship to His own people. This relationship is compared to a marriage. Yahweh is a jealous God, a God who takes revenge against other gods when they seek to embrace Israel, precisely as a husband is jealous when another man goes after his wife. Nor does Yahweh tolerate Israel herself going after those gods; for in so doing, Israel is committing adultery just like a woman who is being unfaithful to her own husband (Jer. 3:8–9; 5:7; Ezek. 23:37; see Hos. 2 and 3). His honor and love are being violated.

The relationship between a husband and a wife, therefore, is not to be expressed in terms of property. To that extent, adultery is something other than simply cheating an owner. It is the violation of a unique relationship—marriage. A married man who has sexual intercourse with another man's wife not only injures the other man (in terms of what belongs to him), but also destroys his *own* marriage. A man may not be unfaithful to the wife of his youth, for then he becomes unfaithful to a covenant witnessed by Yahweh (Mal. 2:14–16).

This last warning is also part of the Old Testament message. It does not emerge when we look up only those verses that speak of "committing adultery" or those verses that strongly emphasize destroying another's marriage. But when we gather together *all* that the Old Testament teaches about marriage, then the commandment "You shall not commit adultery" obtains a much deeper significance. The commandment covers more ground than simply "You shall keep your hands off the woman who belongs to your neighbor." Adultery is much more than a crime against property.

A Still Wider Field of Vision

But we would be setting the limits too narrowly as well if, when discussing the seventh commandment, we restricted ourselves to the *act* of adultery. For in the Sermon on the Mount, Jesus teaches us that, as the One who has come to fulfill the whole meaning of the law, He considers even *looking* at another woman in order to have her to be adultery (Matt. 5:17, 28). Just as in other cases, here too Jesus reveals the depth of the commandment. We must pay attention not only to the letter of the law, but also to the spirit of the law.

When we discuss the seventh commandment in the widest sense possible, we must ask how we ought to live *within the relationship of husband and wife*. Then we end up dealing with far more than adultery.

We have already pointed out the independent status of the seventh commandment in relation to the eighth. "Not committing adultery" is more than "not stealing your neighbor's wife." Not *property*, but *sexuality* is the key word indicating the unique character of the seventh commandment. Our reflection on this commandment confronts us with the biblical principles for sexual relationships.

This appears clearly, for example, in Leviticus 18, where the precept "You shall not lie carnally with your neighbor's wife" (Lev. 18:20) is included in a long series of regulations specifying the *boundaries* for permissible sexual relationships. A man may not have intercourse with his mother, his sister or stepsister, his granddaughter, or other very close family members (Lev. 18:6–18). Moreover, nobody may commit a homosexual act or a sexual act with an animal (Lev. 18:22–23).

We find similar regulations also in Leviticus 20, where "adultery" with a neighbor's wife is included alongside various impermissible forms of "sexual intercourse."

What we have seen in connection with other commandments should be mentioned here as well: the seventh commandment mentions only one sin, but one that includes a wide range of other similar sins.

This is confirmed when we examine how closely adultery and *prostitu-*

tion are linked. Sometimes it can seem as if the Old Testament condemns adultery as a major transgression, while it condones prostitution. Apparently Judah did not think visiting a prostitute was sinful (Gen. 38:15). Samson did the same thing (Judg. 16:1). Rahab was a professional prostitute (Josh. 2). Apparently prostitutes lived in Israel, as we see from the account of Solomon's judgment between two of them (1 Kings 3).

But people did distinguish between visiting an unmarried and a married prostitute. In the latter case, one set foot upon a life-threatening path. The teacher in Proverbs shows the young man who does such a thing that he is destroying himself. For on the day of vengeance, the woman's husband will exercise no sympathy (Prov. 6:34–35; 7:19–27). Someone who visits an unmarried prostitute can be reduced to a crust of bread (Prov. 6:26), but at least his life is not at risk, as in the other situation.*

This set of facts does not mean that in Yahweh's eyes, prostitution could have been a rather innocent matter. No one was to make his daughter a prostitute, certainly not for the purpose of cultic prostitution (Lev. 19:29; Deut. 23:17–18). Cultic prostitution was widely practiced in Canaanite and other pagan temples. People believed that by committing prostitution in these temples, they could guarantee the fertility of flocks and fields. That route was expressly forbidden to Israel.

So cultic prostitution was forbidden, but that does not yet mean that "ordinary" prostitution, sexual intercourse between men and (unmarried) women who led lives of prostitution, would have been permitted. For a woman, the loss of her virginity outside of marriage was in itself a shameful thing (Deut. 22:13–21). How then could prostitution ever have been a good thing?

Adultery and *prostitution* are words that can be mentioned in the same breath. Israel's adultery against Yahweh in Egypt and later in Canaan is simultaneously prostitution and unchastity (Ezek. 16:15–19; 23:1–49). Children born of adultery are called children of harlotry (Isa. 57:3).

That puts not only adultery, but also harlotry in a critical light. And what is said less explicitly in the Old Testament about prostitution is declared explicitly in the New Testament. Christians converted from paganism must, even as their Jewish brothers and sisters, abstain from harlotry (Acts 15:20, 29). The body is not for prostitution, but for the Lord Jesus

---

* J. van der Ploeg, *Spreuken* (Roermond, 1952), 32, and other translators indicate that the contrast is stronger still: A prostitute costs you no more than a crust of bread, but another man's wife costs you your life.

Christ. It is a temple of the Holy Spirit. Therefore, flee sexual immorality (1 Cor. 6:13–14)! Just as one who commits adultery drives a wedge in an existing marriage, so one who commits harlotry destroys the unity established between his own body and the Lord Jesus Christ.

Man and Woman

One who breaks troth breaks marriage. Before proceeding any further to discuss what the seventh commandment forbids, it would be profitable to consider what this commandment presupposes: marriage as an institution of God.

When God created mankind, He created man and woman (Gen. 1:27). As soon as mankind appeared, individuals appeared as man or woman. This datum of creation, seemingly so simple, and confirmed with the experience of every new birth, is of enormous significance for our discussion. Its significance becomes clear once we realize that not everybody agrees that this sexual difference between people has existed "from the beginning." In one of his famous dialogues, the Greek philosopher Plato speaks about the androgyne, literally, the man-woman, as the original human being. This androgyne perfectly embodied the unity of the masculine and the feminine elements. But the punishment of the gods fell upon this androgyne, dividing it in two; now a person is either a man or a woman. Ever since this division, restless human love has been consumed in an endless search for this lost unity.

If this is true, then we should view the duality of man and woman as *brokenness*. In our love, according to this construction, we are constantly searching for the original. Love's restlessness finds rest in the unity wherein man and woman totally encompass each other.

This perspective, which Plato cast in the form of a myth (a story about the gods), enjoys acceptance even today. Consider the French author Elisabeth Badinter, who wrote a book with this revealing title: *L'un est l'autre* ("The One Is the Other"). She divides history into three phases. The first phase was *l'un et l'autre* ("the one *and* the other"). In ancient times, man and woman were each other's complement, with woman exercising the greater influence. That was a rather happy time, compared with the one that followed, when men became the boss and women became the oppressed. Patriarchy meant *l'un sans l'autre* ("the one *without* the other"). The Bible, along with its creation story, fits into this phase, according to Badinter. There is no place for the goddess, since the absolute ruler is the masculine god who is the almighty *father*. It later seemed that Mary, as the

divine mother of Jesus, would bring about a change in this view; but in
spite of this development, the church remained a masculine domain.

Today we live in the third phase, according to Badinter, a phase more
and more governed by *l'un est l'autre*. Differences between men and
women are falling away. Homosexuality and bisexuality demonstrate how
sexuality is not as fixed as the Bible and other books would have us believe. The fact that we act like a man or a woman is not the result of an
innate direction, but a question of nurture. People *teach* their children to
behave as male or female. They *are* not one or the other, but they *become*
one or the other.[2]

The ancient myth of the androgynous man is echoed in various modern
feminist arguments. For example, if people nowadays address God with
feminine terms, so that He must be a "he" and a "she" at the same time,
that conclusion derives not from biblical exegesis, but rather from a
premise nurtured in the world of androgynous thinking.

Because our ethical reflection depends on Holy Scripture as the well
from which we draw, we see the distinction between man and woman to
be one that God has willed, and not as a kind of punishment or fall or
source of misery. When God created man as male and female on the sixth
day, He looked back on that day and pronounced this judgment: "And indeed it was very good" (Gen. 1:31).

But the same Bible tells us on the following pages of the book of Genesis exactly what went wrong between man and woman, and why Badinter
and others have more than enough material from which to draw their portrait of the enmity between man and woman that has existed throughout
history. When mankind fell into sin, the harmonious relationship between man and woman was also distorted. One aspect of the curse that be-
fell the human race was that the man would *rule over* the woman (Gen.
3:16): *l'un sans l'autre*, whereas both of them—created in the image of
God—had originally been called to fill the earth and exercise dominion
together (Gen. 1:26–28)!

The ideal relationship of equality, which was intended at Creation, was
destroyed by sin and is restored only by God's grace in Christ. The new
harmonious relationship between man and woman we can deduce from
the relationship between Christ as husband and His church as bride (Eph.
5:22–33). In this relationship, man and woman love each other and *tenderness* rules, to use the key word Badinter employs to portray the ideal relation between man and woman.

This ideal relation between man and woman does not exclude a certain
rank or order. Just as Christ is presently the Head of His church, so was

Adam, the one created first, the head of his wife Eve. Together they were to rule the world, so that the task of the woman always included more than just "serving." But in fulfilling this common task of ruling, there is indeed an order or rank, one in which the husband is called to function as head of his wife. This applies in the New Testament era as well: In the same way that Christ now leads, nurtures, and protects His church, the husband has the task of leading, nurturing, and protecting his wife (Eph. 5).

This leading of the wife by her husband does not mean that the wife no longer has a governing task. This government consists not only of a mother ruling her children, but also of women using their talents (often not very different from those of men) to cooperate with men in the world-wide program God announced in Genesis 1.

What this means in practice requires no further explication here. For a discussion of the place of women in labor and industry, we refer the interested reader to what we have written elsewhere in this series.[3] We may gratefully observe that the position of women has improved, especially in this century, so that women also may now be engaged in a number of functions formerly closed to them.

At the same time, we must steer clear of emancipation struggles aiming at the androgynous man, where the roles of man and woman become completely interchangeable. This ideal is already rendered impossible by the difference in the build and strength of the human body. "Nature" will always win out over androgynous "doctrine." Where interchangeable functions are possible, however, but forbidden by Scripture, we must obey the order established by God. This refers especially to ruling in ecclesiastical office, something that according to apostolic testimony does not belong to women (1 Cor. 11:3–16; 14:33–36; 1 Tim. 2:11–15). The ravages occasioned by the struggle for interchangeable roles in the area of sexuality will occupy our attention later.

The Goal of Marriage

God created man and woman with a common mandate: "Be fruitful and multiply; fill the earth and subdue it" (Gen. 1:28). In order to be fruitful and multiply, people received sexual organs, constructed in such a way that man and woman could become "one flesh." In the order established by God, "a man shall leave his father and mother and be joined to his wife, and they shall become one flesh" (Gen. 2:24). *Marriage* is the arena for experiencing this repeatedly new unity between one man and one woman, and thus marriage is the route designed for realizing the mandate of Genesis 1.

With two Latin terms for marriage, we can nicely summarize the *goal* of this creation institution, namely, marriage as *matrimonium* and as *coniugium*. The first term emphasizes motherhood. *Mater* means "mother." The man Adam named his wife Eve, because she had become "the mother of all living" (Gen. 3:20). The second term (*coniugium*) emphasizes the common task of life which those two people had assumed.

Both elements are included in Genesis 2:24: A man shall leave his father and mother and *cleave* to his wife and *become one flesh* with her. "Cleaving" to one's wife points to a loving relationship or a friendship, certainly not limited to a sexual relationship. The Hebrew word used here appears elsewhere: Ruth "clung" to her mother-in-law when they were about to part (Ruth 1:14). Shechem "was strongly attracted" to Dinah (Gen. 34:3), even as Solomon "clung" with love to many foreign wives (1 Kings 11:2). The men of Judah "clung" to David when others had abandoned him (2 Sam. 20:2). The "cleaving" mentioned in Genesis 2 refers to an intense love that radiates in body and soul throughout all areas of fellowship.

The expression "become one flesh" must—in view of the mandate to be fruitful and multiply—be taken quite literally. But here too the meaning is not restricted to sexual union. The verse from Genesis is cited by Paul in the passage already mentioned, Ephesians 5:22–33, where the term "flesh" refers to the entire human person (cf. Eph. 5:29, 31). Therefore, those words include reference to the *comprehensive* personal communion of husband and wife.

If we take seriously this communion, which includes body and soul, then *polygamy* is for us something illegitimate. Even though we find polygamy practiced during Old Testament times, that does not justify viewing polygamy as a legitimate possibility for all time. The question is whether the polygamy Yahweh tolerated in Israel really agreed with marriage as He intended it at creation.

The troubles caused by polygamy in the families of Abraham, Jacob, and Elkanah (Gen. 16:4–6; 29:16–24; 1 Sam. 1:6–8) are warning enough. Love can look in only one direction. How could the unique love of marriage ever really be divided between more than one partner?

The Mosaic law offered protection against abuses that often and easily accompanied polygamy. A man with two wives was forbidden to favor the firstborn son of his beloved wife above the firstborn son of his unloved wife (Deut. 21:15–17). We saw that the goal of marriage is at least twofold: having children and forming a living communion. In polygamy (more than one wife) or polyandry (more than one husband), that second aspect is not very possible.

Responsible Family Planning

Having children is one of the purposes of marriage. Nevertheless, a childless marriage is not a failed marriage, for "becoming one flesh" is not achieved only when children are born. In the marriage relationship, unlike any other firm friendship, husband and wife can form a complete unity as a very happy *coniugium*, even without children.

The reverse is not true. If the *coniugium* is not a happy one, such that husband and wife simply coexist or live in enmity, having children will change that very little, if at all. For that reason, we could say that only fellowship in love—with or without children—makes marriage a blessing for husband and wife.

We must not *disconnect* the goal of marriage from having children. Voluntary childlessness conflicts with God's intention for marriage. Those who marry must be willing to have children. Marriage is, in terms of its design, also *matrimonium*. No matter how happy a childless marriage may be, it is natural that such a condition causes grief. Childlessness must not be voluntary, but rather is something that may need to be accepted. And that latter attitude is understandably difficult for many childless couples.

The argument that the earth is already "filled," so that we are not obligated by this part of the mandate in Genesis 1, is not valid. As long as the world turns, a new generation will always be needed. Moreover, in Western countries, the population is aging to such an extent that people are being urged to have more children so the age groups will be more balanced than they are at present. Indeed, on medical or other grounds it can be irresponsible for a couple to have (more) children. This does not bring them into conflict with Genesis 1. The task within marriage belongs to the human race and need not be a demand individually binding every couple in their own special situation.

A discussion of the circumstances in which it might be necessary to refrain from having (more) children requires more space than we have here in our consideration of the seventh commandment. This subject is discussed more fully elsewhere in this series.[4]

Children do not appear automatically, since sexual life too is a matter of *reflection*. This is different than it is with the animals *over* whom God pronounced His blessing and command (Gen. 1:22). God directed Himself *to* man with His message about fruitfulness and multiplying. Conception does not befall us. There is a mandate not only to procreate children, but also to nurture them. That broader responsibility may always be considered in connection with having another child.

May limiting the number of children "be pursued in no other way than that of self-control," as Reformed ethicist W. Geesink argued as a representative of an earlier generation?[5] Or, in addition to abstinence, may couples rely only on those infertile times when a woman is unable to conceive, as the papal encyclical *Humane vitae* of 1968 argues?

It is not clear to us why chemical or artificial means are forbidden when "natural" contraception is permitted. We would argue that *all* these means have something unnatural about them, even the method of total abstinence. Such abstinence for a long period of time is anything but natural, as Paul told us (1 Cor. 7:5)!

If no (more) children may be conceived, we can be grateful that contraceptives have been discovered which serve this purpose without hindering sexual intercourse. In our opinion, there is no principled difference between various contraceptive methods and means (assuming that they work to prevent conception and not to abort an already conceived human being). Which means or methods should be used, up to and including the means of sterilization, depends on the circumstances.

Artificial Insemination

Thus, artificially intervening to prevent conception is not always wrong. But what about artificially intervening to enable conception and birth? Nobody objects to using the technique of delivery by cesarean section to enable birth. Means designed to enhance fertility have been around for a long time. Nobody raises an eyebrow when people undergo operations or use other means to stimulate a wife's ovaries or to elevate the husband's sperm count. But may intervention be allowed in the fertilization process itself?

Consider, for example, *artificial insemination*, whereby sperm is introduced into a woman's reproductive system in order to bring about fertilization and conception which could not occur in the normal way. The official Roman Catholic stand opposes this method on grounds similar to those underlying Roman Catholic opposition to contraceptives. This stand has quite properly been rejected by most Protestant moralists. Why may problems with sexual organs be treated medically in order to make fertilization possible (to stimulate ovaries or to elevate sperm count), yet medical technology may not be used when problems arise with sexual intercourse itself?

However, there is a difference in principle between artificial insemination with sperm from the husband (AIH) and with sperm from a donor

(AID). If sperm from a *donor* is used, the conception occurs beyond the limits of marriage. A third party is involved in getting the wife pregnant. On the basis of what we wrote earlier about marriage as an *exclusive* spiritual and physical relationship between husband and wife, artificial insemination by donor must be morally condemned.

But some argue that in the process of conception via AID, the third party typically remains anonymous. The third party donates "something" of himself (his sperm), but not himself, in order to supply what the husband cannot. But this argument cannot be sustained. True, we cannot speak here of physical adultery; but we can surely speak of *artificial adultery*. The child conceived through AID is the child of another. The facts that both spouses agree to this procedure and that their mutual harmony would not be broken by AID do not make this evil something good. Similarly, exchanging sexual partners, which affects both husband and wife, breaks the exclusivity of their marriage and for that reason destroys what God has intended for marriage.

The truth that AID really involves a "someone," and not merely a "something" of that someone, becomes evident from the comparison between a blood donor or an organ donor, on the one hand, and a sperm donor on the other hand. In the first situation, the woman receives blood or an organ to enable her body to function better. But the second situation involves forming a new human life, of which the biological father is not the husband, but a third party outside the marriage.

Nor can we defend AID by comparing it to the *adoption* of a child. In the case of adoption, biological parenthood belongs to neither spouse, but with AID it belongs to one of the two. But is that biological aspect really so important? Is it not loving nurture that makes people parents, as we see with adoptive parents?

But this comparison between AID and adoption is invalid. With adoption, the interest of the already born child is central. Adoption is a good means for child protection. Children without homes receive the warmth of a normal family, and through their adoption they obtain all the rights that other children enjoy. Moreover, with adoption both parents are in the same relationship to the adopted child. With AID that is not the case, since the wife becomes the child's mother and the husband "adopts" the child. Further, it is true that the biological element is not everything in the parent-child relationship. Emotional, moral, and other factors are just as important. But anybody who speaks about the biological aspect as if it were a *minimal* aspect, in order to suggest that it is dispensable, is fooling himself. With AID that is impossible, since no woman becomes a mother without sperm. Concerning that process we must say that this kind of pregnancy conflicts with what Scripture teaches about marriage and sexuality. This is not the way to become a parent, even though you might possess the most excellent abilities for maternally and paternally nurturing a child.

So much for artificial insemination by donor. Artificial insemination by *husband*, however, we should not reject. The beginning and the conclusion of this process are identical to those of normal fertilization: the husband's sperm is introduced into his wife's uterus, leading to the conception and birth of their own child. The "nature" that has become defective is given a helping hand between these beginning and concluding points. After all, intervening in nature (including our own nature) belongs to human nature, does it not? Nature has come forth from God's hand, to be sure, but that does not make it divine. "For that reason we cannot derive from nature, from creation as it appears before us, any standard for determining whether something is permissible or impermissible, good or evil. Our natural life too falls under the divine commandment."[6]

In passing, we would mention that especially Roman Catholic moral theologians have additional difficulty with artificial insemination in this form as well, since sperm is usually obtained through masturbation. This subject will be discussed later. But in this context of AIH, we can say that *here* masturbation is not isolated from marital communion. The husband does not masturbate in an intentionally chosen isolation which aims at self-gratification. For his act is directed to conceiving posterity. Characterizations like "onanism" or "autoeroticism" are inappropriate in this context.

In Vitro Fertilization

So then, we must not reject every technological intervention in the process of conception. But where should we draw the line? Is *in vitro fertilization* (IVF) acceptable, a procedure that has already led to the birth of many "test-tube babies"? Many people who have no problem with AIH do have difficulty approving in vitro fertilization.

This laboratory technique is employed to fertilize an egg with a sperm cell, and the conceived embryo is then transferred into the uterus. Thus, the fertilization does not occur *inside*, but *outside* the woman's body.

This IVF technique opened up many new possibilities. One of them is *surrogate motherhood*. Suppose that a woman's uterus is not functioning properly, but her ovaries can produce healthy eggs. Using the IVF technique, an embryo can be conceived from her and her husband, which is then transferred into the uterus of another woman. This woman carries the child for nine months, a child whose entire genetic makeup comes from that couple. You could even say that for nine months the child receives loving shelter from another woman.

What are we to think about these already well-developed techniques? We would suggest four conditions which must be (able to be) met in order for us to approve and to use these new techniques.

1. The embryo must originate from the woman and her husband. In other words, the fertilization must occur within the context of marriage. Just as we should oppose artificial insemination with the sperm of a donor, so too it is impermissible to use a sperm donor or egg donor for the purpose of fertilization through IVF.

But that is not the end of the discussion. Must we reject the IVF technique if it can assist a woman and her spouse in combining *her* egg with *his* sperm? The IVF technique is indeed very artificial, but that is not sufficient reason to reject its use under every circumstance. A marriage characterized by love and fidelity is not turned into a "laboratory marriage" if, at a certain step along the way leading from fertilization to birth, medical technology is used to intervene with assistance. Many children are born who have been in the womb only a short time or have left the womb in a less "natural" way than happens with a "test-tube baby."

2. The embryo mentioned in our first condition must be implanted in its *own* mother. If this is her child, then she must carry the child. A surrogate mother carries the child of two other people. No matter how noble the motive may be of helping a family member, a friend, or whomever to have a child, a third party would be entering the relationship alongside father and mother. The womb is not an incubator or guest room for a child who needs temporary shelter elsewhere. It is the place where mothers carry *their* children. If we take this second condition seriously, then we need not be preoccupied with numerous modern possibilities created by the IVF technique. As Christians we simply cannot take advantage of them.

3. Without exception, all the embryos must be implanted. Once we have an embryo, we are dealing with new human life that belongs in the mother's womb, not in a laboratory for experimental studies. Nor may we start selecting among the embryos to use the best ones for implanting, leaving the rest either to be destroyed or to be used for experimental purposes. Otherwise, we would be guilty of abortion at the very earliest stage of human life.

If it is really the case that the IVF technique cannot be used apart from such abortions, then we simply may not use it. But the question is whether IVF inherently involves abortion. It seems quite possible, given further technological improvements, that this third condition can be satisfied.

4. The embryos must be implanted as soon as possible. That should occur at the moment when attachment to the uterine wall is most likely to succeed, no earlier and no later; but certainly as soon as possible, so that the short detour of in vitro fertilization remains a short detour and leads back again to the regular route. Freezing the embryos for a period of time increases the chance that they will not be used or that they will be used for other purposes.

When the embryos cannot be transferred immediately, there is always some risk that they will *not* be transferred. Suppose the mother has a fatal accident. In such a case, our opinion is that the embryo should be treated as though it were in the mother's body already and had died with her, so that the situation would be viewed as a miscarriage.

In vitro fertilization can occasionally correct a defect, and for that reason we believe that this technique cannot be rejected out of hand, as long as the four conditions mentioned above are satisfied. Couples considering IVF in their own situations must become thoroughly informed so that they can take this step with a clear conscience.

The IVF technique must be a *corrective* measure in the fertilization process, a process that subsequently must be allowed to take its normal course. In vitro fertilization may not become a step on the road that leads to making the womb obsolete in the entire prenatal process.

Because of Sexual Immorality

Earlier we saw that marriage has a twofold purpose. As *matrimonium* it aims at forming a family and as *coniugium* it aims at forming a lifelong communion between husband and wife. We can add a third purpose. Paul writes, "Nevertheless, because of sexual immorality, let each man have his own wife, and let each woman have her own husband" (1 Cor. 7:2).

That does not look like a very exalted description, especially when we read immediately before this verse that a man does well *not* to touch a woman (1 Cor. 7:1). Thus, it is better not to marry; but, as a concession, to prevent immorality, you need marriage.

Is this really Paul's view? Is this the same man who could write such fine words about marriage in Ephesians 5, where he compares this institution to the bond between Christ and His church?

It is not altogether certain whether the words of 1 Corinthians 7:1 were those of Paul himself or whether he is quoting them from a letter written by the Corinthians themselves, about which Paul then proceeds to give his commentary. Perhaps among the Corinthians were people who took a rather absolute position about abstaining from sexual contact. Clearly Paul does not share that position. For he says that married men should fulfill their marital obligations and should not suspend sexual relations too long, since lack of self-control can become dangerous (1 Cor. 7:3–5). He says also that the unmarried and the widowed could better marry than burn with desire (1 Cor. 7:8–9; cf. also 1 Cor. 7:36, 39).

Nevertheless, we must be impressed with how soberly Paul speaks about marriage in this passage. He does not counter the assertion "As a Christian you should abstain from sexual contact" by asserting the opposite: "Everyone should get married."[7] Given the situation facing the Corinthian congregation, it would be good for the unmarried and the widowed to remain as Paul himself was—unmarried (1 Cor. 7:8). Likewise, a father would be making an understandable decision were he not to give his daughter in marriage (1 Cor. 7:37–38).

We should, however, be careful not to make these observations into a hard and fast rule of marital ethics for all times and places. Because of the existing crisis in Corinth, Paul expresses the conviction that the unmarried status deserves preference (1 Cor. 7:26, 32–40). In so doing, he is not laying down a binding regulation for all time.

We should also be impressed with how sensibly and plainly Paul speaks about sexual life. Sexual urges are powerful, so that one who does not have the gift of abstinence must know what to expect when he desires to remain unmarried. You then risk slipping and falling, as happened in the Corinthian church, where men were in the practice of visiting prostitutes, mind you. To prevent similar practices, each man should have his own wife and each woman her own husband.

So, marriage exists *also* to prevent sexual immorality. Stated more generally: One of the functions of marriage is to bridle people's lack of sexual restraint. Marriage has more functions, as we have seen, but this is one of them.

Sexual Pleasure

Were we, however, to stare ourselves blind at this third function of marriage, we might easily draw mistaken conclusions. A one-sided appeal to 1 Corinthians 7 often leads people to a negative view of sexual expression. One example is this line of argument: Since most people are so weak in the face of sexual temptations, marriage is useful; but being unmarried is really better than being married. People of high spiritual position, like office-bearers in the church, should not get married. *Celibacy* is more exalted than marriage.

Within the ancient church, this conviction gained rapid acceptance. The ordinary person needs marriage as a safety valve for sexuality, but one who lives spiritually should turn away from "desire." And where does desire reach its most powerful expression but in sexual desire?

Moreover, the criticism within the ancient church of *remarriage* after the death of a spouse arose from the negative evaluation of sexual expression. To marry once was barely acceptable, but to marry again simply betrayed a lack of self-control.

Against this outlook, people properly pointed to marriage as a *holy*—that is, a divinely ordained—institution. This institution originated not after, but before, man's fall into sin. In our sin-corrupted situation, we must indeed speak with Paul about the need for marriage in view of sexual immorality, but that is not all there is to sexuality in marriage. Marriage, and the experience of our sexuality indissolubly connected with marriage, were given to us as part of God's good creation. When God declared that His creative work was "very good," that applied also to the capacity of animals and people for sexual union.

Even after the Fall, we need not be embarrassed about sexual intimacy. Sexual enjoyment is more than an unavoidable concession to weak people who should really be clever enough to suppress their sexual feelings. We hear this view from Augustine and in later Roman Catholic literature. But even in Reformed circles people have occasionally written very narrowly about sexual enjoyment. For example, a seventeenth-century Dutch theologian, P. Wittewrongel (1609–62), wrote many fine things about marriage, but he also declared: "The marriage bed must extinguish, not ignite, the fires of passion."*[8] Here sexual passion is portrayed as a dangerous fire that should be extinguished as quickly as possible.

This kind of outlook hardly fits with Proverbs 5:18–19 and the Song of Songs. The young man of Proverbs must not go to strange women. Let him drink from his own fountain. What he may not seek from another woman he should find with his own wife: "Let her breasts satisfy you at all times;

---

* He appropriately observes that marriage is called *timios* in Heb. 13:4, and that this same word is used for the *precious* stones mentioned in Rev. 18:12 and for the *precious* blood of Christ in 1 Peter 1:18.

and always be enraptured with her love" (Prov. 5:19). The Song of Songs also speaks so clearly about physical *pleasure* as part of the intimacy between husband and wife that it is impossible to be ashamed about it.*

Frequent attempts have been made to interpret the Song of Songs allegorically or to interpret it in a way other than the "ordinary" way. The relationship between bridegroom and bride is then seen as a portrait of Christ's relationship to His church. It seems to us quite proper to see this as an *additional* feature, since Ephesians 5 is also in the Bible. But looking for a deeper background (Christ as bridegroom and His church as bride) should not lead us to ignore the "ordinary" foreground. The delightful union between husband and wife is also a sexual delight.

Voluntary singleness can be good. And we should not criticize involuntary singleness. But to *impose* celibacy, even though merely upon one particular class of people (the spiritual), is wrong. The priests and Levites of the old covenant were married, just as the apostles in the new covenant. The fact that Paul was unmarried was not due to his conviction that an apostle "really" cannot be married. He had the right to be married: "Do we have no right to take along a believing wife, as do also the other apostles, the brothers of the Lord, and Cephas?" (1 Cor. 9:5). If for a particular congregation (Corinth), for a particular apostle (Paul), or for anybody else it was good not to marry, that does not constitute a requirement or even a strong recommendation for all apostles or for everybody else.

Why would remarriage be wrong, even if desire for sexual pleasure plays a role? According to Paul, widows in the Corinthian situation would act responsibly by not remarrying, but he does not forbid them to remarry. Nor do we read that being unmarried is better because then you would be abstaining from sexual activity. In marriage, Paul writes, the husband can be too preoccupied with earthly matters and with pleasing his wife. The same is true of a wife toward her husband (1 Cor. 7:32–34). What Paul writes about "pleasing" the spouse is stated as a generalization and is surely not to be limited to "pleasing" in a physical sense.

At this point, we should mention that, although the Bible sanctions a frank appreciation of sexual intercourse, we should still avoid a glutton-

---

* W. Perkins, *Alle de werken* (Amsterdam, 1659), 3:2, 322, had an eye for the "holy delight" of sexual intercourse, referring to Song of Songs, Prov. 5, Gen. 26:8 (Isaac caressing Rebekah), and Isa. 62:5 (the bridegroom rejoicing in his bride). But then he adds, "Delight and pleasure are more the prerogative of the husband than the wife, and are more seemly for both in their younger years than in their old age"! For this opinion, however, he appeals to no Bible verses for support.

ous, unrestrained surrender to our sexual urges. "One who is unrestrained in marriage, how is he different from an adulterer with his wife, so to speak?" Ambrose is thought to have written once.[9] Married people cannot permit themselves every form of sexual expression. Sexual play has rules that govern pleasing *one another*, not just the individual.

It is quite proper to speak in a figurative sense of adultery within marriage. One who is simply out to satisfy his or her own sexual desires will view the other partner simply as an object, so that it no longer matters whether sexual union belongs to the intimacy of marital union. Coitus becomes a particular form of masturbation. Even someone who, to say it with the words of Proverbs 5:19, is enraptured with the love given by his or her own spouse, can in reality be mentally far away from home.

Within a good marriage, husband and wife will practice the kind of self-control required by sexual abstinence. This need not be only for the reason Paul mentions for temporary abstinence (devoting oneself to prayer, 1 Cor. 7:5); abstinence can also be occasioned by various reasons arising from unselfish and mutually supportive love.

En Route to Adulthood

Genesis 2 tells how Adam got ready in the Garden of Eden to receive Eve. The animals passed by Adam in pairs. What they enjoyed, he missed. God prepared him for marriage and created Eve (Gen. 2:18–22). This course of events contains a lesson for all times. Physically and spiritually, the young man or woman must mature. He or she becomes aware of being alone after the youthful years, so that the longing to share life with someone of the other sex becomes stronger.

That takes time. Giving a wristwatch to a three-year-old would be strange, because a three-year-old is not ready to tell time. Similarly, it is wrong to abuse children sexually. Grapes ripen only in autumn.

For this reason, *pedophilia* causes serious abnormalities in the normal sexual development of a child. A pedophile is an adult who longs either predominantly or exclusively for a love relationship with a child. Pedophilia can be homosexual or heterosexual. Regardless of that, if the pedophile surrenders to his or her desires, children are abused—no matter how much smooth talking people use to make pedophilia acceptable. For children are put in a physical and emotional situation for which they are not ready. In the pedophilic relationship, the adult abuses his or her emotional superiority by confronting a child with things that belong to a later stage of life.

Possibly even more serious is the abuse of children through *incest*. By incest we understand sexual contact between persons who, on the basis of their kinship, may not marry. Leviticus 18 and 20 provide regulations governing Israelite society. If we study the details of various biblical accounts carefully, we will notice that these regulations were not binding for all times.* But the prohibition against sexual relations between especially parents and children or between brothers and sisters is enforced throughout the whole world.

In modern usage, the term *incest* is most often taken in the narrow sense of sexual intercourse between adult family members with *children*. The child is victimized more seriously by incest than with pedophilia. A father who sexually abuses his daughter or a brother who sexually abuses his sister has at his disposal the means to terrorize such a child. Many children are victimized this way for years by sexual practices whose damage remains throughout the rest of life. To alert the outside world to their crisis never occurs to them. Ignorance and naïveté, a vague suspicion of what is really happening, and especially fear of the consequences of telling, hinder the child from coming out into open with this secret. That, in turn, gives the child's closest family members every chance to continue their incestuous behavior for years.

It is very grievous that these sins occur also within the church. Anyone who should ever learn about such circumstances is unquestionably obligated to rise up in defense of these defenseless children. Especially older family members are obliged rather to suffer the shame of exposing other family members than to tolerate their little brothers or sisters being abused any longer. Unfortunately, it happens too often that family members turn away from helping each other. Unmasking those who commit incest will frequently be difficult, even in an "open" society such us ours.

During the time of sexual development, children will likely encounter problems with *masturbation* or *autoeroticism*, also called *onanism*. Currently, masturbation is widely viewed as a normal phase en route to adulthood. Boys and girls discover their own sexual capacities through mastur-

---

* For example, Abraham married his half sister (Gen. 20:12) and Jacob married sisters—two cases of "incest" according to the standard of Lev. 18:9 and 18:18. "Despite the general character of the prohibition against marrying a family member, Leviticus 20 does distinguish between marrying immediate family members and the very next of kin, both of which were subject to the death penalty, and marrying more distant relatives who were afflicted with childlessness. This factor of childlessness played a role already in the narratives of the patriarchs" (J. L. Koole, *De Tien Geboden*, 109–10).

bation. For that reason, in a healthy sexual development during puberty, masturbation is actually indispensable, people say. So who would still dare to say that masturbation is sin?

The Bible says nothing or very little about masturbation. The sin that Onan committed (Gen. 38:9–10) has nothing to do with "onanism" or masturbation. Onan engaged not in self-pleasure, but in pregnancy prevention by means of coitus interruptus. What made him culpable was his refusal to fulfill his levirate duty. He was supposed to beget an heir for the widowed Tamar; he pretended to do his duty, making certain each time that Tamar never became pregnant.

Neither Leviticus 15:16–17 nor Deuteronomy 13:10–11 gives a definitive evaluation of this matter. There we read that a nocturnal emission renders a man ceremonially unclean, just as with female menstruation (Lev. 15:19–28). An ethical judgment regarding masturbating activities is not given in these passages.

Does this mean, then, that masturbation is an innocent pastime? Are the feelings of guilt that so many youngsters experience after masturbating in fact unfounded? Have those guilt feelings simply been handed down by ancestors who were much too puritanical?

Since the Bible nowhere gives an explicit verdict about this matter, we should inquire whether in the masturbating activity—no matter how necessary it may appear to be for sexual development and no matter how widespread this phenomenon may appear to be—there are elements for which the Christian needs to ask for God's forgiveness.

We believe this applies even to nocturnal emission (the so-called "wet dream"). How many impure desires and thoughts accompany this experience? There is an ancient evening prayer, originating in the Middle Ages and adopted during the Reformation, that goes like this: "Moderate our sleep, that it not be inordinate, so that we may in body and soul remain unstained, yea, that even our sleep itself may be to Thy honor." This prayer originates from a medieval hymn containing this line: "ne polluanter corpora"—"so that our bodies may not be stained."[10]

So we cannot say that all of this is "natural," and that in your dreams you are powerless to fight against impure desires and thoughts. For whatever inability exists reflects the inability of a person who in his nightly dreams finds a faithful reflection of the desires and thoughts that spring up during the day. During the day too it is often impossible to control yourself. All it takes is a little nudge to set you sexually ablaze, so then you release the tension by masturbating.

But after that kind of release, it is spiritually very healthy to cry out with Paul, "O wretched man that I am! Who will deliver me from this body of death?" (Rom. 7:24). That is what this apostle said after he too had to confess that it was actually impossible to control himself: "For the good that I will to do, I do not do; but the evil I will not to do, that I practice. . . . I find then a law, that evil is present with me, the one who wills to do good" (Rom. 7:19, 21).

There is no need to be melodramatic about masturbation, sending numerous upright young Christians into despair. Somewhat cynically it is said that except for holy men, heroes, and hypocrites, everybody has masturbated. Most youngsters and numerous older people, single or married, struggle with this. Some struggle with this their entire lives.

But while we need not be melodramatic about it, neither is it correct to treat masturbation as something quite ordinary. For it is far from ordinary for someone who knows what a pure and holy life is. Guilt feelings related to masturbation are not ancestral baggage, but genuine responses of someone who desires to present his or her body as a holy, living, and acceptable sacrifice to God (Rom. 12:1).

Choosing a Partner and Preparing for Marriage

When the time comes for serious courtship, new questions arise. One who chooses a partner must be free in that choice. *Choosing a partner* used to be a family enterprise. The development from seeing marriage as a business proposition to seeing it as a personal decision between two people was a fortunate improvement. Two persons, not two families, marry.[11] If two people love each other, they should not permit themselves to be separated by parents sowing seeds of quarreling, wrote Heinrich Bullinger.[*]

To prevent misunderstanding about the past, it should be added that back then many marriages were entered out of love. Jacob loved Rachel (Gen. 29:18–30), and Michal loved David (1 Sam. 18:20, 28). But even where that was not the case, a marriage did not have to be unhappy on that account. A wife was obtained for Isaac, but when she became his wife, he received her with love (Gen. 24:67). The basis of a good marriage is

---

[*] H. Bullinger, *Huijs-boeck* (Amsterdam, 1607), 65. See also J. Koelman, *De plichten der ouders, in kinderen voor God op te voeden* (reprint, Middelburg, 1838), 171–72, who says that parents must not hinder their children from marrying those to whom they have taken a liking. "Let your children choose, only let them take you along to seek your advice, but don't use fleshly reasons to discourage their plans to marry, especially if their hearts are set on each other and they have made promises to each other."

the *faithfulness* that husband and wife pledge to one another. Where that faithfulness exists, often a mutual fondness grows out of it. A marriage entered for business considerations could thus be quite happy after all.

Freely choosing a life partner does not mean that the choice can be arbitrary. Counsel against starting to court someone widely divergent in age, cultural background, or education is always appropriate. Earlier, in connection with the fifth commandment, we discussed the need for parents to give their input, even though they cannot compel their children to follow their advice.

A Christian who freely chooses a life partner may not marry an unbeliever. Marriage is a covenant that is designed to reflect the relationship between Christ and His church. How then could a believer possibly be yoked together with an unbeliever? For what agreement exists between the temple of God and idols (2 Cor. 6:14–16)?

Someone *already married* to an unbeliever lives in a different situation (1 Cor. 7:12–16). But someone *intending to marry* must marry *in the Lord (Jesus)* and to the glory of God—something applicable to every other activity and decision in our lives (1 Cor. 6:13–20; 10:31; Col. 3:17). Courtship and engagement require a common church basis and a shared religious foundation, so that spiritual unity may be experienced in marriage, too.

Marriage is usually preceded by a rather lengthy time of getting to know each other, dating, and becoming engaged. In former times, *engagement* was equivalent to declaring one's intent to marry, so that breaking an engagement promise was tantamount to divorce. Today that is no longer the case. Engagement and marriage no longer have the same weight. If an engagement is broken, that may well be a sad, and even culpable, matter. To be engaged is to promise fidelity to one's fiancée, a pledge that should be taken seriously, especially since it becomes a public promise through engagement. But the period of engagement is still a probationary period. If, during engagement, it becomes evident that two people are incompatible, it would be better to stop halfway than to go astray all the way. When two people have spoken their vows *before God and His people* on their wedding day, the situation is different. But breaking an engagement is not equivalent to divorce.[12]

Marriage requires a period of *preparation*. This should not last too long, especially in our society where unmarried couples are severely tempted if they wish to remain chaste together.

But couples must get to know each other deeply, so that marriage will be a responsible choice. Many divorces result from marriages entered too hastily. Centuries ago already, B. Smytegelt said, "Casually they come together and casually they split apart."[13] How life will turn out cannot be predicted during courtship. But resolving problems during this time will help make a marriage resistant to disintegration. Couples must learn to understand and accept one another. Two "I's" must become one "we." They learn that love is not simply a matter of emotion, but also of mutual service and self-control. The one whose ego takes center stage will demand too much of the other.

Self-control involves more than the sexual aspect during the time of courtship and engagement. Self-centeredness shows its face in various ways. But surely sexual self-control is an important part of the training leading up to marriage.

If their relationship develops properly, the couple will become spiritually, psychologically, and physically more intimate. How far should physical intimacy go? We agree with the advice of Walter Trobisch: The point where it becomes impossible to stop is usually reached when you begin to lie down together and start undressing each other.[14] Those who stop before that point will not have to think about using contraceptives. Moreover, intimate forms of contact like petting (mutual stimulation of the sexual organs leading to orgasm, so-called "petting to climax") have no place in courtship or engagement.

Besides warning against undressing each other, Trobisch gives one more piece of good advice: The partner with the most tender conscience must help the other. The single, absolutely safe contraceptive is the little word "No!"

Cohabiting Without Marrying?

May courtship include sexual intercourse? This seems like a question only old-fashioned people could get excited about, if we consider how widely accepted *cohabiting without marrying* has become in our society. Marriage now enjoys competition from alternative lifestyles claiming equal rights in our society. Why should people go all out for a wedding if they can find another way? People who want to live together without getting married can decide that for themselves; they do not need the approval or cooperation of family, church, and society.

People do not want to tie themselves down to another person. This is what you do when you get married, because then you have to factor in the possibility of divorce, with all the trouble that usually goes along with it. So people are more comfortable with looser ties, very popular among our modern "Me generation."

The problem is not new; it was around long before people started talking about cohabiting without marrying, which used to be called *concubinage*.* No matter what it is called, this form of living together apart from marriage cannot be reconciled with what Scripture requires of people who wish to share life in body and soul with one another.

Various arguments against cohabiting without marrying can be adduced.

In the *first* place, the Mosaic legislation indicates that sexual intercourse was proper only within the context of marriage. If it became evident on her wedding night that a woman was not a virgin, she was to be stoned to death (Deut. 22:13–21). If a man had sexual intercourse with a girl who was not betrothed, he could be compelled to marry her (Ex. 22:16–17). In the New Testament, we read that Mary, betrothed to Joseph, had not engaged in sexual intimacy with anyone (Luke 1:34). Sexual intercourse may not occur outside of marriage, as we learn from 1 Corinthians 6:12–20 and 7:9. Anyone who cannot practice sexual abstinence should marry, Paul said.

Second, in the Bible, living together as man and woman always affects the broader community—something true also of cohabiting without being married. Taking a woman as wife and a man as husband involved promises and duties toward God and man that were sanctioned before sexual union occurred. Payment of the dowry and giving away the bride preceded consummating the marriage through intercourse.† The village community witnessed the marriage of Boaz to Ruth (Ruth 4:7–13). Forming a new social unit is part of the fabric of communal life, for which reason the community can be summoned to serve as witness when promises and obligations are not fulfilled. This was why Yahweh served as witness to the marriage of Jewish men to the "wives of their youth," when they had abandoned their wives to chase after heathen girls (Mal. 2:14–16).

---

* Concubinage is the cohabitation of a man and a woman outside of marriage, a phenomenon appearing in every age, often sanctioned by law, as in ancient city-states where marriage with a freedman, a foreigner, or a woman without a dowry failed to meet the conditions for a legal marriage. In biblical as well as other times, the childlessness of a man's wife or his own desire for another woman led him to take a concubine as his mistress. Throughout church history, we observe this phenomenon especially among the clergy, who were not allowed to marry, but did live in concubinage.

† See J. Rinzema, *Huwelijk en echtscheiding* (Aalten, 1962), 79, who mentions that consummation of marriage seems to have consisted of three elements: (1) payment of the dowry; (2) the "traditio puellae" (giving away the bride) at the wedding feast; and (3) the consummation of the marriage by husband and wife.

Someone might reply that although things went this way in years past, today we may do things differently. Many things have changed, it is true, and we are not saying that change is bad. But we wish to supplement the preceding two arguments with one more, an argument that is decisive and strengthens the other two.

For in the *third* place, the Bible teaches us that living together as husband and wife is a *lifelong* bond. For that reason we must defend marriage and oppose cohabiting without being married. Couples who cohabit without marrying never promise that they will remain bound to each other for life. No matter how much they love each other, they never declare before God and others their promise of perpetual unity ("until death do us part"). Even as couples begin cohabiting without a marriage license, so too they can leave each other without a divorce decree. The whole thing started out well, and possibly the experiment began in the conviction that they would stay together. Nevertheless, the time came when it seemed wiser to end it.

This human convention, no matter how well intentioned, conflicts with the Bible's teaching about a husband and wife living together. How can cohabiting without marrying ever be viewed as temporary in the light of Genesis 2, such that after a few years a couple decides to separate? How can cohabiting without marrying ever be reconciled with Paul's teaching in Ephesians 5 about marriage as a representation of the perpetual bond between Christ and His church?

By their very nature, the components of love and total life communion between man and woman require a promise of lifelong faithfulness. If so, then obviously such a vow should be made publicly before God and others. No government official is inaugurated unless he or she promises, in the presence of the citizenry, to be faithful to the constitution. Those citizens may call such an official to give an account if that pledge is broken. Why, then, should not the promise of lifelong faithfulness, which we as husband and wife should give each other, require public declaration in the presence of family, friends, acquaintances, and especially the church?

We need not presume immediately that young people living together without getting married simply want to satisfy their lusts, so they "shack up," as people say. The phenomenon of cohabiting without marrying is so widespread that many well-intentioned young people get swept along by it. But that does not eliminate the disorderly character of their behavior. In former times it was properly said that sexual intercourse before marriage violated not only the seventh commandment, since perpetrators were act-

ing in a disorderly manner, but also the fifth commandment, since perpetrators failed to respect the order within civil society.*

Today that argument carries little weight, since government policies
more and more fail to distinguish between being married and cohabiting
without marriage. However, if we are guided not by prevailing opinion,
but by the order found in God's law, then we will understand just how fitting and essential it is for a man and a woman who desire to live together
to speak their wedding vows in the presence of a *public* community.

Therefore, the church should maintain this biblical style by teaching
her youth that the bond between sexual communion and the married state
must remain unbroken, and that a publicly declared vow is required for a
man and a woman to live together.

It is true that such a vow includes many things. The bridegroom must
promise before God that he will guide his wife in love, care for her and
protect her, never forsake her, and remain faithful to her in prosperity and
in adversity, in riches and in poverty, in health and in sickness, as long as
they both shall live. The bride's vow is just as comprehensive. But notice
that we make these vows *before God*, who also bestows blessing upon marriage. The One who instituted marriage makes it possible for fault-ridden,
frightened people to repeat these all-embracing vows with confidence.

Homosexuality

Is it possible to enjoy a homosexual relationship as an alternative to marriage? Ever since the 1960s, the pressure to recognize this as a legitimate alternative has become much stronger. "What is so different about me that I
am not allowed to do this?" is a question being asked even by ministers who
want to live with their male friends in the parsonage and who want openhearted acceptance within the church.[15] If there is a body of elders somewhere who still believe they have the right to exclude from the Lord's Table
homosexuals who live together, such action is considered hurtful and dis-
criminating and is rejected by many as indefensible in our modern age.

We have already encountered other practices that are supposed to be

---

* The Dutch Reformed Synod of Middelburg in 1581 was asked about people who "have
begun their marriage in a disorderly manner by sleeping together." In its reply, the synod
observed, among other things, that such people have transgressed the law of the governing
authorities. See P. Biesterveld and H. H. Kuyper, *Kerkelijk handboekje* (Kampen, 1905),
175–76. More than once, appeal was made to 1 Cor. 14:40, "Let all things be done decently
and in order."

accepted in our modern age, practices we must continue to reject on the basis of our obedience to God's Word, even though people label us bigots. What does Scripture say about homosexuality?

Holy Scripture condemns homosexual relations. That is clear especially from Leviticus 18:22–23 and 20:13, along with Romans 1:26–17. These passages, along with the creation story, show us that the unity between husband and wife is the context for "cleaving" and "becoming one flesh."

The oft-used argument that Leviticus is forbidding *cultic* homosexuality or cultic homosexual prostitution holds no water. If that were the reason behind the prohibition in these verses, then why do we not find in the same context a prohibition against *cultic heterosexuality*? After all, should not cultic heterosexuality have been prohibited with equal force? But when you read the Leviticus verses carefully, you notice that homosexual acts are sinful, quite apart from their practice in a cultic context: a man may not have intercourse with another man "as with a woman." The objectionable element lies in the unnatural character of such an act: a man may not have intercourse with another man as he does with a woman.

The same thing appears in Romans 1:26–27. God punishes people who worship the creature instead of the Creator, by handing them over to their shameful lusts by which they exchange natural relations for unnatural ones. What "nature" means *here*[*] is clear enough from the context: it is the nature created by God and described in Genesis 1 and 2 in terms of the relationship between man and woman.

Some modern interpreters admit that the verses in Leviticus and Romans condemn homosexual practices. They are not impressed by the exegetical contortions required to limit these verses to a prohibition of merely *specific* homosexual behavior (cultic or gross homosexuality). But for these folk, that does not settle the issue. Even if Moses and Paul were opposed to homosexuality, that does not mean that *we* today, who have a better insight into what homosexuality is, need to be against it. Are there not other points at which we no longer follow the Bible's prescriptions? For example, we would not defend *capital punishment for homosexual acts*, would we? This common exception already indicates that we no longer

---

[*] The meaning of this word is not the same throughout the New Testament. For example, 1 Cor. 11:14 describes men wearing long hair as something unnatural. On the basis of this verse, people then argue that what Rom. 1:26–27 prohibits as unnatural need not be unnatural for us today. However, this is an irresponsible way of escaping the prohibition against homosexuality. The meaning of the word *phusis* (nature) must be determined from its context. And that context is clear in Rom. 1.

take seriously part of the Bible's condemnation of homosexuality. Here is another example: We eat meat with blood in it, which the Bible prohibits with the threat of death (Lev. 7:27).*

Such arguments are not persuasive. Regarding capital punishment for homosexual acts, we would argue that the *degree* of punishment can change without thereby eliminating the *moral culpability* for such acts. By analogy, we would not argue that (1) the Bible prescribes capital punishment for adultery; (2) we no longer execute adulterers; *therefore*, (3) we should accept adultery more easily than in times past. Regarding eating meat with blood, a Christian need not object to that, since after the death of Christ we (may) regard animal blood differently than Israel did, whose view of animal blood was closely associated with the function of blood in her sacrificial system.

Those who want the Bible on their side in approving homosexuality must show that the order in Genesis 2 pertaining to sexual relationships is just as relative as using or abstaining from eating meat with blood in it.

We should add that today many in the church no longer appeal to exegetical conclusions in their defense of homosexuality. Something else has become decisive, namely, love. We are supposed to accept each other in love and so we must accept the homosexual Christian in his or her differentness. The direction of our moral argument should be from love to law, not from the law to love. The letter of the law can suffocate homosexuals, but fortunately the Spirit makes alive. Man does not exist for the law, but the law for man.[16]

Given this position, people obviously are no longer concerned about the order and the structures that God has provided in His *commandments*. But we are, because it is not true that love replaces law.[17] For that reason, what Leviticus and Romans teach about homosexuality remains valid. We continue to reject the sexual expressions of homosexuality.

That does not mean we label every homosexual a fornicator. Some homosexuals restrain themselves and do not surrender to their sexual desires. One who has homosexual tendencies is not by definition a homosexual.†

---

* This is the position, for example, of J. Veenhof in *Wie ben ik dat ik dit niet doen mag?*, 113–14—after he had just written on page 112 that the conclusion that both Leviticus and Paul condemn homosexual practices "cannot be doubted."

† For a more extensive treatment of the material related to this question, see volume 9 in the series *Ethische bezinning*, entitled *Homofilie*, 5th ed. (Kampen, 1984). In that book we defend the distinction between *homophilia*, as the *orientation* wherein people are predominantly or exclusively attracted to members of the same sex, and *homosexuality*, as the *practice* of sexual intercourse with members of the same sex. Our use of this distinction does not entail moral approval of homosexual desires.

If a person with homosexual tendencies abstains from acting upon them, just as other single people must abstain from following their sexual desires, then he or she is fighting the good fight and deserves our encouragement and support in that struggle. The person with homosexual tendencies accepts himself, as K. J. Popma puts it, as "God's prisoner" who is bearing his cross.[18] The struggle will often be severe. But it becomes still more severe when the person's own church proclaims another path to self-acceptance by justifying homosexual friendships and homosexual marriages. People who use the Bible this way in their attempt to help homosexuals are simply helping them climb out of the frying pan into the fire.

Adultery and Divorce

If a vow of lifelong troth has been recited, then divorce constitutes breaking that vow. Divorce never happens apart from guilt, either of both parties or of one of them.

It is impossible for Christians to define marriage as a *contract* that can be dissolved upon mutual agreement, leaving both parties free to go on living. Business contracts can be terminated without the opprobrium of "guilt" associated with that termination. But marriage is a *covenant* witnessed by God and other people. If a wife forsakes the companion of her youth, she forgets the covenant of her God, and, along with it, the consecrated character of the bond she entered back then (Prov. 2:17; see Ezek. 16:8; Mal. 2:14). Earlier we saw how the (micro) covenant between two people lies embedded within the (macro) covenant between God and His people, between Christ and His church. One of the consequences of this is that married people are to share life together until death.

What we have just said does not mean that adultery and divorce mean exactly the same thing. That is evident already in the Old Testament. Destroying a marriage by adultery is always judged negatively. It was punished by death (Lev. 20:10; Deut. 22:22–24; Num. 5). But the situation with divorce was different. Divorce was permitted in cases where the husband discovered "something indecent" in his wife (Deut. 24:1 NIV).

What the phrase "something indecent" means precisely is no longer clear. Jewish casuistry pounced on that expression, giving it a broad and a narrow application. Interpreters in the school of Shammai emphasized the second word, "something *indecent*," pointing to some kind of sexual misconduct. Interpreters in the school of Hillel made a broader application by emphasizing the first word, "*something* indecent," such as a wife's physical defect or even the fact that she burned her husband's food while cooking it.

These later interpretations would certainly have been broader than the Lord intended. The expression "something indecent" probably referred to shameful behavior of a serious nature. But regardless of the specific reference, we cannot deny that the Lord permitted divorce in some situations and allowed the use of a certificate of divorce. Elsewhere we read that Yahweh hates divorce (Mal. 2:16), but there Malachi is referring to husbands divorcing their wives apart from any sexual misconduct like that described in Deuteronomy 24.

The existence of the divorce certificate did put a brake on divorce. Husbands had to be able to find "something indecent." A divorce certificate had to be drawn up, and its formulation had to be proper. So a husband would have to enlist the help of a third party, a process that prevented quick divorces. Moreover, the divorced woman who later married another man was not allowed to be taken back by her first husband. Does this not indicate that although divorce was permitted, it could never be treated as something routine? In Israel, marriage was not an institution that allowed a woman to be shunted from one man to another, only to return to her original husband!

We must use a bit more nuance when discussing divorce than when we evaluate adultery. But is that not also true after Jesus pronounced His judgment about the certificate of divorce? In the Sermon on the Mount, He quoted a saying of "the men of old": "Whoever divorces his wife, let him give her a certificate of divorce," and then He proceeded to offer this commentary: "But I say to you that whoever divorces his wife for any reason except sexual immorality causes her to commit adultery; and whoever marries a woman who is divorced commits adultery" (Matt. 5:31–32). Is that not a clear condemnation of every divorce, except for the one legitimate reason (sexual immorality)?

It is not true that Jesus was absolutely opposed to the divorce certificate. In the case of sexual immorality, He considered the certificate permissible, since in His day capital punishment was no longer being administered for adultery. Moreover, we must be sure to distinguish between the regulating activity of the state which simply cannot function without divorce laws designed to restrain human intemperance, and the message concerning divorce that the church proclaims to her members.

For the latter we must listen to the instruction of Jesus. Now, we should not interpret Jesus' words to mean: "Unfortunately Moses instituted the certificate of divorce, but I . . ." Just as with other subjects in the Sermon on the Mount, the contrast is not between Jesus and Moses, but between

Jesus and a *caricature* of Moses. The liberal use among the Jews of the certificate of divorce conflicted with "Moses," certainly with the Moses who had written how it had been "from the beginning": Husband and wife must become one flesh (Matt. 19:4–9). The "hardness of hearts" (Matt. 19:8) compelled Moses to institute the divorce certificate, just as *every* government in this world is compelled to do.

But because the Jews had turned this *necessity* into a *virtue* and made easy use of the divorce certificate of Deuteronomy 24, Jesus opposed them. He does this with remarkable sharpness. Whereas the Jews justified all kinds of divorces and imagined that with their liberal use of the divorce certificate they were miles away from committing adultery and immunized from sinning against the seventh commandment, Jesus shattered their serenity. He blew the dust off the law by saying that the divorce certificate and adultery are cut from the same cloth. In fact, the divorce certificate opens the door for adultery. A divorced woman has sexual intercourse with someone other than the man who should keep on treating her as his own wife. And any man who marries such a divorced woman should know that he is committing adultery! "Therefore what God has joined together, let not man separate" (Matt. 19:6).

It is of interest to note that *two* things are necessary for committing adultery: a marriage that should not have been dissolved is nevertheless dissolved, and one of the divorced partners marries someone else. Adultery has not yet occurred when the divorced partners live separately; however, when a third party enters the picture and forms a sexual relationship with one of the divorced partners, then adultery occurs.

Adultery as constituted by those *two* actions is the focus of all the verses dealing with this matter: Matthew 5:32 and 19:9, Mark 10:11–12, and Luke 16:18. The paraphrase Good News for Modern Man renders Matthew 5:32 with literal precision: "If a man divorces his wife, and she has not been unfaithful, then he is guilty of making her commit adultery if she marries again."

Paul too echoes Jesus' teaching in 1 Corinthians 7:10–11: "Now to the married I command, yet not I but the Lord [Jesus]: A wife is not to depart from her husband. But *even if she does depart*, let her remain unmarried [thus not taking the step rendering her guilty of adultery—J.D.] or be reconciled to her husband. And a husband is not to divorce his wife."

A divorce is already serious enough, but matters become worse if one who is divorced marries someone else. This turns divorce into adultery. Preventing this from happening requires one of two possibilities: the divorced partners remain unmarried, or they become reconciled.

Divorce is not yet adultery. But the former easily paves the way for the latter. For the smoke rising from divorce is so often an indication that the fire of adultery is already burning.

Permissible Divorces

From Matthew 5:32 and 19:9 we see that not every divorce certificate was forbidden, not even in the New Testament dispensation. Otherwise, Jesus would not have said "except for sexual immorality." If a husband sends his wife away on account of unchastity, he is not violating God's will. In the old covenant, such a woman, who in fact had broken troth, was to be put to death, as we have seen.

Traditional Roman Catholic exegetes have argued, in the line of Augustine and other church fathers and on the basis of Mark 10:11–12, Luke 16:18, and 1 Corinthians 7:10–11, that marriage is *absolutely* indissoluble. The exceptive clause about sexual immorality is not mentioned in these verses. That is true, but that does not justify pretending that the exception is absent in Matthew 5 and 19.

In various ways people try to escape this clearly formulated exception. The church father Jerome argued that the exception of Matthew 5 and 19 refers to sending one's wife away, but not to the possibility of a second marriage. To put it in contemporary terms: Separation of bed and board is permissible, but divorce and a possible subsequent marriage are not. Augustine offered another "solution." The word *except* (for sexual immorality) means, according to him, "leaving this case aside." In other words, Jesus supposedly never made a pronouncement regarding a situation of sexual immorality in marriage.

Such explanations are quite contrived. If we were to declare that anyone who assaults another person, except in a situation of war, and kills him, commits murder, then everyone would understand what we were saying. We would not be disregarding situations of war, but would in fact be saying something important about them, namely, that we evaluate assaulting and killing in a wartime situation differently than attacking and killing in any other situation. The latter we would call murder. Now, precisely the same applies to Matthew 5 and 19: If there is a situation of sexual immorality, then the other party does have the right to depart and to marry someone else.

For that reason, Protestant moralists believe that divorce on the ground of sexual immorality conforms to what both Old and New Testaments teach us about marriage. Someone who becomes one flesh with someone other than husband or wife radically sunders marriage. At the point where unity is most intimate, the opposite of unity results in marital breakdown.

Nevertheless, adultery is not *required* to end in divorce. Just as God repeatedly showed grace to His people Israel, even though the nation had become guilty of adultery (see Jer. 3:1; 30:14–22), even so every marriage partner must have a forgiving attitude. Not *falling* into adultery, but *living* in adultery is a legitimate reason to have a marriage terminated.

Most Protestant moralists have followed in the line of Calvin's successor, Beza (1519–1605), in positing a second ground for divorce, in addition to sexual immorality (adultery): *willful desertion*. This is based on an appeal to 1 Corinthians 7:15–16: If a believing husband or wife is abandoned by his or her spouse, the believer is "not bound" (NIV). Paul adds: "God has called us to peace. For how do you know, O wife, whether you will save your husband? Or how do you know, O husband, whether you will save your wife?" Clearly we are dealing here with a frequent situation in the early Christian church where only one partner converted to the Christian faith. If then the unbelieving partner no longer wanted to live with the believer, the latter was not obligated to remain with the unbeliever at all costs.

It should impress us how seriously Paul views the marriage bond in 1 Corinthians 7. The simple fact that within a marriage one of the partners is a believer and the other an unbeliever is, by itself, an insufficient ground for divorce. If the unbeliever is willing to remain married, the couple should remain married.

So even the lack of deep moral and spiritual harmony does not have to lead to terminating a marriage. Paul is looking out in that situation for the children in such a family. If both husband and wife are unbelievers, then you cannot say their children are "holy." But if one partner is a believer, then "the unbelieving husband is sanctified by the wife, [or] the unbelieving wife is sanctified by the husband; otherwise your children would be unclean, but now they are holy" (1 Cor. 7:14).

Even if the precise meaning of these words is difficult to determine, what is abundantly clear is that the believer's Christian faith does (and must) radiate to the other partner and to their children. That faith is such a mighty power that it can provide luster to even a mixed marriage. You should never enter into a mixed marriage (2 Cor. 6:15–16), but once you are in such a marriage, you can continue living in that relationship as a Christian. Grace does not destroy the world; marriage bonds do not need to be severed if both partners have not surrendered to Christ.

So divorce is always regrettable and surely an extreme measure. Members of Christ's church must be aware of that, even if they are married to outspoken unbelievers. But—the possibilities are limited. If the unbeliever refuses to continue the marriage, the relationship cannot be salvaged. The Christian brother or sister in that situation is no longer "bound."

There is difference of opinion about the meaning of this last phrase. If the believer is no longer "bound," is he or she free to marry a second time? Beza and most Reformed exegetes and ethicists have argued that a second marriage is not forbidden. The dissolution of the first marriage is definitive, so that the way is open for a second marriage. We concur with this view. To church members who had married a fellow believer, but had subsequently divorced, Paul said: Do not marry again, or else be reconciled to your spouse (1 Cor. 7:10–11). But he does *not* say this to a church member who divorced an unbeliever.

But does not this conclusion bring us into conflict with what Jesus said about a new marriage by or with the divorced party? To interpret Jesus' words this way would be to absolutize them, for that fails to take into account different situations. *Jesus* confronts His listeners with their responsibility not to divorce. He is pointing out the particular calling of the dismissed woman toward her husband. To keep the way of reconciliation fully open, so that perhaps he might humble himself before God and be converted, she should not marry someone else. Rash divorces must not be followed by rash second marriages.

But *Paul* is talking about a marriage relationship impossible to continue, and he says that it is better that the believer let the unbeliever depart; he or she can no longer exert a positive influence.

In the situations that Jesus was discussing, the divorced woman should not simply acquiesce in her husband's behavior. But apparently there are situations where people simply have no other choice but to acquiesce. If everything has been done to heal the brokenness, the moment comes for acquiescing in a particular divorce.

Therefore, there is no conflict between the two grounds for legitimate divorce. That was formulated clearly by William Ames: There is a ground for *effecting* divorce and there is a ground for *acquiescing* in divorce.* Matthew 5 and 19 indicate the former; 1 Corinthians 7 discusses the latter. The believing partner mentioned in 1 Corinthians 7 honors Jesus' prohibition of "putting away," but must acquiesce in being put away by the unbelieving partner.

In the few passages that deal with this matter, the Bible is not giving us

---

* Ames speaks of the "causa divortii *faciendi*" (Matt. 5 and 19) and the "causa divortii *patiendi*" (1 Cor. 7). See his *De conscientia et eius iure vel casibus* (Amsterdam, 1631), 352.

a recipe for every situation or for all cases of marital breakdown. The second ground offers us a clear guideline for our conduct, but the application of this guideline confronts us with numerous difficulties.

We should mention one of those difficulties here. A wide variety of situations have led people to apply the phrase "willful desertion" to more than simply the single "case" of one marriage partner being converted from paganism to Christianity, discussed by Paul in 1 Corinthians 7. For example, Beza argued that when a husband abandoned his wife and went off to a foreign land, that was *equivalent* to being divorced by an unbeliever as discussed in 1 Corinthians 7. Such a deserter could be equated with an unbeliever, even though he was not a pagan like the Corinthian whom Paul had in mind. Voetius went one step further: Anyone who abandons his wife for whatever reason breaks up his marriage just as ruinously as the Corinthian husband who for religious reasons turned his back on his wife. Suppose, argued Voetius, that this were *not* so. Then a negligent husband could in effect consign his wife to being a lifelong "widow," or a negligent wife could force her husband to be a "widower" his whole life. In this way, such negligent partners could rob their spouses of the use and the fruits of marriage.*

Beza and Voetius are thus arguing at this point *by analogy* to what Paul wrote in 1 Corinthians 7. From the situation mentioned there they extend "willful desertion" to apply to other comparable situations. They show that there are various situations where a divorce is unavoidable and the prohibition against a subsequent marriage does not apply to the party treated in an ungodly manner.† This approach of Beza and Voetius to the

---

* We refer to Theodore Beza, *De repudiis et divortiis* (Geneva, 1569), 205–6, where he subscribes to the norm applied in the church of Geneva and written in *Ordonnances ecclésiastiques*, formulated by Calvin. For Voetius's argument, see his *Politica ecclesiastica* (Amsterdam, 1666), 1:188ff.

† At their Synod of Middelburg (1933), the Reformed Churches of the Netherlands made no pronouncement about the question whether a divorce could be sought also on the basis of willful desertion. In practice, divorces have occurred and still occur on both grounds, namely, for adultery and for willful desertion. At their Synod of Rotterdam (1959), the Christian Reformed Churches of the Netherlands made a careful pronouncement similar to that of the Reformed Churches in 1933.

It is incorrect to argue that the Reformed Churches of the Netherlands (liberated) declared at their Synod of Hoogeveen (1969–70) that adultery is the only legitimate ground for divorce. Such a statement did appear as one of the (in our opinion, debatable) *considerations* in one of the synodical decisions. See the *Acta* of this synod, article 314 (page 333). But the synod never made a *decision* in that direction. To have done so would have required a discussion of the 1933 decision of the Synod of Middelburg.

application of Scripture has been used throughout the history of the church and of Christian ethics. We see it wherever the notion of *equity* surfaces in moral discussions.

The Bible says only a few things about divorce. But these are sufficiently clear to induce us to proceed with extreme caution in this matter and to continue viewing divorce as a great evil. Think of marriage as a lifelong covenant! But these few observations are not so exhaustive that we have a ready-made answer to all our questions. Only biblicism requires a verse for everything. But one who uses Scripture in a healthy way knows that we must pray in order to discern what is excellent (Eph. 5:10; Phil. 1:9).

The church has always understood this, be it ever so imperfectly. Two simple examples relating to our subject illustrate this. If two people marry and one of the spouses refuses to have sexual intercourse, Voetius and others believed this is not a marriage. The Bible says nothing about this particular situation, but a simple analysis of what constitutes marriage makes it grossly unfair to tell someone in this kind of relationship that married is married and that's it. Voetius insisted that in such a situation it may be assumed that married people will live together not as friends or acquaintances, but as husband and wife.

Here is another example: When the Bible verses we have studied speak of sexual immorality, clearly they are talking about heterosexual immorality. But if someone destroys a marriage by homosexual conduct, that too can be a legitimate ground for divorce. Just as in our first example we did not discover a new ground for divorce, so here too; we are simply drawing conclusions from what constitutes marriage and what constitutes sexual immorality.[19]

Anyone who happens to encounter this problem, as a pastor or in some other capacity, will discover again and again that no two situations are alike. The *question of culpability* is not always easy to answer. We are not saying that the question should not be asked; nor are we saying that where two are fighting, two are at fault. Both biblical grounds for divorce do somewhat presuppose that culpability can be assigned. But we can sometimes err very grievously in this matter. Jesus says that the divorce certificate opens the door for adultery. But it can also happen that the lovelessness of one partner drives the other into the arms of a third. Of course this is adultery, and can never be approved. But the "innocent" party had better not run to the judge for a divorce; rather, that partner has every reason to ask whether he or she is the *source* of the trouble. You see, it is also possible to use a biblical ground for divorce very legalistically.

Divorce Without Subsequent Marriage

If there are legitimate grounds for divorce, these can also be legitimate reasons for marrying again. Whether it is prudent to marry again depends on many factors we will not get into. Right now we simply want to observe that someone who is divorced for proper reasons is free to marry again.

But some divorces may not be followed by another marriage. We saw this already in our discussion of the apostle's reasoning in 1 Corinthians 7. Divorced people were members of the church in Corinth. It is not clear why one spouse divorced the other. Some think there was a "spiritual" motive underlying the divorce. Their strong yearning for the return of Christ would have turned some away from the concerns and relationships of ordinary life. They would have considered marital life along with its sexual intimacies to be beneath them as Christians.

It could be that this played a role, in view of what Paul says in 1 Corinthians 7:5 about times of sexual abstinence that should not last too long. But this interpretation has trouble explaining why Paul uses strong language like "put away" and "reconcile" when he is discussing divorces in that church. This language suggests conflict ("put away") that must be resolved if possible ("reconcile"). If spouses went their separate ways because of their conviction that sexual intimacy was no longer appropriate, it is difficult to understand why phrases like "put away" and "reconcile" would need to be used. For that reason, it seems more obvious that the apostle is referring to interpersonal difficulties that unfortunately can alienate even members of Christ's church from one another.

What interests us is the fact that Paul mentions not only the need for reconciliation, but also the apparent impossibility of getting two divorced people under the same roof again—even two people within the same church, where the powers of the Holy Spirit were manifest in many ways (see 1 Cor. 12). It is evil for spouses to part ways (1 Cor. 7:10), but if that has happened, the break is not always repairable. Paul demonstrates pastoral wisdom in facing this reality squarely.

However, matters must not go *from bad to worse* by those who divorce for illegitimate reasons marrying again. In their case, a subsequent marriage would constitute *adultery*. For even though two people are living separately, their marriage can still be valid before God. No matter how thin the thread binding them may become in their day-to-day living, it may not be cut. A break has occurred, but only as a *de facto* separation. Before God, husband and wife are not separated. They are not free to enter a new marriage.

This is a lesson for today as well. Unhappy marriages, even in our churches, can explode. The help offered by church leaders and others to heal the brokenness may do little good. If then we must acquiesce in a divorce, 1 Corinthians 7:10-11 must always remain in our consciousness: "Now to the married I command, yet not I but the Lord: A wife is not to depart from her husband. But even if she does depart, let her remain unmarried or be reconciled to her husband. And a husband is not to divorce his wife."

A practical consequence of this position is that *separation of bed and board* is preferable to divorce. With this arrangement, those who are separated protect themselves legally against the temptation to form new relationships. After all, those separated in bed and board are not legally free to marry anyone else. But they would be free after a divorce.

In modern jurisprudence, separation of bed and board can easily proceed to divorce after a short period. This is possible already if only one of the spouses seeks a divorce. The other spouse will have to acquiesce. But that does not yet allow either party to marry again. The state regulates *civil* relationships among citizens, also when it grants a divorce. But what the state breaks asunder is not thereby broken in heaven. In her teaching and discipline relating to marriage and divorce, the church must proceed from what the Bible says and not from what the state does. Surely the church has her own message to proclaim in response to the vague provisions in most modern Western law codes with all their talk about "incompatibility" and "total and permanent marital breakdown." Someone may be free in terms of the civil law to remarry, but that does not mean that he or she is free in terms of God's law.

There are certain realities, however, no matter how defective, that the church simply cannot ignore. If a marriage has been legitimated with a civil ceremony without the church's blessing, the church cannot act as if the marriage does not exist. Suppose one of the parties gets an unbiblical divorce and remarries (or simply lives with someone apart from marriage); in this situation a new relationship has been formed that has consequences. The first marriage no longer exists, because it has been completely destroyed by adultery. Church leaders can hardly forbid the other spouse (who is now entirely free from the first marriage) to remarry.

Abstaining in Freedom

The message of Holy Scripture concerning marriage and divorce is not always received with delight. Numerous people have a hard time applying its principles in their own lives.

That was the case already with Jesus' own disciples, when He warned them about divorcing rashly. They replied, "If such is the case of the man with his wife, it is better not to marry" (Matt. 19:10). For as a married person, you run a great risk if you must stay bound to your partner in the way Jesus demands. He who finds a wife, finds a good thing (Prov. 18:22)—but the choice does not always work out well. Some husbands could better live in a corner of a housetop than in a house shared with a contentious woman (Prov. 21:9). Women, too, are abused in their marriages, like Abigail, an intelligent woman who had to spend her life with a foolish and surly husband (1 Sam. 25:3).

It is not easy to put up with everything. For that reason, a liberal interpretation of Deuteronomy 24 or modern divorce laws like we have in Western nations come to the aid of many a spouse.

Nor is it easy to remain unmarried after a divorce, for loneliness is terrible and sexual urges remain strong. Homosexuals and numerous other single people can testify to that.

A Christian can be severely tested in his or her obedience to the seventh commandment. Reminding others of this commandment is not so difficult; living according to it ourselves is. For often it requires what Jesus reminded His disciples about: "becoming a eunuch" for the sake of the kingdom of heaven (Matt. 19:12). For many people this means very concretely that they must give up a (subsequent) marriage and/or sexual intercourse.

It has become very difficult for these words of Jesus to resonate with people in a day and age when society gorges itself with every sexual possibility and refuses to hear anything about abstinence. The campaign against AIDS—a dark cloud hanging over the whole world—testifies to that. Unrestrained sexual intercourse with multiple partners must nowadays be rendered safe with propaganda for condoms.

The British bishop Basil Hume has called AIDS the Chernobyl of modern ethics. Just as the catastrophe at the nuclear plant in Chernobyl made us think about what we were doing to the environment, so too AIDS is compelling us to reflect again about our relationships and about the role of sexuality in those relationships, according to Hume.[20]

But the world is so enslaved to sex that the reflection that Hume is calling for demands nothing less than a conversion. People are clamoring for "safe sex" with the help of condoms. But that will only keep the world enslaved in the fetters of sex. It is a slavery to Babylon, the mother of whores and the source of the plagues of the earth (Rev. 17:2; 18:3, 9).

The real remedy is not a condom, but the gospel that puts sexuality in its place and portrays us as travelers en route to a future where people "neither marry nor are given in marriage, but are like angels of God in heaven" (Matt. 22:30). Sexual intimacy will no longer exist. That future must begin taking shape for us already in the present. In the present time we must not fritter away our freedom by throwing ourselves at the feet of idols. It is no mere coincidence that the sins of sexual immorality regularly head the lists of sins summarized in the Bible (for example, Rom. 1:26; 1 Cor. 6:10; and Gal. 5:19).

The seventh commandment, like all the other commandments, comes after the prologue with its declaration of liberation from the house of slavery in Egypt. We are called to be free. If we truly understand that calling, then we will also know what it is to crucify our flesh with its passions and desires (Gal. 5:24). Then too we will know what self-conscious abstinence is. We will be able to abstain in freedom.

Endnotes

1. J. L. Koole, *De Tien Geboden*, 2d ed. (Kampen, 1983), 108–9.

2. Elisabeth Badinter, *L'un est l'autre* (Paris, 1986).

3. J. Douma, *Vrede in de maatschappij*, 2d ed., vol. 12 in the series *Ethische bezinning* (Kampen, 1985), 56–66, 86–88.

4. J. Douma, *Seksualiteit en huwelijk*, vol. 6 in the series *Ethische bezinning* (Kampen, 1993), 144–64 (chap. 7, "Gezinsvorming").

5. W. Geesink, *Gereformeerde ethiek* (Kampen, 1931), 2:289–90.

6. F. Bloemhof, *Kunstmatige inseminatie bij de mens* (Nijkerk, 1959), 50.

7. J. van Bruggen, *Het huwelijk gewogen* (Amsterdam, 1978), 11.

8. P. Wittewrongel, *Oeconomia christiana ofte Christelicke huyshoudinghe* (Amsterdam, 1661), 2:75.

9. Quoted by Augustine, *Contra Julianum*, 7, 20, from a document penned by Ambrose, now lost: "Intemperans enim in conjugio, quid aliud nisi quidam adulter uxoris?" This statement was recalled by, among others, Calvin in his *Institutes*, 2.8.44.

10. Th. Delleman, "Het Zevende Gebod," in A. T. Besselaar et al., *De thora in de thora*, 2d ed. (Franeker, n.d.), 2:61.

11. See, for example, W. J. Kernkamp's essay in *Sinaï en Ardjoeno*, ed. Th. Delleman (Aalten, 1946), 186–88, regarding societies in Indonesia where the family relationship can be a negative and destructive factor for entering into marriages.

12. This is also the view of K. Schilder, *De Reformatie*, 17 (1936–37): 253, who disputed a dissertation thesis that claimed that breaking an engagement would be in conflict with the spirit of the seventh commandment.

13. B. Smytegelt, *Des Christens eenige troost* (reprint, Leiden, 1747), 585.

14. Walter Trobisch, *Liefde moet je leren* (Kampen, 1977), 27.

15. See S. Rozendal, ed., *Wie ben ik dat ik dit niet doen mag?* (Kampen, 1987).

16. This is the argument of J. Veenhof in *Wie ben ik dat ik dit niet doen mag?*, 118ff.

17. See our discussion of this point in *Christian Morals and Ethics* (Winnipeg, 1981), 38–49, 57–63.

18. K. J. Popma, *Levensbeschouwing* (Amsterdam, 1963), 6:289. The expression "God's prisoner" is borrowed from the title of a novel by Wilma, who depicts the suffering of a person with homosexual tendencies.

19. Space does not permit us to discuss various concrete applications of both biblical grounds for divorce in our modern situation. For a more extensive discussion, the reader is referred to volume 7 of the series *Ethische bezinning*, entitled *Echtscheiding*, 4th ed. (Kampen, 1988).

20. According to the Dutch daily newspaper *Trouw*, 15 December 1986.

The Eighth Commandment

You shall not steal. (Ex. 20:15)

Kidnapping

Occasionally the New Testament presents a summary of sins whose *arrangement* leads us to think immediately of the Ten Commandments. That is surely the case in 1 Timothy 1:10, where we read that the law was made "for fornicators, for sodomites, for kidnappers, for liars, for perjurers." The list moves from fathers and mothers mentioned in the fifth commandment (v. 9) to liars identified in the ninth commandment.

Surprisingly, this list contains a reference to kidnappers, whose place in the series suggests that kidnapping is a violation of the eighth commandment, "You shall not steal." A better rendering of the meaning behind the Greek word in the original text would be "man stealers" or "slave traders." That brings us more directly to the eighth commandment, which apparently also forbids stealing *people*.

We read about this kind of stealing in Exodus 21:16: "He who kidnaps a man and sells him, or if he is found in his hand, shall surely be put to death." A similar regulation appears in Deuteronomy 24:7: "If a man is found kidnapping any of his brethren of the children of Israel, and mistreats him or sells him, then that kidnapper shall die; and you shall put away the evil person from among you."

Since the appearance of a publication by theologian A. Alt, this aspect of the eighth commandment has received widespread attention once again. Semitic language scholar J. P. Lettinga appreciates the new perspective of Alt, but rejects out of hand his view that the eighth commandment has a *special* focus on stealing people. You see, Alt and others argue that stealing *property* comes under discussion only in the tenth commandment. But on the basis of the text of the eighth commandment, this argu-

285

ment is incorrect. This commandment forbids robbery in general, without specifying the object of robbery (thing or person). Moreover, the tenth commandment is surely not speaking first of all about stealing, as we will see when we discuss that commandment.

Regardless of the one-sidedness of Alt's exegesis, he has again opened our eyes to an important consideration. We emphasize: *again* opened our eyes. For Alt's observation was very well known to people in former times, but has sunk into oblivion in our modern time. When we investigated old expositions of the Heidelberg Catechism and other treatments written at the time of the Reformation, we were struck time and again by the attention that the commentators paid to this aspect of the eighth commandment. They warned their readers repeatedly about *plagium* (man stealing) and *plagiarius* (a man stealer).*

We owe many new and sometimes surprising insights to Bible interpreters of our own day. But it happens occasionally that what they present as new was known previously.† Interpreters realized that 1 Timothy 1:10 referred to the eighth commandment and expressed this in their translation. Consider, for example, the rendering of "menstealers" in 1 Timothy 1:10 in the King James or Authorized Version.

Perhaps the reader is wondering if this entire discussion is so important after all. Who actually steals people? Permit us first to give an answer from an earlier time. G. Voetius (1589–1676) referred to four instances of stealing people:

---

* Readers are probably familiar with the word *plagiarism*—stealing from another's (published) work and using the stolen material as if it were one's own work. But this modern meaning has totally displaced the centuries-old meaning of *man* stealing or kidnapping. The Latin word derives from the Greek *plagios*, meaning "crooked," "ambiguous," or "unreliable," meanings often attributed in their Latinized forms to "man stealing" or kidnapping.

† After Alt had made his "discovery," someone pointed out that a similar interpretation could be found already in the ancient Jewish Bible commentary known as the Talmud: "Our teachers taught: 'You shall not steal.' Scripture is speaking here about stealing people" (Talmud, *Sanhedrin* 86a). The fact that the rabbis had this view was known already to S. Curcellaeus, who, however, was *simultaneously* critical of this rabbinic interpretation. The text of the eighth commandment is understood too narrowly if we see it as referring only to stealing people: "Quod Hebraeorum magistri exponunt de furto animae, seu plagio; quod gravissimam esse furti speciem constat ea lege [then follows Ex. 21:16—J.D.]. Sed verba praecepti generalia, ita anguste accipere non licet, nisi ratio manifesta id suadet, quae hic nulla apparet" (*Opera theologica* [Amsterdam, 1675], 201).

1. Stealing children, who were robbed from their parents by Roman Catholics and brought to a monastery or enrolled in the Jesuit order.
2. Stealing in the form of slavery. People were sold into slavery, a widespread phenomenon in the East and West Indies.
3. Stealing children from their parents with the aim of using them as beggars. Such children, according to one report, were often mutilated and maimed so that they could arouse sympathy as little cripples when they went around begging.
4. Stealing young girls. Against the will of her parents, a young man carried out his plans to marry a particular young girl.[1]

We can clearly see the stamp of Voetius's own time on the examples he uses. Some time later, Joh. van der Kemp (1664–1718) observed that "these sins [of stealing people—J.D.] do not occur among us very much." He accused only the Jesuits and the monks of this offense.[2]

One fact stands out in Van der Kemp's discussion: He no longer mentioned the evil of *slavery* in the colonial world, which Voetius and others identified with crystal clarity in their discussions of the eighth commandment. Anyone who sells slaves, said Voetius, is robbing them of the precious treasure of their freedom.*

What Voetius is saying here is very important for our understanding of the eighth commandment. With this commandment too we must recall the prologue: "I am Yahweh your God, who has freed you from Egypt, the house of slavery." Because Israel had been freed from a house *of slavery*, she should realize how serious stealing other people is. A slave has lost his freedom. That freedom is what Yahweh now wishes to guarantee for every Israelite; but then no Israelite may rob his brother or fellow Israelite of his freedom by degrading him to the status of a slave.

Slavery did occur in Israel, even with Yahweh's approval. But the slaves were foreigners who were among the spoils of war or who had been obtained in a foreign country. The law contained provisions which—surely

---

* Voetius, *Catechisatie over den Heidelbergschen Catechismus*, 1053. Already in his discussion of the fifth commandment, Voetius had emphatically rejected slavery as an institution whereby one man is perpetually subjected to another (*Catechisatie*, 990ff.). B. Smytegelt was also critical of the robbery involved in the slave trade: "Is it not shameful that Christians have turned this into a trade?" If such slaves could speak, they would cry out "as Joseph of long ago: I have been stolen from my land, Gen. 40:15" (*Des Christens eenige troost* [reprint, Leiden, 1747], 590).

compared to situations elsewhere—were designed to make the life of a slave quite bearable (for example, the fourth commandment; Ex. 21:16; Deut. 23:15–16).

But let us return to the eighth commandment and man stealing. We have already observed that in the post-Reformation period most commentators mentioned stealing people in the form of slavery. At that time, this was a very concrete application of the eighth commandment. Voetius pointed out an evil being committed in the colonies of *his own countrymen*, in the East and West Indies. How concretely is the eighth commandment being applied in our modern time? Can we still speak of stealing people?

We need not wonder very long about this. The "new" exegesis of Alt obtained quick adoption and application in moral treatises. We find one example of that with J. M. Lochman, who argued that what appeared to belong strictly to barbaric societies of the past is very real today as well. He was talking about *terrorism*. People living long ago knew about taking hostages and kidnapping, but today we experience this in a very special way. Television keeps us informed up to the minute about hostage situations and hijackings, events where kidnapping has become a useful tactic in a comprehensive "political" strategy. Powerful governments have been virtually paralyzed for weeks by means of this tactic.

But in such hostage situations we see only the tip of the iceberg, according to Lochman. This is nothing less than *slavery*. Kidnapping is something we have see in the slave trade pursued until the last century among "Christian" nations. But even though the historical institution of slavery has virtually disappeared from the face of the earth, that does not mean that we no longer encounter the threatening phenomenon of kidnapping. Consider the racial discrimination and neocolonial exploitation that exists throughout the world, or the apartheid system once prevalent in South Africa.

We need not restrict ourselves to the Third World. Lochman points to Solzhenitsyn's *The Gulag Archipelago*, an impressive commentary on the applicability of the eighth commandment in the old and new Stalinist regimes. But staying closer to home: Are there not mechanisms at work in our "normal" world of labor and consumption that rob people of their freedom, perhaps even without our realizing it?[*]

---

[*] J. M. Lochman, *Wegweisung der Freiheit* (Gütersloh, 1979), 114ff. Lochman's comment (on p. 114) that in the church's preaching, catechizing, and ethics, the church almost always limits the words "You shall not steal" *exclusively* to larceny or stealing property, betrays a lack of familiarity with the history of the interpretation of the eighth commandment.

Without agreeing with Lochman at every point, we can still learn from him that the eighth commandment has retained its relevance, even to the evil of kidnapping. Slavery occurs not only in the hideous form that Voetius saw in his day, but also in more subtle forms. Slavery occurs wherever people are discriminated against and manipulated.

Stealing the Heart

There is still one other way is which someone can steal another person, having to do with the "being manipulated" we just mentioned. The Bible contains an expression that conveys quite nicely the power of manipulation: "stealing another's heart." If we say that somebody has stolen our heart, that sounds rather favorable. Somebody has won our love, and we are completely taken with him or her. But we can also be *taken in* by another person. Somebody can dupe us, and then we feel taken. We get fooled, or, to put it another way, we get manipulated.

In this way, Jacob "stole" Laban's "heart" by not telling him he wanted to flee (Gen. 31:20). He won Laban's trust surreptitiously. But when Jacob stole away with both his wives and all his possessions, Laban felt *taken;* he said to Jacob, literally, "What have you done, that you have stolen my heart and carried away my daughters like captives taken with the sword?" (Gen. 31:26). By promising all kinds of nice things during his popularity campaign, Absalom "stole the hearts" of the men of Israel. In so doing, he laid the basis for his bid to dethrone David. He duped the people, he took them in—much as people are taken in during election campaigns, until after the election the candidate starts showing his true colors. "Absalom has many disciples. *Democracy* is at bottom *demagoguery;* people-pleasers stand an excellent chance!"[3]

With Adolf Hitler we saw the catastrophic consequences of manipulation. The power of the word is a good gift of God, but abuse of that power can hypnotize millions so that they lend their support to ridiculous schemes. Afterward comes the rude awakening. People allowed their hearts to be stolen.

Just as with these serious forms of manipulation, so too with less serious forms that we encounter sometimes in *advertising*—we must beware that people can *let* their freedom be taken from them. In their naïveté, they become slaves to destructive political policies or slaves to affluence. The situations of those sold into slavery in times past or consigned to forced labor in recent history are different. Those involved simply stealing another's freedom. But one who lets his heart be stolen shares the responsibility. He has not been sufficiently alert. That does not excuse the demagogue, but his opportunity arises when society *wants* to be fooled. People who are inclined to let themselves be easily seduced into thinking they cannot live without this or that luxury should ask themselves how all these "hidden persuaders" (Vance Packard) can exercise such an enslaving power over them. Are their hearts being stolen, or do they allow their hearts to be stolen?

Social Injustice

A second topic appears in later expositions of the eighth commandment less frequently than in earlier commentaries. In addition to discussing kidnapping, the earlier commentators paid special attention to what was often called *land thievery*.* That phrase was understood to refer to sins against the eighth commandment in the social and political arenas, sins like acquiring acre upon acre (see Isa. 5:8), swindling the poor out of their meager possessions, embezzling and mismanaging public funds, expanding one's territory unrighteously through war, and the like.

Regularly in these early expositions of the Heidelberg Catechism, we hear especially *those in power* being reminded of the eighth commandment. Ordinary people commit petty thievery, but the stealing by political nobility on a grand scale, adorned as it is with splash and splendor, is still stealing. Compared to the kings of the earth, all others are but petty thieves. Heinrich Bullinger quoted the Roman Cato to this effect: Thieves who steal private property spend their lives in prison; thieves who steal public property walk about arrayed in gold and purple.[4] As he so of-

---

* Older commentators usually distinguished between:
1. *plagium*, kidnapping;
2. *peculatus*, actually referring to taking *peculium*, "means" or "substance," "savings," and in the broader sense, "land thievery";
3. *abigeatus*, an abbreviation from *abigo*, "drive away," "rob," thus in particular "cattle rustling"; and
4. *sacrilegium*, violating the sacred, often termed "church stealing."

We will not be discussing *abigeatus* any further. Because the Mosaic law contained special regulations about stealing cattle, it is understandable that ancient commentaries devoted special attention to that subject in their discussions of the eighth commandment, all the more so since, in an agrarian society, stealing cattle affected many people at the very center of their existence. This has changed for us in our postagrarian society. We will return below to discuss stealing in the form of *sacrilegium*.

ten did in his preaching, B. Smytegelt aimed his verbal artillery at those in power when he preached on the eighth commandment.

Protesting against social injustice and large-scale theft did not begin with Karl Marx. We encounter sharp denunciations of these already in the time of the Reformation and thereafter. In his Large Catechism, Luther put it this way: "Yea, we might well let the lesser individual thieves alone if we could only arrest the great, powerful arch-thieves, with whom princes and rulers associate. They daily pillage not only a city or two, but all Germany." Such is the way of the world, Luther continued, that "he who can publicly rob and steal runs at large in security and freedom, claiming honor from men, while the petty, sly thieves, guilty of only a small offense, must suffer, to contribute to the appearance of godliness and honor in the other class." In his sermon on Deuteronomy 5:19, Calvin is of the same mind: "And indeed, when God threateneth by His prophet Isaiah, that he which hath spoiled and robbed, shall have his turn [to be spoiled and robbed likewise], He speaketh not of the petty thieves that are carried to the gallows, but of the great princes and monarchs that bear sway in the world." But no matter how esteemed someone may be in the world's eyes, the law of God will have its way.[5]

The special attention devoted to the evil of "land thievery" was entirely in line with the serious warnings that Scripture, in both Old and New Testaments, gives us about every form of exploitation and quest for power. The wealthy power brokers heard this covenantal warning: "Woe to those who join house to house, who add field to field, till there is no place where they may dwell alone in the midst of the land!" (Isa. 5:8). The rich man's mansion was built with his neighbor's money, since he made his neighbor work for a pittance (Jer. 22:13–17). Deceptive practices designed to make the ephah larger and the shekel smaller and to peddle the chaff as wheat led to the destruction of the powerless and to selling the poor for a pair of shoes (Amos 8:4–6). Aided by unrighteous gain, princes feathered their own nests at the expense of other nations. The stones in the walls cry out for vengeance and the beams of the woodwork answer that cry (Hab. 2:9–12).

Jesus spoke words just as sharp against the leaders of the people who acted pious while they devoured the houses of widows (Matt. 23:14). James too had no good word to say about despising the poor (James 2:7). The wages withheld from workers cried out and the cry had reached the ears of the Lord of Sabaoth (James 5:4).

All these forms of exploitation and oppression conflict with the attitude we must have toward the poor and the weak (the foreigner, the widow, and the orphan). They were supposed to share in eating the harvest of the field (Ex. 23:11; Lev. 19:10; 23:22). One may not close his hand toward the poor, but must open it wide to lend money sufficient for his needs (Deut. 15:8, 11). The poor would never disappear (Deut. 15:11; John 12:8); but in a land blessed by Yahweh, where all His commandments are carefully observed, there *did not need to be nor should there have been* any poor (Deut. 15:4–5).

Weights, Measures, Merchandise, and Money

Stealing can happen in a number of ways. The Heidelberg Catechism (QA 110) summarizes several of them. We can rob our neighbor of his possessions "by force or with show of right, as unjust weights, ells, measures and wares, false coins, usury, or any other means forbidden by God." The answer concludes with two other forms of stealing: covetousness and all abuse and waste of God's gifts.

Every explanation of the eighth commandment in the Protestant confessions, catechism expositions, and other treatments offers a catalog similar to what we find in the Heidelberg Catechism.

In addition to what we have written in the preceding section, we should make a few observations about this catalog. First, it speaks of stealing *by using force*. This involves brutal *robbery* in contrast to secret *theft*. "Stolen water is sweet; food eaten in secret is delicious!" (Prov. 9:17 NIV). A person can be *caught* stealing (Deut. 24:7).*

The secrecy by which stealing is covered up often has the appearance of righteousness, by cheating others with false weights, measures, merchandizing, and money (Lev. 19:35–36; Deut. 25:13–16; Prov. 11:1, and other places). Merchants use a heavier weight and longer or larger measure when buying products, but resort to a lighter scale and shorter or smaller measure when it comes time to sell products. If wares needed to be traded, it was profitable to mix water with the wine, flour with the sugar, and chaff with the grain. The one minting false coins saw to it that the metal used was lighter in weight or less pure in quality than people had a right to expect.

---

* Consider this sample taken from the many similar definitions of stealing: Stealing is "to take feloniously, stealthily and deceitfully another's personal property, contrary to the owner's wishes" (Latin: "furtum est iniusta ablatio occulta et fraudulenta rei alienae mobilis invito domino"), Ph. à Limborch, *Theologia christiana*, 4th ed. (Amsterdam, 1715), 517, along with a detailed discussion of each part of this definition.

The examples we find in the Bible and in subsequent literature bear the stamp of an earlier time. Nowadays it is not so easy to defraud with false weights and measures (inspections and laws prevent that), while the modern counterfeiter tries to pass off his paper currency rather than false coins as the real thing. Nevertheless, in spite of all the changes that have occurred, we still face the temptation, in our buying and selling, to act as though our product or possession is better or worse than it really is. The biblical proverb is still relevant: " 'It is good for nothing,' cries the buyer [when he is haggling to get the price down—J.D.]; but when he has gone his way, then he boasts" (Prov. 20:14).

Earlier commentators continually warned against *usury*. Behind this warning lies an entire history that we have treated briefly elsewhere.[6] Initially the church objected without hesitation to loaning money *at interest*. Regulations found in the Mosaic legislation prohibited that. Indeed, Exodus 22:25 and Leviticus 25:35–38 forbid lending at interest to a poor fellow Israelite. More general is the regulation of Deuteronomy 23:19–20: "You shall not charge interest to your brother—interest on money or food or anything that is lent out at interest. To a foreigner you may charge interest, but to your brother you shall not charge interest, that the LORD your God may bless you in all to which you set your hand in the land which you are entering to possess." One could take security from another Israelite, but that too was tied to certain restrictions: If the neighbor's cloak was taken as security for a loan, it was to be returned by sundown, "for that is his only covering, it is his garment for his skin. What will he sleep in?" (Ex. 22:27). Neither the stones for manually grinding grain nor the top millstone were to be taken as pledge, for that would be to take another's living as security (Deut. 24:6).

Especially through Calvin's efforts, the objections to earning interest disappeared. He showed that it was incorrect to identify every form of interest with usury. Usury should be seen and condemned as *exorbitant* profit-taking. But one may responsibly receive interest on money loaned for the purchase of goods which themselves can yield a profit. The prohibition in Israel against taking interest was understandable because it envisioned loaning money to a *poor* brother. In that situation, money was supposed to be loaned without interest. The poor brother was to be given assistance at no cost to him, but someone using borrowed money to buy a field or a house or other property was not a brother in need.

Whether what Calvin and others have written about the Old Testament prohibition against interest is wholly satisfying remains doubtful. This prohibition involved more than simply loaning money to a *needy* fellow Israelite. We should also probably factor into our interpretation Israel's unique status. Israel was a theocracy in which every poor citizen who feared Yahweh would be cared for. Demanding interest upon money loaned, within an economy of a people who were promised everything from the hand of Yahweh, was simply unnecessary.

Reformed Christians continued discussing the interest question, so that various confessions speak of interest in the form of "ravenous usury."* After rejecting usury, the Heidelberg Catechism condemns—but in very general terms—all other means used to obtain another's possessions. The commentaries we consulted referred to such things as forming monopolies so prices could be fixed and raised. Other practices mentioned were borrowing and squandering large sums of money while planning to declare bankruptcy, and nonpayment of taxes or not returning borrowed possessions.

These practices, whereby people appropriate money or property from others (including the government), are just as prevalent today as then. The matter of taxation affects virtually everybody in our society.

The Heidelberg Catechism concludes with a reference to two other forms of stealing that often are not identified as such: the first is greed, and the second is the abuse and waste of our possessions. Apparently we are transgressing the eighth commandment also when we manage or employ our money and possessions that we rightfully own (and thus have not stolen) in a wrong way.

For the *greedy* person, the tightwad, and the miser, money has become the goal rather than a means. Saving is a good practice, but it must be a means toward a good end. We can lay something aside and save it for a collection, as Paul recommended to the Corinthians (1 Cor. 16:1–2). We can save a reserve for the time when our children are older, for a rainy day, or for old age. But laying up treasures on earth, so that money becomes the god Mammon (Matt. 6:19–24), is a form of stealing.

Not without good reason, Abraham Kuyper once made a comparison, in terms of the religion of Mammon, between the miser, who would be the mystic, and the *squanderer*, who would be the pietist in this religion. Just as a pietist likes to walk around showing off his faith, so the squanderer likes to brag that Mammon chose him to be his servant, his choir boy, or priest. He loves to parade before others in the full splendor of his priestly

---

* People used the phrase "voracious usury" (Latin: usura vorax) because the Hebrew word for usury, *nesek*, was at that time thought to be derived from *nasak*, to bite.

status, richly clad and adorned. He donates lavishly; counting and keeping track of his assets are beneath his dignity.[7] The prospect that God will someday require of him an accounting never occurs to him.

This brings us to a very important point: Why is it actually stealing if we use our own possessions—assuming we have obtained them honestly—in a miserly or wasteful manner? Does that kind of behavior rob another person? Even though the Heidelberg Catechism does not mention the term, we need to pause to discuss the truth that man is a steward before God. Only when we take our stewardship seriously will we see the eighth commandment in its fullness.

Being a Steward

We need to search for the roots of the eighth commandment. As we have already observed when we discussed kidnapping, this commandment is designed to protect us from every new form of slavery. Having been led out of Egypt, we must not enter into servitude again. For that reason, we may not steal other people or exploit poor people by making them dependent upon us so that their freedom is lost. For the same reason, too, we are not to sell ourselves into slavery to Mammon.

But there is something still more basic involved here. When speaking about the property and possessions owned by people, we must always remember this is true only in a relative sense. Nobody is an owner in an absolute sense, with absolute sovereignty. Only God Himself is. That fact always sheds a particular light on stealing.

God the Lord is the owner of everything. He created heaven and earth (Gen. 1:1–31). The earth and its fullness belong to Yahweh (Ex. 19:5; Pss. 24:1; 50:10). Man rules over the works of God's hands (Ps. 8:6). Everything we have has been *given* to us. The heavens are Yahweh's; the earth he has given to the children of men (Ps. 115:16). Wealthy Job confesses that the Lord gave him everything and took it all away (Job 1:21). The Lord makes people poor and He makes them rich (1 Sam. 2:7).

When the Israelites went to dwell in Canaan, they took the land as their possession for a perpetual inheritance (Ex. 32:13; Lev. 20:24; Deut. 1:8). But they were always to remember that they were living in Yahweh's land (Hos. 9:3) and that *they* were "pilgrims and sojourners" with Yahweh (Lev. 25:23). It could not be stated more sharply!

The expression describing Israel as a "mere" pilgrim and sojourner appears in a Bible passage that is very important for our discussion. Leviticus 25 contains prescriptions for the *sabbath year* and *the Year of Jubilee*. There is a very important regulation among these precepts, which we have already mentioned: Slaves were to be released in the sabbath year. One Israelite was not permitted to rule over another Israelite like a piece of property over which he had absolute control. But the same was true of the *land*, which could pass into another's possession only temporarily. If an Israelite became impoverished, it could happen that he might have to surrender his land to his creditor. In reality, however, he was selling not his land, but the harvests his land produced, until the Year of Jubilee (Lev. 25:16). The land itself remained the inalienable possession of the original owner and had to be returned to him in the Year of Jubilee (Lev. 25:11).

Amassing huge tracts of land—a form of property ownership that has brought about much grief and little good in this world—would never have been possible in Israel if the people had observed the law of Yahweh. One could rule over the inheritance assigned to one's own tribe and family in that tribe, while one's own land could fall into other hands only temporarily. Moreover, Israel was familiar with the right of redemption, whereby the next of kin could step in to help an impoverished blood relative buy back what he had been forced to sell (Lev. 25:25; Ruth 3:12–13; 4:1–12).

From the attitude of Naboth toward King Ahab, we learn how weighty the possession of one's ancestral inheritance was in Israel. When Ahab wanted to buy Naboth's vineyard, which bordered the royal estate, in exchange for another vineyard or for a hefty sum, Naboth answered: "The Lord forbid that I should give the inheritance of my fathers to you!" (1 Kings 21:3). Even a king was not permitted to appropriate the land belonging to his subjects, no matter how generous a bargain he might offer to close the deal. The land was the property of Yahweh, and had been loaned for use to a particular family and to nobody else, with the result that someone could thwart even a king who wanted to annex fields and acres to his estate.

We have already mentioned that the stealing of *cattle* or *other property* was punished less severely in Israel than in surrounding nations. Someone guilty of kidnapping was to be put to death, as we saw earlier, but the punishments for other forms of stealing were more lenient. This is surely evident in comparison to the penalty for murder and adultery. If livestock had been stolen, the thief was to pay fivefold or fourfold restitution, depending on whether it was an ox or a sheep (Ex. 22:1), or he had to pay double if the stolen animal was found alive (Ex. 22:4). In other situations, the fine was quite light: the thief had to make restitution for whatever had been stolen, extorted, or entrusted to him or found by him, and add one-fifth of the value of the stolen property (Lev. 6:1).

Why were there such (relatively) lenient penalties, when crimes against property throughout human history have often been punished much more severely?* We could say that murder and adultery cannot be undone, whereas in the case of stealing, adequate restitution can usually be made to the original owner. But another argument is just as relevant: here too we must recall the relative right to property that the Israelite enjoyed even in terms of his "own" possessions.[8] Yahweh is the great owner. The Israelite did not enjoy a strict and absolute right to property. For that reason, a clear distinction was made among the penalties for violations of the sixth and seventh commandments, on the one hand, and transgressions of the eighth commandment, on the other—that is, as long as the crime involved stealing possessions, not people.

Expressing the matter juridically, we could say that, strictly speaking, in terms of his relationship to God, man does not own property, but simply has things in his possession. There is a distinction between these two concepts. *Owning property* carries with it the right to call something one's own; it then becomes a matter of legal title. But *having something in one's possession* gives that person actual control over the thing possessed, as if it belonged to him and he owned it. An owner has the right of possession, but one who has something in his possession is not thereby the owner. A legal right must be distinguished from actual control. Thus, God is the absolute owner, and He has placed the earth in the possession of man.

This becomes clearer when we view man as a *steward*. He manages the goods belonging to Another. The term *steward*, as a description of man's position in relation to God, appears nowhere in the Bible.[†] But clearly the concept is present in Scripture, in view of the material we have considered above. The time is coming when we will have to give an account of what we have done with the possessions entrusted to us, as we learn from the par-

---

* In early catechism expositions and other documents, we regularly find a warning against capital punishment for crimes against property, with reference made to the mild punishments prescribed in Israel. For example, see Curcellaeus, *Opera theologica*, 634ff.; P. van der Hagen, *De Heydelbergsche Catechismus* (Amsterdam, 1743), 460; and G. Voetius, *Catechisatie over den Heidelbergschen Catechismus*, 1066.

† In the King James Version, the Greek word *oikonomos* is often rendered by the word "steward." Modern translations and paraphrases render the word differently. (For example, in Rom. 16:23 the Greek word is rendered "treasurer" [NKJV] and "director of public works" [NIV].) The image of the steward as one who collects rent and manages the estate of an owner is prominent in the parable of the shrewd manager told in Luke 16:1–9; it also appears in 1 Peter 4:10, where Peter summons believers to serve one another according to the gifts they have received, "as good stewards of the manifold grace of God."

ables of the talents and the minas (Matt. 25:14–31; Luke 19:11–27). Just as the steward in Luke 16 had to give an account, so we too will be required to do the same on the Day of Judgment (Matt. 12:36; Rom. 14:12).

The metaphor of man as *steward* is preferable to that of man as *tenant*, though they are used interchangeably. A tenant is one who, after paying a specified rent, has the right to use the land and its produce. He works for himself. The amount of profit he can produce beyond the cost of rent is his to keep. He may do with it what he wishes. But the steward manages property on behalf of the owner's interests. For this reason, the concept of "steward" communicates more clearly that everything man has received from God to manage must be cared for and used not according to man's wishes, but according to God's will.

This comes out very nicely in the Heidelberg Catechism, when it states that we may not be covetous or wasteful. Even though these are my own things, I am not yet free to use them as I please. This catechism goes on to insist that I "further my neighbor's profit wherever I *can* or *may*" (Answer 111). I must devote my possessions, wherever I *can*, to my neighbor's well-being. But there are times when I *may not* do that. For example, I may not help my neighbor evade paying taxes. Perhaps both he and I would benefit from doing that, but we may not, and therefore as good stewards we must keep the rules God established for the proper management of His possessions. If they were my own property, then I myself could determine what "can" and "may" be done. But as a steward, I manage *my* possessions as God's property.

Private Property

In terms of our relation to God, we are not owners, but stewards. Strictly speaking, nothing belongs to us. But in our relation to other people, we do deal in terms of "mine and thine." One may legitimately claim that something belongs to him. Abraham went through a lot of trouble to buy a burial plot that would belong entirely to him (Gen. 23:3–18). Each of the tribes of Israel received its own territory (Josh. 13–21), and Naboth refused to sell his ancestral inheritance to Ahab (1 Kings 21:3–6). People like the patriarchs and like Job, David, and Solomon were blessed by God with great wealth. So possessions and wealth were distributed. One person received more than another. And all could say that it was their own possession or property.

There was private property within the New Testament church as well. Ananias had a piece of land that belonged to him before he sold it and whose sale generated income that lay at his disposal (Acts 4:4). Mary, the mother of John, Lydia the seller of purple, and Philip the evangelist owned their own homes (Acts 12:12; 16:14–15; 21:8). The church included prominent and wealthy members, along with poor members (Luke 8:3; 1 Cor. 1:26; 1 Tim. 6:17; James 2:2).

The fact that we are stewards before God does not mean that we must *together* manage the possessions entrusted to us, as if they were community property. There are certainly communal aspects to stewardship, since we must further our neighbor's profit wherever we can. But that does not make stewardship a communal activity. Each of us will one day have to give a personal account of what we have done with the talents entrusted to us (Matt. 25:14–31).

What we are told in Acts 2:44–45 and Acts 4:32–37, concerning the Jerusalem church in which nobody said "that any of the things he possessed was his own, but they had all things in common," does not alter this conclusion. For these verses describe the *style* in which the church members managed their possessions. With great unselfishness they made their perishable and durable goods available for the benefit of the entire church.

But there is no indication that a *judicial structure* was created that would have made it impossible to speak of private property any longer and that would have introduced a kind of communism. Not the church, but the people themselves sold their possessions. In this way, the *management* of possessions remained an individual matter, whereas the *use* of possessions bore all the traces of commonality. We mentioned earlier that Ananias could have retained possession of his land as his own property if he had not sold it. His sin, and that of his wife, was hypocrisy (acting as if they were donating the entire proceeds to the church, and not the relatively smaller contribution they were giving to the church).

In the Jerusalem church, stewardship was being practiced in an excellent way. Each managed his or her property individually; but this management kept in view the benefit of the neighbor in such a way that togetherness and the well-being of the group governed their attitudes. Their use of, and attitude toward, possessions were "freed from their neutral autonomy and self-centeredness, and directed toward the loving service of God and the neighbor." What should impress us is "not the usurping or abolishing of the right of private property, but *restoring* that right by *reinstating* it in the service of love."[9]

Rarely is it necessary to imitate what happened in Jerusalem. Equally true is that what occurred in Jerusalem is hardly ever imitated when it is necessary. The contrast between rich and poor has worked destructively within the church. We have observed the difficulties in Corinth (1 Cor. 11:20–34) and other churches (James 1:9; 2:2–16; 5:1–6), where lack of love distorted people's attitudes toward possessions. Spiritual life became impoverished, with the result that people sought their own interests instead of the interests of others (Phil. 2:4). Paul viewed generosity as part of imitating Christ, who "though He was rich, yet for your sakes He became poor, that you through His poverty might become rich" (2 Cor. 8:9).

To say that owning private property is good is not to say that communal or collective property is evil. The eighth commandment says nothing about the distribution of land and goods.* Appealing to this commandment in defense of either capitalism or socialism is senseless. Every existing social and economic system recognizes in practice some form of distinguishing between "mine and thine." Total collective management of all property is an ideal on paper that never existed in reality.

Reality is always complicated. "Pure" capitalism is just as bad as "pure" communism. The intermediate form found in the tightly controlled free-market economies in North America and western Europe is perhaps the least harmful system. But even in that system one observes much injustice and precious little resembling Christian stewardship.

How property is obtained does not require much discussion. There are various routes that have led or can lead to legitimate property ownership. The straightforward acquisition of land and property that does not yet belong to anybody—referred to with the Latin term *occupatio*—is rarely possible anymore today. Acquiring property by means of *labor* is quite common. Other ways include receiving property through *inheritance* and *bequest*. In older commentaries, these latter methods of acquiring property were discussed somewhat (too) extensively.†

Private property need not be condemned, as long as it is managed within the parameters of Christian stewardship. Nor is it proper to consider *poverty*

---

* A. Kuyper, among others, warned: "Let's be extremely careful, especially nowadays, with our inferences from God's Word." It is not true that a society "as envisioned by most social democrats would necessarily conflict with the eighth commandment" (*E Voto Dordraceno*, 4:188).

† We can well imagine that *occupatio* played the largest role in acquiring property in a still undeveloped world. Currently this factor has been reduced to a minimum, and *work* is virtually the exclusive means for acquiring property. For a discussion of *theories* about acquiring property, see J. Douma, *Vrede in de maatschappij*, 2d ed. (Kampen, 1986), 113–18. Other subjects not treated in depth or omitted entirely from our discussion of the eighth commandment have been explored in *Vrede in de maatschappij*, such as labor and the division of labor, income, social relationships, and our global task.

to be better than wealth. Agur's proverb applies here: "Give me neither poverty nor riches—feed me with the food You prescribe for me" (Prov. 30:8). Bed and board should suffice for us (1 Tim. 6:8). For both poverty and riches have their dark side. The rich man easily asks, "Who is the LORD?" And one who is impoverished takes up stealing and profanes the name of his God (Prov. 30:9). Wealth can be a divine blessing (Prov. 10:4, 22), and we may enjoy riches (1 Tim. 6:17); but one who *desires* to be rich and *longs* for wealth falls prey to many foolish and harmful lusts (1 Tim. 6:9).

Nor is it correct to insist that we must become "inwardly detached" from our possessions. The eighth commandment simply assumes that we and others have possessions. Otherwise there would be no talk of stealing. We can go one step further: Viewed "anthropologically," people and possessions go together. Being human and having possessions are not in tension with one another, because as lord in this world, the human race attains its development and progress with these possessions.

The observation is correct that in the Bible, the owner either increases or decreases together with his possessions.[10] He is what he has. Property is an extension of man and not "simply" something he must be able to lay aside easily. A man's property constitutes his environment, his adornment, and his name, all of which are very valuable to him. Thus we really need not be embarrassed to be happy with things we have, for that is quite human.

Therefore, we need not become "inwardly detached" from our possessions. We infer this from Jesus' words to His disciples: "Assuredly, I say to you, there is no one who has left house or brothers or sisters or father or mother or wife or children or lands, for My sake and the gospel's, who shall not receive a hundredfold now in this time—houses and brothers and sisters and mothers and children and lands, with persecutions—and in the age to come, eternal life" (Mark 10:29–30). Apparently the desire for family and for durable property is quite human and quite acceptable. We need not detach ourselves from them. We harm people psychologically when we demand this of them.[11]

But we must indeed *be ready* to lose our property for the sake of Christ's kingdom. The error of the rich young man was that he refused to do this en route to following Jesus, unlike the other disciples (Matt. 19:16–29). The present dispensation is going to disappear, and in the time remaining, it may be necessary to forsake things, so that the married live as if they had no spouse and buyers live as though they did not possess what they bought (1 Cor. 7:29–31). We must be ready to forsake everything *external*, which requires being prepared *internally*.[12]

Equally true is the warning against being *preoccupied* with storing up treasures on earth, where moth and rust consume and where thieves break in and steal (Matt. 6:19–20). Wealth is always relative. We have brought nothing into the world, and we can take nothing out, either (1 Tim. 6:7).

Work

In connection with the eighth commandment, we should also pay some attention to our mandate to work. That is obvious in view of the clear connection that the Bible makes between laziness and stealing. The sluggard comes to poverty (Prov. 6:6–11), and poverty tempts a person to steal (Prov. 30:9). The one who used to steal must steal no more, says Paul, but must exert himself to perform work with his hands, so that he will have something to share with the needy (Eph. 4:28). One who minds his own business and works with his hands conducts himself appropriately toward those who are outsiders (1 Thess. 4:11–12). The general rule is that one who refuses to work shall not eat (2 Thess. 3:10). Laziness leads to the servitude of forced labor (Prov. 12:24), precisely the opposite of being freed from the slavery of Egypt.

On the one hand, the Bible views work as a harsh necessity, even as in fact it remains for the larger part of the world's population to this day. Trouble and sorrow attend our work (Gen. 3:17–19; Ps. 90:10). But, on the other hand, work is also a divine mandate attended by God's blessing.[13] Already in Paradise man received the mandate to work (Gen. 2:15). So work is not the sad consequence of man's fall into sin. By his labor, man would rule over the world (Gen. 1:28). The sluggard falls into slavery, but the hand of the diligent will rule (Prov. 12:24). Blessing upon work means that man can be genuinely joyful (Deut. 16:15).

The calling to work comes to everyone who can work. In our labor we develop the gifts we have received from God and must now employ as good stewards. For that reason, wealthy people are appropriately taught that they too have a duty to work, even though it is unnecessary for their sustenance. After all, as good stewards we work not first for ourselves, but for God. Nobody may bury his talent in the ground (Matt. 25:24–30), but instead must render it profitable for the master who provided it to him.

To this we should add something else. Work also has a *social* function. People must exercise dominion over the earth through collaboration. Within Israelite families, each member was expected to contribute something. A son who was a profligate and a drunkard could be brought before the court by his father (Deut. 21:18–21).

In the Bible we occasionally read about employers who worked together alongside their male and female employees in a way that might
serve to illustrate for us today the meaning of collaboration in the labor
arena. Abraham entrusted his servant with the important job of seeking a
wife for his son Isaac (Gen. 24:2–9). Boaz was on friendly terms with his
employees (Ruth 2:4). Perhaps the pauper, the widow, and the foreigner
stood outside the labor arena, but they certainly shared in enjoying the
produce of the field, as we saw earlier.

The Hebrew word for "work" actually means "to serve." This suggests,
on the one hand, the difficulty involved in work. It does *not* mean that we
are slaves to our work. For God's blessing does not depend on the toil of
our labor (Deut. 8:3; Ps. 127:1–4). Therefore, "work as service" means, on
the other hand, service to the Lord and service to our neighbor.

Our stewardship for the benefit of our neighbor also comes to expression when we help him through our labor. To say it with the Heidelberg
Catechism (Answer 111), God commands me to labor faithfully that I
may be able to relieve the needy. This observation brings us to our next
subject.

Stewardship and Generosity

Not everyone is equally happy with using the term *stewardship* to describe
the management of our property. Dutch theologian P. J. Roscam Abbing
prefers the phrase *church warden* instead of *steward*, since his phrase nicely
accents not only the relationship to God, but also to the church. Church
members, according to Roscam Abbing, should be lay church wardens.

We find this suggestion of Roscam Abbing to be no improvement.
Highlighting the relation between our use of money and the church is
valuable, but life is too diverse for capturing our *entire* pattern of spending
with such an ecclesiastical organizational phrase as "church warden."
Nevertheless, it is important that we reflect on the generosity we should
be showing as members of Christ's church.

In this connection, we should recall the concept of *sacrilegium* (sacrilege) mentioned in older treatments of the eighth commandment alongside stealing people (kidnapping) and land. The Latin noun was often
translated as "church robbery" or "church thievery." This covered various
forms of sacrilege. Writers mentioned Achan, who stole from the "devoted things" (things consecrated to God) after the fall of Jericho (Josh.
7:1, 11). They went on to mention the duty of Israel to pay the tithe and
the freewill offering, gifts Israel nevertheless often withheld from Yahweh:

"You are cursed with a curse, for you have robbed Me, even this whole nation. Bring all the tithes into the storehouse, that there may be food in My house" (Mal. 3:9–10). Judas Iscariot, as manager of the benevolence fund, was guilty of "church robbery" because he stole that money (John 12:6). Paul accused the Jews of a similar sin: "You who abhor idols, do you rob temples?" (Rom. 2:22). Scripture references in these older expositions often mentioned Simon the magician (Simon Magus), who offered to pay money to purchase the ability to dispense the Holy Spirit through laying his hands on someone (Acts 8:18–23). From this narrative, the term *simony* was later derived, referring to the practice of buying and selling spiritual benefits and offices.

The sin of "church robbery" has always been severely condemned. Money and possessions intended for God or the poor of the church may not be stolen. Therefore, it should never happen that churches become wealthy while the poor remain poor. This kind of imbalance can be observed repeatedly throughout church history. What we see in the nations around Israel, namely, that the priestly class must often have been wealthy (see Gen. 47:22, 26), contrasted remarkably with what God commanded regarding provision for the priest and the Levite. But both Israel and the New Testament church frequently fell off the path. When church buildings were golden, charity became wooden. Bitter battles have been fought over the enormous estates that the church once possessed (and occasionally still possess). The portrait of the Vatican has throughout the centuries looked remarkably different from that of Peter and his friends, who were instructed not to take with them gold, silver, or copper (Matt. 10:9).

People can be guilty of "church robbery" in other ways. The Erlauthaler Confession of 1562 numbered among thieves those preachers who fail to preach rightly and piously. They walk off with a salary they really do not deserve![14] Further along we read that selling or buying ministerial charges renders one guilty of something we saw earlier, called "simony."

It is clear what may *not* be done. More difficult is specifying what should be done today. Do the requirements of generosity still obligate us to give a *tithe*?

In the commentaries we consulted, not much is written about this question, while giving the tithe appears regularly in the Bible. The practice was already an ancient one, as we see from the history of Abraham (in his encounter with Melchizedek) and Jacob (Gen. 14:20; 28:22). The Mosaic legislation prescribed that a tenth of the harvest of the produce of the land, of the trees and of the flocks, be given to Yahweh (Lev. 27:30–33). Unlike the other tribes, the tribe of Levi was not assigned any land in Israel, but instead received every tithe as an inheritance, as payment for the service Levites performed before Yahweh (Num. 18:21). They in turn paid Yahweh a tithe of these tithes (Num. 18:28). The foreigner, orphan, and widow were supposed to share in receiving the tithe, "so that they may eat within your gates and be filled" (Deut. 26:12–13). The New Testament indicates that the practice of tithing was often followed very strictly in Jesus' day (Matt. 23:23; Luke 18:12).

Some churches require tithing today. Is that proper? We should remember that in Israel the tithe was virtually the only form of taxation each Israelite was obligated to pay. The ecclesiastical and political spheres were not as distinct as they are among us today. Often we have to pay high taxes to the state and, in addition, we are called to exercise generosity in the realm of the church. The New Testament church is nowhere bound by the word of Jesus or His apostles to giving a particular percent.

From the Bible's description of care for priests and Levites, as well as for the poor, we can indeed learn that we have an obligation to support the church and her poor. Our annual fixed voluntary contributions to the church remind us of the institution of the tithe. The requirement that the Levite in turn give away a tithe of Israel's tithe is a good example for preachers as well. They live from the gifts of church members; but they themselves are also church members. Why should a contribution not be expected from them, too?

It should be an honor for the church herself to underwrite the costs of maintaining her worship, rather than becoming dependent on government assistance. The same goes for theological training, which is tied so closely to the well-being of Christ's church that the financial costs of such training should be borne by church members.

The church of Christ has more than a task within. She must care for the maintenance of worship and help her own poor who receive no help from others out of their financial and spiritual distress. But this *diaconal* task extends beyond the brotherhood. Paul instructs us to do good to *all*, even if we focus especially on fellow believers (Gal. 6:10). The fact that in the early centuries, the Christian church did so much for others who were not members, led many in that time to reflect about the nature of genuine love. The Roman emperor Julian, a renowned persecutor of Christians, had to acknowledge that Christians fed not only their own poor, but "ours" as well.[15]

Today as well, we have not finished our task by supporting our own church and the organizations connected with the church. A task of immense proportions awaits us in a world where millions of people still live

below the subsistence level. We will always have the poor among us, Jesus
said (John 12:8), but currently we have them farther away from us than in
the past. Seen in its larger context, we have a tremendous responsibility
in our relationship to the Third World, one that surely falls within the
realm of our stewardship. This stewardship has acquired a global dimension.

Enjoying Without an Aftertaste

Let us assume for a moment that we are generous with our charity. Can we
ever be too generous? Can we really do anything else but give all our goods
away, since there are still so many people living in appalling poverty? Is it
still possible to enjoy a glass of fine wine or a vacation or a festive celebration, as long as others dwell in the deepest of misery?

Even if we could make it a rule that we all would give away ten percent
of our disposable income, we would still be able to ease only a tiny bit of
global suffering. Can we enjoy with an honest and quiet conscience what
we have left over after deducting our donations for various worthwhile
causes? Should we not use the remaining funds to ensure that another two
or three people on the other side of the world can stay alive? May we enjoy
our earnings without the sour aftertaste that the money we used for our vacation could have been spent to keep others alive?

These kinds of questions should engage us first of all on a personal level.
It is not a mere coincidence that we see pictures of raw misery on television. They should stimulate us to give just a little bit more than we have
been giving. They also give us pause to reflect about our budgets and our
plans to acquire new things. It is difficult to imagine that we could sit
watching television reports of wretched poverty without examining our
own lifestyles.

But that is not all there is to it. We may also enjoy the wealth God gives
us. Even without a bitter aftertaste.

This is permissible on the basis of *biblical* principles. When God blesses
people with wealth, they ought to be generous toward others. Nor should
they be miserly toward themselves and their own families. For the Israelites
were commanded to feast "before the LORD your God," along with their
families, their servants, and the Levites, from the tithes of grain, new wine,
oil, and the firstborn of their herds that they brought to the temple (Deut.
12:6–7, 17–19; 14:22–23). Job never refused the poor anything they
needed, and he never ate his bread by himself (Job 31:16–17), but he did
not take offense when his children enjoyed feasts of celebration (Job 1).

Jesus was acquainted with the misery of the poor and the widows of His day, but He also attended a wedding feast (John 2) and ate meals at the homes of wealthy people (Luke 7:36–50; 11:37; 14:1, 12). When some became indignant about pouring a flask of costly perfume on Jesus' head, feeling that the money spent for the perfume could just as well have been given to the poor, Jesus took the side of the "wasteful" woman, saying: "You have the poor with you always, and whenever you wish you may do them good; but Me you do not have always" (Mark 14:7).

This saying of Jesus also means that there are more things we may be concerned about in this world besides hunger and misery. There is a time to be shocked by the hollow eyes and distended stomachs of crippled children. There is a time to humble ourselves and do something about our selfishly imbalanced budgets. And there is also a time to go on vacation and to enjoy without an aftertaste. During that time, we are not to think about all the misery in this world, but to rejoice in our prosperity.

In the latter situation we are good stewards when our enjoyment (just as our shock and humbling) occurs before the face of God.

Here too we should mention an *economic* argument that can prevent us from being too embarrassed to enjoy our prosperity. Suppose for a moment that all of us quit taking vacations, quit buying books and compact discs, and gave all our money to poor people in the Third World, except the money required for our own basic necessities of life. We would then throw hundreds of thousands of people in our own country out of work, we would disrupt our own economy, and with all our good intentions, we would simply be helping people in the Third World to jump from the frying pan into the fire.

We are fully aware that these observations are not exhaustive, since for the sake of improved relations between rich and poor in this world, we should be able (and will have to be able) to give up part of our prosperity. But even then, a *portion* of our prosperity must still be left for us to enjoy. For the poor do not become richer when the rich become poor. When prosperity can be found nowhere, poverty will be found everywhere. For that reason too, we should not restrict our concern to the needy in faraway places, but extend it also to the television salesman, the bookseller, the resort owner, and the hotel manager in our own neighborhoods.

Forced to Steal?

Can circumstances arise in which we simply must steal? In the Bible several situations arise that we should consider in connection with the eighth commandment. When Israel left Egypt, the Israelite women took articles of silver and gold and clothing from their Egyptian mistresses (Ex. 3:22; 12:35–36). This "thievery" did bear a special character. We read that the Israelite women *asked* their Egyptian mistresses for these things, and that Yahweh ensured that the Egyptian women were inclined to grant this request. So this was not stealing by force, but rather acquiring things Yahweh wanted to give the Israelite women.

We see here that as absolute owner of everything, the Lord can ensure that Egyptian treasures were put at the disposal of His own people. Possibly this was also a kind of compensation for all the persecution the people of Israel had to endure in Egypt.

We find another situation in Proverbs 6:30: "People do not despise a thief if he steals to satisfy himself when he is starving." Hunger can drive people to steal in order to stay alive. Nevertheless, this verse is followed immediately by the warning that if he is caught, he must restore sevenfold; he may have to give up all the wealth of his house (Prov. 6:31). That is surely a relatively severe penalty, more severe than the Mosaic legislation prescribed. Sympathy for the plight of such a thief does not alter his culpability. Perhaps this proverb is talking about a hungry man whose own laziness is responsible for his desperate situation (see Prov. 6:6–15).

Within Christian ethics, an exception has been made for the starving person who in a case of extreme necessity steals food. Where life itself is at stake, then the scales of justice were tipped in favor of the communal use of vital necessities. The Latin proverb, "In extrema necessitate omnia fiunt communia," means something like this: "In cases of extreme necessity, everything is public property."*

These situations of extreme necessity do occur. During World War II, when food and fuel were extremely scarce, Cardinal Frings van Keulen declared that stealing *in periculo mortis* (in a life-threatening situation) was not a sin.† The danger is real that in such situations people may interpret

---

* See W. Geesink, *Van 's Heeren ordinantiën* (Kampen, 1925), 4:334–35, who approves of stealing "in cases of extreme necessity," but then warns against going any further. Pope Innocent XI did go further when he declared that stealing was permissible not only in cases of *extreme* necessity, but also in cases of *serious* necessity ("Permissum est furari non solum in extrema necessitate, sed etiam in gravi").

† Helmut Thielicke tells of this in his *Theological Ethics* (found in the German original, but not the English translation). In those circumstances, too, abuse occurred, for people soon imported the cardinal's name into their vernacular description of such stealing: "Come, Hans, let's go 'fringsing' "!

"life-threatening" very broadly. But such abuse cannot contradict the reality of circumstances that require people to choose between stealing or starving.

Aside from those exceptional situations, are there legitimate reasons to approve stealing? People exploited by others understandably suppose they can steal to recover what was withheld from them. They stole from me; why then may I not steal from them?

When oppressed people escape those exploiting them, God's wrath against those exploiters becomes evident. But that gives no one the right to avenge himself by giving the thief some of his own medicine.[16]

We should remember this also when we think the taxes imposed by the government are too high. It is rather inflammatory in this situation to start prating about "legalized theft" by the government. Even if the state were to impose an illegitimate tax burden strongly resembling theft, our calling continues to be to pay what we owe (Rom. 13:6–7).

Protesting unfair and impractical laws must follow the channels established for that. Sometimes during busy seasons, employers simply cannot get workers unless they pay them in cash (which is then not reported as income). Employers who occasionally operate on a cash basis are not necessarily seeking to enrich themselves, but they face a critical choice— during the harvest season, for example: either plow the crop under or pay (unreported) cash to seasonal workers. However, the Christian joins the struggle against the illegal underground economy in earnest precisely at the point where he himself is willing to sacrifice, not whining too quickly that he is about to go under. Businessmen must believe that "the blessing of the LORD makes one rich, and toil adds nothing to it" (Prov. 10:22, following RSV margin).

Proverbs like "Everybody is a thief in his own trade" or "Business is business" perhaps portray reality accurately, but they surely do not describe a Christian lifestyle.[*]

Within the church, the question becomes seriously real: Can a Christian be a businessman? Around the year 400, a minister with whom we are unacquainted preached a sermon about the temple cleansing (Matt. 21:25), in which he said: A man who is a merchant can hardly, almost never, please God. Therefore a Christian should not be a merchant, and if he still wants

---

[*] This is how Voetius evaluates the first aphorism: "Understood in terms of people's conduct or their wicked customs, true enough; but understood in terms of what is legitimate, this is false" (*Catechisatie over den Heidelbergschen Catechismus*, 1056).

to do that, then let him be driven out of God's church, as Jesus once drove the buyers and sellers out of the temple. A businessman, according to this preacher, cannot do business without lying and dishonesty.[17]

To evaluate fairly this sermon dating from around 400, we should not understand the term *merchant* to refer to the modern retail businessman, but to the haggler and huckster described in Proverbs 20:14, whom we met earlier. Moreover, around 400 the route connecting production and consumption was usually short. The farmer and the craftsman were the important people, not the merchant. But as civilization flowered, the more developed society became, the more indispensable the merchant became, for it was his class of workers that moved products from East to West and vice versa.

During the period of Dutch colonial supremacy, G. Udemans, preacher at Zierikzee, wrote an entire book about merchandising, entitled *'t Geestelyck Roer van 't Coopmans Schip* ("The Spiritual Rudder of the Merchant's Ship").[18] In this book he explained that alongside dishonest trade, there was also honest trade. In addition to the verse about the temple cleansing, the Bible contains Proverbs 11:26 as well: "The people will curse him who withholds grain, but blessing will be on the head of him who sells it." There were business merchants in biblical times, and they obtained their wares from faraway places, such as cypress wood from the coast of Cyprus (Ezek. 27:6) and gold from the land of Ophir (1 Kings 9:28). An entire fleet returned with gold, silver, ivory, apes, and monkeys for Solomon, who had already been blessed by God with surpassing wealth (1 Kings 10:22).

The abilities required to become a businessman come from God just as much as those required to become a carpenter, an artist, a journalist, and a scientist. Enterprise is part of his work. Trading is in his blood, and he wants to make a profit, of course. This profit motive is not the same as greed.[19] Just as a narrow-minded moralism brands the adventuresome spirit of a mountain climber as recklessness, the same thing happens to the entrepreneurial spirit of the merchant. The mountain climber might fall down the side of the mountain, and the entrepreneur might suffer heavy financial losses, but the drive to compete and to win are still good gifts from God. There are grocers who do well to stay put at the foot of the mountain, but there are enterprising businessmen and salesmen who desire and are able to explore higher altitudes.

The businessman is no less or more a sinner than other people. Certainly people differ in the sins they commit. One person may be in greater danger than another of cheating on his income tax form. The entrepreneur will be harder pressed in various areas to remain honest and to keep his integrity than a teacher or professor with his fixed salary.

However, evil does not lie in our occupations, but dwells in our hearts. Augustine said this about businessmen already in his day. He reports a Christian businessman saying: If I sin, then the sin is mine and not a sin of my *trade*. Anyone expecting me not to lie and not to make false promises must show me just one occupation in which that does *not* happen.[20]

Being a businessman is an honest calling, as long as the merchant ship has a "spiritual" rudder, as Udemans put it. Respect for the eighth commandment steers us as we do business. God gave us this commandment not only for easy situations, but also for those difficult circumstances in which it sometimes looks as though we cannot go through life being honest.

Endnotes

1. G. Voetius, *Catechisatie over den Heidelbergschen Catechismus*, ed. A. Kuyper (Rotterdam, 1891), 2:1052–53.

2. Joh. van der Kemp, *De Christen geheel en al het eigendom van Christus in leven en sterven*, 10th ed. (Amsterdam, 1737), 802–3.

3. For this section, we have relied on F. H. von Meyenfeldt, *Tien tegen een* (Goes, 1980), 4:70ff.

4. H. Bullinger, *Huijs-boeck* (Amsterdam, 1607), 78.

5. For Luther, see *Dr. Martin Luther's Large Catechism* (Minneapolis, 1935), 90; for Calvin, see *Sermons on Deuteronomy* (Edinburgh, 1987), 230 (with punctuation and English modernized).

6. See J. Douma, *Vrede in de maatschappij*, 2d ed. (Kampen, 1986), 135–40.

7. A. Kuyper, *E voto Dordraceno*, 3d ed. (Kampen, 1892–95), 4:223–24.

8. J. L. Koole, *De Tien Geboden*, 2d ed. (Kampen, 1983), 124.

9. A. Troost, "Het Achtste Gebod," in *De thora in de thora*, 2d ed. (Franeker, n.d.), 2:116.

10. See W. A. van Es, *De eigendom in den Pentateuch* (Kampen, 1909), 22–23, and F. H. von Meyenfeldt, *Tien tegen een*, 4:83ff.

11. See also A. Troost, "Het Achtste Gebod," 101–2.

12. Ibid., 102.

13. For this section we are making grateful use of J. L. Koole, *De Tien Geboden*, 120ff.

14. Quoted by J. Koopmans, *De Tien Geboden* (Nijkerk, 1946), 58.

15. Quoted by Martin Hengel, *Property and Riches in the Early Church* (Philadelphia, 1974), 45.

16. For a discussion of the "right of revolution" in extreme circumstances, we refer the reader to our earlier treatment of this question under the fifth commandment, and to J. Douma, *Politieke verantwoordelijkheid*, 2d ed. (Kampen, 1987), 193–203.

17. This sermon is found in J. Wiarda, *Mercatura honesta* (Groningen, 1964).

18. Published in 1640 in Dordrecht, reprinted in 1965, again in Dordrecht.

19. See the address given on this subject by I. J. de Bussy, *De koopman uit een zedekundig oogpunt* (Amsterdam, 1905).

20. Augustine, *Corpus Scriptorum Ecclesiasticorum Latinorum* (Vienna, 1865), 954–55 (Ennarationes in Ps. 70:17).

The Ninth Commandment

You shall not be a lying witness against your neighbor. (Ex. 20:16)

You shall not be a false witness against your neighbor.
*(Deut. 5:20)**

In a Court of Law

The ninth commandment involves first of all judicial or courtroom matters. We have tried to convey that in the translation we are using. The Hebrew text speaks literally about a lying (false) *witness*, one who might appear to testify against his neighbor before a judge.

This is not to say the ninth commandment has no meaning or relevance for another kind of "testifying," one that could harm a neighbor *outside* the courtroom. The lie as such must be considered in any adequate discussion of the ninth commandment. But this commandment (just like other commandments) has a primary meaning or reference requiring our thoughtful attention at the very outset of our reflection. The ninth commandment leads us into the arena of the practice of courtroom justice in ancient Israel.

Jurisprudence was exercised by the elders of a particular locale, who formed a jury of sorts. We find an example of this in the life of Boaz, who took ten men from among the elders of Bethlehem, before whom he set forth his case at the city gates—the place where court was held (Ruth 4:1–2). In addition, we read of specially appointed professional judges (Deut. 16:18–20; 2 Chron. 19:5; Ezra 7:25), of a circuit judge like Samuel, who

---

* The difference between a "lying" and a "false" witness is small and, in our opinion, insignificant for the interpretation of this commandment.

313

traveled annually from town to town to hear court cases (1 Sam. 7:16–17), and of kings who were also judges (David, 2 Sam. 14:4–11; Solomon, 1 Kings 3:16–28).

In Bible times, courtroom justice was rather uncomplicated. There were no lawyers, fingerprints were not used as evidence, nor were there detectives like Sherlock Holmes or Hercule Poirot.

Everything could depend on what the *witnesses* said. Naboth was killed because two witnesses had accused him unanimously of blaspheming God and the king (1 Kings 21:13). Unanimity among (false) witnesses played a role also in the trial of Jesus (Matt. 26:60–61) and that of Stephen (Acts 7:13–14).

So witnesses could hold decisive sway over life and death. At the testimony of two or three (unanimous) witnesses, a defendant could be sentenced to death (Deut. 17:6; 19:15). In view of the seriousness of their role, it is no wonder that the ninth commandment warns against the lying witness. For such a witness functioned as an *accuser* against his neighbor and could even be held responsible for his death.* His words could be fatal. "A man who bears false witness against his neighbor is like a club, a sword, and a sharp arrow," we read in Proverbs 25:18.

In view of the seriousness of this matter, then, we see how the Lord seeks to safeguard the exercise of justice. The testimony of one witness is insufficient for pronouncing a death sentence, no matter how serious a crime has been committed (Deut. 17:6; 19:15). Further, the witness-accusers must throw the first stones in carrying out the sentence against the accused (Deut. 17:7). To stone someone to death with your own hands requires more courage than a few lying words!

Moreover, someone unmasked by the judges as a false witness was to receive the punishment that the accused would have received (Deut. 19:16–19). The judges too were to remain impartial by not letting themselves be bribed (Ex. 18:21). Bribes blind even wise men, easily leading to twisting the words of the innocent (Deut. 16:18–20). Fair justice must be administered, without favoritism toward class or rank: the poor may not be treated preferentially, and the rich may not be singled out for favor

---

* J. L. Koole, *De Tien Geboden*, 2d ed. (Kampen, 1983), 130, points out that the Hebrew word for "witness" can also mean "accuser" (Deut. 19:16; Jer. 29:23; Mal. 2:14). Today we are familiar with the distinction between the witness *à decharge* or defense witness (for disproving an accusation) and the witness *à charge* or prosecution witness (for supporting an accusation).

(Lev. 19:15). Even when the majority of the people want wickedness, *justice* may not be perverted (Ex. 23:1–3).

Someone has properly observed that from these regulations two principles emerge: In the administration of justice, the neighbor must be protected against the false witness, and the administration of justice itself must be safeguarded.[1] At issue is the protection both of the neighbor and of the system of justice itself.

This system of justice exists for human welfare. Yahweh prohibited murder, adultery, and stealing in the preceding commandments; but in order to achieve this, so that life, marriage, and property are truly safeguarded, good legal institutions are needed. The lying witness is a great danger, but if the entire system of justice no longer functions and the judges are corrupt, the situation is even worse. For then society itself totters on the edge of collapse (see Isa. 1:17, 23, 26; Jer. 7:5–6; Amos 5:7; Eccl. 3:16). "If the foundations are destroyed, what can the righteous do?" (Ps. 11:3).

Therefore, the ninth commandment involves a crucial issue. The phenomenon of a false witness brings into our field of vision the entire judicial system required to safeguard human honor, life, marriage, and property.

Perhaps this was more evident to the Israelite than to us. For unlike today, back in Israel the court of law was part of *everyday* life. Justice was administered at the gate of the town where a person lived. The ninth commandment was not designed for exceptional situations where an Israelite involved in a court case would have to travel to a distant city. As often as he went through the town gate, he was reminded of the justice administered there regularly.

Moreover, although the courtroom today is farther away and has become an institution most people seldom, if ever, encounter *directly*, nevertheless we can now understand clearly its significance for our society. We are acquainted with countries where justice is not administered impartially and where trials are little more than a sham. The judge passes judgment in terms of a politician's wishes, and dissidents are sentenced to confinement in psychiatric institutions. False witnesses and prejudiced judges, who must of course be faithful members of "the party," ensure that trust vanishes and people spy on each other. Freedom vanishes and fear reigns. People are no longer neighbors to each other; instead, they become wolves preying upon one another.

Therefore, in our interpretation of the ninth commandment, we must always include reference to the significance of the system of justice. Past interpreters of the ninth commandment never hesitated to mention various persons who have a role in administering justice. These interpreters would demand of a *judge* that he be incorruptible and not judge rashly. "Audi et alteram partem"—"Hear the other side too"! They required of the *accuser* that he never accuse somebody unnecessarily, out of antipathy or revenge. They expected the *witness* to tell the truth and nothing but the truth. The *lawyer* was forbidden to call black white and white black, even when he had the valuable function of coming to the aid of the accused and demanding that proof of guilt—if there was any—be airtight. These interpreters required the *accused* to confess his guilt where such guilt was proved.*[2]

The court of law is very important. Where justice reigns, peace also reigns (Ps. 72:1–3). Righteousness and peace kiss (Ps. 85:11).

Forms of Untruthfulness

It is not a big step from the courtroom lie to other forms of the lie that can harm our neighbor's reputation. True, the ninth commandment does not say, "You shall not lie"; but neither can we separate what the ninth commandment forbids from what the Bible says in general about the outrageous character of lying. Already in the Old Testament, lying could be denounced without mention of any court procedure. Hosea 4:2 mentions five different sins, clearly recalling the Ten Commandments: swearing, lying, killing, stealing, and committing adultery.

In the old dispensation, an Israelite was forbidden to be a lying witness against another member of God's people; similarly in the new dispensation, Paul instructs us, "Therefore, putting away *lying*, each one speak truth with his neighbor, for we are members of one another" (Eph. 4:25).

The ninth commandment aims at preserving the reputation, the good name, of the Israelite.[3] That reputation was especially at risk in the courtroom, but it could be attacked outside the courtroom as well. A number of ways can be mentioned.

Someone can chip away at the good name of his neighbor through *backbiting* and *gossip*. These need not be lies, because gossip can spread many things that are true. But it is still frivolous prattling behind a per-

---

* G. Voetius points out (with reference to John 7:51) that even if someone is guilty, he is not obligated to acknowledge his guilt to the court if his guilt has not been *proved*. No one hates his own flesh; no one can be compelled to betray or to hate himself or members of his family. Every truth must be established out of the mouth of two or three witnesses (*Catechisatie over den Heidelbergschen Catechismus*, 855, 1074).

son's back. Perhaps the one spreading gossip is not lying, but he or she is being untruthful: saying things that are true, but in the context of slander, is deceitful.* The neighbor's mistakes, faults, and shortcomings are discussed in minute detail. People realize this kind of chatter gets them an attentive audience. For it is a universal phenomenon that we would rather hear something bad about our neighbor than something good. And something dirty always sticks long after the conversation has died. As Martin Luther put it in his Large Catechism, reputation is something quickly stolen, but not quickly returned.

Gossip can even be presented piously by conveying the impression of reluctance as we repeat what we know about our neighbor. "I've known for a long time, but never said anything." Or, "I'm telling you this in confidence and would not want you to repeat it." We can sugarcoat the bitter pill by starting or ending our story with a trumpet blast of praise for our neighbor: "Even though I've told you this about him, he has his good points, too."[4]

Even if we see someone doing something wrong, that is still no basis for talking about it to a third party. There is a big difference, said Luther, between "knowing about sin" and "talking about sin."[5]

Another form of sinning against the ninth commandment is *judging rashly.* David believed Ziba's slander about Jonathan's son Mephibosheth and rendered a judgment without further investigation (2 Sam. 16:4; 19:24–28). Jesus' disciples came to Him with the report that Galileans had been killed by Pilate as they were bringing their sacrifices. Pilate had mixed their blood with that of the sacrificial animals. Surely that must have meant those people were wicked sinners (Luke 13:2)! As the disciples were passing by a man blind from birth, they asked Jesus who had sinned, the blind man or his parents (John 9:2). The answer to their serious question was contained already in the terms with which they framed the dilemma. They assumed that where there is suffering, there must be personal guilt, on the part of either the man or his parents.

Rash judgments occur often. Anyone who depends on the media—press, radio, and television—has seen how the most contradictory judgments about the most complicated problems can be pronounced as quick as a wink. Government officials are torn apart without mercy. Justified criticism of small details gets blown up to such an extent that soon the

---

* Older versions of the Heidelberg Catechism, Lord's Day 43, speak of "backbiting," which modern versions correctly render as "gossip."

politician's entire person or his entire administration is subjected to destructive condemnation.

Therefore, it is no coincidence that in the Sermon on the Mount, Jesus says very bluntly, "Judge not, that you be not judged. For with what judgment you judge, you will be judged; and with the same measure you use, it will be measured back to you. And why do you look at the speck in your brother's eye, but do not consider the plank in your own eye?" (Matt. 7:1–3).

This does not eliminate the right to make judgments about various matters. Judges must render verdicts, church leaders must make judgments, and all of us must evaluate many matters and persons as we try to fulfill our God-given task. When we discuss the tenth commandment, we will see that in various situations we can and must evaluate what proceeds from the heart of another person. But too often we judge rashly, so that our neighbor's reputation is harmed. We judge without sufficient knowledge of the situation. Or we judge without being called to render judgment. The question becomes appropriate at that point: Who made you a judge over us?

In connection with the third commandment, we discussed situations where we should be quiet rather than speak. "Speaking is silver, but silence is sometimes golden," we said. The same is true in situations where we have not been called upon to render judgment, even though the words are on the tip of our tongue. We simply may not say everything that comes into our head.

Here we can learn a lesson from the archangel Michael, who dared not bring a slanderous accusation against even the Devil (Jude 9). The Great Judgment is coming, along with an infallible assessment of all that has been done, said, and thought. That should deter us from rendering premature judgments (1 Cor. 4:5).

The lowest form of lying is *libel*. One who libels is lying openly and intentionally. We are no longer dealing with slander behind someone's back or with "just" rash judgment. For rashness has given way to an intentional attempt to rob one's neighbor of his reputation. Libel is lying when we know better.

Of course, here too the lie seeks to clothe itself in the garment of truth. In the trial of Jesus, the false witnesses claimed that Jesus had said, "I am able to destroy the temple of God and to build it in three days" (Matt. 26:61). But Jesus had not said it this way, for John 2:19 reports that He said to the Jews, "[You] destroy this temple, and in three days I will raise it up," referring to His own body.

Often libel is accompanied by *twisting someone's words*. Giving a little

turn to what someone has said can communicate exactly the opposite of
what was intended. When we realize this, we begin to understand why
rash judgment, which seems so much more innocent, is very close to libel.
Has anyone ever met two people involved in a dispute who did not claim,
"I didn't say that"?

Truth is a matter of precision, but how often do we not profit by bend-
ing someone else's words just a bit? In discussions and public polemics, it
is hard to be completely nonpartisan and to treat our opponents with
openhearted fairness.

This is quite a challenge even in scientific research, where, for example, our judgment may be sought about facts and people from the past. We
so easily tint the portrait according to our tastes. Objectivity is a moral virtue and part of our obedience to the ninth commandment.[6] We must try
to judge people and events from the past and the present as honestly as
possible. For all of us look at people and events from our own historically
specific vantage point. But for that very reason we must strive for as much
objectivity as possible, so that the picture we give may be reliable.

The opposite of these forms of lying and untruthfulness that we have
been discussing is summarized briefly in the Heidelberg Catechism: In
court and everywhere else, I must love the truth, speak and confess it honestly, and do what I can to defend and promote my neighbor's honor and
reputation (Answer 112). The tongue does incalculable evil, being full of
deadly poison. But you can also use the tongue for putting into practice
the wisdom from above. That wisdom is peaceable, friendly, considerate,
full of kindness and good fruits, impartial and sincere (James 3:17). This
is how we are peacemakers (James 3:18).

Who Is My Neighbor?

The ninth commandment says that we may not be a lying (false) witness
against our *neighbor*. In the preceding commandments, the protection of
life, marriage, and property obviously involves our neighbor, too. But
now, for the first time in the Decalogue, our neighbor is expressly mentioned. Perhaps one acceptable explanation can be discovered by putting
the third commandment alongside the ninth. Both commandments involve names and reputations; both also involve being a false witness. But
the third commandment deals with attacking the name of *Yahweh* by using it idly, as, for example, when people misuse God's name when swearing an oath in a court of law. In contrast to the third commandment, the
ninth deals with attacking the name of our *neighbor*.

More important than the question why the ninth commandment expressly mentions our neighbor is the question, To whom does "neighbor" refer? Is everyone our neighbor? We have already given something of an answer to this question in our discussion of the sixth commandment. For the Israelite, the neighbor was (especially) his *fellow Israelite*. He was indeed required to love his enemy, but that too referred first of all to the enemy *among* his own people (Ex. 23:4–5; Prov. 24:17; 25:21).

In the New Testament, the circle is drawn more widely, although there too we read that the neighbor is to be found first of all within the new people of God, namely, the church of Jesus Christ (Rom. 15:2; James 4:12). Love for one's neighbor is first of all love for one's brother.[7] Everyone must speak the truth with his neighbor, "for we are members of one another" (Eph. 4:25).

But we cannot stop here. Recall the parable of the good Samaritan (Luke 10:25–37). Paul wrote about pagan governments and immediately thereafter proceeded to summon his readers to love their neighbors, who can be identified very generally as "another" (Rom. 13:8–9). Our Savior's lovingkindness and *love toward men* has appeared (Titus 3:4)—a love as wide as the world.

Therefore, we cannot restrict the application of the ninth commandment to the circle of "our own kind," whether church members, fellow citizens, or any other group. We should keep our word, for example, even to our enemy. Just before the Prague reformer John Hus (1370–1415) laid his case before the Council of Constance, he had received a promise of safe conduct from Emperor Sigismund of Bohemia. This would have guaranteed his safe return to Prague. However, in spite of this promise, Hus was apprehended and burned at the stake. His executioners ignored his promise of safe conduct, because, after all, nobody needed to keep a promise made to a heretic. This is how the concept of "neighbor" is emptied of meaning. If someone is declared a heretic, then people can treat him as they like. He loses all his rights, despite nice promises.

Another example involves promises made to terrorists who have seized hostages. It has happened that terrorists have negotiated with law enforcement officials that they be given an escort to fly to a specified country if they release their hostages unharmed. Here too the proverb applies: "It is better not to vow than to make a vow and not fulfill it" (Eccl. 5:5 NIV). Even when officials promise terrorists that they can leave unharmed, they must keep their word.

The attitude of Joshua toward the Gibeonites is instructive at this point. As residents of the pagan land of Canaan, the Gibeonites were actually supposed to be destroyed. But their envoys tricked Joshua into thinking that they had traveled from a distant country and had come to make a treaty with the people of Israel. Joshua made a treaty of friendship with them, discovered their ruse several days later, and let them live, because otherwise God would have punished Israel for not keeping their sworn oath (Josh. 9:1–27). Even pious arguments cannot release someone from his word. Bloodguilt came upon Saul and his family because years later he killed the Gibeonites. The excuse that he did this "in his zeal for the children of Israel and Judah" evidently did not exonerate him (2 Sam. 21:1–14).

In a little while, we will say something about the "lie of necessity," related to military deception and other forms of duplicity. But even in war not everything is permissible. One who grants authority for negotiations or makes agreements or signs treaties may not change his yes to no whenever it suits him.

Lying Lives Deep

As we have seen, the lie appears in many forms. Courtroom perjury is but one of them. Moreover, the ninth commandment applies in our relationships with everyone, whether friend or foe.

Evidently we have a hard time being honest. Even if we have never given false testimony in court, we still catch ourselves gossiping, judging rashly, and twisting another person's words. Even the slanderer finds a ready audience. His words are like tasty morsels; they slide down easily to the inner recesses of the heart (Prov. 18:8; 26:22). Lying or believing lies both come easily for us.

The verbal inflation rate is high and a lot of verbal counterfeit enters circulation. So we need a variety of methods to verify what we are saying. Everything needs to be documented with invoices and receipts. Licenses, customs officials, speed checks, and tax inspectors are all proof positive that we need a network of supervision because we compromise the truth very easily. We are not inherently trustworthy.

Why does the lie slide down so easily, and why do we devour it like delicious pastry? Dutch theologian W. J. Aalders insists that we do not take life seriously enough, that we have too much time for fun and for games of chance, for fiction and theater. In our conversation we reduce the life of the other person to a game and a stage performance. The lie entertains and diverts us. With the lie we play a game with our neighbor. We become oblivious to the fact that our neighbors are living persons with their own interests, honor, and reputation. Abraham Kuyper said something similar. The world of fantasy is bigger and more interesting than the real world. Everyday life bores us. Gossip is the spice people need to enhance their otherwise dull lives.[8]

But our question still remains: Why do we fall into this kind of game and into this world of fantasy? The sin of lying apparently lies very deep. We all stumble in many ways, James says. "If anyone does not stumble in word, he is a perfect man, able also to bridle the whole body." We put a bit in the mouth of a horse and with it we steer its whole body. Huge ships have tiny rudders, which the pilots use to keep the vessel on course. Similarly, the tongue is a small member of the body, but the damage it does is terrifying: "The tongue is so set among our members that it defiles the whole body, and sets on fire the course of nature; and it is set on fire by hell." We can tame all kinds of wild animals, "but no man can tame the tongue. It is an unruly evil, full of deadly poison. With it we bless our God and Father, and with it we curse men, who have been made in the similitude of God. Out of the same mouth proceed blessing and cursing" (James 3:2–10).

This passage shows clearly that the tongue is set afire *by hell itself*. There dwells the father of lies, the Devil (John 8:44). Jesus spoke this against the Jews who were boasting that Abraham was their father. He pointed out that they did not understand the truth, so they were not free sons of Abraham, but slaves of sin. "You are of your father the devil, and the desires of your father you want to do" (John 8:44). That statement irritated the Jews. How could they be slaves and children of the Devil, they who were descendants of Abraham and pious Jews?

Jesus' criticism is revealing, not only for the Jews of His day, but for all of us. Lying lives very deep within us, because we have been defiled with lying by the father of lies. Even that is put too weakly. Through his fall into sin, man has not simply been defiled with the lie, but dominated by it. The truth of God is exchanged for the lie, so that the creature is worshiped instead of the Creator (Rom. 1:25). The world of idolatry is a world of lies. The apostle Paul writes about men who were *walking* in that world with a mind that was darkened, alienated as they were from life with God, because they dwelt in darkness and their hearts had become hard (Eph. 4:17–18). The lie is not an incidental phenomenon, but is characteristic of fallen man. All men became deceitful (Rom. 3:9–18).

It is instructive to hear the description theologian A. C. Kruyt provides of the hold the lie has over the lives of pagans. When a Toradja wants to take his dugout down the Posso River, he announces in a loud voice that he will be doing this tomorrow, intending thereby to fool the river spirits and to ward off dangers threatening him from these spirits. Never tell a child that she has pretty eyes and a pretty face; it is much better to insist she has the eyes of a pig and the hair of a dog. Otherwise the spirits will become jealous and hurt the child. Do not bother asking if anybody has ever been eaten by a crocodile in a particular river, because the only answer you will ever get is: "Nobody from our tribe has ever been eaten by a crocodile."[9]

Among such primitive tribesmen, but among ourselves as well, we observe how all of us try to preserve ourselves by lying. We want to keep the controls of our lives in our own hands, and that simply cannot be done without lying. Lying betrays our striving for self-preservation and self-redemption.

No cure for this ailment exists other than radical conversion. That is how deep lying lives in us. In our conversion, we must put off *the old nature;* but in that same context Paul says that we must put away *lying* and start speaking the truth (Eph. 4:22–25).

We can do this only through the grace of God's liberation. Also above the ninth commandment stands the preamble: "I am Yahweh your God, who has freed you from Egypt, the house of slavery." This is not self-redemption, which enslaves us to the lie; rather, this is liberation by Yahweh, who rescues us from bondage to lying. Jesus Christ says, "I am the way, *the truth,* and the life" (John 14:6).

Now we begin walking a different path. Through redemption in Christ, we know God as Father and our neighbors in Christ's church as our brothers and sisters. We may not lie anymore; we do not need to lie anymore. For the troubles we used to have in lying to safeguard our own lives against the wiles of "the gods" and other people need not continue when we live with Christ. Self-denial replaces self-preservation. Speaking the truth leads us down a safe path, even though lying quite often seems to be safer. It is because we so rarely really live by faith that we often want to rescue ourselves from our difficulties by lying.

Clearly those difficulties exist. A. C. Kruyt mentions that conversion to Christ leads to the disappearance of head-hunting, idol feasts, and rituals for the dead, replaced by various Christian practices like church attendance, holy communion, prayer, and the like. But, he adds, changes *in attitude* are less visible.[10] To quit lying is a tremendous challenge. Lying lives deep. We struggle not simply with a vice, but against our entire old nature caught in the net of lying. We must wage this struggle in the *faith* that only by speaking the truth will we live safely before God and among our neighbors.

Even though Christians are fortunate to know the way, the truth, and the life, they do not always walk in the truth. By contrast, sometimes non-Christians compel respect for their honesty and integrity, even though they unfortunately do not know the way, the truth, and the life. You can speak the truth and still walk in the lie. Lying and being deceitful are two different things, just as there is a difference between speaking the truth and being truthful.[11]

Knowing now how deeply the lie lives in the human heart, it becomes clearer why the Bible fulminates so vehemently against *false prophets*, those teachers of the lie. False prophets lead people back into idolatry and slavery, seducing them to surrender the freedom they have obtained (Deut. 13:1–18).

People led astray will fall away from God. The god of this age (the Devil) can strike people with blindness, so they cannot see (any longer) the light of the gospel shining upon them (2 Cor. 4:2–4). In fact, as punishment for despising the truth, God Himself sends a powerful delusion, which induces people to believe the lie (2 Thess. 2:9–12).

On the basis of this reality, it is no wonder that throughout her history the church has experienced, in addition to much backsliding, a constant struggle to preserve the truth. After all, we cannot effectively battle the vice of lying if we let the church's vision of the truth be obscured. How can we live in the world as people of integrity if we make room in the church for truth and falsehood to live side by side? Fighting for the pure gospel means fighting for the preservation of the truth among people. This is why "lying in the church"[*] must be fought with all our might, and this is why every church reformation, which exposes such lying, constitutes a blessing for society.

Three Kinds of Lies

For centuries, lies have been categorized in three classes: the malicious lie, the jocular lie, and the lie of necessity.

Concerning the *malicious lie* (Latin, *mendacium perniciosum*) we need not say very much, in view of what we have already written. This kind of

---

* This phrase is the title of a chapter in Abraham Kuyper's pamphlet entitled *Church Visiting* (Utrecht, 1868), where he criticizes the deceptive conduct of the church in his day, in terms of abuses relating to baptism and holy communion, catechizing and profession of faith, and receiving ministers and church members.

lie is to be condemned. It is always a violation of the ninth commandment. For we may never harm our neighbor by lying, which we do in all those forms of lying we discussed earlier.

The *jocular lie* (Latin, *mendacium iocosum*) is a bit more complex. We amuse each other with "untruths." When someone amuses us with a tall tale, he is not necessarily guilty of lying. For usually we sense immediately that he is speaking in jest. "Lying" intends to deceive. This is more than telling someone something that is untrue.*

The situation is different, however, when the elements of truth and untruth cannot be distinguished in the jocular lie. We can lead someone along to the point where telling untruths harms him. Someone who deceives his neighbor and then says, "I was only joking!" is compared in the Bible to a madman shooting firebrands or deadly arrows (Prov. 26:18–19).

Genuine humor does not employ "objective truths," but is nevertheless still a healthy component of human interaction. Laughter is healthy, and when someone creatively pulls our leg about our idiosyncracies and pretensions, that is good, no matter how "stretched" the humorous parody may be. That kind of humor will not hurt us. But it is different when humor is designed to deceive and deride our neighbor. That is no longer a form of joking. Humor turns sour and the joke becomes a lie.

The third kind of lie, the so-called *lie of necessity* (Latin, *medacium officiosum*) requires a lengthier discussion. The Latin phrase describes better than the English what this kind of lie involves: lying for my neighbor's *benefit*.† This kind of lying intends no harm against my neighbor (which harm is a violation of the ninth commandment), but the opposite—to

---

* We should mention here that there are various definitions of "lying." Some see the decisive element to be the *voluntas falsum enuntiandi* (the intent to communicate something false). Others limit lying (correctly, in our opinion) to the *voluntas fallendi* (the intent to deceive someone). See B. M. Lee, *Mendacium officiosum*, 58ff., 119–20. With this definition, the jocular lie (and the white lie, discussed below) are not really forms of lying forbidden in the ninth commandment, since they lack the element of "intent to deceive."

† Although we are using the phrase "lie of necessity," the French language speaks of *mensonge pieux* ("the pious lie").

Translator's note: Because this kind of lie characteristically intends to avoid anticipated *harm* (rather than embarrassment), we are using the phrase *lie of necessity* to render the Dutch term *noodleugen* and the German term *Notlüge*. Although some translators render this with the phrase *white lie*, in popular English usage *white lie* usually denotes a polite fib told to avoid embarrassing oneself or another person; it comes closest to what will be discussed below as the *hoffelijkheidsleugen*, or polite lie.

In summary, then, a lie of necessity is a lie made critically necessary by the situation.

help him. This is not a lie *against* my neighbor, but for his *benefit*. How could this possibly violate the ninth commandment?

Hiding a Jew during World War II has become a classic example. How could someone hiding a Jew from the Germans tell the truth to soldiers making house-to-house searches? In that situation, speaking the truth would have resulted in surrendering the fugitive to the Germans, whereas he could have been spared with the use of a falsehood. Should this kind of beneficial lie be condemned?

Should We Reject the Lie of Necessity?

Following in the footsteps of Augustine, the church has throughout her history rejected the lie of necessity almost universally.[12] How does Augustine answer the question about what we should do when someone seeks refuge with us, whose life we may have to save by lying? His answer is very simple: This person may die in body, but not in soul, whereas one who lies dies in his soul (Wisdom 1:11). God destroys everyone who speaks falsehood (Ps. 5:6). No lie proceeds from the truth (1 John 2:21).

You may indeed wish to help someone, but you may never do this at the cost of your own soul. Here Augustine appeals to the words: "You shall love your neighbor *as yourself*." This is not achieved when we sacrifice our own eternal salvation to save the temporal life of our neighbor. Similarly, we may not comply with the demand to commit unchastity even if the one demanding threatens to hang himself if we refuse, may we?

Is Augustine then telling us simply to tell the truth and lead the questioner to the fugitive we were protecting? No, we may not speak falsehood, but neither may we betray anyone. We avoid both by *being silent* or by declaring that we will not tell the questioner whether or where we are hiding a fugitive.

Augustine's conviction deserves our respect. He knows the issue and dares to face the consequences of his position. Nevertheless, the question remains whether Augustine has led the church down the right path with his rejection of the lie of necessity. He appeals to a number of Bible verses that he considers to be absolutes. But he does not handle these verses the same way he handles others. For example, when Jesus says that we must not swear any oath at all (Matt. 5:34), Augustine argues that there are times when we must swear an oath. Sometimes we need not turn the left cheek when our right cheek is struck. For various *examples* or stories in the Bible show us, says Augustine, how we should interpret the *words* or verses. But, the Bible contains a number of surprising examples of the lie of necessity, examples that should caution us about condemning *every* lie.

The midwives Shiphrah and Puah let the baby boys of Israel live after birth, contrary to Pharaoh's command. When interrogated about this, they declared that the Israelite women gave birth too quickly. By the time Shiphrah and Puah arrived for the delivery, the baby had been born already and hidden away (Ex. 1:15–21). Clearly that was a falsehood, but the falsehood was spoken by two midwives described as fearing God and as being blessed by God because of their attitude (Ex. 1:17, 20).

Rahab spoke a falsehood when she told the king of Jericho that she did not know where the spies she had hidden earlier had come from or where they might have gone (Josh. 2:4–6). She is praised for her faith, because she had received the spies in peace (Heb. 11:31). She was justified from her works (Greek, *ex ergon*, out of [her] works) when she gave lodging to the messengers and helped them leave by another route (James 2:25). Especially this latter comment is significant. Had she spoken the truth, she could not possibly have helped the spies escape by another route!

The woman in Bahurim hid two men in her well, allies of David, and she camouflaged the hiding place. In answer to the question of Absolom's servants as to where the men were, she pointed in the wrong direction, saying: "They have gone over the water brook" (2 Sam. 17:19–20).

To us it seems impossible to claim (as many have claimed) that the midwives and Rahab were praised for their faith, but not for their lies. For their faith was expressed precisely in their works. It is an abstraction to disconnect the *effect* of their acts from the *path* they took to achieve that effect.

Clearly all of these women performed a service to their neighbors by means of the *mendacium officiosum*. This kind of lie is different from the lie told for personal survival, told sometimes at the cost of our neighbor's life. This kind of lie also appears in the Bible. Recall Abraham and Isaac who, when they were in Egypt, pretended that their wives were their sisters (Gen. 12:11–20; 20:2–18; 26:7–11). Their half-truth or full-blown lie, intended to rescue them from their own personal distress, could have resulted in other men committing adultery with their wives.

We must reject such lies, but is it possible to condemn *every* lie? Those who do, encounter serious problems. If every lie is wrong, what about strategies of *military deception*? This is clearly a form of deception. One can hardly condemn this kind of deception, since the Lord Himself recommended such tactics in Joshua's battle against Ai and in David's fight against the Philistines (Josh. 8:1–26; 2 Sam. 5:22–25).

The response of those opposed to any and every lie is usually that these military strategies certainly involve deception, but not lying. Pretense is part of war, but not lying. But this distinction is artificial.* Essentially it means that deception is permissible, but lying is not. But if I may not mislead the enemy with words, may I mislead him with deeds? You cannot defend military deception and condemn the lie of necessity.

The characteristic feature of the lie of necessity is its capacity to mislead. Whether that misleading occurs through words, deeds, or gestures makes no difference in principle. Even with words that are "true" we can achieve the same misleading as with the lie of necessity. Consider what is called *dissimulation*. The church father Athanasius was once asked by his pursuers, "Where is Athanasius?" Deftly he answered, "Athanasius is not far away; with a little effort you can find him!" The Mennonite Hans Busscher was asked a similar question when he was being pursued. In the cart where he had been sitting with others passengers, he *stood* up and asked the others if Hans Busscher was *sitting* among them. The formally correct answer was "No."†

This misdirection is just as evident as with so-called *simulation*, where one pretends. Someone who cries without any genuine sadness is lying not with words but with his face. He misleads just as with military deception and with the lie of necessity. The so-called *restrictio mentalis* is another form of misleading. With this technique, we use words that, taken absolutely, are untrue, but become true with the addition of some unspoken mental addition. To a visitor at the door, someone says, "My husband is not home," thinking the extra words, "for you, that is."[13]

One form of misleading is not better than the other. What is decisive is whether in particular circumstances we are permitted to mislead. The form in which that happens is of secondary significance.

---

* Therefore, Rousseau was not completely wrong in his remark about this matter of lies of necessity, a moral issue evaluated in two quite divergent ways: "It is disapproved in ethics books, where defending the most uncompromising morality costs the authors nothing. It is approved in the real world, where book-morality is gibberish because it cannot be put into practice anyway" (quoted by W. Geesink in *Van 's Heeren ordinantiën* [Kampen, 1925], 4:381).

† These examples are found in B. M. Lee, *Mendacium officiosum*, 72, where the author mentions the definition of "Mennonite lie" found in the authoritative Dutch dictionary of Van Dale: "A statement formulated in such a way that the hearer can understand it differently than it was in fact intended." This kind of lie, Lee argues, is wrongly associated with the name of Menno Simons.

Dire Circumstances

We can easily understand why many hesitate to approve the lie of necessity. Read the ancient commentaries on the ninth commandment and you will repeatedly encounter warnings about the dangers of the lie of necessity. Will we not have to give an account of every idle word (Matt. 12:36)? Surely we may not do evil in order that good may result (Rom. 3:8), may we? Is not silence the only alternative? Is not Augustine's observation correct, that we may not rescue someone's life by stealing or committing adultery? How can the judge still trust the word of a witness if there are situations where we may lie?

Indeed, it would be sad if everybody took the law into his own hands, so that we could no longer trust one another's spoken word. Agreeing that lying is *sometimes* permissible is dangerous. Soon we may be sliding down the slippery slope. But other things are dangerous, too. Saying that we may *never* lie, so that we cannot help Jews or other fugitives because we will have to speak the truth to those pursuing them, is also dangerous.

The argument that in such circumstances we could better *remain silent* rather than lie, is weak. In this situation silence says a mouthful. For if you answer, "I'm not telling," you can figure on your house being searched with double thoroughness, since you are apparently hiding something or someone. Nor can the argument that we may not rescue someone's life by stealing or committing adultery suffice as a basis for rejecting the lie of necessity. B. M. Lee has shown that the Bible distinguishes between stealing and adultery. In Proverbs 6:30–35 we read that a thief is not despised if he steals to satisfy his hunger. If he is caught, he must repay sevenfold. But concerning adultery, the text observes: "Whoever commits adultery with a woman lacks understanding; he who does so destroys his own soul." Theft can be made right through restitution, but adultery with its consequences cannot be repaired.

We must not condemn the lie of necessity. We are dealing here with a borderline situation, something that can arise with other commandments too. David violated the law when he ate the consecrated bread given to him by the priest Abimelech (Lev. 24:9; 1 Sam. 21:3–6), and the priests who work on the Sabbath in the temple desecrate (!) the Sabbath without being guilty (Matt. 12:5). We must honor our parents (fifth commandment), but it can be necessary to deny them obedience for the sake of Christ. We must be subject to the government, but if the state conducts itself tyrannically, it is not impermissible for the right of revolution to be invoked. Murder is forbidden (sixth commandment), but the Israelite is free of bloodguilt if he catches an intruder and fatally wounds him (Ex.

22:2). We may not steal (eighth commandment), but Yahweh permitted the Israelites to rob the Egyptians just before the Exodus (Ex. 3:22; 11:2; 12:35–36). Jesus' comment about the priests who work in the temple on the Sabbath can be applied to other situations: the law is "broken," but without guilt.

However, a lie of necessity may be used only in *dire circumstances*, that is to say, only in situations where life is at stake, either our neighbor's or ours. This does not refer to various *difficult* situations, where we can escape our problems by speaking a falsehood. Even though we incur no guilt when we tell a lie of necessity, we do make use of a sinister and dangerous means.*

It is also better not to smooth things over by saying that lies of necessity may be used against people who have no right to the truth.† Or, to put it more strongly: Lies of necessity may be used against people I need not view as my neighbor.‡ More than once the lie of necessity has been called a *poisonous* remedy, compared by John Cassian (died ca. 430) to a kind of sneezing powder that was beneficial as an antidote for a deadly disease, but quite fatal if used unnecessarily.[14]

Situations where the lie of necessity may be used are rare, if we deal honestly with the ninth commandment. Our examples involve situations

---

* For that reason, we must be sure a lie of necessity is called a *lie* and not try to turn it into a *truth*. It is a form of intellectual gymnastics to play off the "Hebrew concept of truth" (being true to God or our neighbor) against the "Greek view of truth" (not concealing the facts), in order to transform the lies of Rahab and the others into truth. See B. M. Lee, *Mendacium officiosum*, 111ff. After all, we use the lie of necessity to mislead someone, which is the essential characteristic of "lying." A lie of necessity is something other than a *mere* lie, a *mere* deception.

† Undoubtedly there are situations where someone has no right to certain information. Secrets entrusted to us should not be revealed, even when we are asked. But Hugo de Groot, S. Pufendorf, and others use this fact to justify distinguishing between *mendacium* and *falsiloquium*. According to them, an untrue statement (*falsiloquium*) would be a lie (and thus impermissible) only if it were directed to someone entitled to hear the truth. So, for example, if one were to embarrass a physician by inquiring about the condition of his patient, without having the right to that knowledge, the physician may provide incorrect information. But an untrue statement intended to mislead our neighbor is always a lie, even though that neighbor has no right to hear the truth. See B. M. Lee, *Mendacium officiosum*, 76, 133.

‡ We cannot agree with the Dutch writer K. J. Popma, who argues in his *Levensbeschouwing* (Amsterdam, 1963), 6:231–32, that Hitler's henchmen, who trampled the Netherlands in 1940, "most assuredly" were not his neighbors in the biblical sense. "They had no business in our country; God didn't put them in our neighborhood, the devil did. . . . It was our sacred Christian duty to give these bandits wrong information, the more confusing the

in times of war or extreme need, circumstances where life itself is at stake. W. Geesink mentions the situation of a deranged man who is bent on murder and demands to know the location of his victim.* The number of cases requiring use of the lie of necessity is not large.

If we would rather not tell a person who is seriously ill that he or she is about to die, are those dire circumstances? Is *lying to a patient* permissible? In a publication on this subject, J. J. Buskes draws attention to the fact that in daily life we often have to tell each other things we can hardly cope with. Dying "is such a traumatic event that an obvious requirement of humaneness is not to use deception to rob a loved one, whom we know is dying, of the opportunity to prepare for death."[15] In this situation, a lie would not be to benefit our dying neighbor, but to conceal our own inability to talk with someone about his impending death.

Speaking the truth is often not easy; it presupposes insight into difficult situations and wisdom for finding the right words. That is why it makes a difference who is lying in such difficult situations. Dietrich Bonhoeffer gave a memorable illustration of this. A child was asked by his teacher in front of the entire class whether his father came home drunk very often. Although it was true, the lad denied it. His teacher's question had put him in a situation that he could not cope with. He did not want to hear his family's misery broadcast to the class, so he denied the truth. A family has its own secrets to keep, and the teacher had failed to recognize this. In commenting on this illustration, Lee adds that, had the boy been older or more mature, perhaps he would have replied, "May we discuss this privately during recess?"[16] But such an answer presupposes a maturity possessed by few schoolchildren. So then, when we ask who sinned more grievously against the ninth commandment, the teacher or the pupil, the answer is obvious.

What Is Courtesy, What Is Pretense?

Occasionally, in addition to the three kinds of lies mentioned above, a fourth is mentioned: the *polite lie* (Latin, *mendacium humilita-*

---

better." The Dutch could not give free reign to their animosity, not even against the Germans, *precisely* because they were their neighbors in the biblical sense. The command to love our enemy applies also to enemies of war. Indeed, many times it was the Christian's duty to mislead Hitler's henchmen. We agree with Popma's conclusion, but not with his argument justifying this behavior.

* Typical of Geesink's approach is his approval of the deception used to mislead the deranged man, but his refusal to approve telling the man a falsehood. Both the deception and the lie of necessity constitute forms of misleading (see *Van 's Heeren ordinantiën*, 4:386–87).

tis).* Do we really mean what we write when we sign a letter, "Very truly yours" or "Sincerely yours"? Is it honest to answer our host's question, "Have you had enough to eat?" with a polite "Yes, thank you," even though we would really like another helping?

In general, we can say that here we are dealing with customs of politeness, not lying. For a lie intends to deceive, but we are not deceiving when we show respect to whom it is due or follow rules of etiquette.

Something else needs to be said about this. It is a blessing that we cannot and do not say everything that comes into our head, but instead have to follow fixed customs in our conversations with each other. It is possible to write a very critical letter to someone whose conduct has made it hard for me to respect him; but if I respect rules of etiquette, then I cannot give free rein to my feelings. By signing the letter "Respectfully yours," I must remember as I write the letter that there are limits to my criticism. Such rules of etiquette temper our anger. We keep the way open for reply and subsequent discussion. By saying "No, thank you" at the meal table, when we would really enjoy another helping, we restrain ourselves. It may *seem* entirely honest to write exactly what we feel (without the "Dear" or the "Respectfully") and to do what we would like (to eat our fill), but that would be pure egoism.

Politeness is thus something other than refined insincerity. Rules of etiquette are a blessing. These rules help us give shape to our love. Love covers much and endures much (1 Cor. 13:6; 1 Peter 4:8). Love shuns the kind of "honesty" where we always say what we think. Very often that is exactly what we should not do. Fortunately, rules of etiquette come to our aid by offering us conventional ways of speaking so that we can deal more considerately with each other than if we would "just let ourselves go." Politeness is an air cushion, so goes the saying: there's nothing inside, but it absorbs life's bumps![17] "Conventions of language are necessary, especially since we ourselves are so often unconventional."[18]

We can corrupt anything, including etiquette. Conventions of courtesy must not become so calcified through overuse that they begin to function like a crusty filter that no longer lets anything through.[19] That would make these conventions a mere pretense. A person who fawns and flatters you appears courteous, but is in fact a phony. In that case, politeness really does become a *mendacium humilitatis*, a lie.

Pretense has many faces, some of them alarming. A. C. Kruyt tells how

---

* *Translator's note:* In English this is usually called a "white lie." See the preceding translator's note.

among primitive people, children are trained to pretend. Children are mocked when they are playing; boys are forced to show masculine emotions that they do not feel; expressions of tenderness are suppressed.[20] In our own world as well, some children and adults live in a straitjacket and cannot really be themselves. An alarming incidence of deformed growth patterns has led to artificial and insincere interaction in various human relationships. People either cannot or will not be honest with others. Stubbornness or inability prevents them from openhearted conversation and clearing the air.

A common form of pretense is the contradiction between doctrine and life. A Christian's talk may conflict with his walk. To a certain extent this is true of every Christian, since even the most holy, as the Heidelberg Catechism says in Lord's Day 44, have but a small beginning of new obedience. But there is a difference between a weak Christian life and a deceptive Christian life. In the latter, words and deeds *clash*. Such people talk piously, but live wickedly. They honor with their lips, but their hearts are not in it (Matt. 15:9); they load burdens on others, without lifting a finger to help carry them; they resemble whitewashed tombs: they look nice on the outside, but inside they are full of bones and rottenness (Matt. 23:4, 27).

Secrecy and Concealment

The ninth commandment forbids lying and (thus) requires us to love the truth, and to speak and confess the truth uprightly. But we have already seen that often we serve the truth by keeping silent. Many things we know about we must keep secret.

For many, this duty obviously belongs to their professional code of conduct. Physicians, ministers, nurses, social workers, and many others must maintain confidentiality about what, in the practice of their professions, they have come to know about church members, patients, or clients.

In particular situations, one may be obligated to divulge confidential information, not to just anyone, but only to those authorized to ask us to speak. A patient must be able to trust the doctor's confidentiality regarding his disease. But if the disease is dangerously infectious, then the physician may be required to divulge that information. Or if national security is at stake, telling what we know may be required. In 1605, when some people plotted to assassinate James I at the opening of the British parliament by blowing up the parliament building, the plot was discovered, and two Jesuit priests who had known of the plot because of their work in the confessional, but had remained silent, were executed. Someone who, by keeping silent, becomes an accessory to murder, cannot excuse his guilt by appealing to rules of confidentiality. The limit upon an obligation to confidentiality is reached at the point where keeping something confidential would cause great harm to others, or to the person himself who entrusted us with the secret information.[21]

To parade the vices of another person is a violation of the ninth commandment. We dislike it when children tattle, because often they *take pleasure* in telling father or mother about the misdeeds of their brothers or sisters. But such telling can become necessary in various circumstances, for old and young alike. We are not tattling when we complain to the elders about a sin of a fellow church member, but only after we ourselves have previously, though unsuccessfully, pointed out his sin to him. Nor is it gossip when people warn from the pulpit or in the public press against wrong ideas concerning doctrine and life, even naming those who propagate such ideas. As long as our communication builds up the Christian life of ourselves and others, without taking a personal delight in ruining those defending those wrong ideas, who can object? Nevertheless, engaging in polemics properly is as difficult as it is necessary.

We may not betray the secrets entrusted to us. Without the assurance that secrets will be kept, good relationships among people are impossible. There are numerous matters about which we may not—or may not yet— talk to another party. But keeping silent is different from concealing the truth. For this latter refers to *concealing* matters and hiding things that should be told to other people. A husband may not conceal from his wife that he has a relationship with another woman. If children are in danger of going astray, that should not be hidden from their parents. He is a friend who tells me my faults, but an enemy conceals them from me, perhaps telling them to others behind my back. One who conceals is not helping his neighbor, but is causing him harm.

The ninth commandment asks us to work for our neighbor's well-being. We may not be false witnesses. But we are *true* witnesses when we help our neighbor with our words, even when we have to *oppose* him. True friends do not wear velvet gloves. Words that hurt us are not always in conflict with the ninth commandment.

Endnotes

1. B. M. Lee, *Mendacium officiosum* (Groningen, 1979), 95–96.

2. For these views, see G. Voetius, *Catechisatie over den Heidelbergschen Catechismus*, ed. A. Kuyper (Rotterdam, 1891), 2:1073ff.; J. d'Outrein, *Het gouden kleinoot van de leere*

der waarheid (Amsterdam, 1724), 680ff.; W. à Brakel, *The Christian's Reasonable Service*, trans. Bartel Elshout (Pittsburgh, 1994), 3:228.

3. J. J. Stamm and M. E. Andrew, *The Ten Commandments in Recent Research* (London, 1967), 109.

4. Luther's Large Catechism; see also Pictet, *De Christelyke zedekunst* ('s-Gravenhage, 1731), 529–30, where he quotes Bernard of Clairvaux concerning the evil of gossip.

5. Luther said, "Wissen magst Du sie wohl, aber richten sollst Du sie nicht" ("You may know about it, but you may not pass judgment about it"). Do not act as if you are the emperor or the government.

6. Helmut Thielicke, *Theological Ethics*, vol. 1, *Foundations*, ed. William H. Lazareth (Philadelphia, 1966), 522–29. See also Herman Dooyeweerd, *A New Critique of Theoretical Thought* (Amsterdam, 1955), 2:152, who mentions "logical morality" and integrity.

7. J. L. Koole, *De Tien Geboden*, 145–46.

8. W. J. Aalders, *De Tien Geboden* (Zeist, 1932), 55; A. Kuyper, *E voto Dordraceno* (Kampen, 1892–95), 4:238–39, 251.

9. A. C. Kruyt, "Het Negende Gebod," *Sinaï en Ardjoeno*, ed. Th. Delleman (Aalten, 1946), 235, 248ff.

10. Ibid., 263.

11. B. M. Lee, *Mendacium officiosum*, 114.

12. Much of what follows can be found in the study of B. M. Lee, *Mendacium officiosum*, in which he devotes considerable attention to the opinions of Augustine, Aquinas, and others.

13. B.M. Lee *Mendicum officiosum*, 71ff., where he mentions still more distinctions.

14. Ibid., 143.

15. See ibid., 150. The quotation is from J. J. Buskes, *Waarheid en leugen aan het ziekbed* (Baarn, 1964), 127.

16. B. M. Lee, *Mendacium officiosum*, 152.

17. For several examples, see Helmut Thielicke, *Theological Ethics*, vol. 1, *Foundations*, 545–51.

18. B. M. Lee, *Mendacium officiosum*, 119.

19. Thus A. D. Müller, *Die Wahrhaftigkeitspflicht und die Problematik der Lüge* (Freiburg, 1962), 292.

20. A. C. Kruyt, "Het Negende Gebod," 245ff.

21. W. Geesink, *Gereformeerde ethiek* (Kampen, 1931), 1:442–43.

The Tenth Commandment

You shall not set your desire on your neighbor's house; you shall not set your desire on your neighbor's wife, or his male slave, his female slave, his ox or his donkey, or anything that belongs to him.
(Ex. 20:17)

You shall not set your desire on your neighbor's wife; you shall not set your desire on your neighbor's house, or on his field, his male slave or his female slave, his ox or his donkey, or anything that belongs to him. (Deut. 5:21)

Not Two Commandments

As we mentioned at the beginning of this book, there are different ways of numbering the Ten Commandments. The Jews, Greek Orthodox, and Reformed assign to the tenth commandment the text we have printed above. But Roman Catholics and Lutherans believe we are dealing here with *two* commandments, namely, the ninth and tenth commandments. What we view as the first and second commandments, they combine. But in order to end up with ten, they are forced to divide one of the subsequent commandments. They do that here, with the tenth commandment, where it says *two* times: "You shall not . . ." Is it not consistent to follow the preceding commandments, "You shall not kill unlawfully, you shall not commit adultery, you shall not steal, and you shall not be a false witness against your neighbor," with two separate commandments?

But Roman Catholics and Lutherans differ from one another. Roman Catholics start with the text of Deuteronomy, Lutherans with the text of Exodus. This yields the following results.

337

In the *Roman Catholic version*, the ninth commandment reads: "You shall not covet your neighbor's wife" (Deut. 5:21a), and the tenth commandment: "You shall not desire your neighbor's house, his field, his male servant, his female servant, his ox, his donkey, or anything that is your neighbor's" (Deut. 5:21b).

In the *Lutheran version*, the ninth commandment reads: "You shall not covet your neighbor's house" (Ex. 20:17a), and the tenth commandment: "You shall not covet your neighbor's wife, nor his male servant, nor his female servant, nor his ox, nor his donkey, nor anything that is your neighbor's" (Ex. 20:17b).

We need not spend much time on this matter, since it makes little difference in practice. When you read Roman Catholic and Lutheran explanations of the Decalogue, you will notice that often they do not treat "their" ninth and tenth commandments separately, but discuss them together as one.[1] This fact alone minimizes any need for splitting the tenth commandment into two.

Moreover, the fact that Roman Catholics and Lutherans differ with each other leads to another embarrassing problem. If the ninth commandment, according to the Lutheran version which uses Exodus 20, should say, "You shall not covet your neighbor's *house*," why then does the ninth commandment in Deuteronomy 5 say, "You shall not covet your neighbor's *wife*"? Precisely the reverse question may be raised about the Roman Catholic version, which begins with Deuteronomy 5.

In our opinion, given the *content* of these verses, the notion of dividing this material is far from obvious at first glance. The need to come up with ten commandments forced the division! The *form* of speaking (twice "You shall not . . .") is indeed striking, but in itself not a compelling reason for concluding that these are two distinct commandments. This is one commandment—You shall not covet—and it does not make that much difference whether the list begins with your neighbor's "house" or his "wife," as the varied order in Exodus 20 and Deuteronomy 5 suggests.

Our conviction is strengthened by the way the New Testament quotes the tenth commandment. Paul says that he would not have known coveting if the law had not said, "You shall not covet" (Rom. 7:7). Evidently this is but one commandment, seen also in Romans 13:9, where the following commandments are listed: " 'You shall not commit adultery,' 'You shall not murder,' 'You shall not steal,' 'You shall not bear false witness,' '*You shall not covet*,' and if there is any other commandment, are all summed up in this saying, namely, 'You shall love your neighbor as yourself.' " Clearly, "You shall not covet" must be understood as one commandment, even though various aspects are enumerated in the subsequent text of the commandment.*

Only Our Inward Attitude?

What is the tenth commandment about? To answer this question correctly, there is one view we need to discuss at the very outset.

Often people reason as follows: The preceding commandments have already condemned various wrong desires. A proper interpretation of the seventh commandment would condemn not only adultery, but also looking at a woman to *desire* her (Matt. 5:28). A thorough investigation of the eighth commandment turns up not only flagrant theft, but also the love of money as a root of all kinds of evil (1 Tim. 6:10). What is love of money if not the *desire* for money?

But if such desires have already been condemned in the preceding commandments, why then should the tenth commandment still forbid them by saying, "You shall not covet"? Is not that warning actually superfluous?

To provide a satisfactory answer to this question, Calvin[2] and others distinguished between *plan* and *desire*. You can entertain desires, which consolidate into a *plan*, which then leads to harming your neighbor. These desires do not stay inside your heart, but find a passageway to the outside. A man who desires another woman undertakes strategies to have her for himself. The greedy man develops plans for realizing his desire for more money through various deceptive tactics. In such cases, the *will* concurs self-consciously with a desire. The man goes beyond *dreaming* about another woman or about a huge sum of money, to the point of wanting to *possess* these objects of desire.

But other desires stay within and never come to outward expression. A man can desire another woman without ever making an attempt to let her notice. This kind of desire can pass by quickly. It might not pass by quickly at all, such that he is always internally preoccupied with it. But in both cases the desire need not lead to a particular plan designed to realize or

---

* The Roman Catholic version distinguishes between sexual desire ("your neighbor's wife") and covetous desire ("your neighbor's house, field, slaves, and so forth"). This is less clear in the Lutheran version. In his Small Catechism, Luther distinguishes between desiring "your neighbor's house" and desiring "your neighbor's wife, slaves, ox, and so forth." "House" refers then to our neighbor's property, which we may not appropriate to ourselves by deceit or show of right. Concerning "wife," "slaves," "animals," and the rest, Luther goes on to say that we must leave them to our neighbor so that they can perform their duties.

possess what one desires. Not everything dwelling in the heart comes to outward expression.

Thus, there are stages of desire. Someone can be caught off guard by an immoral desire. He can continue to *nurse* that desire.* He takes another step by surrendering his *will* to that desire and thus develops a *plan* to satisfy that desire. Finally, he translates that desire into a *deed*. These are four stages discussed frequently in the literature dealing with this commandment.

Now then, which stage is the tenth commandment dealing with? According to Calvin and others, the tenth commandment is aimed at the first two stages of desire. The tenth commandment supposedly forbids the evil that lies within our hearts and is nurtured there.

Often people go on to say that these immoral desires cannot be punished by church or state, simply because they are a matter of the heart and never find outward expression. The government can punish murder and the church can discipline adulterers. But God goes further, since He knows the human heart. He comes to us with this tenth and final commandment as the Judge who knows the deepest recesses of our hearts and therefore is able to condemn "even the slightest inclination or thought contrary to any of God's commandments" (Heidelberg Catechism, Lord's Day 44, QA 113).

It seems to us that this interpretation of the tenth commandment is not entirely correct. We would not deny that the tenth commandment renders a verdict about the human heart. But where Calvin and others *begin* in their understanding of the tenth commandment is where we would rather *end*. Just as with the other commandments, we should begin with the literal and direct meaning of the tenth commandment and only then move to its deeper significance. We will come then, just as Calvin does, to the deepest interior level, but only at the conclusion of our study. For when we follow our usual route and begin with the literal text of the tenth commandment, then we notice soon enough that not only man's "inward attitude," but also his "outward behavior" and that of his society are thrown into confusion by human desires.

You Shall Not Set Your Desire On . . .

The tenth commandment uses a word most often translated "covet." A somewhat more accurate rendering, suggested by Semitic language scholar

---

* In the Latin literature on this subject we regularly encounter the word *titillatio:* desire titillates a person!

J. P. Lettinga and others, would be, "You shall not set your desire(s) on your neighbor's house, wife, etc." If we set our desire upon something, we are out to get what we desire. Thus, to set our desire on something *already* involves forming a *plan* (recall what Calvin said!) ready to be put in motion as soon as opportunity arises.

A number of examples of this use of the word in the Bible could be mentioned. After the fall of Jericho, Achan set his desire on a magnificent Babylonian robe, on pieces of silver and gold, and he took all of it to his tent (Josh. 7:21). Here, "covet" means concretely that Achan could not keep his hands off all that nice stuff.* In Micah's day, there were people who had set their desire on fields, which they then also stole (Mic. 2:2). Here too, "covet" is clearly not simply a matter of inner attitude, but included the plan for getting their hands on the objects of their desire. We read that the Israelites were forbidden to "covet" the gold and silver of the graven images that they would find in the land of Canaan. Here again, the warning not to "covet" means that the Israelite was not permitted to appropriate this gold and silver for himself (Deut. 7:25).

We find another clear verse in Exodus 34, where Yahweh promised Israel (if she remained faithful to Him) that no one would "covet" the land of the Israelites (Ex. 34:24). That obviously means that no people would set their desire on the land of the Israelites and (thus) *attempt* to get their hands on it. Perhaps the surrounding nations did desire in their hearts to conquer the land of the Israelites, but *in this instance* their "coveting" would not be satisfied through armies marching in to take over the land of milk and honey.

Stated briefly, we could also say it this way: Anyone who sets his desire(s) on his neighbor's house, wife, employees, or animals will not be able to keep his hands off. With premeditation he intends to strike. That is the primary meaning of the tenth commandment.

Therefore, we may properly insist that the "coveting" of the tenth commandment lies somewhere between the disposition and the deed.[3] The deed has been condemned by the preceding commandments, especially "You shall not commit adultery" and "You shall not steal." But the tenth commandment looks behind those deeds to the passionate heart *and* to the steps a person takes to implement the plans he has forged in his heart.

---

* The Good News Bible renders Achan's excuse this way: "I wanted them so much that I took them."

Desire as a Spreading Fire

What we have discovered up to this point makes us a bit cautious in simply repeating the claim that church and state cannot punish sins against the tenth commandment since those sins belong to the inner disposition. You could compare the human heart to the boardroom of a corporation. From this room, all kinds of messages and orders proceed to various departments within the company. This boardroom is definitely not open and accessible to just anybody, but some things do leak out to others. Decisions made behind closed doors generally do not stay inside the room, so that eventually outsiders get a pretty good idea of what happened inside the room.[4]

The same thing happens with our evaluation of the human heart. That evaluation can never be complete or exhaustive. Often we miss the target. Man looks at the outward appearance, but God looks at the heart (1 Sam. 16:7), which means that we humans often judge superficially, sharply, or arrogantly, so that Jesus' word is well deserved: "Judge not, that you be not judged" (Matt. 7:1). But the illustration we used above also suggests that many times we can also evaluate what lives in the human heart. For desire does not just burn on the inside; that fire spreads. What lives in the heart never stays hidden.

Here are several examples arising from the text of the tenth commandment. "You shall not set your desire on your neighbor's *wife*," it says. What unspeakable misery enters a marriage when a husband no longer finds his own wife desirable because he is completely infatuated with another woman. Even if he denies the fact, his wife senses in all kinds of ways that something is terribly wrong. He is no longer there for her and the children, as he used to be; he is gone a lot and covers up with reasons that are no more than transparent nonsense. Even though his wife may not know everything he is brooding about in the "boardroom" of his heart, she knows enough to realize that there is another woman in his life. Perhaps it may never get as far as divorce, but even apart from divorce, a person can make a terrible mess of his marriage and family life.

"You shall not set your desire on your neighbor's *land*." When you study how many wars have been fought in history out of the desire to increase one's territory, then you understand what must have lived—and still lives—in the hearts of many emperors, kings, dictators, and their advisors. God is the One who ultimately judges the human heart, but, on the basis of the tenth commandment, we also know what goes on inside a person, when we see the kind of destruction he commits in the world. The airplane hijackings by terrorists of the Palestine Liberation Organization betray their heartfelt passion to drive the Jews from Israeli land. But more pervasive than the misery they inflict upon a countless number of victims is the cost they make the world pay for their fanatic desire: fear among millions, permanent tension in international politics, and increased security measures around the world that resemble a climate of war more than of peace.

The acts of adultery and murder are serious wrongs, but the tensions en route to both of them disrupt society even more.

Passions may rage somewhere between "inclination" and "deed" without ever reaching their goal. Think, for example, of the situation where a conspiracy to overthrow a government is hatched but never carried out. If the conspirators are collared, they can expect a severe sentence. Even though they never fired a shot or assassinated any head of state (sixth commandment), it has nevertheless become very clear what they had been setting their desire on (tenth commandment).

This is one of many examples that clarify how a government can actually pronounce a judgment on the basis of certain actions having more to do with the tenth commandment than with the sixth. What lies brooding in the human heart does become so manifest, and the harm to society so enormous, that this tenth commandment is needed to bring home to us this sin and misery.

Out of the overflow of the heart the mouth speaks, people say (see Luke 16:45). It simply cannot stay inside.

One could also say that a person's entire body reflects what is living inside him. Love of money radiates from the eyes, quickens the pulse, excites the mind, and stretches the nerves.[5] The eyes have rightly been called the mirror of the heart, and you can often read on someone's face what is going on in his heart. When the king's face is bright, that means life (Prov. 16:15); but a downcast face betrays a different state of mind (Gen. 4:5; Est. 7:6).

A Sprawling Territory

Anyone with eyes and ears has plenty to talk about if he traces the twists and turns of passion. Even though someone knows how to hide his hatred ever so well, his wicked intentions are revealed openly (Prov. 26:26). Cloaking desire and deceit with a show of right does not help. Both king and commoner fall prey to the everyday sin of covetousness, no matter how fancifully people in high positions may dress up their behavior. When a captured pirate was forced to tell Alexander the Great how he got it into his head to commit piracy and make the seas unsafe, the prisoner sneered: "I was merely doing the same as you, when you make the world unsafe. But since I work with a small ship, I am called a pirate; you are called a king, because you work with a whole fleet."[6]

You could describe the history of the human race, of entire nations and families, under the theme: "You have coveted what belonged to another." In this connection, we cannot help but think of *envy*. Our first parents desired to be like God, and their sin plunged the whole human race and the creation into misery.

Cain's envy led to the murder of his brother Abel, after God had warned Cain that sin was lying at the door, and its desire was for him. God exhorted Cain to master that desire (Gen. 4:7). But history testifies to a different reality: ever since Cain, desire masters us. If you describe world history strictly in terms of the wars people have fought, you will repeatedly stumble upon the desire for more power and more property, because people simply cannot stand it when others possess more power and more wealth than they do.

Envy generates unrest in our lives. Envy recognizes no boundaries. Envy cannot tolerate somebody having something more, even if that "something" has little value. Nathan showed David in a parable that he was envious of his neighbor's ewe lamb, even though David himself had a corral full of animals. Envy blinds a person to everything he has and allows him to see only the thing he does not have.

The territory covered by the tenth commandment is sprawling. The cares of the world, the deceptiveness of riches, and the *desire* for other things can dominate a person (Mark 4:19). Not possessing, but craving to possess, is forbidden in the Bible—not wealth itself, but *wanting* to be wealthy is the great danger (1 Tim. 6:9). Beware of all covetousness (Luke 12:15). Covetousness can so dominate a person that it should really be called a form of idolatry (Col. 3:5). It leads to shamelessness in sexuality (Eph. 4:19; 5:3), and just like the love of money, covetousness is the root of all kinds of evil (1 Tim. 6:10). Moreover, covetousness lies behind false prophets preaching their heresy (2 Peter 2:3, 14).

Christians are not immune to covetousness. Just as in the wilderness Israel longed to return to the fleshpots of Egypt (Ex. 16:3), dissatisfied as she was with the spiritual food and drink she received from God (1 Cor. 10:1–13), so too the New Testament church faces a perpetual struggle between a lifestyle led by the Spirit and a lifestyle led by the desires of the flesh (Gal. 5:16–26). The power of desire is so strong that when speaking about the "world," John refers to "the world *and* its desires" (1 John 2:17).

Covetousness appears in every day and age. Dissatisfaction with what he was and had lay behind man's fall in Paradise. The fruit of the tree was desirable, and by eating it man would become "like God" (Gen. 3:5–6). Ever since then, a voice has been whispering in every person's ear that he should have been more than he was and should have had more than he had. The forms may vary, but the substance remains the same.

Do Not Forfeit Your Freedom

The tenth commandment proclaims another message in contrast to the message of these desires. We may *not* set our desires on our neighbor's house or wife or anything else. The apocryphal book called Sirach formulates the same thing in this remarkable way: "Don't chase after your desires" (Sirach 18:30). All that hustle and bustle conflicts with the tone of the tenth commandment. Do not forfeit your freedom, which Yahweh obtained for you when He led Israel out of Egypt, out of the house of slavery.

Our explanation of the tenth commandment, just as with the others, must recall the prologue to the Decalogue. Yahweh liberated Israel, and now provides in His commandments the fence within which His people can remain genuinely free. Worshiping no other gods, observing the Sabbath, respecting authority, life, marriage, property, and the truth—all of that keeps Israel in the freedom received from the Lord. In the language of the New Testament, all of this keeps us in the freedom we have in Christ.

Thus, we can live in the bodies we have, in the houses we own, with the husband or wife God has given us, with the jobs we have. There is no objection against striving for a better position. But there is an unchristian chasing after affluence, the kind that leaves us constantly looking with a jaundiced eye at what somebody else has (more than we have). In contrast to this, the starting point of the tenth commandment is very simply this: Your own house is the best one *for you*, your own spouse is the most pretty or handsome *for you*, in your own job lies the most fruitful development of *your abilities*, even though your house may be smaller than your neighbor's, though your wife may be less attractive than other women, though your job may rank lower on the scale of values than those of your friends and acquaintances, and so on.

Advertising and Gambling

Ever since Paradise, man has been instigated by the Devil ("You will be like God") always to want to be and have more. A few paragraphs ago, we used the phrase "whispering in every person's ear" to describe this. For you see, desire can attack us, suddenly and powerfully, with silent strength. By contrast, when people try to induce us to chase after "more," that force is far from silent. One very intensive form of talking us into getting "more" is the *advertisement*. The word comes from an old French verb that meant "to warn, to give notice to," and naturally this warning was made audibly, often raucously. Advertising is a form of mass communication whose purpose is to influence the behavior of buyers in regard to consumer goods and services.

Advertising is an age-old phenomenon. The screeching market merchant has always been around. Medieval patrons bequeathing stained glass windows to a cathedral were also probably involved in advertising when they commissioned symbols and scenes from their own professions to be depicted in these workpieces. But modern advertisements are far more persuasive and pervasive. The craftsman's signboard, drawing the attention of passersby to his business, has been replaced with the psychologically well-designed television commercial, with its constant appeal to people's lust for consumption.

Advertising has become a world all its own. It has not been without its critics. Advertising is misleading, is wasteful, and fuels the capitalist engine. Advertising nurtures a mistaken consumptive mentality, and is the handiwork of "hidden persuaders" (Vance Packard), who cleverly exploit all kinds of human needs and instincts.

Nevertheless, we should be careful in making advertising the scapegoat. Someone who delivers a good product should be allowed to recommend it. Certainly advertising embodies an insidious power, but that is true with other fine things as well. Advertising can also be quite charming and rather intriguing. We should not act or talk as if advertising involves a kind of mass hypnosis capable of steering mindless zombies to the store to buy things they really do not want to have.[7] Just because children find a little fun in television commercials does not require us to pontificate ponderously about "our materialistic youth."

Some have properly observed that it is dishonest to speak only about the moral principles that should guide the advertisement *producer*. There is also the advertisement *viewer/listener* who reveals his character in the way he receives the appeal coming to him, either surrendering to it or spurning it. Advertising would have no tomorrow if today no goods and services were sold by advertising. The customer is king. Advertising and the masses are not polar opposites. The customer is king and the advertiser is his court jester. The court jester lives only by leave of the king himself.[8]

Advertisements reflect what lives within man. The beautiful and the ugly come to expression. The questionable side of advertising would not exist if *we* were different people, not driven to live as materialistically as we do today. Modern advertising is aimed squarely at that feature of the modern human personality. The remedy for that malady is not to get rid of advertising (which we could limit at best only on radio and television), but rather a Christian lifestyle that takes the tenth commandment seriously: *You* shall not covet—*you* must realize that life is more than consuming; *you* must become the master of the hidden persuaders in your life.

If it would be wrong only to criticize advertising, the situation is different with *gambling*. State-sponsored lotteries, betting pools for sporting events, pari-mutuel betting, and slot machines are a few of the forms of gambling, all of which involve spending money in the hope of receiving a large return if we are lucky. A gambler's experience and ingenuity can help increase his chances of winning. If you know next to nothing about football, your chances of winning the football pool will be far less than those of the fellow who has studied the relative strengths of the various football teams. But the variables of chance and of the draw play an important role as well.

When we discussed the third commandment, we indicated that using the variable of chance in playing games is not wrong. The older view that games involving dice had no place in a Christian home cannot be defended. Throwing dice is not a form of praying, we observed. But at this point we must see clearly the difference between using chance in playing a board game and using chance in gambling, which is designed to appeal to human greed. The latter conflicts with what the tenth commandment demands of us.

The same must be said about all those television shows where huge prizes are awarded for "achievements" seldom deserving that name. Winning a two-week vacation to the Bahamas for guessing the name of France's current president, or missing that prize just by a hair because of a wrong answer, defies all sense of proportion, because the accomplishment bears no relationship to the prize received.

Occasionally such events are associated with raising money for a good cause. The money will flow, but first a particular incentive is needed to pique the donor's interest—the chance to win a car or a trip or a color television. We must guard against covetousness, and for that reason we should be willing to show charity without getting something in return. Someone has correctly observed that charity fundraising events that offer a chance to win a big prize in exchange for a small contribution will eventually bankrupt benevolence.

We need not go so far as to condemn every gift or memento given a donor in recognition of his donation. Just as a business perquisite need not constitute a bribe, so too winning a prize at a fundraising bazaar need not taint a donor's charitable intentions. Here, simply having fun and being entertained by the element of surprise do not necessarily arouse covetousness.

When merely small gratuities are given as amenities, nobody should object. Why should a merchant not offer something to the hundredth customer entering his store, or why should a publisher not give a prize to his thousandth subscriber? But the situation becomes more difficult for a Christian storekeeper who stands to lose customers by refusing to cooperate with sales promotions involving prizes obtained through drawings, raffles, and the like. These tactics are designed to increase sales, promising huge prizes for customers who play the game. May a Christian merchant participate? It has happened that a grocer has had to reshelve an entire grocery purchase when the customer became irate at not receiving any lottery tickets as promotional items. The customer was seeking the kingdom of consumer delight, wanting still more things to fall into his lap by winning the lottery. A Christian storekeeper gives a good testimony by refusing to engage in these kinds of practices for luring customers.

A Christian lifestyle is required of us, also with regard to the tenth commandment. This is different from a nervous moralism that has no room for playing with dice or an anxious ethic that can only criticize what is no more than a fun-filled fundraising bazaar. By contrast, a Christian lifestyle does require spending money responsibly as we compare our own luxuries with the poverty predominant in a large part of the world. Realizing human need *elsewhere* can help make the enjoyment of luxuries *here* more responsible. To say it once more: Possessing is not condemned, but the desire to possess is. Therefore, we do not participate in gambling and other activities that stimulate our desire to possess, our covetousness.

The Good Desire and Autarchy

When the tenth commandment says, "You shall not covet," God is not intending to condemn every possible desire. The Bible does not propagate any form of Buddhism, whose supreme objective is freedom from everything earthly and the complete suppression of all desires. This is how man supposedly enters nirvana, a state of complete oblivion to external stimuli and internal passions.

That is not the Bible's message, not even in Matthew 6, where we are warned against worrying about tomorrow's eating, drinking, and clothing. Indeed, we can desire to meet our daily needs in such a way that we forget something still more important: "Seek first the kingdom of God and His righteousness, and all these things shall be added to you" (Matt. 6:33). In other words, certain priorities in life are easily pushed aside if we become too preoccupied with eating, drinking, and clothing.

Our "natural" desires are not sinful. Jesus Himself knew what it was to be hungry (Matt. 4:2), to be thirsty (John 19:28–29), and to need sleep (Luke 8:23). The opening chapters of the Bible and the Song of Songs speak in exalted terms about the sexual love between a husband and a wife (Gen. 2:22–23; Song of Songs).* We may long for children (Gen. 30:22–23; 1 Sam. 1:17; Ps. 127:3–5) and to improve our position (Prov. 24:27). The lazy man is covetous, but in vain; the plans of the diligent lead to plenty (Prov. 13:4; 21:5).

We may and should desire other things as well. We may thirst for God, as a deer thirsts for water (Ps. 42:1–2). One can long for God without desiring anything else on earth (Ps. 73:25). Paul desired to depart and be with Christ (Phil. 2:23). We must pursue various virtues. In this connection, Philippians 4:8 has properly been called a song of tribute to good desire:[9] "Finally, brethren, whatever things are true, whatever things are noble, whatever things are just, whatever things are pure, whatever things are lovely, whatever things are of good report, if there is any virtue and if there is anything praiseworthy—meditate on these things."

Wrong desire is in league with sin; good desire, with love.[10] Good desire lies embedded in living with Christ and is satisfied with what He gives. Throughout the centuries, this has been termed *autarchy*. This term is derived from the Greek word *autarkeia*, meaning "sufficiency." Paul declares to the Corinthians this promise: "And God is able to make all grace abound toward you, that you, always having all sufficiency in all things, have an abundance for every good work" (2 Cor. 9:8). This verse shows clearly that Christian autarchy has nothing to do with *self*-sufficiency. Paul is not speaking about philosophical or economic self-sufficiency, where someone assumes he can save himself entirely independently of others. Nor is it the self-sufficiency of the Pharisee who stands before God boasting that, compared with the publican, he can be quite satisfied with

---

* W. J. Aalders is right to point out that the forbidden desire refers not to desiring the neighbor, but to desiring something belonging to him, at a cost to that neighbor himself (*De Tien Geboden* [Zeist, 1932], 60).

himself (Luke 18:9–14). In 2 Corinthians 8:9, autarchy means that a believer has *received enough*.[11] A Christian indeed has received enough for "self," so that he or she can employ this sufficiency by overflowing in good works on behalf of God and neighbor.

This sufficiency must be *experienced* as contentment—not with oneself, but with what one has received. Godliness brings great profit, Paul writes in another place, if it is coupled with "autarchy," with contentment (1 Tim. 6:6). Paul himself knew what both poverty and abundance were, and he had learned to be "autarch" or content in every circumstance (Phil. 4:11). This contentment must not turn into a bourgeois satisfaction that finds its comfort in one's personal equilibrium. A person can be so content with his circumstances that he loses sight of the task that comes along with the gifts he receives. We have received in order to give. Christian autarchy does not rest in what it has received, but works with it.*

Penetrating More Deeply

"If we measure by the outside, the Pharisee looks like a saint; if we survey the inside, the best of saints is worthy of hell."[12] Our guilt lies buried deeply in our hearts, underneath all those desires that have become a *plan*, desires we try to realize. We have seen that "desiring," in the sense used in the tenth commandment, concerns first of all that planning stage. It concerns those desires that set a person in motion, leading him to reach for his neighbor's wife or house or property. But there is another "desiring" not easily discernible in one's behavior, though it still falls under the condemnation of the tenth commandment.

So we need to go down still more deeply to uncover the heart of the tenth commandment. Some sinful desires arise within the human spirit without setting a person in motion and without driving him to outward action. In the courtroom of human opinion, these are called "innocent thoughts" or "daydreams," but such thoughts are not so innocent before God.

Already in the Old Testament, human guilt was not restricted to visible

---

* K. Schilder pointed this out in his *Dictaat ethiek,* January 1934–June 1937 (unauthorized publication, Kampen, n.d.), 1:32: *Autarkeia* is not the kind of liberal contentment belonging to the "bourgeois satisfait," who contents himself with his life circumstances without ever being gripped by the obligation of his office before God, who requires him to bestow upon others what he has received.

actions. Some transgressions are unobserved, but nevertheless sins for which we must pray, "Cleanse me from secret faults" (Ps. 19:12). Our secret sins stand in the light of God's countenance (Ps. 90:8). We ourselves often do not realize what kind of wrongdoing dwells in our hearts: "Search me, O God, and know my heart; try me, and know my anxieties; and see if there is any wicked way in me, and lead me in the way everlasting" (Ps. 139:23–24). "The heart is deceitful above all things, and desperately wicked; who can know it?" (Jer. 17:9). Before and after the Flood, all the imaginations of man's heart were evil from his youth on (Gen. 6:5; 8:21). Evil courses through our veins! We do not merely *do* sinful things, we *are* sinful people.

Consequently, in line with these realities, Paul formulates the tenth commandment very generally: "You shall not covet," without quoting the additional specifications found in Exodus 20 and Deuteronomy 5, but rather with the observation that sin arouses *all kinds* of desires within us (Rom. 7:8). It is even the case that we live under the power of sin so much that this principle applies: "I find then a law, that evil is present with me, the one who wills to do good" (Rom. 7:21). No good desire exists without evil desire lurking nearby.

Are we then responsible for those desires that assail us? Can we help it that we glanced at another man's wife or at another person's property, and suddenly began to desire them? Can we help it that desire overwhelms us even in our dreams? Are we not responsible only for what we do intentionally and self-consciously? Are we not responsible only for those desires that we *nurture* and for the plans conceived on the basis of those desires?

Within Reformed ethics, these questions have received a radical answer. For example, H. Bastingius realized full well that some desires arise within us just as suddenly and spontaneously as dizziness overcomes someone afraid of heights who happens to look down from a tall building. Even then Bastingius held people responsible for their condition.[13]

We might join the Roman Catholic theologians who distinguish between three kinds of desire: (1) spontaneous desires, (2) nurtured desires, and (3) fulfilled desires. But in contrast to Roman Catholic doctrine, which assigns human responsibility only for nurtured and fulfilled desires, Reformed thinkers add responsibility for spontaneous desires, in line with what Paul says in Romans about man's total depravity. Not only our active desires, but also the hearth where these desires ignite into the flame of action, come under divine condemnation. Evil desires arise from an evil heart.

In 1546 the Council of Trent declared concerning spontaneous desires that they "still survived in order that we fight against them."* Such desires are—to express it with a biblical metaphor—like the Canaanites who survived after Israel had conquered the land of Canaan. They remained to test Israel. Would they be resisted or would they be left alone to do their work? Those "Canaanites" are still around, and the decisive question is simply this: How are you going to deal with them (see Judg. 2:21–22)? The same is true of spontaneous desires. In themselves, they are not sinful, but the point is that you may not give those desires a chance. We will receive the crown if we have competed according to the rules (2 Tim. 2:5)! But this analogy is not persuasive. For in the days of Israel, those Canaanites should not have been there. Israel's guilt becomes evident in the very presence of Canaanites, for Israel had been commanded to spare no one (Judg. 1:28–35; 2:2–3).

We cannot be satisfied with the excuse that we just happen to be this way—hassled all our days by sinful desires that happen to pop into our minds. Because our love toward God and our neighbor must be radical love (with all our heart, all our soul, all our mind, and all our strength, Matt. 22:37–40), *all* those storm troopers who threaten at every moment to climb from our subconscious and take control of our lives must be enlisted into the service of Christ. The issue is not simply putting our evil desires to death, but replacing those evil desires with *good* desires.

Love's radical claim is satisfied with nothing less. Consequently, the Heidelberg Catechism is not exaggerating when it asserts as a demand of the tenth commandment that "not even the slightest inclination or thought contrary to any of God's commandments shall ever rise in our heart; but that at all times we shall hate all sin with our whole heart and delight in all righteousness" (Lord's Day 44).

Understandably, every legalistic view of religion insists that this is going too far. We can well imagine that a tribal chief among the Toradjas once declared, "I would rather have the 7777 commandments and prohibitions of the Toradja *Adat* than the Ten Commandments of the Christians, for the Ten Commandments demand my whole heart, whereas the 7777 ancestral commands and prohibitions leave room for a lot of freedom!"[14]

---

* Denzinger, 792: "quae cum ad agonem relicta sit, nocere non consentientibus et viriliter per Christi Iesu gratiam repugnantibus non valet," with reference to 2 Tim. 2:5. This desire (*concupiscentia*) is termed *fomes*, dried kindling that requires ignition from without in order to burst into flame.

If we see clearly the nature of love toward God and the neighbor, then we will also see clearly how far from home we have wandered. In the light of love's radical demand, we discover our radical depravity. Along with Paul we must cry out, "O wretched man that I am! Who will deliver me from this body of death?" This is the answer he gives: "I thank God—through Jesus Christ our Lord!" (Rom. 7:24–25). That is the New Testament fulfillment of the words with which the Ten Commandments begin: "I am Yahweh your God, who has freed you from Egypt, the house of slavery."

The proper interpretation of the tenth commandment—just like that of the other nine commandments—is impossible without going back again and again to the beginning: from the house of slavery known as sin there is but one who has delivered us and can always deliver us again: Yahweh, the God of Israel, who has revealed Himself in Jesus Christ.

Endnotes

1. For example, this is what you find in the official Catechismus Romanus of 1556 (3:10), published by authority of the Council of Trent. Luther does the same in his Large Catechism (but not in his Small Catechism, where he treats these commandments separately).

2. J. Calvin, *Institutes of the Christian Religion*, 2.8.49, and the Genevan Catechism, QA 213–16.

3. J. L. Koole, *De Tien Geboden*, 2d ed. (Kampen, 1983), 142–43.

4. M. R. van den Berg, *Gij geheel anders* (Amsterdam, 1982), 99–100.

5. K. J. Popma, *Levensbeschouwing* (Amsterdam, 1963), 4:268.

6. Augustine, *De civitate Dei* 4.4.

7. A. van der Meiden, *Reclame en ethiek* (Leiden, 1975), 26.

8. Ibid., 27.

9. W. Fijn van Draat, "Het Tiende Gebod," *De thora in de thora*, 2d ed. (Franeker, n.d.), 2:188.

10. J. A. Heyns, *Teologiese etiek* (Pretoria, 1982), 1:346.

11. F. W. Grosheide, *De tweede brief aan de kerk te Korinthe* (Kampen, 1959), 258.

12. F. Ridderus, *Sevenvoudige oefeningen over de catechismus* (Rotterdam, 1671), 495.

13. H. Bastingius, *Verclaringe op den catechismus der Christelicker religie*, ed. F. L. Rutgers (Amsterdam, 1893), 657.

14. Quoted by Th. Delleman in *Sinaï en Ardjoeno*, ed. Th. Delleman (Aalten, 1946), 6–7.

Appendix:
The Use of Scripture in Ethics

Literature

Bahnsen, Greg L. *Theonomy in Christian Ethics*. Rev. ed. Phillipsburg, N.J.: Presbyterian and Reformed, 1984.

Barth, Karl. *Church Dogmatics*. 2/2, 3/4. Edinburgh: T. & T. Clark, 1957, 1961.

Bavinck, Herman. *De navolging van Christus en het moderne leven*. Kampen: Kok, 1918.

——. *Gereformeerde dogmatiek*. 4th edition. Kampen: Kok, 1930.

Berkouwer, G. C. *Sin*. Translated by Philip C. Holtrop. Studies in Dogmatics. Grand Rapids: Eerdmans, 1971.

Blank, J. "Het probleem van 'ethische normen' in het Nieuwe Testament." *Concilium* 5 (1967): 11–24.

Bockmühl, K. *Gesetz und Geist*. Giessen/Basel: Brunnen Verlag, 1987.

Childs, Brevard S. *Biblical Theology in Crisis*. Philadelphia: Westminster Press, 1970.

Douma, J. *Christian Morals and Ethics*. Winnipeg: Premier Publishing, 1981.

——. "Prof. Troost over scheppingsgeloof." *De Reformatie* 51 (1975/76): 613–95.

——. *Voorbeeld of gebod?* 4th edition. Kampen: Van den Berg, 1983.

Fabius, D. P. D. *Mosaïsch en Romeinsch recht*. Amsterdam, 1890.

Frame, J. M. *Medical Ethics*. Phillipsburg, N.J.: Presbyterian and Reformed, 1988.

Gustafson, James F. *Christian Ethics and the Community*. Philadelphia: Pilgrim Press, 1971.

——. "The Place of Scripture in Christian Ethics: A Methodological Study." In *The Use of Scripture in Moral Theology*, edited by Charles E. Curran and R. A. McCormick. New York: Ramsey, 1984.

Heyns, J. A. *Teologiese etiek*. Vol. 1. Pretoria: N. G. Kerkboekhandel Transvaal, 1982.

Hoek, J. "Het gezag van de Schrift in de ethische vragen van vandaag." *Theologia reformata* 30 (1987): 132–46.

Hoffecker, W. A. "Ethics Revealed by God." In *Building a Christian World View*, edited by W. A. Hoffecker and G. S. Smith. Vol. 2: *The Universe, Society and Ethics*. New Jersey: Presbyterian and Reformed, 1988.

Jonas, H. "Response to James M. Gustafson." In *The Roots of Ethics*, edited by D. Callahan and H. Tristram Engelhardt, Jr. New York: Plenum Press, 1976.

Kloosterman, N. D. *Scandalum infirmorum et communio sanctorum: The Relation Between Christian Liberty and Neighbor Love in the Church*. Neerlandia, Alta.: Inheritance Publications, 1991.

Krusche, W. *Das Wirken des Heiligen Geistes nach Calvin*. Göttingen: Vandenhoeck & Ruprecht, 1957.

Kuitert, H. M. "De rol van de Bijbel in de Protestantse theologische ethiek." *Gereformeerd theologisch tijdschrift* 81 (1981): 65–82.

———. *Het algemeen betwijfeld Christelijk geloof*. Baarn: Ten Have, 1992.

———. "Het schriftberoep in de ethiek." In *Anders gezegd*. Kampen: Kok, 1970.

Mieth, D. *Moral und Erfahrung*. 3d edition. Freiburg, Switzerland: Universitätsverlag, 1977.

Muether, John R. "The Theonomic Attraction." In *Theonomy: A Reformed Critique*, edited by William S. Barker and W. Robert Godfrey. Grand Rapids: Zondervan, 1990.

Neilson, L. *God's Law in Christian Ethics*. Cherry Hill, N.J.: Mack, 1979.

North, Gary. *The Dominion Covenant: Genesis*. Rev. ed. An Economic Commentary on the Bible. Vol. 1. Tyler, Tex.: Institute for Christian Economics, 1987.

Pesch, O. H. "Sittengebote, Kultvorschriften, Rechtsatzungen." In *Thomas von Aquino. Interpretation und Rezeption*, edited by W. P. Eckert. Mainz: Matthias Grünewald, 1974.

Pronk, P. *Against Nature? Types of Moral Argumentation Regarding Homosexuality*. Translated by John Vriend. Grand Rapids: Eerdmans, 1993.

Rushdoony, Rousas J. *The Institutes of Biblical Law*. Phillipsburg, N.J.: Presbyterian and Reformed, 1973.

Schilder, K. *Dictaten kompendium der ethiek*. Vols. 1–4. Compiled by G. J. Bruijn. Kampen: Van den Berg, 1980.

Schillebeeckx, Edward. *Christ: The Experience of Jesus as Lord*. Translated by John Bowden. New York: Crossroad, 1989.

Troost, A. "Christian Alternatives for Traditional Ethics." *Philosophia reformata* 38 (1973): 167–77.

———. *Geen aardse macht begeren wij*. Amsterdam: Buyten en Schipperheijn, 1975.

Velema, W. H. *Wet en evangelie*. Kampen: Kok, 1987.

Verhey, A. *The Great Reversal*. Grand Rapids: Eerdmans, 1984.

———. "The Use of Scripture in Ethics." In *The Use of Scripture in Moral Theology*, edited by Charles E. Curran and R. A. McCormick. New York: Ramsey, 1984.

Waltke, Bruce K. "Theonomy in Relation to Dispensational and Covenant Theologies." In *Theonomy: A Reformed Critique*, edited by William S. Barker and W. Robert Godfrey. Grand Rapids: Zondervan, 1990.

1. The Possibility of Using Scripture in Ethics

1.1 *The use of Scripture within Scripture itself.** The question whether we can use an appeal to Scripture in order to find proper solutions to moral problems would not have arisen in the early Christian church. Repeatedly in the New Testament writings, appeals are made to the Old Testament Scriptures for this purpose. Paul appeals to what was written in Deuteronomy 32:35 in order to convince Christians that they should not avenge themselves (Rom. 12:19). A stimulus toward a sacrificial attitude is grounded in "what is written" in Exodus 16:18 and Psalm 112:9 (2 Cor. 8:15; 9:9). Israel's experience in the wilderness is recorded as a warning for us (1 Cor. 10:11). The regulation of Deuteronomy 25:4 that a threshing ox must not be muzzled was established "for our sakes" (1 Cor. 9:9). To learn the place of women in the church, we are pointed to what the law says (1 Cor. 14:34). If the issue is marriage or the evils of divorce and prostitution, then we are directed by both Jesus and Paul to Genesis 2:24 (Matt. 19:5; 1 Cor. 7:16; Eph. 5:31). More than once the Ten Commandments are cited (Matt. 19:18f.; Rom. 13:8ff.; Eph. 6:2f.; James. 2:11).

Here we are not asking whether moral questions were answered in Scripture by other methods than an appeal to "it is written." Rather, we are limiting our discussion to the question whether an appeal to texts of Scripture was authoritative for the New Testament church. The answer is obvious. It is written in the law what one must do (Luke 10:26f.). Everyone who wants to avoid error must know Scripture (Matt. 22:29); its authority is fixed: it cannot be broken (John 10:35).

1.2 *The use of Scripture throughout church history.* What we observe with Jesus and His apostles we see happening repeatedly in subsequent history. In their reflection upon human behavior, Augustine, Thomas Aquinas, Luther, Calvin, and thousands more appeal to the authority of Scripture. As long as people continued to accept the unity of Scripture and its reliability as the Word of God, they simply assumed that an appeal to Scripture as *regula fidei et regula morum* ("the rule of faith *and* the rule of conduct") was decisive. At this point, the fact that we might often find their appeals unacceptable is not really relevant, since we realize that various behaviors were incorrectly defended by appealing to the Bible. Nor are we interested at this point in discussing the degree to which the authority of the church fathers, or of reason, or of natural law, or of conscience, or of any other standards played a role alongside the appeal to

---

* Depending on its context, the Dutch term *schriftberoep* requires various translations, as either "Scriptural warrant," "use of Scripture," or "appeal to Scripture."

Scripture or even contrary to it. Our interest is simply to observe that until our modern era, the appeal to Scripture in moral matters was considered self-evident and decisive.

The way in which the above-mentioned theologians appealed to Scripture varies. If you consult Aquinas's *Summa theologiae*, you will observe that where he deals with ethics, his use of Scripture is quite sparse. After formulating objections to a particular thesis, he often cites one or more Bible verses under the heading "Sed contra est." Clearly, by citing Bible texts, Aquinas considers the case closed by virtue of the authority inherent in the quoted passages. Of course, he continues to answer paragraph by paragraph every possible objection with the use of rea-soned arguments. Moreover, in his "Sed contra est" sections, Aquinas occasion-ally appeals to other authorities instead of the Bible, such as Augustine or "the philosopher" (Aristotle). One often wonders whether, in a given argument, any-thing would be missed if Aquinas had omitted any appeal to Scripture.

Augustine's use of Scripture is often broader and more meaningful. There are good examples of this in *De vera religione*, *De mendacio*, and *Contra mendacium*.

The close connection between moral reflection and Scripture is quite evident with Luther and Calvin. See, for example, Luther's Larger Catechism (explana-tion of the Ten Commandments) and Calvin's *Institutes* (2.8, explanation of the Ten Commandments, and 3.6ff., the Christian life). After their time, the innu-merable catechism explanations constitute abundant proof that the appeal to Scripture formed an indispensable and decisive authority in ethical as well as in doctrinal matters.

1.3 *A significant transition.* The situation changed fundamentally when many people surrendered the unity of Scripture under the influence of his-torical criticism. Faith in the one, multifaceted, but therefore still inter-nally consistent Word of God was exchanged for the conviction that the Bible is a collection of human documents containing a plurality of mutu-ally contradictory theologies (the theology of the Yahwist, of the Elohist, of Isaiah, of Mark, of John, of Paul, etc.). Attention shifted from God's message to men's perspectives.

Obviously, this had consequences not only for doctrinal reflection, but for ethical reflection as well. Publications appeared that treated Old Tes-tament ethics and New Testament ethics (seldom both together), each in turn organized according to various theologies. Thus, one book on New Testament ethics pays special attention to Jesus' eschatological ethic, an-other to the ethic of the early church, or to the Christological ethic of Paul, or the ethic of the deutero-Pauline writings and of the Johannine writings. Each group of biblical writings has its own interpretation of Jesus, leading to its own views about Christian conduct.

Moreover, comparing biblical precepts with those of nations surrounding both Israel and the early Christian church yields the view that the Bible supposedly offers little that cannot be found elsewhere. Were not the household regulations in the New Testament, for example, simply a faithful reproduction of Stoic ethics?

Beside the opinion that Scripture was not so unique and its morality not so distinct, a particular development in philosophy further strengthened the sentiment that the age-old view about using Scripture in ethics was outdated for good. Especially as a result of existentialist philosophy, it became impossible any longer to speak of fixed truths and moral directives that were valid for all times. No book of universally valid prescriptions and prohibitions could be inserted into the I-Thou relation between God and man or between people themselves. The old viewpoint was characterized as "idealist," and had to give way to an existentialist viewpoint in which human actions must be characterized by freedom and self-realization, apart from fixed patterns of behavior.

We find a clear example of moral reflection colored by existentialism in Karl Barth. According to him the command of God is "the particular command which faces each of our decisions, the specially relevant individual command for the decision which we have to make at this moment and in this situation." Barth says, "The command of God meets us not in the form of rules, principles, fundamental precepts, or universal moral truths, but in the form of pure historically unique and temporally concrete commands, prohibitions, and directives."

This kind of situation ethics renders impossible a direct appeal to Bible texts that are universally valid. Barth rejects any kind of obedience tied to moral rules from Scripture and accepts only the kind of obedience to the command of the Person of the living God reaching the individual in a very direct and very concrete sense (*mandatum concretissimum*) (*Church Dogmatics*, 2/2:662, 669).

1.4 *From text to paradigm.* Was every appeal to Scripture impossible after the transition we have just described? For anyone who values the term "Christian" and still wants to be a theologian, such a result is of course impossible. Instead, we observe that something quite different happened. Those who could no longer accept the unity of Scripture found themselves compelled to construct or manufacture that unity. As a special book, the Bible continued to function as the pillar undergirding Christian reflection. But a particular motif or theme in the Bible acquired the status of being the core or center of the gospel. The authority once ascribed to the whole Scripture as God's Word now applies to only a selection. Thereby it remained possible to continue appealing to Scripture, as long as this appeal could pass through the sieve of what people considered central to Scripture. Texts made room for themes or—formulated in more contemporary fashion—for paradigms.

The authority ascribed to such paradigms can hardly remain unchallenged, if for no other reason than the multiplicity of these paradigms. Simply choosing a paradigm and legitimizing it with the claim "The Bible's primary concern is . . ." immediately presents us with an unavoidable question. Let us assume for the sake of discussion that we can no longer say, by way of a direct appeal to Bible texts, "This is what God wants of us." Can we then say this on the basis of a paradigm that we have distilled from the very same Bible? How can one legitimize his claim to be speaking on the basis of a particular paradigm about the "binding authority of revelation" (Blank) or the "immutability of God's will" (Kuitert)? Are these not qualifications of paradigms formed on the basis of particular biblical information? Why does one permit himself the liberty of appealing to divine authority this way, but not when discussing the whole content of Scripture? What legitimate criterion exists for this particular selection?

J. Blank (1967: 20ff.) presents a case for working with "ethical paradigms." The precepts in the New Testament are historically and sociologically antiquated, but from such historically limited circumstances and precepts viewpoints can be derived, according to Blank, which point "as a typical paradigm" beyond those circumstances. As a fixed revelational-historical type it supposedly protects the binding character of the revelation that must be required from Scripture. At the same time, as a "type" it supposedly makes possible the freedom of reflection on the "typical" which in turn requires a new explanation for each age. As an "ethical paradigm," the New Testament ethos would serve as a pointer.

H. M. Kuitert (1970: 85f.) agreed with Blank. He too found the most responsible hermeneutical grasp of biblical commands in the portrayal of these commands as "examples of earlier faith-obedience" (W. Schweitzer), or as ethical paradigms. Such phrases discount "the immutability of God's will without becoming unhistorical and also the reverse: they honor the historicity of biblical paranesis without falling directly into a situational ethic" (1970: 86).

Specific paradigms include, for example, the *Exodus* paradigm and the *Sermon on the Mount* paradigm. See Schillebeeckx (1989: 553, 597), who says of such paradigms that in them, "we find an ethical sensibility which, inspired by the Christian view of the grace of God, the faith and the disquiet of love, and driven by eschatological hope, becomes the realization of salvation in a lost world" (1989: 597).

We can use the Exodus paradigm to illustrate just how selective a paradigm can be. The exodus from Egypt has become the locus classicus of liberation theology. "Let my people go!" is its cry. But in this modern theological call to liberating action, there is virtually universal silence about the need for faith in, and conversion to, God. When James Gustafson once wrote, "Where there is oppression God wills liberation; where there are movements for liberation, there is the presence of God," H. Jonas replied (1976: 200f.) that this must be said differently: "Where there is oppression, God wills liberation—*on condition* of a 'covenant,' i.e., on the condition that the liberated will henceforth serve Him, i.e., that liberation is charged with a new obligation." When we sing "Let my people go!" we must ask immediately, "Go *where?*" "Mount Sinai, not the Golden Calf, was the divine interest in the liberation," Jonas said.

One could make similar remarks concerning ethical systems that work with the *love* paradigm. Understandably, love (as the "great and first commandment," Matt. 22:38) occupies a central place in Christian ethics. But by what right does anyone ascribe biblical authority to the theme of love when his concrete applications bring him into open conflict with biblical commandments, as in the situation ethics of Joseph Fletcher?

The route from text to paradigm is clearly evident also in Karl Barth. From what we have quoted of him in §1.3, it is already clear that for him, too, the route formerly traveled in appealing to Scripture is no longer passable. If we had no more from Barth than what was quoted in §1.3, then it would be inexplicable how appealing to Scripture from his actualistic starting point is possible at all. But in reality Barth himself continually appeals to Scripture in those ethical sections of his *Church Dogmatics* (1957, 1961), in spite of his talk about "the many events of the encounter between God's command and human action in a singularity and uniqueness which cannot be anticipated and which scorn regimentation" (1961: 17). How then does Barth justify the hundreds of pages where, with continual and extensive appeals to Scripture, he provides directives that are anything but singular and unique?

This is possible because Barth pays attention to the *horizontal* line alongside the *vertical* line. That is to say, Barth inquires about the continuity and constancy of the divine commanding and the human acting, about which we can speak in terms of Scripture. We know God as Creator, Reconciler, and Redeemer; we know man as creature, sinner, and child of the Father. Ethics describes not only the *point* indicating the event of the encounter between God and man, but also the *field* in which this event occurs (27). Therefore, we need not settle for "a monotonous, colourless and formless reference to the vertical" (19f.), since as a "commentary" on the history between God and man, ethics can provide us with a definite lead ("*geformter* Hinweis") (26, 30–31).

This "definite lead" is to be found nowhere else than in Scripture. But, at the same time, by equating the Word of God with Jesus Christ, Barth selects what must then provide legitimacy for his appeal to Scripture made on the basis of his imposingly constructed Christology.

For the rest, it still remains valid that "to make decisions about the content of the divine command and good and evil in human action cannot be the task of ethics, nor can it be suggested to us by a knowledge of the spheres in which divine command and human action take place. More than the general form of the particular truth of the ethical event . . . cannot be the content of this knowledge" (30). We can lead in the *direction* of an answer, but the *answer itself* each person must provide in his relationship to God and his fellowman.

When you study Barth's ethics, however, you will discover that in many cases he talks about God's command for everybody. He does indeed talk about the *mandatum concretissimum;* but we fail to understand why in many instances he could not speak just as well about what might be called the *mandatum generalissimum*—when he deals, for example, with discussions about Sunday (47–72), about prayer (87–115), about monogamy, which Barth characterizes as "self-evident" (195–203), about the prohibition of homosexuality (166), about suicide (404–12), about abortion (415–23), and so forth. If in such matters God's command is so clear for everybody, how can he maintain the "singularity and uniqueness" of the *mandatum concretissimum* without bringing God into conflict with Himself?

Barth is perhaps the most impressive example of a theologian who, on the one hand, wants to distance himself from the centuries-old way of appealing to Scripture and, on the other hand, comes up with opinions bearing a strong resemblance to what is condemned in others as biblicism.

1.5 *Biblicism.* We have seen that even modern theologians appeal to Scripture for their ethics, no matter how selectively they proceed. Thereby they admit that using Scripture is possible. They reject biblicism, but apparently not every appeal to the Bible. By *biblicism* we understand that appeal to Scripture which uses Bible texts in an atomistic (isolated) way by lifting them out of their immediate contexts or out of the whole context of Scripture.

Much biblicism is characterized by its neglect of the difference in circumstances between then (the time in which the texts being cited were written) and now. The consequence is that biblicism is thoroughly conservative.

Here are a few less modern examples of biblicism: Tertullian (*De cultu feminarum,* 2,7) found it improper for women to wear hairpieces made from someone else's hair. For proof he referred to Matthew 6:27, from which Tertullian inferred that it is forbidden to increase not only one's height but also one's weight by, as it were, allowing "some kind of rolls, or shield-bosses, to be piled upon your necks" (see *The Ante-Nicene Fathers* [Buffalo: The Christian Literature Publishing Company, 1885], 4:21). The curse of Ham (Gen. 9:25) has been used often to justify slavery (of blacks, for example). The eight-hour workday was opposed with an appeal to Jesus' words that we must work as long as it is day (John 9:4a), which means "for twelve hours." A five-day work week was thought to contradict the command to work six days (Ex. 20:9). Nationalizing land has been rejected with an appeal to Ahab's stealing of Naboth's vineyard (1 Kings 21). Using dice for games has been condemned because Proverbs 16:33 ("The lot is cast into the lap, but its every decision is from the LORD") is thought to teach that the lot is sacred.

Not every form of biblicism bears marks of conservatism. On the basis of my definition of biblicism, we can with equal right call, for example, the Exodus paradigm a form of modern biblicism. See §1.4. This example shows also that it is a mistake to think that biblicism appears only in circles that people today term "fundamentalistic."

1.6 *Inherent biblicism?* It would be a hopeless situation if by definition every appeal to Scripture were biblicistic. For then a pure appeal to Scripture in ethics would be simply impossible. In fact, H. M. Kuitert and others are of this opinion. According to Kuitert, the standard in terms of which anyone distinguishes between those texts in the Bible which contribute to the construction of a biblical worldview, and those texts which do not, is formed by the "cultural point of view" that the reader adopts already before coming to the Bible.

Here is a radical departure from viewing Scripture as the authoritative and foundational court of appeal for ethics. This perspective views biblicism as something quite different from the atomistic use of Bible texts, a use that can and should be replaced with a better use of Scripture. Rather, biblicism is here defined simply as using *any* Bible texts or *any* premises appearing in the Bible to support an ethical argument (Kuitert 1981: 71). According to this view, biblicism is inherent in every appeal to Scripture in ethics.

In this view, the Bible cannot be employed as it has been in earlier centuries, but neither can it be used in the way contemporary paradigm thinkers use it. The Bible might be significant for other purposes, but apparently no longer for the answers we need about good and evil.

Already in his 1970 publication (63ff.) Kuitert spotted behind the seemingly arbitrary use of Scripture on the part of writers like Calvin a working concept of *lex naturalis (moralis)*, which functioned as a hermeneutical key "in order to separate, within the whole chaos of biblical commands, the temporary, historically determined command from the non-historically determined, universally valid ones" (1970: 72). Calvin and his cohorts supposedly did nothing else than "scrap what they could not use from the totality of biblical commands, and keep what in their estimation was necessary for human society of their own day. *Lex moralis* = the moral order as they thought a Christian order should look like in that day" (1970: 74).

In 1970 Kuitert did not yet reject every appeal to Scripture in ethics, and he

was comfortable with paradigm thinking. For him, then, biblicism was an atomistic use of Scripture that failed to see Scripture according to its true nature (1970:
77). But in a 1981 essay he went further, as we mentioned above. According to
Kuitert, the Bible exists not for its moral, but for its story. For knowing what we
may and may not do, we are no longer directed to the Bible (1981: 81; see also
1992: 267f., 289).

In the 1981 essay, Kuitert made "a remarkable discovery": If you put the (Protestant) ethics which claim to be based on special revelation alongside (Roman
Catholic) ethics which claim to be based on natural law, you can hardly see any
significant differences (1981: 80f.). Naturally, this confirms Kuitert's conviction
that the same cultural starting point must lead to the same destination, with or
without appealing to the Bible.

In Kuitert's line stands P. Pronk (1993: 283), who claims that with *every* appeal to Scripture we do not *deduce* our standpoint from the Bible, but rather *read
it back into* the Bible. According to him, our moral viewpoint precedes our theological perspective. One begins with his moral viewpoint even before theology
and its accompanying appeal to Scripture are invoked (1993: 301ff.).

1.7 *Our own position (1)*. When it comes to formulating our own position
concerning the relationship between ethics and appealing to Scripture,
our starting point is faith in the unity and reliability of the Word of God.
This is a clear presupposition, although by itself it does not resolve all
questions involving our use of Scripture (presuming they can ever be resolved). But this presupposition is something completely different from a
"cultural starting point" which functions in ethics to permit Scripture to
say what culture has already said. Anyone believing in the power of the
still-living Word of God, which by the work of the Holy Spirit is sharper
than a two-edged sword (Heb. 4:12), believes also that it is possible for
people who are gripped by the Holy Spirit and moved by the testimony of
Scripture to be converted and thereafter to demonstrate another pattern
of behavior. Such a believer sees in the life pattern of Luther, Calvin, and
their followers, for example, the outworking of a new and better reading
of Scripture. History teaches that people (and thus we, too) can be converted from an incorrect and often biblicistic use of Scripture.

Doctrine and life should not be separated—neither should dogmatics
and ethics. Why may we use proof-texts in systematic theology and not in
ethics?

By itself, the discovery that in a culture still strongly stamped by Christianity, ethics grounded in God's revelation and ethics not so grounded should come to similar conclusions is not so remarkable. The same thing is happening here as

happened with the proofs for God's existence: people could act as if they had proved God's existence by means of reason, but because people were Christians who accepted the Bible, the conclusion about the existence of God had already been reached before it was proved. This is how it goes with Roman Catholic ethics, no matter how much they rely on natural law. The similarity of their system to ethical systems based on Scripture is understandable, not because they rely on natural law, but because their system belongs to the category of Christian ethics.

But what would happen if *today* we would pursue a similar investigation in our much more strongly secularized society? What would happen if we used for that investigation a comparison of, *on the one hand*, the conclusions of our own ethical system plus those of ethical systems originating from orthodox Roman Catholics (grounded in natural law or not) with, *on the other hand*, the results of Kuitert's ethical system plus those of ethical systems built by liberal Roman Catholics? Would not the difference be much greater than in the comparison Kuitert had in view between ethical systems of at least forty years ago? Among other things, would not the differing judgment regarding matters like abortion, euthanasia, premarital sexual intercourse, and homosexuality indicate that a common "cultural starting point" no longer exists, and that it is precisely the appeal to Scripture made by one side that prevents its adherents from accepting the cultural starting point of the other side?

1.8 *Our own position (2)*. Although appealing to Scripture in ethics is possible without thereby necessarily being a biblicist, the history of Christian ethics shows more than adequately just how frequent and dangerous a biblicistic use of Scripture can be. We all read the Bible as we stand within a tradition; nobody begins with an empty slate, and everybody's tradition generates some difficulties in terms of using Scripture. But what is decisive is whether we give the last word to our "cultural starting point" or to Scripture. The fact that we accept the whole Bible as the Word of God does not mean that we would not do any selecting, in contrast to advocates of paradigm solutions. In the following section, you will see that it is impossible simply to take over everything that Scripture, from Genesis to Revelation, commands and forbids. Moreover, dealing with the Bible requires something other than obedience to a legal code that needs merely to be fleshed out from the Bible.

Nor is the difference between the selectivity of paradigm thinking and our use of Scripture simply that advocates of paradigms pay attention to their own day and age, while we can suffice with Scripture alone. We too must consider the "cultural starting point" and use our understanding to find various answers not given by Scripture itself. The difference is rather that paradigm defenders selectively remove data out of Scripture as being unbelievable or antiquated on the basis of their cultural starting point, without beforehand being able to advance from Scripture itself well-grounded reasons for their decision.

Here is an example to clarify the difference in principles of selection: One who views as outdated every difference in rank between husband and wife in marriage comes into conflict with clear declarations of Scripture (1 Cor. 11:2ff.; Eph. 5:22ff.; Col. 3:18; 1 Tim. 2:9ff.; 1 Peter 3:1). The headship of the husband over the wife is anchored by Paul in the Creation (1 Tim. 2:13; 1 Cor. 11:9). But this has become unacceptable to modern thinking. So what do people do? Supposedly the texts listed above can no longer function today. If people nevertheless wish to appeal to the Bible to defend the complete equality of man and woman, they begin to select: the texts mentioned are no longer authoritative, but are overshadowed by other texts like Galatians 3:28 ("There is neither male nor female . . . in Christ"). Such selectivity is completely arbitrary and necessarily leads to playing off the writer (Paul) against himself in order to maintain the appearance of appealing to Scripture.

Kuitert (1981: 72) points to this example and correctly observes that the "cultural starting point" is deciding the issue at this juncture. However, he is incorrect to insist that the cultural starting point is always decisive, so that maintaining scriptural proof as an authority within ethics becomes meaningless. For we can *resist* the cultural starting point by holding fast to the order between husband and wife because Scripture says some things about it that remain valid for us.

But where this latter is not the case, we will have to deal with the cultural starting point. Earlier, we saw that there is a kind of biblical morality in the sense of "people used to do that," which does not obligate us to do it that way now (ceremonial actions, vigilante justice, polygamy, slavery, and the like). That can also be valid for giving expression to the relationship between male and female, without thereby denying the headship of the husband. In the *maintenance* of the universally fundamental order between husband and wife, much has changed.

2. The Method of Using Scripture in Ethics

2.1 *Varieties of Scripture usage*. The preceding discussion suggested already that our use of Scripture will need to show some variety. Often we can appeal very directly to the Bible. In such cases, we speak about Scripture as a *guide* (§2.2).

We cannot always appeal so directly to Scripture. But also in matters about which Scripture provides no direct evaluation, we can still appeal to Scripture. In addition to being a guide, it is also a *guard* (§2.3–4) that does not point out the way (positively), but rather warns (negatively).

In the third place, we can use Scripture as a *compass* (§2.5–6) that points out the direction we must walk, without specifying what exactly must happen. Scripture points to constant factors that can serve as directives for our actions.

In the fourth place, we can use Scripture for its *examples* (§2.7–8). From the examples provided us by Christ and others flow forth not particular actions as such, but a much more general Christian ethos.

2.2 Scripture as guide. In many cases, our appeal to Scripture provides no difficulties, because a simple reference to Scripture can suffice. Like many other commands and prohibitions, the command to love our neighbor and the prohibitions against murdering him, and against stealing or lying, can be substantiated with a clear appeal to Scripture texts as *loca probantia* (proof-texts).

Whatever difficulty we face in not living in anger with our brother (Matt. 5:22), in being friendly toward our adversary (5:25), in not looking at a woman lustfully (5:28), and in loving our enemy (5:44ff.)—this difficulty lies not in the obscurity of God's (Christ's) will, but in ourselves. Making a simple appeal to the Decalogue, or quoting an adage from Proverbs or a saying of Jesus from the Sermon on the Mount, can tell us in a number of situations exactly what God's Word is for us or for others.

In all these cases, Scripture functions as a *guide*. Just as in a mountainous region we take along a map to indicate the passable route and to warn us about the impassable route, so Scripture functions in many situations as a guide who tells us specifically what good and evil lie in our path.

2.3 Scripture as guard (1). Often a direct appeal to Scripture is not possible. When you take into account the great difference in situation between the biblical time and now, you will admit this. Husbands and wives, parents and children, governments and citizens, now deal with one another in different ways than in biblical times. Then fathers arranged their daughters' marriages (1 Cor. 7:36ff.), something we today would find strange. Today we view slavery, which is certainly limited but not condemned in the Bible, as an evil. Even good kings like David did not shrink from torturing their enemies (2 Sam. 12:31), while today we pay attention to human rights and such things. Freedom of religion, or the right to change religion, was unimaginable within Israel. A democratic system of government is nowhere recommended in the Bible. At the same time, given the changes in family relationships, the development and refinement of judicial legislation, the rise of human rights, and the spread of democracy, it is impossible to return to the situations prevailing in Bible times.

It would be saying too much to argue that the developments toward a better jurisprudence, better forms of government, and the like constitute extensions of *Scripture*. For Scripture nowhere summons people to make these changes that we have mentioned. They certainly constitute extensions of *history*, which sooner or later drives cultures with irresistible force toward the modification of outdated structures. This happened with religious persecution, slavery, child labor, and colonialism. Various Christian, but also non-Christian, influences have played a role in the process of raising awareness leading to major changes in human society. The correctness of many such changes is evident to everybody, though to one person more quickly than to another.

If at this point Scripture cannot function as a guide, but does serve without the possibility of a direct appeal to the Bible, this does not mean that, in matters like those mentioned above, the Bible plays no role. For how must we explain the fact that Christians accept these various changes as evidently necessary? Because without being a manual for various cultural changes and improvements, Scripture is nevertheless a guard that warns against corrupt developments. Old Testament prophets left behind no blueprint for political and social relationships, but they certainly denounced abuses where God was not being honored and people were not being respected. Scripture does not choose for or against democracy and other matters that we today value highly. But the Bible does sharpen our vision for seeing where people are abused and oppressed, regardless of political or economic system.

Therefore, we can speak of Scripture as a *guard* alongside the use of Scripture as a guide; this guard warns us against despising God and oppressing people.

In the "impingement" of developments that we find naturally acceptable, we may trace the work of God and His Spirit. We know God from special revelation in Holy Scripture, but we also know Him as He reveals Himself in the creation and in the history of the world. In order to form our moral judgment in many situations, it is not enough simply to know the Bible. We must also know the history in which God reveals Himself ("general revelation").

When we speak of what is "evident," that does not mean for us something that is automatically apparent to human consciousness. We do not find something evident simply because it is the consequence of a process that enjoys the agreement of the majority. What is evidently good is not what surveys reveal to be the opinion of the majority (e.g., in connection with abortion and euthanasia). For example, many people today, even some theologians, believe that homosexual relations can no longer be condemned because this phenomenon impinges upon us as an evident expression of someone's psychological formation, something not yet known to Bible writers.

But what if Scripture condemns homosexual relations? Then we do not have the right to consider them permissible. So then, the simple fact that something impresses many people as being good is not the last word. But some things do impress human consciousness as being good, so that we can connect these things *simultaneously* with God's leading of history aimed at the restraint of evil and the development of the good.

2.4 *Scripture as guard (2)*. In "reading" history, we can make mistakes. Did not German Christians say that God's will could be read in Hitler's rise to power? Was that not for them an "impingement" of God's revelation? Using this example, we can clarify what it means that Scripture is a guard for us. Hitler's national-socialist ideology, with its practice of Jewish persecution and territorial expansion, clearly contradicted the "critical" meaning of Scripture (thus its function as guard), so that we would consider it blasphemy to connect Hitler's conduct with God's name. Scripture always retains its critical function, even when it provides no specific prescriptions (when it does not function as guide), whereby we are taught to eliminate slavery and colonialism, to choose democracy above aristocracy, and to practice capital punishment less frequently than in ancient Israel or perhaps not at all. Scripture does not always declare what is good in a particular situation, but even so it can still show us what is evil in that situation.

2.5 *Scripture as compass (1)*. Thirdly, Scripture is also a *compass*, indicating the direction we should be traveling to find an answer to the question of what is good or evil in a specific situation. The Bible as guide and the Bible as compass are related as the answer itself is related to the direction(s) for finding the answer.

Take, for example, new problems facing us today, like DNA-research and in vitro fertilization. Does Christian ethics have anything to contribute here? After all, Scripture says nothing about DNA, in vitro fertilization, and many similar modern questions. But even when we can find no verse in the Bible that speaks about DNA discoveries, there are biblical *themes* that can be applied to these questions. Consider the themes of creation and of the place of man in creation. Anyone who reflects on modern issues like in vitro fertilization and genetic engineering will need to take into account what we read in the Bible about man as creature of God, about marriage as a monogamous institution, and similar matters. One begins to realize that the Bible contains *constant principles* that remain valid for every age, factors that are therefore also relevant for our judgment about the most advanced scientific developments.

The difference between this and the appeal to Scripture as a guide we have already indicated above. But we would like also to illustrate the difference between this and the appeal to Scripture as a guard. This latter appeal is certainly relevant when it comes to the modern issues we have mentioned. When in vitro fertilization involves selecting embryos, which after all are persons in development, the guard calls out: "Thou shalt not kill." But, while the guard warns us about what we must *not* do, the compass indicates those themes which help us discover what we *must* do.

Using specific Bible verses and appealing to general themes are not necessarily contradictory. Thus, using the Bible as a guide does not contradict using the Bible as a compass. Heyns (1982: 169) correctly terms it a false dilemma to say, "We must work scripturally rather than textually." Anyone who appeals to a biblical theme must be able to muster textual support for that theme. Using isolated verses leads to biblicism, as we have seen. But using themes apart from verses would lead to speculation. Nevertheless, although we cannot separate the guide-function of Scripture from its compass-function, we can distinguish them. A direct appeal to the Bible in reference to matters like DNA is impossible, but indirect appeal is certainly possible.

Here we encounter those *constant principles* that Schilder spoke about in his definition of ethics (1980: 16; see Douma, 1981: 26): "Ethics is the science which investigates the constant principles, the changing dispensations and the relevant, concrete specificity of the obligation of the human will for obedience to God's revealed will." With the phrase "constant principles" (grounds), Schilder was referring to those fundamental principles that remain valid amid every change: Man is a creature; man (in contrast to the animals) is brought into covenant with God; man is God's image bearer; and so forth.

Heyns (1982: 159ff.) is less clear when he speaks of ten biblical coordinates. He describes them as the context within which the Bible's precepts can truly become relevant for today. What we stated above concerning Scripture as guide and as guard already suggests that we do not need coordinates first before biblical precepts become relevant. Moreover, Heyns's choice of coordinates is so diverse that in our opinion they cannot be used efficiently in practice. Heyns mentions: (1) divine authority, (2) the covenant, (3) the historical existence of a people, (4) the historical relationships among nations, (5) the historical revelation of redemption, (6) the perpetual and the changing elements, (7) the paradigms and norms of obedience, (8) the leading activity of the Spirit and the creative activity of the believer, (9) the total intention of revelation, and (10) the total realm of revelation (that is, the individual believer exists within the fellowship of the church). See also the critique of Velema (1987: 75). We wonder whether these coordinates can in fact be derived from Scripture (especially coordinates 3 and 4).

2.6 Scripture as compass (2). Often Scripture gives us the direction we must
go, but for determining within that general orientation what is and is not
responsible, we are left to our own understanding of the issue and to our
own insight. We must employ our own understanding in order to arrive at
correct decisions. Naturally, that applies as well to matters illuminated for
us by Scripture's function as guide or as guard. But that happens to a larger
degree with circumstances involving progress and new developments.
What then is the relationship between using our understanding and using
Scripture?

Calvin distinguishes between the *ratio ingenita*, which everyone has by
nature; the *ratio vitiosa*, which results from human depravity; and the *tertia
ratio*, which is led by the Word and Spirit. The *ratio ingenita* can lead people to good insights and good behavior in various circumstances, even
though they do not know the Bible. Calvin and others have always connected this possibility to divine providence and to the gifts distributed
among men by the Holy Spirit (Krusche, 1957: 95ff.). For various moral
developments, the *ratio ingenita* can be of positive interest, while the *ratio
vitiosa* operates destructively. But, at the same time, the Christian allows
himself to be led in the use of his *tertia ratio* by the Spirit and the Word in
Scripture.

It is precisely the knowledge of those constant factors as the Bible
speaks about them that prevents us from thinking that various new situations will embarrass us as Christians. Perhaps new issues seem to demand
a complete reorientation, so that appeal to the Bible is no longer possible.
In fact, however, the moral decision will be determined by our answer to
the question whether we will hold fast to Scripture as our compass.

What is involved here is not the use of *paradigms*, against which we raised our objections in §1.4ff. Although we reject the paradigms selected by higher criticism,
we can nevertheless pay meaningful attention to elementary biblical givens like
those mentioned above, using them as coordinates for our moral reflection. It certainly seems strange that some advocates of the school of Reformational philosophy reject any appeal to Scripture in the field of ethics on the basis of what they
call *creational faith*. Although they reject paradigm ethics, even as we do, because
they accept the Bible as the Word of God, nevertheless they do consider it rationalistic and scholastic to appeal to the Bible in connection with various specific
questions.

For example, A. Troost declares that Scripture is the Word of God, that life
outside of Christ disintegrates, and that we are directed to the one revelation in
Christ (1975: 44f., 96, 138). But at the same time, he considers it a reactionary
desire to search for the proper scientific direction and vision needed for our mod-

ern problematic "directly from Scripture" (88). We can agree with him insofar as this word "directly" refers to the kind of appeal to Scripture addressed in §2.2 (Scripture as guide).

But Troost goes beyond this. According to him, Scripture is given merely for the strengthening of our faith, so that by means of this strengthening of our faith, we come to the position of being able to read the revelation in creation and to discover the normative structures, even though our work always remains unfinished (105). It is science which uncovers the irreducible aspects of the totality of human life—in great diversity God created everything "according to its nature" (127); science, not the Bible, tells us what we must do in a particular situation. The Bible tells us nothing else than to look upon Christ and to believe in Him (1973: 175). There is certainly a "tertia ratio," but one that is fed and filled with knowledge taken from creational structures and not from Scripture.

This view generates a number of questions, as we have explained elsewhere (1975/1976: 613ff.). Here we will restrict ourselves to the matter of appealing to Scripture. Is it not strange that this advocate of the school of Reformational philosophy thinks he can refer to Genesis 1 in order to abstract the irreducibility of normative structures (everything is created "according to its nature"), while in ethics we have no right to go to the Bible to discover norms for a specific structure like marriage (monogamy, homosexuality and heterosexuality, the unity expressed through intercourse and marriage, etc.)? The sharp opposition between professing Christians and non-Christians over these and other matters would be simply unimaginable if Scripture had nothing to say about such matters. But it does have something to say, for the Bible is more than a lens which corrects our blurred vision in order to provide a clear view of creational structures. The Bible provides also a *content* that is indispensable for a correct view of specific structures.

2.7 *Scripture provides examples* (1). We must be impressed by the fact that Scripture often points us to the example others have given. We must follow in the footsteps of the saints whose lives are described in the Old and New Testaments (Luke 4:25ff.; 1 Cor. 10:1ff.; Phil. 3:17; 2 Thess. 3:9; Heb. 6:12; Heb. 11–12:1ff.; James 5:17f.). The great example is Christ Himself (Matt. 16:24; 19:21; John 13:15; 1 Cor. 11:1; 1 Peter 2:21).

If we would use the Bible only in the senses explained above, as guide, guard, and compass, we would shortchange its relevance for our moral conduct. For Scripture is more than a book for gathering verses to defend or oppose certain actions. It is the book of the covenant between God and man; it tells us the history of God's redemption of man through Christ. It shows us how through faith we are engrafted into fellowship with Christ and His own. Within this fellowship, the Christian ethos is born. We could also say that in following Christ and His people, *virtue* is born.

When we are told the story of Christ and of all who have followed Him, we are moved to act: "But you have not so learned Christ, if indeed you have heard Him and have been taught by Him, as the truth is in Jesus" (Eph. 4:20–21).

The importance of example appears from the fact that the apostles do more than repeat what "is written." In situations where a simple appeal to the Decalogue would have sufficed, they point to our life "in Christ." The one can go together with the other. In Ephesians 6:2f., Paul points to the fifth commandment, but he does not begin there. The first thing he says is, "Children, obey your parents *in the Lord* [Jesus]" (Eph. 6:1). As in so many other situations, the main idea here is that of following Christ. The Christian must walk differently from the pagan, not (only) because the Ten Commandments require this of him, but because he has learned to know Christ (Eph. 4:20). He must have an attitude of forgiveness, even as God in Christ has forgiven him (Eph. 4:32). He must find out what is pleasing to Christ (Eph. 5:10). In their marriage, husband and wife must reflect the relationship between Christ and His church (5:22ff.). Christians must flee fornication because their bodies are members of Christ (1 Cor. 6:3ff.).

A proper use of Scripture must always include wanting to abide in a living relationship with Christ and His church.

When the ancient church was confronted with the problem of abortion, she did not possess a norm, but certainly a paradigm (example), namely the unconditional acceptance of human life from God, according to Mieth (1977: 85). The example of Jesus' love toward lepers, toward the blind and the deaf, toward women and children, was for the ancient church impressive enough for her to determine her position in this matter spontaneously. Kuitert's conclusion that the Bible is given to us for its story rather than its moral (see §1.6) should rather be that the Bible is given to us for both, but in the proper order: first the story and then the moral that arises from the story. Ethics without proclamation is blind, just as proclamation without ethics is empty (Smelik, 1967: 13). It is not example *or* command, but example *and* command.

2.8 Scripture provides examples (2). The example of Christ and His followers summons us to be united to the church as His body, so that in and with that *fellowship* we may search for God's will. This is certainly of interest with regard to our reflection on the matter of the Christian lifestyle. A simple appeal to Bible verses is impossible in many instances. Taking into account the example of the preceding generation as well as our own with regard to questions of proper Christian lifestyle is not being old-fashioned, but testifies to respect for the fellowship of the church, within which we are not the first who know Christ and read Scripture.

But the example that Christians gave and give is not always worth following. Within the church of Christ, differences of insight and corresponding differences in conduct remain. Occasionally the differences can be so serious that on the basis of clear pronouncements of Scripture, they cannot be allowed to continue alongside each other. But this does not apply to every difference, and in such cases we must exercise great care. In such circumstances, we may not say to each other, "Thus says the Lord!" or, "The Lord wants you to behave this way and not that way!" Paul's discussion of the conflict between the "strong" and the "weak" in the earliest Christian congregations (Rom. 14f.; 1 Cor. 8ff.) is very instructive for us. He holds before these Christians that each must be convinced in his own mind (Rom. 14:5), and that the one must accept the other in spite of differences of insight and conduct (Rom. 15:7; 1 Cor. 8:1). The conduct of the one Christian does not need to be followed by the other Christian, though as members of Christ's church they must certainly respect each other's behavior.

With reference to the "strong" and the "weak" in Romans 14 and 15, Hoek writes (1987: 145f.):

> We must leave room where we sense that our knowledge is partial, where also Bible-believing interpreters occasionally demonstrate significant differences in the interpretation of certain texts, as well as in their definition of the abidingly normative core of certain commandments. We must allow room in view of the tangled and often frustrating character of the questions put to us today.

The boundaries of this room lie "where people no longer wish to be held accountable by the full content of Scriptures."

Kloosterman (1991: 72ff.) understands the weakness of the "weak" mentioned in Romans 14 and 1 Corinthians 8–10 not to be *culpable* weakness, which would need to be removed through further instruction. According to him, weakness consists of "an incapacity for a particular moral undertaking caused by a knowledge deficient in applying certain elements of the Christian faith to life" (81). Clearly in the church of today, not everyone draws the same conclusions from the same (scriptural) data. On that basis, differences in personal lifestyle arise, in social and political opinions, and so forth. Each person may be expected to live carefully before God and to be "fully convinced" within himself regarding his insights and conduct, especially when these depart from what others in the Christian church think and do. In those cases where opinions differ, where disagreement neither can nor need be removed, each person may be expected to accept the other in love.

2.9 Fulfillment in Christ (1). The significance of Christ for our moral reflection is not exhausted by using the example provided by His life. We cannot employ Scripture very well in ethics unless we also know Him as the *fulfiller* of the Old Testament Law and Prophets. For this fulfillment brought with it a significant alteration, so that we can no longer use the Mosaic legal code, for example, as a guide in the sense outlined in §2.2. Regulations dealing with Israel's sacrificial worship no longer specify our worship. This applies even more to the Mosaic penal code, which stipulates capital punishment for more than twenty crimes. Prescriptions in the area of economics (dealing with property, ceasing work during the sabbatical year and the Year of Jubilee, and the like) are nowhere enforced today. But our use of Scripture as a guide would be quite arbitrary unless there were some basis in Scripture itself for viewing these kinds of prescriptions as no longer binding.

Christ has come not to destroy the Law or the Prophets, but to *fulfill* them so completely that not one jot or tittle of the law will pass away (Matt. 5:17ff.). But this word "fulfill" means something a bit different from "establish," in the sense that whatever the law meant for Israel is what it still means for us. For *pleroō* means that this law and these prophets, which *are* not full (filled-out), Jesus is going to *make* full or fill them out. And this fulfilling involves a significant alteration. Because the law was fulfilled in Christ, the Old Testament worship, along with its multitude of prescriptions, has fallen away. Jesus Himself relativized the regulations governing ceremonial purity (Matt. 15:1ff.). Later, Peter learned clearly that he was permitted to eat foods earlier forbidden as unclean (Acts 10:9ff.). With regard to eating and drinking, feasts, new moon, or Sabbath, all of which served as shadows of the reality of Christ, Christians were supposed to enjoy more freedom than was formerly permitted to the Jews (Col. 2:16). In connection with the fourth commandment, "not destroying, but fulfilling" means for us that we find the Israelite Sabbath in the Christian Sunday.

"Fulfill" means also that Jesus brings the finishing or capstone revelation. Especially in the Sermon on the Mount, he shows how far-reaching the Old Testament commandments are. If not one jot or tittle of the law will pass away, this means that in its deepest parts the law must be taken seriously. Jesus did not abolish the law, but made it transparent all the way to its heart and center.

Not murdering and not committing adultery mean more than the letter of the law indicates. Many jots or tittles of the law would pass away if one were to violate the command "Thou shalt not kill" by being bitter against a fellow believer and insulting him by calling him "dummy" or "idiot." Similarly, many jots or tittles would pass away if one were to evaluate divorce, after the instruction of Christ, on the basis of Deuteronomy 24 and not by going back to the situation of the beginning (Gen. 2:24; Matt. 19:1ff.). Similarly, one shortchanges the law in its "fulfillment" by insisting, as the Judaizers did, on something like bloody circumcision in order to obtain forgiveness of sins (Gal. 5:2ff.). The spiritual reading of the Mosaic law often renders it impossible to hold to the letter, or merely to the letter, of the law.

2.10 *Fulfillment in Christ* (2). This fulfilling has consequences not only for what we term "ceremonial" laws, but also for the "civil" ordinances belonging to the Mosaic legislation. It is not easy to determine where the boundary line exists between ceremonial and civil laws. Are regulations pertaining to the years of sabbath and Jubilee, to the quarantine of lepers, and to sowing seed in a field, ceremonial or (also) civil? Identifying what is embraced by the ceremonial element in the Mosaic legal code is not possible. Nor is it necessary. Through Christ's fulfilling of the law, an end has come to the exclusivity of Israel as a holy nation and a holy people (Rom. 9:25f.; Gal. 3:29; 6:16; Eph. 2:11ff.; Heb. 8f.; 11:13ff.). Therefore, we may say that the ceremonial and civil laws no longer possess juridical authority for us. Calvin says that freedom is given to all nations to make laws that they deem profitable, as long as they agree with the precept of love (*Institutes*, 4.20.15f.). We may prefer other laws than those in the law of Moses, says Calvin, because they correspond better to the circumstances of our time, place, and people. He makes the cynical remark that in such circumstances a nation is not casting off the Jewish law at all, since Moses' law was never given to it anyway (*Institutes*, 4.20.15f.).

This last observation appears already in the Old Testament. Yahweh gave His law to Israel and not to other nations (Ps. 147:19f.). He placed the Israelite under other commandments than the non-Israelite living in Israel. Foreigners and children of sojourners could be kept as slaves and could remain part of someone's inherited property, something impermissible for Israelite slaves (Lev. 25:39ff., 47ff.). Interest could not be charged to poor fellow Israelites, but could be charged to foreigners (Deut. 23:19f.). Israelites could not eat carrion, but sojourners within the gate were permitted to do that; carrion could be sold to foreigners as well (Deut. 14:21).

The end of the temple ministry and the decision of the ecclesiastical gathering in Jerusalem "to lay upon you [Gentiles] no greater burden than these necessary things" (Acts 15:28) brought the Christian church, out of inner necessity, to the point of having to distinguish among the Mosaic laws, between what still needed to be observed and what no longer needed to be followed. Although in the early church various distinctions tended toward the triad familiar to us, it was Thomas Aquinas (*Summa theologiae*, 2/1:99.2–4) who crafted the distinction between moral, ceremonial, and civil laws.

There is no objection to maintaining this distinction as long as people use it merely as a guideline and avoid the notion that these are airtight compartments. We must remember that this distinction never functioned in Israel and (put more strongly) never *could* have functioned. For the Israelite, there was throughout the entire land, with its tabernacle or temple, with its administrative structures and penal codes, only one law. The civil and moral commandments were religious ordinances just as much as the ceremonial commandments. Israel was a theocracy, in which the civil and religious aspects of life were not distinguished.

Aquinas linked the threefold distinction to the distinction found in Deuteronomy 6:1 between *mitswah* (moral), *huqqim* (ceremonial), and *mishpatim* (civil). See Pesch (1974: 491ff.). We meet the distinction again in, for example, Melanchthon (*Loci communes*, 6) and Calvin (*Institutes*, 4.20.14ff.), and in the Westminster Confession of Faith (19.3, 4). Concerning Israel, this Confession says, entirely in the spirit of Calvin: "To them also, as a body politic, he gave sundry judicial laws, which expired together with the state of that people; not obliging any other now, further than the general equity thereof may require."

With regard to the *ceremonial* laws, involving the temple ministry, cleanness and uncleanness, bloody sacrifices, festivals, etc., already from the beginning of Christendom it was said that in Christ they had obtained their fulfillment and could be considered no longer applicable. The *civil* laws, directed as they were toward the civil society of Israel, including among other things a penal code, were no longer considered fully binding for the Christianized world. Naturally, it was a long time before the Mosaic civil laws as a whole no longer enjoyed the force of law. Thus, as recently as 1735 the States of Holland declared that in the jurisprudence of the Netherlands the Mosaic penal code would be inapplicable from that point on (Fabius, 1890: 7).

Only with regard to the *moral* laws, whose core is the Ten Commandments, was it declared that they retained their direct validity.

2.11. *Is Moses still binding after all?* An entirely different opinion regarding the validity of the Mosaic legal code is promulgated by the school of Rousas J. Rushdoony, Greg L. Bahnsen, Gary North, and others, who are attracting to the Christian Reconstruction movement a significant number of Protestant Christians, especially in the United States. This school believes that the entire Mosaic legal code remains valid for us and should be reinstated in modern civil life. Idolatry, witchcraft, blasphemy, apostasy, adultery, homosexuality, and rebellion against parents should be punished today with execution. What Calvin wrote about the freedom of nations to make their own laws Rushdoony calls "heretical nonsense" (1978: 9).

The opinions of the school of Rushdoony and his associates function in a postmillennial context: contemporary society is going to collapse, and the human race will realize that only a return to biblical (Mosaic) law will rescue society. When that happens, a golden age will dawn for the whole world. The new and dominant element in this form of postmillennialism is its plea for the fully integrated reinstatement of the Mosaic legal code. The only exception is the ceremonial laws, which have obtained "permanent validity and embodiment in Christ" (Bahnsen, 1977: 207).

This position brings us back to a time in history before the fulfilling of the law by Christ, making Golgotha a second Sinai and Christ a second Moses.

The opinion that *pleroō* in Matthew 5:17 might mean "fulfill," "supplement" or something similar is rejected completely by this position, because the law was already perfect (Pss. 19:7f.; 119:128) and thus had no need of a supplement. *Pleroō* can only mean "confirm and restore in full measure" (Bahnsen, 1977: 54ff.). The law of God is "re-established as a result of the New Sinai, Golgotha, by the greater Moses, Jesus Christ" (Rushdoony, 1978: 209).

This "theonomic" vision is quite assailable for the following reasons:

a. Such an interpretation of the "fulfillment" of the Mosaic law makes inexplicable why Scripture exalts the new covenant so far above the old covenant. The law was given through Moses; grace and truth came through Jesus Christ (John 1:17). The old covenant had ministers of the letter, the new covenant has ministers of the Spirit (2 Cor. 3:6). Christ is the mediator of a better covenant (Heb. 8:6), whose superiority consists also of this, that God's law is placed within people's hearts (Jer. 31:33f.; Heb. 10:16). The commission that Christ gave His apostles was to teach the nations what He (not what Moses) had commanded them (Matt. 28:19).

b. If *pleroō* means that the Law and the Prophets remain binding without alteration, why then are the ceremonial laws nevertheless excluded? And if it is true of ceremonial laws that their fulfilling has led to a transformation of (bloody) sacrifices into the sacrifice of Christ, why then could not and should not a similar transformation apply to the whole Mosaic legal code? Why is the shadowy character of the legal code (Col. 2:17) restricted to what we now term "ceremonial" laws? Is not the separation of Israel into a distinct nation just as "shadowy"?

c. The subsequent teaching of Matthew 5 suggests clearly enough that the scope of Christ's word about "fulfilling" the Law and the Prophets is not directed to establishing the Mosaic legal code for civil life. One can hardly argue that the death penalty should also be applied to everyone who says "Raca!" or "You fool!" (Matt. 5:22) and to everyone who looks at a woman lustfully (Matt. 5:28), although Christ does indeed explain what murder and adultery mean according to the Law and the Prophets. However, Christ is directing His teaching not toward the external civil order, but toward the internal spiritual and moral meaning of the law. On those terms, He can free Himself from the letter of the law in order to indicate the depth of it. He does the same thing with regard to the civil ordinances involving divorce. According to Rushdoony (406ff.) and Bahnsen (97ff.), divorce is still permissible on the basis of Deuteronomy 24. So then the ground for divorce is not only adultery, but unchastity in the broader sense (related to the expression "some uncleanness" in Deut. 24:1). The word used by Jesus (*porneia* in Matt. 5:32 and 19:9) is then interpreted in the broader sense of Deuteronomy 24 (Bahnsen 97ff.). It appears as if Bahnsen and his associates let no jot or tittle of the law fall into irrelevance. In reality, however, they want no old legal *regulation* to fall into disuse, so that in this way they close their eyes to the depth with which Jesus "fulfills" God's law with regard to the evil of divorce. Jesus goes behind the regulation of Deuteronomy 24, which had been adapted to the "hardness of hearts," all the way back to God's law in Genesis 2, as this appears in Matthew 19:8. Christ does *not* establish or confirm the certificate of divorce, but unmasks it as arising precisely as a result of "hardness of heart."

d. It is striking that Christian Reconstruction pays a lot of attention to the reformation of the world, but hardly any to the reformation of the church. Within the Reconstruction movement, Reformed and charismatics join together enthusiastically to show everybody how salutary the Mosaic legal code will be for the world. But one finds little trace of a similar zeal with regard to what is needed in the church (Muether, 1990: 252ff.), while Jesus and the apostles continually focused attention on the life of believers together. In Rushdoony and his associates we read quite a bit about physical execution, but little or nothing about spiritual excommunication, to which Paul obligated the Christian community *in conformity to the Mosaic legal code*: "Put away from yourselves that wicked person" (1 Cor. 5:13; cf. Deut. 13:5; 17:7; 19:19; 22:24; 24:7).

e. Predictably, it is impossible to apply the Mosaic legal code consistently in modern society. People within the Christian Reconstruction movement itself disagree among themselves about what should and what should not apply. Should Sabbath breakers (= Sunday desecrators) and adulterers be executed today? Bahnsen (228ff., 445f.) says yes, while Rushdoony (301, 411) says no. Does the prohibition in Leviticus against sowing two kinds of seed in a field still have legal consequences today (Rushdoony 255) or not (Bahnsen 209, who views this as a ceremonial regulation)? How must we apply today the prohibition against charging interest, which functioned in Israel in terms of the distinction between fellow Israelite and non-Israelite? Should we agree with Rushdoony that voluntary slavery is still today a "legitimate way of life, although a lesser one" (120, 286), keeping in mind the fact "that some people are by nature slaves and will always be so" (251)? Concerning the quarantine regulations in Leviticus 13–15, it is said that the *details* can no longer be adapted "to our times, in that they have an earlier era in mind," but that "the *principles* of these laws are still valid" (Rushdoony 293). But does not the entire Mosaic civil code have "an earlier era in mind"? And if we were to reinstate the Mosaic legal code, how would we determine what is a detail and what is a principle? Is twofold, fourfold, or fivefold restitution of stolen goods (Ex. 22:1ff.) a detail that has passed away or an abiding principle? May somebody be sold as a slave if he cannot restore stolen goods (Ex. 22:3), or is that a detail that has passed away, while the principle must apply that such a person is placed "today [in] some kind of custody" (Rushdoony 460)?

Conclusion:

> Reconstruction does not actually provide the clear, simple, incontestably "biblical" solutions to ethical questions that it pretends to. . . . Reconstructed society would appear to require a second encyclopedic Talmud, and to foster hordes of "scribes" with competing judgments, in a society of people who are locked on the law's fine points rather than living by its spirit. (R. Clapp, quoted by Waltke, 1990: 80)

Theonomy deteriorates into nomistry.

2.12. *Using the Old Testament.* If those parts of the Old Testament administration which we term "ceremonial" as well as "civil" can no longer be the law for our ecclesiastical and civil life, how then must we use the Old Testament writings in our moral reflection?

Of course, the apostles had to deal with various changes already after the coming of Christ. We observe that for their answers they regularly appealed to "Moses." They saw no break with the law, which had not lost its significance as the "holy law" and as the "holy and just and good" commandment (Rom. 7:12).

Anyone who avenges himself forgets that it is written: " 'Vengeance is Mine, I will repay,' says the Lord" (Rom. 12:19; Deut. 32:35). A serious sin had to be eradicated from the Corinthian congregation on the basis of various arguments, the last of which is borrowed from the Old Testament: "Put away from yourselves that wicked person" (1 Cor. 5:13; Deut. 13:15 and parallels). Both Jesus and the apostles appealed to the Decalogue (Matt. 19:18ff.; Rom. 13:9; Eph. 6:2f.; James 2:11). This points clearly to the possibility of appealing to specific texts from the Mosaic legislation in order to know God's will.

For us, the fulfilling of the Law and the Prophets in Christ means that we must read the Old Testament spiritually, and that we cannot be satisfied with following its letter. There is no cleavage between law and gospel, because Moses and all the prophets bore witness to Christ (Luke 24:27; John 5:46; 1 Peter 1:10ff.). When we read the Old Testament "spiritually"—that is, Christianly—then that is in order "to confirm us in the doctrine of the gospel, and to regulate our life in all honorableness to the glory of God, according to His will" (Belgic Confession, Article 25). The shadows have come to an end, but the "*veritas et substantia*" ("truth and substance") remain in Christ (Belgic Confession, Article 25).

To that substance belongs the revelation of God as the holy and merciful God, as well as the summons to man to live in holiness and mercy. The form of the cult has changed, but not the substance. The bloody sacrifice of animals, the distinction between clean and unclean animals (Lev. 11), quarantine regulations regarding lepers (Lev. 13 and 14), and the prohibition against sowing two kinds of seed in the same field or manufacturing a garment from two kinds of material (Lev. 19:19) no longer have any legal force, but the message contained in these regulations—to live before the Lord as a holy people and thus completely different from the pagans—remains in force today for the church of Christ. The form of fasting may have passed away, but the substance—namely, the need to humble oneself before God—remains. The years of sabbath and Jubilee are no longer familiar to us, but our moral reflection today must continue to confess God as the owner of the harvest, the landlord of our fields and the Lord of mankind. The wrath of God, which could be poured out in Israel in a number of executions, must also be taken seriously in the church, but then by means of spiritual excommunication rather than by the civil execution of a former era (see 1 Cor. 5).

From these examples it becomes clear what "fulfill" means.

Christ's word in Matthew 5:17–18 preserves us on the one hand from the Scylla of denigrating the Mosaic legislation (which says, "The Mosaic legislation is no longer relevant for us"), and on the other hand from the Charybdis of nomism (which says, "The Mosaic legislation is still valid in the same way as it was for Israel").

If we use the Old Testament this way in ethics, then we honor the character of Scripture as the revelation of the *history* of redemption. The Mosaic legislation is like a "tutor to bring us to Christ" (Gal. 3:24)—a stage in that redemptive history. In Christ a better covenant has arisen, one in which elect Israel expands into the universal church. The temporal character of the old covenant forbids us from still living according to the laws of Moses. Scripture itself provides us, by means of the spiritual understanding of the law, the hermeneutic with which we can devote continuing attention to the Old Testament in Christian ethics.

Nevertheless, it will remain difficult to say precisely what in the Mosaic legislation is the "moral" element—that element about which we say that it remains valid not only in its Christian transformation, but also in its literal significance. The New Testament provides us with important assistance at this point. On that basis, we may believe in the continuing validity of the Ten Commandments, even though the fourth commandment contains a "ceremonial" element when it talks about the Sabbath. But these Ten Commandments, Israel's constitution written by the Lord Himself on two stone tablets, can still function appropriately as a constitution for the New Testament administration. They function this way, distinct from the various further regulations that were made, for example, in the book of Deuteronomy (Deut. 6–27).

W. H. Velema (1987: 90ff.) speaks of the "redemptive historical paradigm" that we need in order to use Scripture properly. Although our objections against paradigms discussed in §1.4f. do not apply to Velema's paradigm, we still think that the proper use of Scripture cannot be captured by the "redemptive-historical" concept. It has already become apparent to us that we need to pay attention not only to the progress of redemptive history, but also to the progress of "ordinary" history. It is not enough to say that "we live after Christ" and "we are not Israel." Minimally, we must add that "we live in the twentieth century." When we say this, then other developments beside redemptive-historical developments must be brought into the discussion.

2.13. *Using the entire canon.* Our use of Scripture must be a complete use, and must therefore involve the *entire* canon. This is already evident on the basis of the foregoing. For it can be said of the whole Scripture that it testifies of Christ (John 5:39) and finds its unity in Him. In ethics, Scripture does not function as a collection of laws and rules, but it does reveal to us the law of God as it has been given within a history of redemption in Christ.

Paying attention to the whole canon means also that both Old and New Testaments have canonical authority. We read the Old Testament in the light of the New, but also the reverse may apply: we must not use the New Testament without the light of the Old Testament.

Basing our argument on Scripture is often a difficult business, because we are inclined to look for those Scripture texts that fit in with our already chosen point of view, and to lay aside those texts that do not fit our standpoint. For example, an advocate of pacifism faces the temptation to quote the Sermon on the Mount, but to ignore what the rest of the Old and New Testaments say about force that is exercised by God or permitted by Him. Someone who opposes pacifism runs the risk of failing to consider adequately the message of the Sermon on the Mount and of many other parts of the Old and New Testaments. Precisely for that reason, we need to evaluate critically our use of Scripture when reflecting on controversial ethical subjects, and to ask the question, Are we allowing the *entire* Scripture to speak?

A fine example of allowing the entire canon to resonate when treating a particular subject is provided by Childs (1970: 186ff.) when he writes about sexuality and marriage. He shows the different (but not contradictory) ways in which Proverbs 7, the Song of Solomon, and 1 Corinthians 7 talk about this subject. "Once Paul's remarks were cut loose from their Old Testament setting in the process of Christianizing the Greco-Roman empire, a new stance to sex and marriage emerged that was completely alien to the Old Testament" (199). Often people point to the hermeneutical rule that we must read the Old Testament in the light of the New. But the reverse is also true:

> The Pauline discussion of the role of sex and marriage is a good illustration of the need of the theologian to understand the New Testament in the light of the Old. Two obvious, but faulty, hermeneutical moves are thereby avoided. Either one seeks to absolutize the Pauline teaching for Christian ethics in every age or one dismisses the Pauline teaching as a distorted and time-conditioned human judgment. By insisting on its place within the normative tradition, and yet subjecting it to the criticism and balance of the other witnesses, another theological alternative is opened up for the serious handling of Scripture in the life of the church. (1970: 199f.)

2.14. *The testimony of the Holy Spirit (1).* In the preceding discussion, we observed more than once that the answer to ethical questions cannot always be drawn in a simple, direct way from Scripture. Often we must search for God's will. In fact, that was the case also in Bible times. In the Old Testament, the "way of the LORD" was not always so clear. On the one hand, the "way of the LORD" can refer to an already familiar commandment (for example, Deut. 5:32f.; Pss. 18:22f.; 119:13f., 30ff.; Jer. 7:23). On the other hand, this expression may point to the implicit search for the as yet unknown commandment, as that relates to God's leading in human living (for example, Ps. 25:4, 12, "Show me Your ways, O LORD; teach me Your paths. . . . Who is the man that fears the LORD? Him shall He teach in the way He chooses"; Ps. 27:11, "Teach me Your way, O LORD, and lead me in a smooth path, because of my enemies"; Ps. 86:11, "Teach me Your way, O LORD").

From the New Testament, we know that we are led along life's pathway by the Holy Spirit. In accordance with Christ's promise, the Holy Spirit will lead us into all truth (John 16:13). He has been given not only to the apostles, but also to other members of Christ's church (1 Thess. 4:8).

We must take into account the special position of the (inspired) apostles, but nevertheless we may liken ourselves to them in terms of seeking the path we must walk. Through experience and exercise, our senses are sharpened to distinguish between good and evil (Heb. 5:12ff.). We must try to discover what pleases the Lord (Eph. 5:10). Love produces "knowledge and all discernment, that you may approve the things that are excellent" (Phil. 1:9–10).

Does the Holy Spirit grant us knowledge *alongside* the knowledge that Holy Scripture bestows for moral reflection? We cannot answer this question with a simple yes or no. If we simply say yes, we fall into spiritualism. If someone wants to explain to others that he is following the will of the Holy Spirit as he understands it, they should be able to ask him to verify the legitimacy of his claim. And where is that to be found except in the Word of God given to all of us in Holy Scripture? If someone appeals to the leading of the Holy Spirit, and we have to tell him that his decision contradicts what Scripture asks of a Christian, then his appeal to the Spirit is improper. Every appeal to the Spirit may be *evaluated* according to the analogy of faith (*analogia fidei*, Rom. 12:3; 1 Cor. 14:29). Scripture always continues to function as our guard and compass, even where it does not lay down for us express commands concerning what we must do concretely and personally. Whoever is really led by the Holy Spirit cannot behave in any other way than in the spirit of Scripture. To that extent we must say that the Spirit works *per verbum* ("through the Word") and not *extra et praeter verbum* ("apart from and without the Word").

On the other hand, neither can we reply with a simple no to the question whether the Holy Spirit comes with His own message. For what is involved here are concrete decisions that we take without Scripture telling us what those decisions ought to be. To him who asks, it shall be given; he who seeks, will find; to him who knocks, it will be opened, because the Father will give the Holy Spirit to us (Luke 11:9ff.). If, in time of persecution, you must give an answer, you need not worry about what to say, for it is not you, but the Holy Spirit who will speak (Mark 13:11; Luke 12:12). To that extent, we must say that the Spirit works not only *per verbum* ("through the Word"), but also *cum verbo* ("alongside the Word").

The distinction between *per verbum* and *cum verbo* is familiar from the field of dogmatics, and often refers to the difference between Reformed and Lutherans. According to H. Bavinck (1930: 437), Reformed theologians ordinarily employ the formulation that the Holy Spirit ties Himself to the Word (*cum verbo*), while the Lutherans strongly emphasize that the Spirit works through the Word (*per verbum*) as an instrument. H. Bavinck points to the distinction made by Reformed theologians between the ordinary and the extraordinary way in which God works grace in the human heart, while the Lutherans, fearing Anabaptism, more and more abandoned the extraordinary manner and placed all their emphasis on the Holy Spirit's activity by means of the Word.

Whether the difference between the two schools is so clear is doubtful. G. C. Berkouwer (1971: 213–21) points out that both *cum verbo* and *per verbum* are used by both sides. The phrase *cum verbo* is needed to emphasize that preaching does not have an automatic effect and that the Word can be received only through the power of the Spirit through faith.

This distinction is also significant for ethics. It is used by K. Bockmühl (1987: 418ff., 427, 438f.), who believes that Calvin restricts the activity of the Holy Spirit subsequent to the period of prophets and apostles to a *power* that certainly enlightens Christians and motivates them in their conduct, but provides no unique content. He judges that according to Calvin the Spirit's speaking, as we read of that in connection with, for example, Simeon (Luke 2:26) and Paul and Silas (Acts 16:6ff.), does not occur today. What is decisive for our conduct is the biblical command along with God's providence shown in our vocation, in our circumstances, and in our life's history. According to the summary of Calvin's thought given by Bockmühl, the Holy Spirit leads us by "Schrift und Schicksal" ("Scripture and fate"). In contrast to Calvin, Bockmühl does not want to restrict the *testimonium internum* ("internal testimony") of the Holy Spirit to a *power* that opens our eyes to Scripture, that inflames our hearts, and motivates us. The testimony of the Holy Spirit can also have its own *content*.

2.15. *The testimony of the Holy Spirit (2).* Even after the special apostolic period, it is responsible to speak of the *testimonium internum* as more than a power that opens the Bible for us. The Holy Spirit opens our eyes to Scripture, but also to the path of life along which we must walk. The latter does not simply follow from the former. The addition is that we may know ourselves to be steered very personally and particularly when we do certain things and omit others.

This applies to what is called the "Differential-Ethik," that is, the individuation of God's will for our personal lives. What is God's will for my life? What occupation should I choose? Should I get married, and if so, to whom? How must I live within a church fellowship? What is my task in this world? Within a life of faith and prayer, it is not at all strange to speak of a personal leading of the Holy Spirit.

But is it not possible to be mistaken about the Holy Spirit's leading in our lives? People sometimes argue that God is calling them to a certain profession, when in reality it seems unlikely that He is. This should caution us to be careful when we appeal to the testimony of the Holy Spirit, certainly when we present this testimony to others as God's will. What Bockmühl says along with Calvin remains valid: What we need is the harmony, the *coniunctio* or the *consonans*, of two voices, Spirit and Scripture. Everything new may be tested by the standard of the *analogia fidei* ("analogy of faith"), here the *analogia praecepti* ("analogy of precept"). It is not wrong for people to be convinced for themselves that the Holy Spirit is directing them in a certain way in their own lives, but when people try to lay on others, without proof from Scripture, that the Holy Spirit wants to lead these others in a certain way, then they are going too far. The Holy Spirit can shows us new paths, but these will always be in harmony with, and not contradict, the Word of God as we have that in Scripture.

Bockmühl (1987: 220) employs the concept of "Differential-Ethik," by which he means "the moral specificity and differentiation with regard to the individual person and situation that goes beyond the Decalogue as such."

Here is an example of the very personal and particular leading of the Holy Spirit: In the church wedding ceremony, we dare to say in the wedding prayer that God has brought bride and groom together and called them to their marriage. This "call" we derive not merely from the fact that two people have just said "I do," and are thereby called by God to marriage. We believe that the two people *knew* of this calling from God (possibly after quite some vacillation), and that therefore they entered their marriage together. For that, they must have received an answer from above, even though it came not as with Simeon and Paul, who received voices. But if we believe that prayers are heard, then we also believe that they are answered, with or without words. Sometimes they are answered with words, as for example in situations like those of Mark 13:11, when it is not the believer, but the Holy Spirit Himself who is in the believer, who speaks before the judge.

A question similar to the one we are discussing here arose in §2.4. Scripture, as a guide, can condemn a particular action or development, even though people appeal to God's general revelation to justify it. The *cum verbo* is at stake. In the same way, Scripture can condemn every appeal to the leading of the Holy Spirit that contradicts the *cum verbo*.

2.16. *Exercising care in our use of Scripture.* Appealing to Scripture is not always simple. In those cases, we must exercise care in making our pronouncements. We should realize that we can also *ask too much* from Scripture. The fact that Scripture is a lamp for everyone's feet and a light upon everyone's path (Ps. 119:105) does not therefore mean that Scripture offers blueprints for every sector of life. It is not hard, on the basis of Scripture, to condemn political oppression and social exploitation (Scripture as guard), but we fall into biblicism when we employ Scripture as the guide for discovering appropriate structures and laws in the areas of politics, economics, and medicine. Reflecting on our use of Scripture is continually necessary, so that our appeal to Scripture continues to serve as the basis for our decisions and is not reduced to a bit of Christian frosting on the cake.

We find an example of *asking too much* from Scripture when Gary North argues that only one economic system is possible, namely, "revelational economics" (1987: xxix). One is left to wonder what *perspicuitas Sacrae Scripturae* can mean today if a "treatise on Christian economics" could be written only after North delivers an "economic commentary" on Genesis through Revelation. He began this work in 1973 as a "preliminary study," and he believes that it will take him the rest of his life to complete it. He presumes that only after he is finished will people be writing "many treatises and monographs on economics from a Christian perspective."

But what North delivers in his commentary on Genesis exhibits all the traces of biblicism. In that book he does not travel from exegesis to his (Christian Reconstructionist) vision for economics, but in the opposite direction: he reads his already adopted perspective into specific Scripture texts. For example, already on pages 9–11 he makes a choice of cardinal importance for economics when he discusses the first verse in the Bible, Genesis 1:1, and strongly implies that only the free-market principle can be called Christian (9ff.).

Our criticism of this way of using Scripture does not mean that North's books are without value, or that economics has nothing to do with Scripture. This last point North correctly denies, and he proves it, too. But he does indeed fall into biblicism when he thinks that he can "exegetically" derive an economic system from Scripture.

A second example: Often John Frame's *Medical Ethics* is not convincing because he wants to prove too much with the Bible. For example, Frame argues on the basis of the Bible that the family and the church community must make decisions in the case of incompetent patients. "It is clearly appropriate that the church, represented by its elders, plays a role in determining the proper treatment of an incompetent patient. . . . A family that will not hear the church is by definition incompetent. . . . The Bible defines [!] competence in moral, spiritual, physical, and mental terms: competence is conformity to God's will." In order to define the principle of informed consent, we are pointed to the parable of the good Samaritan, who lent spontaneous and unrequested assistance (1988: 39f., 43).

2.17. *Summary.* We use Scripture in our moral reflection in more than one way. Our appeal to Scripture can be more direct in one case and less direct in another. In our direct appeal to Scripture, the Bible serves as a *guide* to indicate specifically and concretely what is good and evil. In other situations, Scripture serves us as a *guard*, warning us against wrong developments (despising God and man), but without giving us a blueprint showing what good developments might look like. The Bible also functions as a *compass*. In such cases, we take into account biblical themes as directives for our conduct. Fourth, Scripture gives us *examples*, especially that of Christ Himself, which call us to imitate them and which form and feed our moral consciousness.

Christ is not merely the great example whom we must follow, for He is also the fulfiller of Scripture. When we take into account this *fulfillment in Christ*, it is impossible to view the Mosaic legal code in its totality as still being the guide for today. Moreover, the unity of Holy Scripture presupposes that in our moral reflection we will always use the *entire canon* of Scripture.

The *testimony of the Holy Spirit* leads us not only along the ancient paths known from Scripture, but also along new paths (*cum verbo*). Indeed, the new cannot contradict the old, and must as such be tested by the old (*per verbum*).

Exercising care in our use of Scripture is required. We must not ask too much of Scripture, and we must continue to test critically our own appeal to Scripture.

Others have pointed out the necessary variety in the use of Scripture. Thus, James Gustafson (1984: 159ff.) distinguishes various ways of using Scripture to evaluate the actions of persons and groups. These can be tested according to (1) the "revealed morality" in the Bible (as the Jews do with the Torah and its related halacha), (2) the "moral ideals" given in Scripture, (3) via the "method of analogy" (liberation from oppression can be seen as analogous to Israel's liberation from Egypt, for example), and (4) "a great variety of moral values, moral norms and principles through many different kinds of biblical literature: moral law, visions of the future, historical events, moral precepts, paranetic instructions, parables, dialogues, wisdom sayings, allegories."

Gustafson himself chooses for the fourth method, by which "the Christian community judges the actions of persons and groups to be morally wrong, or at least deficient, on the basis of reflective discourse about present events in the light of this variety of material as well as to other principles and experiences." Gustafson has in view here what we have termed Scripture as *guard*, especially since he formulates the result of the fourth method negatively (Scripture can condemn something as "morally wrong, or at least deficient"). So he does not choose the first or the second possibilities (parallel to what we have termed Scripture as *guide* and as *compass*). We think that on this point one needs to combine them, rather than choose between them.

In regard to the authority of Scripture, Gustafson absolutely rejects two extreme solutions: "It does not have the authority of verbal inspiration that the religiously conservative defenders of a 'revealed morality' would give to it, nor is it totally without relevance to present moral judgments" (1984: 175). Now this last opinion is indeed extreme. If Scripture has no relevance for today, then appealing to Scripture in ethics is superfluous. But the first view is not extreme. The Bible is relevant for today because it contains the Word of God for every age. Therefore, it has decisive authority and is "sufficient in itself to make any particular judgment authoritative."

With Gustafson we can certainly say that there are more sources for ethics than Scripture alone. But what can be said of no other source can be said of Scripture alone, namely, that as *iudex controversarium* it has the last word. This is in contrast to what Gustafson argues explicitly: "Scripture *alone* is never the final court of appeal for Christian ethics" (1984: 176).

Scripture Index

391

16:1–2—294
16:2—111
16:22—98

2 Corinthians
1:23—92
3:6—379
3:7–11—46
3:17–18—46
4:2–4—324
4:4—50
5:10—10
5:11—70
6:14–16—264
6:15–16—275
8:9—300, 350
8:15—358
9:8—349
9:9—358
11:31—92
11:32—202
12:14—161

Galatians
1:8—98
1:20—92
3:7–14—6
3:10–14—135
3:24—382
3:28—367
3:28–29—6
3:29—377
4:1–5—142
4:1–11—149
4:8—30
4:10—111, 135, 136
5:1—7
5:2—377
5:13—9
5:16–26—344
5:19—282
5:24—282
6:10—305
6:16—377

Ephesians
1:4—7
2:1–3—17n

2:8—170
2:8–9—6
2:10—7
2:11—377
2:11–13—233
2:11–22—5
2:12—30
3:14–15—21
3:14–19—171–72
4:17–18—322
4:18—30
4:19—344
4:20—30, 374
4:20–21—374
4:22–25—323
4:24—52
4:25—316, 320
4:28—302
4:32—374
5—249, 256, 259, 267
5:3—344
5:10—278, 374, 385
5:22—367, 374
5:22–33—248, 250
5:24—180
5:29—224, 250
5:31—250, 358
5:33—180
6:1—178, 374
6:1–2—162
6:1–3—180
6:2—166–67n, 168, 358, 374, 381
6:5–8—180

Philippians
1:8—92
1:9—278
1:9–10—385
1:23—222
2:4—300
2:9–11—21, 79
2:10—21
2:10–11—6
2:15—7
2:23—349
3:6—85

3:17—373
3:19—17
3:20—167–68
4:8—349
4:11—350

Colossians
1:13—6
1:15—46, 50
1:15–18—17n
1:19—50
2—136
2:5—48
2:9—50
2:15—17n
2:16—376
2:16–17—5, 111, 123, 136
2:17—137n, 379–80
2:18—136
2:19—137n
2:20–23—68
2:21—136, 149
3:5—17, 344
3:10—52
3:17—264
3:18—182, 367
3:20—178
3:21—177

1 Thessalonians
4:8—385
4:11–12—302
5:15—237

2 Thessalonians
1:6—237
2:9–12—324
3:9—373
3:10—302

1 Timothy
1:2—164
1:5—12
1:9—285
1:10—285, 286
1:13—85
2:5—21

2:9—367
2:11–15—249
2:13—181, 367
3:16—44
4:4—32
4:8—168
5:4—173
6:6—350
6:7—302
6:8—301
6:9—301, 344
6:10—339, 344
6:15—202
6:16—42, 43, 213
6:17—299, 301
6:20—22

2 Timothy
2:5—352
4:2—100
4:14—237

Titus
1:4—164
2:5—80
2:9—182, 198
3:1—180, 198
3:4—320
3:4–7—31

Philemon
10—164

Hebrews
4—129, 130, 141
4:7—129
4:9–10—129, 141
4:11—129
4:12—365
4:13—42
5–10—5
5:12—385
6:12—373
6:13–20—92
6:16—90, 92
8—377
8:6—5, 379

9:15—5
10—80
10:16—379
10:25—149
10:26—80
10:26–31—80
10:30—237
10:31—70
11–12:1—373
11:13—377
11:23—162n
11:24–26—9
11:27—46n
11:31—327
11:32—224
11:39—224
12:6—28
12:9—44, 48, 199
12:11—169
12:18–21—2
12:24—5
12:29—2
13:4—258n
13:17—180

James
1:2–4—28
1:9—300
1:25—4
2:2—299
2:2–16—300
2:7—291
2:11—358, 381
2:25—327
3:2–10—322
3:9—52, 211
3:17—319
3:18—319
4:7—198–99
4:12—320
5—92
5:1–6—300
5:4—291
5:11—29
5:12—92
5:17—373

1 Peter
1:10—382
1:15–16—7
1:18—258n
2:9—6
2:13—197, 198
2:13–17—180
2:13–20—8
2:17—180
2:18—198
2:18–24—178
2:21—373
3:1—367
3:5–6—181
3:9—237
3:15—100
4:8—332
4:10—297n
5:5—180, 182n, 198
5:6—29

2 Peter
2:3—344
2:14—344

1 John
2:16—17–18
2:17—344
2:21—326
3:15—230
3:24—22
5:2–3—22
5:5—16
5:21—16

3 John
4—170

Jude
9—318

Revelation
1:10—111, 138
3:19—28
4:11—6
5:5—202
5:12—202
5:12–14—79

General Index

Please consult the expansive table of contents at the beginning of the book and the detailed outline introducing the Appendix. Many subjects identified there are not indexed below.